CONTEMPORARY EUROPEAN WRITING ON JAPAN

COVER ILLUSTRATION

The Shōhō map, the earliest Japanese printed map of the world, published in Nagasaki in 1645.
Courtesy The British Library.

IAN NISH has been Professor of International History in the University of London at the London School of Economics and Political Science (LSE) since 1980.

He has published a number of works in the field of Japanese foreign policy, notably on the Anglo-Japanese alliance. His most recent publication is *The Origins of the Russo-Japanese War* (1985).

He was President of the European Association for Japanese Studies from 1985 to 1988.

CONTEMPORARY EUROPEAN WRITING ON JAPAN

SCHOLARLY VIEWS FROM EASTERN AND WESTERN EUROPE

Edited by Ian Nish

Paul Norbury Publications
Woodchurch Ashford Kent England

PAUL NORBURY PUBLICATIONS
Woodchurch Ashford Kent England TN26 3TW

First published 1988

© European Association for Japanese Studies

ISBN 0-9044-04-69-0

British Library Cataloguing in Publication Data

Contemporary European writing on Japan :
    scholarly views from Eastern and Western
    Europe.
    1. Japanese civilization, 1700-1978
    I. Nish, Ian, *1926*- II. International
    Japanese Studies Conference   *(4th: 1985:
    Sorbonne and College de France)*
    952

    ISBN 0-904404-60-9

This book has been photoset in Plantin Roman
10 on 11 pt by Visual Typesetting, Harrow
Printed in Great Britain by A. Wheaton & Co. Ltd, Exeter

Contents

List of Contributors

ACKERMANN, Peter	Basel University, Switzerland
ALLEN, Louis	University of Durham, UK
ALTMAN, Albert	Hebrew University, Jerusalem, Israel
BLOMBERG, Catharina	Sweden
BOHACKOVA, Libuse	Naprstek Museum, Prague, Czechoslovakia
BREEN, J.L.	School of Oriental and African Studies, University of London, UK
BREMEN, Jan van	University of Leiden, Netherlands
CHABOT, Jeanette Taudin	Netherlands
CORNELL, John B.	University of Texas, Austin, USA
FÄLT, Olavi K.	University of Oulu, Finland
FERRETTI, Valdo	University of Rome, Italy
FORRER, Matthi	Rijksmuseum voor Volkenkunde, Leiden, Netherlands
GETREUER, Peter	University of Vienna, Austria
GÖSSMANN, Hilaria	University of Trier, FRG
GOODMAN, Roger	University of Oxford, UK
GROMKOVSKAYA, L.L.	USSR
HENDRY, Joy	Oxford Polytechnic, UK
JALALI-ROMANOVSKY, Ulrike	Vienna, Austria
JENSEN, Nini	University of Copenhagen, Denmark
KARGL, Ingrid	University of Vienna, Austria
KAWATAKE, Toshio	Waseda University, Tokyo, Japan
KIM, J.Y.	Switzerland
KOCKUM, Keiko	University of Lund, Sweden
KRISTEVA, Tsvetana	University of Sophia, Bulgaria
LATYSHEV, Igor A.	USSR
LEIMS, Thomas	University of Bonn, FRG
LINDBERG-WADA, Gunilla	University of Stockholm, Sweden
LINHART, Ruth	Vienna, Austria
MASSARELLA, Derek	Chuo University, Tokyo, Japan
MOESHART, H.J.	University of Leiden, Netherlands
MOUER BORNER, E.	Würlingen, Switzerland
MONNET, Livia	University of Heidelberg, FRG
MONTUPET, Pascale	Paris, France
NEARY, Ian	University of Newcastle, UK
NISH, Ian	London School of Economics and Political Science, UK
POSPELOV, B.V.	USSR
SAUNDERS, Valerie	University of Oxford, UK
SHACKLETON, Michael	Osaka Gakuin, Japan and University of Manchester, UK
SISSAOURI, Vladislav	University of Paris, France
SUGITA, Kurumi	Japan
TAKAMURA, Tadashige	Soka University, Japan
TOLSTOGUZHOV, A.A.	USSR
TYLER, Susan C.	Oslo, Norway
VERBITSKY, S.I.	USSR

Foreword

THE FOURTH International Japanese Studies Conference organised by the European Association for Japanese Studies was held at the Sorbonne and the College de France, Paris, from 23 to 26 September 1985. It was organised by Professor Hartmut Rotermund, Ecole Pratique des Hautes Etudes, University of Paris, and his associates, to whom the Association owes a great debt.

Some 136 papers were presented to the conference in specialised sections. In view of the large number, it was not possible to consider publishing them in a single volume. The papers of the Economics and Economic History section were published under the editorship of Professor Erich Paver in the *Bonner Zeitschrift für Japanologie,* Band 8, under the title 'Silkworms, Oil and Chips...' (Bonn, 1986). Those in the Linguistics and Language Teaching section were also published in 1986 in the *Travaux de Linguistique Japonaise,* Vol. 8 (Université de paris 7) with Professor André Wlodarczyk as editor. The papers of the three sections devoted to the History of Science, Technology and Medicine, Linguistics and Language Teaching, and Religion and Philosophy are due to be published separately by their section organisers in France.

This volume includes papers from the following sections: History, International Relations and Contemporary Politics; Sociology and Anthropology; Theatre, Music and the Arts; Literature. Many of the papers delivered at the conference were not offered for publication by their authors. But it is hoped that those that were may be a display-case, showing the range of research being done on Japanese civilisation in the universities of Europe.

In the arranging of the Paris conference, the European Association was grateful to the Japan Foundation *inter alia* for financial support to Japanese scholars who came specially from Japan in order to present the conference with the findings of Japanese experts in their particular fields. It was also assisted in bringing participants from the Soviet Union and Eastern European countries. The presence of these scholars in large numbers gave a perspective to the conference deliberations which was both new and welcome. The papers which they presented have been included in this volume.

In terms of geographical distribution, the papers carried in this volume come from Austria (4), Finland (1), France (2), Germany (3), Israel (1), Italy (1), Japan (5), Netherlands (4), Scandinavia (5), Soviet Union and Eastern Europe (7), Switzerland (3), United Kingdom (9), United States (1). While these numbers are not of course representative of the strength of Japanese studies in Europe, they give an indication of the spread of these studies.

The European Association for Japanese Studies wishes to express its sincere thanks to the Great Britain-Sasakawa Foundation for their interest and support in the publication of these papers.

As editor, I should express my thanks to those who have played a vital part in this publication of the Association. In the first place, I should like to place on record my gratitude to Professor Olof Lidin and Professor Rotermund, the President and Secretary (respectively) of the Association at the time of the Paris meeting. Secondly, thanks are due to the conveners of sections whose papers are included in this volume: *History, International Relations and Contemporary Politics* — Dr John Chapman, University of Sussex; *Sociology and Anthropology* — Professor Sepp Linhart, University of Vienna; *Theatre, Music and the Arts* — Dr Thomas Leims, University of Bonn; *Literature* — Professor Irmela Hijiya-Kirschnereit, University of Trier.

I have also been greatly assisted by Dr Philip Harries and Dr Helen Ballhatchet of the School of Oriental and African Studies, University of London. My thanks are also due to the publisher of these papers, Mr Paul Norbury, whose professional drive and good counsel about this project were much appreciated. Finally, I should thank my wife, Rona, who has assisted in ways too numerous to mention.

IAN NISH
Autumn 1987

SECTION 1:

History
International
Relations
Contemporary
Politics

1

The Position of Japan in the Pacific Era

TADASHIGE TAKAMURA

Recently, we have often been hearing such expressions as 'the opening of the Asian-Pacific Era,' 'the twenty-first century will be the Century of the Pacific,' and so on. We could say that one of the reasons for the inauguration of the Pacific Era may be attributed to Japan. One reason for this is that Japan's economic growth and progress in the technological sciences has stimulated economic activities and trade between the countries in the Pacific area. Another may be that for the past twenty years, Japan has been promoting the idea of cooperation among nations in the Pacific Basin. As a matter of fact, the first concrete and systematic proposals on Pacific Basin Cooperation were put forward in the 'Report on the Pacific Basin Cooperation Concept,' (19 May 1980) and announced by the then Japanese Prime Minister, Ohira, who has since died.

Since Japan is one of the promoters of the concept of Pacific Basin Cooperation and supposedly one of the driving forces behind it, she also has an obligation to take responsibility for ensuring the further, stable progress of economic cooperation in the region. Fulfilling such a responsibility will often entail discarding self-interested pursuits and making sacrifices for the good of the whole.

If Japan, at present the economic and technological giant in the region, exerts herself in contributing to, and actively supporting, political stability and economic growth in collaboration with the other countries concerned, I am certain that it will be possible to achieve overall stability and prosperity in the Pacific Basin. If successful, the results of this Pacific Basin Cooperation concept will have a far-reaching, positive effect on more than just Asia and the Pacific. I believe that the Asia-Pacific Area is not merely a regional matter, but rather that it could provide hints for solving similar problems on a world-wide scale, thereby paving the way to the establishment of a 'New Global Era.'

PROBLEMS FACING THE ASIA-PACIFIC COOPERATION CONCEPT

When contemplating the problems facing our world today, there are two things which we must keep in mind before attempting to draw any conclusions: one is the growing threat of nuclear war, the other is the undeniable necessity for mutual cooperation. It would be useless for us to make future plans or take any action without first putting these two into their proper perspective in relation to any problem currently under deliberation. Consequently, the Asia-Pacific Cooperation concept and all actions implemented in order to further political, economic and cultural stability in the region must also be examined with due consideration in relation to these two factors.

Naturally, there are both pros and cons about the Asia-Pacific concept.

Negative attitudes can be divided into two basic categories, one being strategic, and the other based on doubts about feasibility. As far as the first category is concerned, one question seems to be whether the military alliances such as NATO and SEATO are actually intended to be constructive or not. This doubt arises from the opinion that the cooperation concept is nothing more than a means towards the end of achieving the western policy of 'containment' as exercised towards the Soviet bloc or a means of maintaining some sort of military balance. In short, many people, both on the western and the Soviet side, fear that such cooperation is part of a US-Japanese military alliance with the purpose of encircling the Soviet Union.

Another doubt relates to the notion that this concept is a plan aimed at forming a closed economic bloc — a misgiving which the West European countries, eager to rebuild their economies successfully, seem to entertain. A third suspicion is that the concept is a contrivance by means of which larger, more powerful countries can dominate smaller, less powerful ones. This is a concern felt strongly by the countries in the Asia-Pacific region itself, especially the ASEAN countries and the small island nations in the Pacific Basin. To them, such a concept of cooperation appears to be a measure by which the larger countries within the region, namely Australia, Canada, Japan and the United States, might seek to satisfy their own national interests to the detriment of those of smaller countries.

One reason these suspicions remain is negligence on the part of the promoters of the cooperation concept to clearly explain sufficiently to these smaller countries what they have to gain from it. Another is the fear that regional integration will be detrimental to the national identity of each country, which contradicts their current efforts to establish such a strong national identity. What this means is that the promoters of cooperation must work to eliminate both the real danger and the fear that smaller countries stand to lose their national integrity through participation in regional integration schemes.

The second category involves scepticism as to whether cooperative relationships among various countries are possible in view of the variety and complex differences in race, religion, language, habits and customs, and stages of economic development, not to mention the influence of east-west confrontation and north-south problems. Considering all the problems and how they are all intricately intertwined, it may even be said that the Asia-Pacific region reflects the problems facing the rest of the world in miniature.

Another opinion belonging to the second category argues that economic growth and increases in trade within the region are to be attributed to natural evolution, and that active measures should not be taken to further cooperative relationships in case this results in an unfavourable reaction, causing the present favourable conditions to degenerate. After all, the development of the region is dependent, not on any single grand design but on many factors, including the economic growth of Japan, the shift of the economic structure from the east to the west in the United States, the development of ASEAN, the rise of NICs, and the opening of China's economy.

The Asia-Pacific Cooperative concept, therefore, finds itself facing a multitude of problems. Although in principle, it could promote a number of hopes, ideas, and opinions, the problem is that some of these collide head on with one another so that, at the present, there is no agreed concrete format for implementing the concept.

JAPAN'S ATTITUDE TOWARDS CONCEPT OF ASIA-PACIFIC COOPERATION

What is the current response of Japan's decision-makers to these misgivings about regional cooperation?

First, in response to the notion that regional cooperation is a means of forming a military alliance, Prime Minister Nakasone announced the so-called Nakasone Doctrine on Pacific Cooperation in November 1984. In it he stressed the development of cooperation in non-military areas, in other words along the lines of economic cooperation, cultural exchange, education, and vocational and technical training programmes. He also advocated that it would be better to use existing civil organisations for furthering the concept of cooperation. In addition, he was able to gain the support of the American and Australian governments on this matter. He seems to have made his decision based on advice received from the Pacific Basin Economic Council (PBEC), a Japanese businessmen's organisation which reported to him on 24 December 1984. The PBEC recommended that Pacific Basin Cooperation should be promoted with civil bodies taking the lead, while the government should only play a supportive rôle. Through the emphasis on non-military and non-political intentions and allowing civil organisations to take the initiative in cooperation-promoting activities, the leaders of Japan are attempting to calm fears that implementation of the cooperation concept would lead to a military alliance.

The 'Nakasone Doctrine' was also to serve as a response to suspicions that a cooperative system in the Asia-Pacific region would create an exclusive economic bloc and thus constitute a form of withdrawal into closed regionalism, by asserting that such a cooperative body should be open and non-exclusive. As the Japanese government sees it, the establishment of a cooperative organisation in the Asia-Pacific region should not aim at binding the region's countries in a closed regional organisation, but rather provide opportunities for deeper and widened economic ties and cooperation between Asia-Pacific area countries and Atlantic-area countries.

Trepidation that an Asia-Pacific Cooperative would serve to build an exclusive economic bloc is a misconception mainly held by the Western European countries. To these countries, Nakasone replied in a lecture given at the International Institute for Strategic Studies, London, in June 1984 by saying:

'The idea of the cooperative system should not be perceived from the point of an alternative view of the Pacific or the Atlantic. It is true that the development of the Pacific Region, including Japan and the United States, will be connected with the whole profit of the Western European countries and it cannot be realised without the cooperation and mutual dependence of the West.'

Regarding the third problem of the first category, Japan has taken great care to avoid the suspicion that the formation of a new regional body could become a means for the larger countries, especially Japan and the United States, to dominate or even integrate the smaller countries of the area. Japan's former Foreign Minister, Miki, stated as early as 1967 that a new organisation should not be a 'club of the rich,' and the late Prime Minister, Ohira, hoped that ASEAN and Australia would take the lead with Japan and the United States keeping a low profile in a supportive rôle. Prime Minister Nakasone, at the beginning of his 'Doctrine,' stressed the need to respect the initiatives taken by Oceania and the ASEAN countries. This point was also reconfirmed at a top-level conference between the United States and Japan at the beginning of 1985. Both countries also agreed on the following:

(1) ASEAN's Expanded Ministerial Conferences, in which the six ASEAN countries plus Australia, Canada, Japan, New Zealand and the USA participate, should be used as a place for inter-governmental discussion on the matter of, and the problems facing, an Asia-Pacific Cooperation body;

(2) Japan and the United States would support the activities of the PECC (Pacific Economic Cooperation Conference).

Returning to the apprehensions about whether a cooperative body would, in fact, be open and non-exclusive or not, we would have to wait and see how the organisation develops after it is founded. Actually, the key to whether an open and non-exclusive organisation could be realised and maintained lies largely in how successful the leadership of ASEAN and other smaller countries turns out to be.

As regards the second category of negative attitudes, the question of whether or not countries with different socio-cultural infrastructures can form a union of sorts in such a cooperative organisation is more or less a cognitive problem. There are some who feel that integration and unification within a cooperative organisation will gain strength from their differences, while there are others who are convinced that the complexity of differences will make harmony impossible. At this point it may be worth noting that Ohira once said that the establishment of a cooperative relationship between nations with some sort of common cultural background would be a major event and an experiment as yet unknown in the history of the world.

Attempts to compare the Pacific Basin concept with the relatively homogeneous EC are undesirable and perhaps even useless. The Pacific Basin concept does not aim at the realisation of an organisation of the same type as the EC but rather a system based on functionalism. There is also the worry that to tamper with the economic-cooperation system as it exists today by establishing a cooperative body would invite disaster by interrupting the natural progress of things that has taken place thus far.

One is that, as difficult problems cannot be satisfactorily solved by means of bi-lateral negotiations or negotiations between small groups of nations, it is imperative that preparations be made to provide an opportunity for holding multi-lateral conferences where all concerned parties can get together to make their positions clear and hammer out agreements which will be beneficial to all.

5

Another is that, precisely because of the multifarious differences which certainly do exist between the countries of this region, it is absolutely necessary to make ready now for the establishment of a cooperative body for ironing out differences between the interests of each nation before a major problem occurs. If the initiative is not taken at an early date, we may find ourselves facing problems which have developed to an insurmountable degree because they suddenly first occurred during the absence of such an interest-coordinating, cooperative body.

Bearing all this in mind, the Japanese policy-makers have adopted policies towards the Asia-Pacific Cooperation concept as follows:

(1) ASEAN's Expanded Ministerial Conference should serve as the central opportunity for holding inter-government discussions on the Cooperative concept;

(2) Governments should support civil organisations, such as PECC's in their efforts to contribute to cooperation;

(3) The rôle of the Japanese government should be limited to talks with the leaders of the United States and Oceania in order to formulate ideas and work out the framework of the cooperative body;

(4) Policy on the actual work of a cooperative body has it that activities should begin first in fields where few difference-resulting problems are likely to occur, and that these activities should be based on functionalism. As these activities would serve as an initial step, they serve as stepping-stones in widening and strengthening the cooperative system.

For example, the Japanese PBEC committee at the end of 1984 formulated a proposal for the establishment of a 'Pacific Economic Community' and presented it to Prime Minister Nakasone. This proposal recommends projects which aim at establishing a pan-Pacific information network system a pan-Pacific cultural exchange organisation, a pan-Pacific cooperation fund, and an institute for the development of the oceans. In response to the proposal's recommendations, Prime Minister Nakasone at the beginning of 1985 announced at a press conference in Australia that, in reference to the Asia-Pacific Cooperation concept, he would like to see a system adopted whereby a quick start could be made to be followed by gradual progress, which he considers better than recklessly rapid progress.

Other ASEAN leaders have stated very similar opinions over the past few years. For example, Prime Minister Mahathir of Malaysia announced that, in spite of differences in ideology and political systems, we had better set about creating a system in fields in which real cooperation is feasible. Be that as it may, for the moment the Japanese government intends to realise a cooperative system covering a wide range of fields by moving forward step by step and building it block-by-block. I might also add here that, when establishing a cooperative organisation like this we will have to face the problem of deciding which countries will become members of the organisation. The late Prime Minister Ohira once said that the Soviet Union and China should be permitted to join if they so desired, countries should be free to join or withdraw as they please and that different conditions of membership might be considered for each cooperative body

6

within the whole organisation. Ohira also expressed the opinion that such a cooperative organisation should open its membership to all Pacific countries interested in promoting cooperative relations in the region. Judging from this, it can be safely said that Ohira's concept is quite open-minded and flexible. Although the realisation of such an organisation as he seems to have foreseen would be ideal and therefore most desirable, it would in reality be quite difficult to put into practice as it is obviously too optimistic.

THE KIND OF POSITIVE ACTION JAPAN SHOULD TAKE

I would like to mention three points which are necessary for Japan to bear in mind when promoting the concept of Asia-Pacific Cooperation. First, concerning the fundamental principle upon which a cooperative body should be based, the Japanese must respect the ideals of equality and justice. Frankly speaking, care should be taken to avoid the misuse of such a cooperative body as a means for the North to control the South, and we must comply with late Prime Minister Ohira's assertion that the cultural identities and political independence of all nations must be observed and respected.

Professor Sakamoto once said that coexistence is a system whereby each country pursues its own interests separately, resulting in weakened mutual relationships with other countries. In contrast, cooperation is a system whereby nations seek common interests and purposes together, with the consequence that mutual relations are strengthened. We can safely say that it is under cooperative relationships based on the principle of equality that the potentials and the creativity of the member countries can be best developed. The important thing in this case is that, when these cooperative organisations are first conceived and established, all the countries in the region concerned should be able to participate in the planning and construction of the organisation; a cooperative organisation of this sort conceived and implemented by a single nation and imposed on its neighbours would lead to disaster. It is worth recalling that Japan put forward in the early 1940s the concept of the 'Greater East Asia Co-prosperity Sphere,' conceived and put into practice by only one country, and what that led to. Clearly, such an organisation should be a collaborative project.

Second, if Japan's decision-makers want to use this cooperative organisation as a means for contributing to the stability of international society as a whole, they must discard the negative attitude they have in which they maintain that this organisation should not handle any political or military problems. They should alter this attitude, and adopt a more positive stance, perhaps by proposing that the Asia-Pacific region be made a non-nuclear zone, or something similar. Needless to say, two major trends can be observed in the region in recent times: one is the rise of the threat of nuclear war, the other, a movement towards the establishment of a nuclear-free zone. As for the latter, there is a nuclear-free zone in South and Middle America, and Japan has three non-nuclear principles. ASEAN adopted a policy of non-alignment and neutrality, and we can also observe steady progress towards the realisation of a nuclear-free zone in the South Pacific. It is, therefore, quite possible to imagine that the day may come when the Pacific is free of nuclear weapons, especially if nuclear-free zones could be established on the Korean peninsula, in China, the Soviet Union, the United States, and Canada. If such an ideal nuclear-free zone could be realised, the Pacific Ocean would become a 'pacific ocean' in the most literal sense of the words. The realisation of such a nuclear-free zone would also guarantee the kind of comprehensive security plan Japan is seeking. Although this kind of non-nuclear policy seems quite unrealistic at first glance, it is by no means impossible. It would not be correct for Japan to further the realisation of the Asia-Pacific Cooperation concept openly, but it is her duty to make efforts towards the establishment of a nuclear-free zone in the region as the only nation on earth which has had the experience of being nuclear-bombed, as well as the duty to abide by the peace constitution and uphold the three non-nuclear principles.

My third point is the importance of cultural exchange. The Pacific Basin region has a wide variety of races, languages, and religions. The most essential element in exchanges between peoples having a complexity of socio-cultural differences between them is the importance of establishing heart-to-heart friendships. No true and strong cooperative relationship will appear under conditions of cultural segregation. Brisk cultural exchanges form the basis for regional consolidation. I agree in essence with the concrete propositions put forth in the Ohira report calling for the promotion of cultural, educational, and academic exchanges on an international level. Professor Sakamoto proposed in 1972 the establishment of the Organization for Asian Cultural Cooperation to promote cultural and communication exchanges. Although economic cooperation dare not be ignored, the exchange of culture, technology and human resources between concerned countries is essential for building all international relationships.

In conclusion, as a possible alternative to the Pacific Cooperation concept, I would like to propose the establishment of a Pacific Basin non-nuclear zone through the promotion of cultural exchanges. Naturally, this would be a cultural organisation based on principles of equality and non-nuclear policy. I think that it is important for us to adopt a culturally-oriented policy instead of one of political priorities, as well as one of non-nuclearism for the purpose of applying the brakes to the nuclear arms race.

THE SIGNIFICANCE OF THE ASIA-PACIFIC COOPERATION CONCEPT TO JAPAN

Japan is now being showered with criticism from various countries around the world, including many in Asia as well as the United States and European countries. The criticism is especially vehement when directed against the closed nature of Japan's market, her excessive exports, and her unjust economic assistance programmes. To correct these problems at their roots, we often hear that Japan must alter her 'closed society'.

On the other hand, Japan is also called upon to play a more active rôle to help ease the tense international situation through the full use of her economic power, technical capabilities and peace-oriented nature.

Japan is also advised to promote technology transfers, programmes for training skilled workers, and the horizontal division of work for the purpose of assisting developing countries. I believe that Japan, big economically but small militarily, should change her closed nature to an open one and take the lead in promoting cultural exchanges while becoming a driving force towards peace. Japan should be involved in the Asia-Pacific Cooperation concept from such a point of view. I think that Japan's positive participation in making such a regional cooperation concept into a reality will favourably influence her attitude in the area of diplomacy as follows:

Firstly, Japan has often been criticised for not having a specific policy of her own since the end of the Second World War. Her policies have always been formulated for only short-term effect. Now that Japan has grown into a major economic power, she must abandon such a haphazard attitude. It is now necessary for Japan to set forth her own explicit diplomatic policies to international society, and especially to her neighbouring countries. The Asia-Pacific Cooperation concept has the potential to become one of Japan's more efficient diplomatic policies as we progress towards the twenty-first century, so long as the aforementioned guidelines of behaviour and attitude are put into practice. It is very significant that Japan is trying to show clear direction in her diplomatic policy and undertake the responsibility to contribute to solving the difficult problems facing the international community with a positive and independent attitude while cooperating with a number of other countries. Up till now, Japan has absorbed both oriental and western cultures. It is no exaggeration to say that, since Japan has the ability to ingest and synthesise various cultures, she should sincerely undertake action to help form some sort of cooperative body in the Asia-Pacific region which will be able to embrace harmoniously a wide variety of different cultural elements and mentalities.

Secondly, Japan's efforts in tackling the problems of establishing such an emulsification of cultures in a cooperative body will greatly influence her transition from a closed- to an open-natured society. It has been often pointed out that Japan has never had the experience of changing her attitude positively without first receiving some sort of external stimulus. Therefore, when Japan takes a positive rôle to iron out the differences between other countries in the region, it will provide her with the opportunity to transform her closed nature. Japan is now entering a new stage in her development where, if one wishes to improve one's own lot, one must first revolutionise oneself from within.

2

Heretics in Nagasaki: 1790-1796

J. L. BREEN

On the night of the 17th of the seventh month in 1790 a small army of local officials raided the village of Urakami near Nagasaki. The raid, which was the result of a tip-off, was led by Takatani Eizaemon, the *Shōya* of Urakami. Nineteen villagers were arrested, all accused by the *Shōya* of being involved with Christianity. Their arrests began some six years of high-level investigations into heretical practices in the village.

The year 1790 should be noted in passing, for traditionally the 'discovery' of the Urakami Christians is given as 1865, almost a century later, when a small group of villagers professed their faith to French missionaries in the new Catholic cathedral in Nagasaki. While this event undoubtedly marked the discovery of the Christians by the French and while it was something of a surprise, too, for the French themselves, it was no discovery for the *Bakufu* and its representatives in Nagasaki. Already in 1857 the *Bakufu* had persecuted the Urakami Christians; and still earlier in 1842 there had been another persecution. But, to the best of my knowledge, the first incident involving Christians from Urakami takes us back to 1790. This date, to all intents and purposes, marks the official discovery of Japan's hidden Christians.

My purpose here is to reconstruct the major episodes of this first Urakami incident in order to examine the official response to the discovery: how rigorously would the prohibition of Christianity be enforced; would the guilty villagers be summarily executed or would they be tortured into apostasy as had happened in the seventeenth-century persecutions; or had the policy and attitude of the *Bakufu* and its officials in Nagasaki perhaps changed?

*   *   *

The evidence against the villagers had been provided by a man called Sakujirō, himself a self-confessed former Christian, and it concerned principally the mysterious burial practices of the villagers. Sakujirō revealed, for example, that the ritual head-shaving of the deceased was not performed, that incense was not burned at funerals, that coloured cloths were placed on the heads of the deceased, and that hair was burned. Other accusations were that villagers gave their morning offerings to the destitute who wandered through Urakami.[1] Sakujirō had also provided the names of men who owned statues of what he called 'evil Buddhas' — among them statues of 'Santa Maruya' and a 'crucified Buddha'.[2]

Statements later made to the *Daikan* by the *Shōya* suggest this was a straightforward case of a local official dutifully acting upon reliable information and arresting men obviously guilty of heresy.[3] However, statements made by the nineteen tell a different story. They maintained that the *Shōya* had a personal grudge against them because they had declined earlier in the year to make special contributions towards the building of some statues for a local temple. The project had been the *Shōya's* own idea, and the villagers claimed that, because of their refusal to cooperate, he had spread malicious rumours of their involvement with the forbidden religion. They were quick to point to the fact that every year in the presence of the *Daikan* they performed the *fumi-e* ceremony; they were all on the temple register; and they all made regular offerings to Buddha.[4]

From the verbal evidence presented by Sakujirō and others, it seems certain that the nineteen were indeed Christians, but it is equally clear that some sort of personal grudge and not concern for the law was the principal reason why the *Shōya* arrested the villagers when he did. It emerges, for example, that the *Shōya* had long been familiar with the activities of the villagers, but had till then turned a blind eye. The *Shōya* may indeed have been a Christian himself at some stage. Moreover, he did not report other villagers he knew to be involved such as Hikozaemon, the head Christian in Urakami, or Enkichi, or his son, Yasuzaemon, who was to be a key figure in later developments.[5]

It was only with the arrests of the nineteen that the Nagasaki *Daikan* had been informed of the rumours of Christianity. He now became involved and prepared statements from all those concerned for the Nagasaki *Bugyō*. The initial refusal of the *Bugyō* himself to become involved was apparently owing to the fact that, despite abundant rumours, no material evidence had yet been produced. This in turn would explain why the *Shōya* now planned to fabricate evidence. *Sakujirō* knew of a man in Amakusa who owned a 'crucified Buddha' and was sent there at official expense to purchase it. He found on his arrival, however, that the Buddha had been buried with its recently deceased owner. So, after returning empty-handed to Urakami, he set off again at official expense to Omura, from where he finally succeeded in returning with a statue. This he had stolen from his grandmother.[6] Upon his return, the statue was handed in to the Bugyō. Apparently neither the Nagasaki *Daikan* nor the *Bugyō* were aware of any irregularities at this stage. Before the *Bugyō* could act on this new 'evidence,' however, — if such indeed was ever his intention — he was visited personally by Yasuzaemon.[7] Yasuzaemon who was himself a local official, reported rumours that the statue in the *Bugyō's* possession was in fact a 'plant' and also mentioned other irregularities committed by the *Shōya* and his men.

It was only now that the *Bugyō* himself became concerned, and it is of considerable interest that in his investigations he seemed much more preoccupied with the illegal activities of the officials — misuse of funds, fabricating of evidence — than with the grave accusations against the imprisoned. As a result, direct or indirect, of Yasuzaemon's visit to the *Bugyō*, the *Bugyō* ordered the release of all the nineteen villagers, and at the same time meted out severe penalties to the officials that had been involved.[8] The *Shōya*, for example, was imprisoned, and dismissed from his post, while, according to the Nagasaki *Hankachō*, the original

11

informant, Sakujirō, was tattooed, given 100 lashes and expelled from Nagasaki.[9]

The severity of the punishments given to the officials and the swift release of the villagers possibly suggest that the *Bugyō* genuinely believed that the rumours of Christianity were quite unfounded and were, as the villagers themselves protested, all part of a plot concocted by the *Shōya*. It seems much more likely, however, that the *Bugyō* was anxious both to bury the incident and to discourage further informers. Had he been determined to uncover the truth, he could, for example, have ordered the opening of the graves belonging to the suspects' families. Prior to the arrests of the nineteen, the *Shōya*, acting without the *Bugyō's* knowledge or consent had attempted to do just this. But confronted by stick-wielding villagers, he had been forced to retreat. The opening of the graves would have been justifiable on this occasion not least because it was learned that all nineteen used distinctly odd-shaped gravestones, and there was ample historical precedent for disposing of these. Had the *Bugyō* done so, he would have uncovered countless objects of worship and clear evidence of Christian burial.[10] Perhaps, he feared something of the sort. Subsequent events in Urakami tend in any case to support the suggestions here that official policy towards Christians had indeed undergone something of a change.

That the *Shōya* was released from prison after just one year was due to his having bribed officials of the *Bugyō's* office.[11] Within two months of his release he had contrived to have Yasuzaemon arrested, again on suspicion of involvement with the forbidden religion. In the meantime, however, a new *Bugyō* had been posted to Nagasaki, who, in the first instance at least, seemed more intent than his predecessor on discovering the truth about the rumours of unorthodoxy. It was largely due to his efforts that a mass of circumstantial as well as some material evidence began to emerge. For the first time, practising Christian villagers began to confess their involvement, to reveal details of their beliefs, and to report on other believers to the authorities. All these developments threatened the very existence of the Urakami Christians; as indeed did the arrest of Yasuzaemon himself, who, in all probability, was *mizukata* or baptizer in the community. Just how much of a blow Yasuzaemon's arrest was can be judged from the drastic action taken by one of his servants, a man called Kumejirō.

At the end of 1792, while Yasuzaemon was in prison, Kumejirō left Urakami with a pass to visit a shrine in the province of Chikuzen. After visiting the shrine, he did not return to Urakami but instead proceeded to Edo where he submitted to the *Bakufu* a *Kakekomi-uttae*.[12] This was an urgent appeal for the release of his master. It presented to the *Bakufu* in clear and convincing detail the corruption of the *Shōya* in the incident of two years before; it explained how the *Shōya* had then been able to bribe his way out of prison, and had proceeded once again to trump up charges of heresy against his master. The *Kakekomi-uttae* stated that, unknown to the *Bugyō*, the local officials had tortured his master so badly that he would never work again, and all because Yasuzaemon had two years before revealed the *Shōya's* corruption to the *Bugyō*. The appeal, however, made no mention of the abundant rumours and indeed the irrefutable evidence of Christian activities that was beginning to emerge in Urakami. Kumejirō's aim was most likely to divert the *Bakufu's* attention from the Christians towards the easily verifiable activities of the village officials, thereby effecting, as in the previous incident, the release of the villagers and the arrests of the officials.

Extant documents do not say whether Kumejirō's *Kakekomi-uttae* won the release of Yasuzaemon.[13] But it was passed on to the *Bugyō* resident in Nagasaki, and certainly provided him with some reason for looking with suspicion on the accusations brought against Yasuzaemon and the others associated with his *kō*.[14] These include accusations, for example, that Yasuzaemon would pressurise customers at the inn which he owned into joining the 'sect,' and then would have a friend of his, Heisuke, bring along water in a bowl over which he made the sign of the cross before pouring it onto the 'convert's' head.[15] Equally revealing were accusations that men in Yasuzaemon's *kō*, such as Risuke, owned statues of 'evil Buddhas.' Risuke's Buddha was, in fact, the first piece of material evidence to be secured.[16]

Material evidence of a different kind next emerged against Yasuzaemon's friend, Heisuke, and his family. The former *Shōya,* acting on a tip-off from a local doctor, had accompanied the doctor to Heisuke's house and returned with a picture which he claimed to have found hidden in a wall.[17] Heisuke himself was already in prison and his son was now arrested too.

The *Bugyō's* response to these two discoveries is of interest. In spite of the fact that Risuke confessed to worshipping the confiscated 'Buddha' with the words 'Amen Iezusu,' the *Bugyō* in his final report to the *Bakufu* on the incident in 1796, declared Risuke's 'Buddha' to be 'insufficient proof of heretical activities in the village.'[19] As for the picture, Heisuke's son denied all knowledge of it and was soon released, while the doctor was arrested and imprisoned. It is, of course, possible that the picture had been planted — this is the implication of the doctor's arrest. Moreover, the *Bugyō* does appear to have made fairly extensive inquiries into the possible significance of the crudely drawn picture of a man 'holding something like a sword.'[20] Equally, however, the possibility exists that the picture was what the hidden Christians called *'nandogami'* or 'gods of the closet.' Typically, these were pictures of Christ or one of the saints drawn intentionally crudely in order to confuse the authorities and are known to have been kept hidden in such places as garden walls.[21] The picture seems, in fact, to be the one genuinely ambiguous piece of evidence and was set aside because it was hampering other investigations. These appear to have concerned two developments of a much less ambiguous nature. Firstly, the attention of the *Bugyō* was drawn to the unorthodox gravestones of the suspects' families; secondly, a quantity of highly incriminating literature was procured by the *Bugyō*.

We have seen that as early as 1790 irregularities concerning the gravestones of the nineteen had been discovered by the *Shōya*.[22] Under interrogation in that year it emerged that none of the nineteen used *sekitō*, the orthodox Buddhist gravestones. Nor did they know the *kaimyō* or posthumous name of their deceased relatives.[23] Evidently, they were not orthodox Buddhists. It is not clear, however, whether any action was contemplated against the gravestones or the priest of the local Shōtokuji temple, whose responsibility it was to detect such unorthodoxy. Still, it is quite clear from extant documents that no action was actually taken. It was, in fact, not until 1794, some four years after the first disclosures, that the *Bugyō* ordered the first detailed on-site investigations to be carried out. Orders were given to all temples in Nagasaki to investigate graveyards in their parishes, but only the Urakami Shōtokuji reported anything out of the ordinary.[24] The accompanying sketch (see page 275), styled *Urakamimura Yonogo Fukahori Yasuzaemon narabi ni kinpen bosho zumen*, is thought to be one of several sent by that temple to the *Bugyō* and is a good example of what was found.[25]

The large stone in the top right-hand corner is the orthodox Buddhist *sekitō*. It is of a distinct shape, vertically placed and carries the *kaimyō* of the deceased. The remaining stones, most of which belonged to Yasuzaemon's family, are of three quite different shapes: gable-shaped as in (a); hewed flat stones as in (b); and so-called natural stones as in (c). The special characteristics of all three types appear to be that they are horizontally laid and that, if they carry any name at all, it is not the posthumous Buddhist name but the deceased's ordinary name. Confronted with these facts, the *Daikan* summoned the owners of the gravestones, interrogated them and reported the results of the interrogations to the *Bugyō*. Even though all the villagers protested their innocence, the stones were not orthodox and again, perhaps, one would have expected some action to have been taken. Nothing was done, however, and two years later the *Daikan's* attention was drawn to the fact that the number of gravestones had actually increased. So once again the *Daikan* summoned and interrogated the owners.[26] For men like Chūeimon, this was for the third time.

Unfortunately, extant documents do not make clear what finally became of either Yasuzaemon or Chūeimon or how the gravestone episode was ultimately disposed of.[27] It is interesting to note, however, that no mention of this incriminating episode was made in the otherwise comprehensive *Oshiokiukagai* report submitted by the *Bugyō* to the *Bakufu* in 1796. It is of still greater interest to note that the gravestones of Chūeimon and many others still exist today in the Kyōnomine graveyard in Urakami.[28] Clearly they and their dead were left untouched.

A final and most interesting piece of evidence of heretical practices (in Urakami in the 1790s) concerns a selection of Christian literature procured by the *Bugyō* in 1793. Takatani Eizaemon, the ever alert former *Shōya*, reported to the *Bugyō* that he had access to suspicious documents. The literature, he said, belonged to a man by the name of Genzaemon, a portion of it had been written by his son, Kisuke, and it was now in the keeping of another man, Kusaburō. Takatani had the literature somehow borrowed and copied, and copies were submitted to the *Bugyō's* office.[29]

There is good reason to believe that the literature obtained by Takatani corresponds to an extant collection of documents now known by the name of *Yasokyō Sōsho*.[30] One reason for this is that the extant *Yasokyō Sōsho*

14

also includes a document signed by Kisuke. The document is a Christian calendar detailing the major feast days of the year and is signed 'Tomiiusu Kisuke' and dated 1787.[31] The remainder of the *Yasokyō Sōsho* contains such titles as 'An Invitation to Martyrdom,' 'Preparation for Martyrdom,' and 'Proof of God's Existence,' along with a refutation of Buddhism and one also of Shinto.

It is difficult to know whether all these works or just some of them were obtained by the *Bugyō* at this time since the statements of Takatani and others are vague. They tell us nothing of the quantity of literature, and of its content they simply record that 'it looked to be suspicious heretical material,' it contained 'European words' and several references to 'Santa Maruya.'[32] This alone would seem to be evidence of heresy in Urakami, and accordingly Genzaemon, his son, Kisuke, and Kusaburō were all interrogated. Genzaemon denied all knowledge of the literature; Kisuke declared he 'could not recall copying any suspicious literature.' Both were released.[33] As for Kusaburō, regarding whom it was also alleged that he recited the 'Abe Maruya' every morning, he apparently escaped custody and fled, with his family, to the Gotō islands.[34] Despite this evidence, however, the *Bugyō* saw fit to conclude in his report as follows:

'Having cursorily examined the documents, it does not appear that they are of the sort used by people believing in a forbidden religious sect. It is difficult, therefore, to use them as evidence in our investigations into heretical practices in the village.'[35]

The question we must ask is, was the *Bugyō* prepared to accept anything as proof of Christian activity? Was not the *Bugyō's* real concern, having grasped the enormity of the problem in Urakami, to make as little as possible of the revelations? In the final sentence of his lengthy report, the *Bugyō* concludes of the Urakami affair as a whole:

'... all the rumours of people believing in a heretical religion seem to be rambling and incoherent. Still, the fact that such rumours exist means that there must be reason for them.[36]

If one thing can be said, it is that times had changed since the ruthless Christian inquisitions of the seventeenth century, when inconclusiveness such as this would certainly have been viewed as gross negligence and incompetence. Is it possible that knowledge of Christianity had so faded with the passage of time that successive *Bugyō* were genuinely ignorant of the real issue? It is true, after all, that in the documents the religion is referred to not as *Kirishitanshū* but simply *Ishū*, the standard term of reference for all the forbidden sects. Undoubtedly, the authorities were ignorant of both Christian doctrine and customs. So, perhaps, could they have mistaken the Christians for adherents of, for example, the forbidden sect of Nichiren Buddhism known as *Fujufuse?* This is no idle question because subsequent incidents in Urakami and elsewhere in Kyushu were actually ordered by the *Bakufu* to be taken as cases of *Fujufuse* heresy.[37]

Unfortunately, the *Bakufu's* reply to the *Bugyō's* 1796 report is not extant so how the *Bakufu* chose to view this incident is a mystery. Still, the *Bakufu* was intimately familiar with the activities of the *Fujufuse* sect, and to refer to the Urakami religion as Nichiren Buddhism or even as *Ishū* was undoubtedly an expedient. For Christianity in Nagasaki was hardly a forgotten issue. In Nagasaki, there stood public notice-boards warning of the evil of Christianity; moreover, every year the *fumi-e* ceremony was performed.[38] And the absence of accurate knowledge was well filled with myth and legend. Indeed, from the late eighteenth century onwards, particularly as foreign vessels began to appear off the shores of Japan, there was something of a proliferation of anti-Christian chapbooks.[39]

There were, of course, any number of political reasons for making as little of the affair as possible. Clearly, for the *Bugyō* to uncover a community of thousands of Christians in territory under his control would be to risk personally having to bear the responsibility for this flouting of the Christian prohibition styled *Kokka no daiichi genkin* by the *Bakufu*. Moreover, the villagers themselves were very much an unknown quantity. Legend depicted Christians as subversives, who, inspired by their religion, were capable of fearful acts of rebellion. Could the authorities be sure they would not react in like manner if provoked? Finally, by a strange coincidence — if indeed a coincidence it was — the *Shūmon Aratameyaku*, the Edo headquarters of the state's department for Christian investigation, was abolished in 1792.[40] It would be extremely awkward for the *Bakufu* to acknowledge that a Christian community had been thriving in secret for 150 years, now that the *Bakufu's* office concerned with Christians and Christianity had been abandoned.

Whatever the reasons for playing down the Urakami affair, it has to be emphasised that the official disposition of this Christian incident marks a great departure from the ruthless practises of the seventeenth century. There is no evidence that the *Bakufu* or the *Bugyō* ordered executions or torture to induce villagers to apostasise. Indeed, one is struck by the perfunctoriness of much of the investigation. Nevertheless, we must be very wary of interpreting all this as heralding a new and enlightened approach towards Christians and Christianity, for as later nineteenth-century history was to demonstrate, the trials and the tribulations of the Urakami Christians had only just begun.

3

Carl Peter Thunberg, a Swedish Scholar in Tokugawa Japan

CATHARINA BLOMBERG

The eighteenth century saw the spread of certain philosophical concepts in Europe which gave birth to the so-called Enlightenment. The new ideas of freedom of thought and utilitarianism for the common good also took root rapidly in Sweden and resulted in a number of epoch-making discoveries and inventions. Among the famous names of this period may be mentioned: Kristofer Polhem the technical genius in mining engineering, Jonas Alströmer, who after several years in England returned home to introduce manufacturing skills on an industrial scale, Torbern Bergman, the analytical chemist, Anders Celsius, the inventor of the centigrade thermometer, Emanuel Swedenborg, the religious philosopher, and Carl von Linné (Linnaeus before he was ennobled) who revolutionised botany with his sexual system of classification.

During his years as professor of botany at Upsala University Linné gathered around him many outstanding pupils. A number of these scholars were sent out on long voyages in order to collect botanical specimens in foreign parts, several of them dying abroad — victims of tropical diseases or fevers. Valuable collections, also of ethnographica, were sent back to Sweden from practically all parts of the world. Per Kalm went to North America, Peter Forskål and Jacob Jonas Björnståhl travelled in Arabia, Daniel Solander accompanied Captain Cook on his first voyage in the Pacific, Anders Sparrman went to India and South Africa as well as to the Pacific on Cook's second voyage, and Carl Peter Thunberg visited Japan between 1775 and 1776.

Thunberg, the son of a clergyman, was born in Jönköping, in Linné's own home province of Småland in 1743. He went to Upsala University in 1760 to study medicine, and received his doctorate in 1770. Shortly afterwards he departed for the continent, and in December 1771 sailed to South Africa as ship's doctor on a Dutch merchantman. He stayed in the Cape for over three years, collecting specimens and travelling in the countryside. Early in 1775 he sailed to Batavia, the flourishing Dutch trading port in Java. Immediately upon arrival Thunberg was appointed chief surgeon on the Dutch East India Company's ship for Japan that year, and after about a month the ship set sail for Nagasaki in June 1775.

Land was sighted on 13 August, but it was not until a few days later, after the very rigorous customs inspections to which the Japanese authorities subjected the Dutch (or rather those whom they imagined to be Dutch — the ship's crew and officers in fact consisted of many nationalities: Swedes, Danes, Germans, Portuguese and Spaniards, as well as Dutchmen) that he was able to set foot on Japanese soil, in the form of Deshima island, where all foreigners were confined. Of his sixteen months in Japan, Thunberg spent all but four at Deshima and, being an inquisitive and curious man, as well as an ardent botanist wistfully viewing the green grass on the other side of the fence, he found life at Deshima extremely restricted. 'The European condemned to spend the rest of his life in this solitude would in reality be buried alive,' was his verdict on the monotonous existence of the small European colony.

Due to his status as ship's surgeon, Thunberg was one of the three Europeans who visited the Dutch embassy in Edo in 1776, and to judge from his lively account he appears to have enjoyed every moment of the journey. After brief stops at Osaka and Kyoto the party followed the Tōkaidō road across Hakone, and on the return journey the travellers were shown the Tōdaiji at Nara and the Rengeoin, better known as Sanjusangendō, in Kyoto. This seems to have been the standard sightseeing tour, since Olof Eriksson Willman, another Swede in Dutch service, who made the journey to Edo in 1651, mentions seeing the very same temples.

The Edo embassy afforded a welcome change from the tedium at Deshima, although Thunberg appears to have used his time wisely there also, in daily conversations with the interpreters and other Japanese allowed to visit him. By nature observant, he carefully noted everything that passed before his eyes.

On 3 December, 1776, Thunberg left Japan with a sigh of relief at regaining his freedom of movement and sailed for Batavia. After six months in Java he went to Ceylon, where he spent another six months visiting different parts of the island.

In February 1778 Thunberg left Ceylon for Europe, arriving in South Africa in April. There he met a Swedish ship carrying letters from home and learned about the death of his teacher, Linné, in January of the same year, and of his own appointment as demonstrator in botany at Upsala. On 1 October, 1778, Thunberg landed in Texel, Holland. 'filled with happiness,' but in no great hurry to return to his native country. He spent some time in Holland before going to England in December in order to meet Sir Joseph Banks and his own countryman, Solander, as a guest of the Royal Society. It was not until March 1779 that he at last returned to Sweden after nine years absence.

Thunberg returned a famous man, and was soon given the chair in Botany and Medicine at Upsala, where he remained until his death in 1828. He was made a member of more than fifty learned societies in Europe, as well as elected President of the Swedish Academy of Sciences in 1781, and in 1785 he received from King Gustaf III the order of the Wasa. Of his many publications the most famous work is the *Flora Japonica*, published in Leipzig in 1784, but his *Voyage to Europe, Africa, Asia*, published in Upsala (1788-91) which was immediately translated into German, English and French, naturally has a wider appeal than his purely scholarly work in Latin.[1] He was a very popular professor; and there are stories in Upsala about the way his students used to carry their teacher from his carriage to the lecture-room when walking became difficult towards the end of his life. His mind, however, was anything but feeble, and there is among his papers a brief and extremely sharp note written to a university official who had annoyed him during one of his last years. His portrait in the Medical Faculty Room in Upsala University shows a rather sinewy man with sharp features and intelligent eyes with more than a glint of humour.

Thunberg's main purpose in visiting Japan was the collection of botanical specimens but, as he himself states, his aim was to bring back to Sweden a comprehensive account of as many different facets of Japanese life as he could possibly gain insight into. No sooner had he set foot on Deshima than he began sifting through the fresh fodder brought for the cattle kept by the Dutch, in order to examine the plants. He rapidly made friends with the Japanese interpreters who came daily to Deshima and he enlisted their aid. They brought him many plants and flowers from the countryside around Nagasaki, and these were carefully pressed, catalogued and shipped back to Sweden. His medical training proved very useful, and the suspicions of the Japanese authorities, who regarded all foreigners

18

as spies, were somewhat allayed when it became clear that his entire interest was directed towards medicine and botany.

Thunberg discovered the medicinal properties of a number of wild herbs, and tried very hard to obtain permission from the authorities to be allowed to collect plants and seeds on the outskirts of Nagasaki. His repeated requests were stoutly refused but, judging from his *magnum opus*, the *Flora Japonica*, it must be said that he made the most of the material available to him. During the journey to Edo, however, he saw his chance and, although he is enthusiastic on the comforts of travelling in a *kago*, he seized every opportunity to stretch his legs. He tells, not without a certain glee, of his passage through the Hakone mountains, and how he led the guards who were dogging his footsteps a merry dance among the cliffs over which he sprang with ease, stooping down here and there to collect rare plants and flowers in his handkerchief before his panting guards could catch up with him. The season was spring and could not have been more suitable for his purpose.

While his main interest was botany he did not neglect either the geography or the geology of Japan, and his *Voyage* contains a catalogue of various minerals which he had examined. He also made meteorological observations throughout his stay, recording the temperature, precipitation and prevailing winds. Furthermore, there is in his book a section on the fauna of Japan, including birds and insects. He was much taken with the scenery along the road and frequently described the beautiful landscape he was travelling through.

Thunberg's first contact with the Japanese authorities took place when the customs officials came on board in order to take all arms and books of religious content into custody. The officers were allowed to keep their swords, and in fact a small collection of firearms and gunpowder had been prepared for this event, while the rest of the ship's arms were hidden in the hold. All Bibles and other religious works had to be locked up in a chest, while some books for amusement were allowed, and Thunberg notes that any books in Latin, French, Swedish or German passed, since the interpreters could not read them. The Europeans were frisked before being allowed ashore, and Thunberg, in fact, expressed some understanding for this procedure, stating that practically all of them habitually tried their hand at smuggling. He describes in some detail the manifold restrictions imposed on the Europeans at Deshima, and the extensive bureaucratic paperwork which accompanied every transaction, however trifling, and, although he frequently expresses admiration for the organisational skills of the Japanese, he was also considerably irked by them.

The Japanese system of government interested him and, apart from committing the usual mistake made by westerners at that time of providing Japan with two emperors, one secular, (the Shōgun) and one ecclesiastical, (the Emperor), he gives a concise and reasonably accurate account of the historical development of the Japanese state and of its rulers. The local organisation won his approval, and in his opinion the system of government was for the common weal, keeping order and in principle protecting the weak from the strong. The legal system he found to be a severe deterrent from crime, with swift and harsh punishment even for minor crimes. He also mentions the fact that innocent bystanders were often considered guilty if a crime happened to take place near their dwelling and were punished together with the real culprit. In the towns he found the police organisation excellent for maintaining public order, as well as for purposes of fire protection, and generally comments very favourably on the prevailing order and cleanliness everywhere. Although the Japanese had some notions of liberty — Thunberg commends them for abhorring the Dutch slave trade — he concludes that theirs was a despotism which, although it possessed some traits of justice, made Japan in reality a police state.

One of the chief preoccupations of the Enlightenment in Europe was utilitarianism, and Thunberg looked with keen interest at manufacturing, industry and trade in Japan. He found Japanese agriculture efficient and productive, and noted that there was an abundance of vegetables, rice, cereals and other agricultural products. Foreign trade was quite extensive, and among the goods exported Thunberg mentions soy sauce and silk, but states that the latter commodity was not as popular in Europe as it might have been, due to the narrowness of the loom. He was surprised to find that barter was still a common form of trade in Japan. The quality of Japanese cloth and paper won his admiration, and he also comments admiringly on the excellence of Japanese swords.

The sciences were still in their infancy in Japan, but with his professional interest in medicine Thunberg had the opportunity to meet a number of his Japanese colleagues and even converse with them, as some of the doctors he met while he was in Edo spoke Dutch. Two of these doctors were leading *Rangaku* scholars. Nakagawa Jun'an (1739-1780), a physician of the Obama daimyo in Edo, and Katsuragawa Hoshū, also known as Kuniakira (1751-1809), had collaborated together with others on the translation of the Dutch work *Tafel anatomia* which was published in 1774 as *Kaitai shinsho* (New Text on Anatomy). He gave them lessons in physics, botany, medicine and surgery, and the brand new set of the latest surgical instruments which he had brought with him from Paris and Amsterdam was a great success. The Japanese doctors brought him various drugs, minerals and plants, and taught him their Japanese names and uses, while he gave them the corresponding Latin and Dutch terms. Thunberg was often consulted concerning the patients of the court doctors and, although on one memorable occasion he was not even allowed to learn the age or sex, much less the name of the ailing person, many of them were cured through his instructions and prescriptions.

Methodical and inquisitive as he was, Thunberg also found time to compile a small but comprehensive Japanese vocabulary, with the help of his interpreters. This had to be done with great stealth, and Thunberg claims that both he and his Japanese friends would have been in grave danger had the authorities got wind of this enterprise. The list includes the rudiments of a grammar as well as a number of useful phrases, and is of great interest to modern philologists. Thunberg also managed to form a collection of some forty Japanese coins, ancient as well as those in current use. These had to be smuggled on board, hidden in the soles of his shoes. The collection was the subject of Thunberg's inaugural speech upon entering the Royal Academy of Sciences in 1779, and was presented by him to the King, Gustaf III.

Because of his position Thunberg came to meet Japanese from different social strata, from the Shōgun down to the servants at Deshima and the porters of his *kago*, and he was able to form quite a shrewd opinion of the character of the people. Always cautious and disinclined to rash and sweeping statements, he noted that the Japanese, like all other nations, have both good and bad qualities, but that in his opinion the good qualities predominated. Prudence, docility, sobriety, economy, loyalty and courage were some of the character traits which he found most commendable, together with the equality in dress, which he claimed made it impossible to tell masters from servants. This uniformity in clothes did not signify any real equality, he hastened to add; and he found Japan to be a strictly hierarchical society, adhering to many petty formalities. Thunberg often comments on the insatiable curiosity of the people for anything the Europeans did, said, or brought with them. He himself was subjected to thorough interrogations wherever he went, and found himself being considered a veritable oracle, expected to be able to answer all questions.

The virtue which impressed him most in the Japanese was their great sense of economy and thrift, among all classes of society. There was no idle waste, and Thunberg was moved by the patience and infinite care with which the peasants cultivated the soil. He also states that beggars were seldom seen, and that crime was rare. The personal cleanliness of the people he found admirable but, being a medical man, he considered the public bath-houses unhygienic and regarded them as an exchange for contagious diseases. Thunberg highly approved of the Japanese dress, which he thought both functional and becoming, and the food was also to his liking. He described it as nourishing and tasty, and commented on the fact that most people he saw appeared well fed and healthy. While he was in Japan his own diet seems to have consisted largely of European food, prepared by the cooks attached to the Dutch factory, who also accompanied the embassy to Edo. He states quite emphatically that he much preferred a glass of good wine or beer to green tea, a brew which he claims ruins the stomach.

One chapter of Thunberg's *Voyage* is devoted to the customs of the Japanese, and throughout his work there are many mentions of things which caught his eye. He mentions the Japanese custom of never visiting anybody without bringing a gift of some kind, and comments on the strict rules of polite behaviour, which, as he points out, sometimes differ rather drastically from European etiquette. He found the fact that cosmetics were used by all women, and not only by prostitutes; like other Europeans in Japan, he was shocked to see women bathing nude by the roadside — in full view of passers-by. The tenderness and indulgence towards children impressed him, as did the public educational system.

Religion was another sphere of great interest to Thunberg, who as a child of the Enlightenment was able to view foreign religions in a fairly dispassionate and unbiased light, whereas 125 years previously, his fellow countryman, Willman, had only seen heathen idolaters and devil worshippers, noting their strange customs in passing. Although he sometimes appears rather vague as to the distinction between the many Buddhist sects and Shinto, Thunberg was aware of the existence of two main religions in Japan, as well as a third, Confucianism. He states that the Japanese have an idea of a Supreme Being, but found their cult riddled with what he called superstitions. He was amazed by the size of the Nara Daibutsu, which inspired both awe and respect and, when confronted with the serried ranks of the more than one thousand nearly life-size gilt Kannon sculptures in the Sanjusangendō in Kyoto, he was greatly impressed. Among Shinto shrines he especially mentions Ise, stating that he met many pilgrims bound for Ise on his way to Edo. Monks and nuns he frequently saw along the way, and he particularly mentions meeting *yamabushi* and mendicant nuns. He was well aware of the brief Christian epoch in Japan, and in the New Year of 1776 he heard about the *e-fumi* ceremony from a Dutch officer who had witnessed it when visiting a Japanese official on business. This ceremony lasted for four days in Nagasaki, and the entire population was assembled, quarter by quarter, and made to tread on bronze plaques bearing pictures of Christ or the Virgin and Child. This was done, observed Thunberg, to prevent Christianity from re-entering Japan, and to keep the Portuguese merchants away.

The Confucian scholars were treated with as much reverence as the Buddhist priests, and Thunberg notes the extent to which Confucian doctrines had permeated the Japanese code of behaviour. In his chapter on religion he also remarks on the fact that in Japan suicide was not only permissible but even regarded as an heroic act to which no social stigma was attached, much less any concept of sin — something which even today does not fail to astonish foreign observers.

Among the many festivals occurring throughout the Japanese calendar Thunberg mentions what he called the lantern festival, i.e. the Buddhist *O-bon*, which he himself observed in Nagasaki. He mentions being invited with the other Europeans to a large Shinto *matsuri* in Nagasaki in the autumn of 1776, and gives a vivid description of the festive throng. Thunberg was also able to attend various kinds of secular entertainment, and saw Kabuki performances both in Nagasaki and Osaka. He found the costumes as well as the mannerisms of the actors highly bizarre, and made unfavourable comparisons with the European theatre. Japanese music did not appeal to Thunberg, and of the other arts, such as literature and poetry, he could by necessity have no opinion. There is in his *Voyage* scant mention of the decorative arts, although he does speak highly, for example, of the quality of the lacquer-ware.

In spite of the drastic restrictions on freedom of movement and the added difficulty of the language, Carl Peter Thunberg through his innate curiosity and talent for observation was able to write a surprisingly comprehensive account of Japan as he saw it. The rather formidable list he gives of the characteristics of the Japanese, which was naturally somewhat modified throughout his writings, is still worthy of contemplation. 'The characteristics of the nation,' he writes, 'are commonly to be sensible and cautious, free, obedient and polite, curious, industrious and dexterous, thrifty and sober, clean, good-humoured and friendly, frank and righteous, honest and faithful, suspicious, superstitious, haughty and magnanimous, implacable, brave and invincible.'

It was with no regrets that Thunberg sailed from Japan, a country where restrictions he found too stifling. However, he appears to have inspired confidence in his native informants, and it is clear that he possessed charm as well as honesty, sincerity and an open mind. He felt genuine affection for his 'beloved disciples' Katsuragawa Hoshū and Nakagawa Jun'an, who had spent almost every day with him during his month in Edo, 'often remaining late into the night.' For several years after his departure he maintained a correspondence with them, as well as some friends among the interpreters, exchanging books for seeds and other specimens, thus providing a rather touching link between Japan and Sweden more than two centuries ago.

4

Some Features of Japanese Feudalism

A. A. TOLSTOGUZOV

According to Soviet historians, feudalism in Japan has existed for about a thousand years and since its forms have changed radically during that period, there is no point in simply comparing certain parameters of the social system of medieval Japan and oriental countries, on the one hand, and Western Europe, on the other. For example, if one takes land as the ultimate hallmark of status then Japan in the eighth century with its allotment system could be compared to the Asian type of feudalism. However, already by the fifteenth century feudally-split Japan was an example of private property feudalism as was the case in Western Europe. Was that by chance or was it the result of some form of administrative planning? To answer this question, it is necessary to single out the mainspring behind the development of Japanese society.

Japan moved from being an early centralised state, through to a fragmented one and then, between the seventeenth and the middle of the nineteenth centuries to being a relatively centralised state once again with a bourgeois society. The economy of the country developed without any substantial failure. This is seen from the data on population and cultivated lands, inasmuch as it is precisely agriculture that makes for the foundation of an economy in a pre-capitalist society.

Thus, Japan's population was 6 million in the seventh century,[1] 10 million in the twelfth century,[2] 16-17 million in the sixteenth century,[3] 25 million at the end of the seventeenth century,[4] and 34.8 million in 1872.[5] Cultivated land amounted to 860,000 chō[6] in the twelfth century (1 chō is equal approximately to 1 hectare), 940,000 chō[7] in the fourteenth century, 1,600,000 chō[8] in the sixteenth century, and 3,000,000 chō at the beginning of the eighteenth century. Although the data are approximate, they show a rather even growth of the two indicators.

Since Japan never experienced foreign invasions, her economic and demographic difficulties could in no way be compared with the situation in neighbouring countries in the Far East where internecine wars and foreign invasions inflicted colossal damage. Some scholars have claimed that although Japan's development has emerged as an isolated case within Asia the actual geographic factors in the Philippines and in Indonesia could have been even more favourable for social and economic development. It seems to me that from the viewpoint of stability the location of these two countries could have been more beneficial near a big centre of civilisation. It is the balanced influence of these two factors that matter.

Bearing in mind the constant economic development of Japan, let us try to trace the changes in the basic typological features of her development. A common feature for all medieval societies in the East was the supreme ownership of land by the state. The extreme form of it in Far Eastern countries was the allocation system when the state interfered to the greatest extent in both production and land cultivation. The introduction of the allocation system in Japan in the seventh century was tantamount to the elimination of the old tribal community as the fundamental economic unit which was already in a state of considerable decay. The allocation farmstead thus became the basic economic unit. It was a closed autarchic family community and often numbered more than a hundred people. In view of the low level of development of the productive forces at that time, a separate small nucleus family was unable to maintain an independent economy. A big family community satisfied its needs in handicraft products, giving part of them in the form of tax to the state or to the feudal rulers. The head of the community paid all duties and taxes.

The introduction of the allocation system was, as a matter of fact, the nationwide implementation of the principle of the community reallotment of land and, at the same time, a step towards its elimination because, after 743, under the allotment system, private property of peasants in the form of personal plots, kitchen gardens and water fields was recognised. By the tenth century the aristocracy had formed big private land plots, according to rank and status. The shōen estate system was thereby established in Japan. Although big family communities continued on the whole to exist as economic units, the shōen estate, headed by the patriarchal heads of Myōshu families, became a higher socio-economic unit of society in which Myōden big family communities which included a considerable amount of non-free population were the main unit subject to tax. In the most economically developed central region, the heads of Myōden and Myōshu were often heads of small families who cultivated land by themselves and did not use hired labour. At that time the economic ties in the countryside were at the level of the estate which had its own artisans. Markets also came into being.

After the fourteenth century the estates began disintegrating, and the principalities — the territorial possessions of the big feudal lords — were formed. The Shōen system fell into decay due to the development of methods of production, trade and economic ties which destroyed the closed limits of the natural economy after the appearance of patrimonial markets which in their activities exceeded the limits of separate estates. This necessitated the establishment of a new economic and political structure. The sixteenth century saw a single princely ownership of land, while its other forms sharply decreased, including ownership of the aristocracy, of temples, part of small and medium feudals, of commercial and usury capital. The formation of big feudal principalities promoted in itself further development of the productive forces because more favourable conditions were created for the development of crafts, trade, and mining. This contributed to a broader social division of labour and growth of towns. Certain specialisation of areas, as to the types of production, could be traced by the sixteenth century.

When the trade and economic ties became nationwide, a relative unification of the country was brought about, which found its expression in the formation of the Tokugawa shogunate. With the aim of increasing the number of tax units, the feudal authorities took the census of land plots and their owners, equalised the rights of different categories of holders, eliminated their dependence on each other and standardised taxes. This created the impression that such measures were close to the introduction of the allocation system, though they were unequal to it. This was in no way a return to the former allocation system. In the eighth century the allotment of land was carried out through a big family community, whereas now, in view of the considerably increased level of productive forces, the reallotment was based on the desire to eliminate the remnants of the family community and make individual peasant farms payers of taxes.

Thus, in view of the need to preserve peasants' farmsteads as the main economic unit, the fundamental forms of economic organisation, of the development of trade and economic ties and of exploitation of the peasantry in the course of the uninterrupted economic development of Japan, the growth of the division of labour and the formation of territorial economic ties went through the following stages: from allotment peasant farmsteads towards the autarchic Shōen estates, and further to the separated feudal principalities. Later on, the Tokugawa feudal empire emerged — one which was considerably tied up with nationwide economic relations, and inside it the prerequisites of capitalism matured. That is why, if the allotment system of Japan in the seventh to the ninth centuries can serve as a typological feature, the elements of the allotment system in the seventeenth century have no independent significance, nor have they any typological meaning.

In other Asian countries the strengthening of state property ownership took place frequently, while in Japan it happened only twice. Moreover, after the second time the country embarked on the capitalist road of development. What was the reason for this? In Japan the favourable geographic location made it possible to live through the troubled times of internecine wars and fragmentation when economic ties were formed but were not yet completed. One should bear in mind that the insular location of Japan, practically the only big country in Asia, helped her defend herself from the Mongalian invasion. Several centuries later when Europeans came, internal prerequisites for unification had already matured in the country, and its feudal rulers, by closing Japan, succeeded in warding off

25

the external threat. In Asia, at the stage of the intensification of private feudal elements and the weakening of the state, the latter was invariably the victim of its aggressive neighbours which often were at different levels of social and economic development. Here one may agree with the remarks by L. B. Alayev concerning the specific features inherent in the development of Japan: 'Each of the stages lasted long enough to bring to light the possibilities inherent in each of the systems which replaced one another.[10]

Objections may arise regarding the fact that the problem lies not in the existence of external forces which retarded Asian states in their economic and social development but rather in the regular intensification or weakening of agricultural societies and their states. Some scholars believe that the tendency towards the establishment of private property at the expense of state property could not develop because it resulted in the decay of agriculture and the economy at large, and that the consolidation of state power and state property was usually linked with the expansion of production and economic prosperity.

It should be pointed out that in the Middle Ages both internal and external factors of development played a particularly important rôle, and it was under their influence that a number of countries — objects of typological studies — totally disappeared — the Byzantine empire being a case in point. On the other hand, the mention of the periodical strengthening and weakening of agricultural societies and their states is of no use because in such a case there would be a reason for bringing about such periodical weakening. The example of Japan where there was no decisive influence exerted by external factors shows that development (through internal factors only) can and should be uninterrupted.

The thesis concerning the connection between state power and economic prosperity in the Middle Ages is doubtful. It seems to me that academician N. I. Konrad was right when he wrote: 'The allotment system can be one of the powerful instruments for the overall raising of the productive forces in agriculture ... When is it necessary? It is imperative when there was a drop in the productive forces, when the country was ruined, when the fields were abandoned by peasants and poverty reigned supreme. All this could happen as a result of uprisings, protracted internecine wars and enemy invasions.'[11] Thus, the introduction of the allotment system or the consolidation of the state ownership of land served as an extraordinary measure taken by the feudal authorities, rather than as a reflection of normal development of the economy and a means for consolidating the condition of the entire feudal class. It is a rare case in the history of big Asian countries when, after a relatively long period of normal development (here it was invariably characterised by intensified private feudal tendencies), a sudden transition to the state-feudal principle of land ownership occurred.

The onward development of Japan's economy reflected changes in the social structure of Japanese society. In the early feudal state, after the reforms introduced by Taika in the seventh century, with the exception of the thin layer of aristocracy and 'mean' people, the entire population was regarded as 'good' people, that is, farmers. Since the beginning of developed feudalism in the twelfth century, noblemen-*samurai*, peasants and town-dwellers were the basic categories of population, whereas after the seventeenth century (the period of late feudalism) the latter category was subdivided into artisans and merchants and the famous *Shi-No-Kosho* gradation, i.e., soldiers-peasants-artisans-merchants were established. The complicated nature of the economic life of society manifested itself in the complicated nature of the social structure.

As the structure of production was developing, it was reinforced by legal, juridical and class norms. Clear-cut estates signified that craftsmen and merchants finally kept aloof in the process of the social division of labour. The Japanese 'third' and 'fourth' estates played the part of the European 'third' estate. At the same time, the establishment of a rigid class framework in no way signified a protracted social stabilisation. Up to the fiteenth century class interrelationships proceeded from principles based on land ownership. During the fifteenth and sixteenth centuries the existence or absence of capital, wealth independent of land ownership, began exerting increasing influence on the formation of social assessments. This led to the actual breach of class gradations, even under the Tokugawa feudal empire. They were fully eliminated in the course of the bourgeois revolution.

How did Japanese handicrafts develop? During early feudalism when the feudal system in the country was marked by all the basic 'Asian' features, handicrafts were at a low level of development, with peasants themselves producing handicraft items when required for their own use and for paying taxes. There were big cities — Nara and Heian (Kyoto) — but at that time those were typical Oriental cities: aristocrats, officials, monks, their servants and artisans subordinated to them lived in the cities. As in the early medieval towns of Europe, many city-dwellers were engaged in agriculture. There were two markets in Kyoto but they were under the control of the city administration. On sale were unused surpluses of agricultural or handicraft duties produced by the peasants and the products of artisans dependent on the imperial court, aristocracy and monasteries rather than freely manufactured products of craftsmen and peasants.

At the junction of the two millennia handicrafts and agriculture were not yet completely divided: plots of land were given to craftsmen to support their subsistence, while the greater part of artisan products were made by the peasants themselves. During the twelfth and thirteenth centuries a number of specialised artisans and merchants appear in country and town; regular markets are formed; residential areas for artisans and merchants emerge in Kyoto and Nara, and other towns spring up. After the twelfth century artisans were united in guilds, which points to the process of separating handicrafts from agriculture. However, the guilds were under the control of the aristocracy and the monasteries; and they were not free associations of artisans. In other words, handicrafts were in a typically 'Asian' situation. Work on the basis of orders predominated at that time rather than work for selling at markets.

By the end of the sixteenth century the share of production for market had grown considerably. Due to the increased marketability of handicrafts, guilds of merchants came into being. At the end of the sixteenth century

27

and the beginning of the seventeenth century the guilds were largely independent, the relations between them and the feudals were changing and, instead of personal dependence of artisans on feudals, economic relations began to prevail. Apart from dependent artisans, free ones appeared. In the seventeenth century the number of guilds increased, and the rôle of commercial-usury capital in them became greater. During the latter half of the eighteenth century, alongside the development of handicrafts, capitalist production in the form of disintegrated manufacture emerged in Japan. Thus, the example of Japan shows that, as in Europe, the dependence of artisans on the feudal class was observed during the early stages of the development of feudalism and is characteristic of a lower level in the development of the productive forces. In the case of normal economic development, an Asian country also witnesses prerequisites for the capitalist development of industry.

What rôle was played by the community in the history of Japanese feudalism? As has already been mentioned, the Taika reforms and the establishment of the allotment system resulted in the disintegration of the tribal community, and a family community came to the fore as the economic cell of society. It was under the rigorous control of the state and lacked sufficient rights to the basic part of the cultivated land. There were no free population and free communities. Such patriarchal family communities (Myoden) became fundamental units in the private Shōen estates which had grown up. The association between the heads of the patriarchal family communities was fragile. Certain community functions in the estates were in the hands of the ruling class, and this intensified the private-property rights of the peasants as a counterbalance to the community rights. In the areas where a neighbouring community took shape, only the upper crust of peasants was regarded as its members.

The countryside during the fifteenth and sixteenth centuries witnessed the process of disintegration of the family community and the formation of neighbouring communities. Rich peasants and petty feudals still played a leading rôle in them. That was the period of the flourishing of the community when the latter, as a mainstay for petty feudals, obtained considerable rights to self-government. After Japan was unified and the feudal rulers promulgated their reforms, it was turned into a body of extra-economic coercion and a tool for obtaining taxes. The top echelon peasants (*Hombyakusho*) had the right to inherit land, that is, actually the right to private ownership.

Thus, throughout the period of the existence of feudalism in Japan, the ruling class kept in its hands the property of the basic means of production and enjoyed strong power over the peasants. The rôle played by the community was not so important as in other Asian countries, and this led to the early emergence of peasant land ownership.

The vague nature of the class division in the East, the protracted existence of the intermediate strata which combined the features of a producer and an exploiter, shows that it took a long time for the classes of feudals and peasants to form. In Japan the classes of feudals and peasants became clearly recognisable only after the elimination of Myōshu in the seventeenth century. This phenomenon occurred at the beginning of the stage of late feudalism. In Europe the similar process was completed earlier by the beginning of developed feudalism. Rich peasants who came into being during the stage of late feudalism in Japan were already the result of the stratification of the class of feudal peasants. They possessed great economic independence; the trade and usury element was strong in them; and many feudal peasants became initiators of the primary forms of capitalist production.

Now a few words about the forms of exploitation of Japanese peasants. First, under the allotment system the corvée work played an important rôle — it reached 100 days a year. However, as time passed, the number of these days was reduced, while the share of natural duty increased. When the system of estates emerged in the ninth century, about 20 per cent of the land was cultivated by means of corvée work. After the tenth century the latter quickly disappeared, and the whole land was leased to peasants who paid natural rent for it. Of course, peasants were still enlisted to take part in different building and other works. The thirteenth century sought a gradual process of the commutation of rent. According to some data, money was paid in the thirteenth century in 38 estates, while at the beginning of the fourteenth century in 126 estates. In the fifteenth century during the flourishing of the self-governing communities, corvée work was frequently ended, and natural and money payments were used. At the turn of the sixteenth and seventeenth centuries a return to the natural tax on rice took place but this should not be regarded as direct regression because at that time rice became a marketable product on a wide scale. Simultaneously, the number of land plots owned by the 'new landlords' (from among the peasants, merchants, and so on) who purchased land for money and no longer had any administrative or juridical rights over the peasants (that is, the sphere of economic coercion) was expanding.

It should be stated in conclusion that Japan's example shows how favourable geographical and geophysical conditions can provide maximum stimulus as regards the manifestation of a society's potential for the internal development of the productive forces in that society. In this case simultaneous changes in the state structure, forms of economic life and social organisation of society take place both in European and Asian countries.

5

'The Loudest Lies:' Knowledge of Japan in Seventeenth-Century England

DEREK MASSARELLA

The comment contained in the title of this paper was made by James I after being shown a 'long scrole of fyne paper,' probably a Japanese almanac, and an account of the estates and revenues of the *daimyo* 'most of them, equally or exceeding the revenues of the greatest Princes of Christendom,' and a letter which had all been sent by Richard Cocks, head of the English East India Company's factory at Hirado during its entire existence from 1613 to 1623. Cocks's letter and the two items had been sent to his patron, the then keeper of the records, Sir Thomas Wilson, who had shown it to James with a covering note stating that he had received it 'from the most remote part of the world.' The letter describes in considerable and acutely observed detail the new capital of the Tokugawa, Edo, the *shōgun's* magnificent retinue as he led a falcon-hunting party, the great *daibutsu* of Kamakura, the sights of Kyoto, including Sanjusangendō, and recent political developments relating to the banishment of the Jesuits and friars. Wilson felt, rather obsequiously, that the letter, written in January 1617, which has only recently come to light in the Kent Archives Office, 'were a good recreation for Your Majesty if you had any idle hours' and declared that 'neither our cosmographers nor other writers have given us true relation of the greatness of the princes of those parts.' But James could 'not be induced to believe' what was written, and dismissed the letter as 'the loudest lies that ever (he) heard of.'[1]

Regardless of this curt dismissal, the letter, and no doubt, too, the other items presented to James which have no longer survived, is a good example of the high quality of the material reaching England from Japan during the existence of the Hirado factory and especially of that written by Cocks, a man who obviously enjoyed writing and whose descriptive powers had been sharpened by intelligence activity in south-west France during his stay there as a merchant from 1603 to 1608.[1] From this material a fairly vivid picture of Japan emerges, a picture seen through European eyes, of course, but eyes that had no notions of superiority, cultural or otherwise, to colour what they saw and how they recorded their vision. The authors of the material were not intent upon pushing any particular line, especially religious, and they were not writing with a view to being published and sold. This puts their output into a different category from much contemporary travel literature.

The discovery of new material relating to the Hirado factory and a closer examination of existing but largely unused sources have added even more detail and depth to what constitutes the fullest archive of the Company's factories in the Far East (that is East and South-East Asia) in the seventeenth century (the only comparable one is Tonkin in present-day Vietnam later in the century). In addition to providing information about such diverse matters as freight charges within Japan, the cost of sending letters, the factory's business operations, the social life of its members, their personal relations with each other, with other foreigners, especially Iberian and Dutch, and with the Dutch, the archive also provides important information about Japan at a time when the Tokugawa regime was still trying to consolidate its power both within Japan and in relation to foreign powers, a process not without its parallels in the quest for legitimacy of successive regimes in England after 1649.

The contents of the records, then, tell a much fuller story about England's early contact with Japan and paint a more three-dimensional picture of Japan than does much of the printed material that came off the presses later in the seventeenth century and during the eighteenth. By then details of the factory had been very much forgotten and the numerous travel collections which appeared were little more than a recycling of Hakluyt and Purchas. Indeed, in the early eighteenth century, Dr John Harris, the compiler of one such collection, dismissed the rather short account of Japan by Cocks that appears in Purchas as 'long and tedious (sic) and besides intermixt with abundance of vulgar, frivolous, and unprofitable matters.'[3] Harris's remarks reflect the self-confidence of a Europe on the threshold of optimism. If the world was in truth the best of all possible ones, then there was by this time little doubt that Europe was the best 'world' within the world. Whatever else the great Lisbon earthquake shook to the ground it was not the burgeoning European sense of superiority *vis-à-vis* other cultures.

The fact that much of the material available today about Asia, including Japan, from the early modern period remained unpublished until the nineteenth century has often been pointed out since the first critical reviews of Professor Donald F. Lach's monumental series *Asia in the Making of Europe*.[4] It has recently been reiterated by Professor C. R. Boxer.[5] Lach concentrates solely on printed sources, which had limited circulation and which, if the comments of James I are anything to go by, may not have had as great an impact on the educated literate classes as Professor Lach implies. Far from being merely a wise fool, James had from his earlier days as King of Scotland built up an extensive library of geographical and cosmographical works.[6] But why did this discrepancy between the printed and manuscript sources occur? In the case of the English and Japan a large part of the explanation is to be found in the East India Company in whose extensive archives most of the early Japan-related material is located.

Whatever interests some of its eighteenth-century servants may have had in their leisure time, the company was not an organisation dedicated to the creation of a corpus of knowledge about distant lands. Nor, contrary to Professor K. N. Chaudhuri's view, did it have a 'highly developed sense of corporate history' by the mid-seventeenth century. In reality, the company did not treat its records with care or respect. This was true from its earliest years. In 1604, for example, when certain documents were sought for consultation they could not be found, the Court of Committees ordered that in future records should be better preserved; but the order met with little success.[8] There were occasional bursts of enthusiasm from time to time for putting in order the vast amount of documentation that accumulated in London. In March 1669 the secretary was instructed to supervise the indexing of the Court Books (that is the minutes of the Court of Committees) from the company's foundation. However, in April 1682 it was reported that there were many 'old books and papers which are in a confused manner layd up in the garret of the (East India) House.'[9]

Confusion and neglect of documents no longer considered to be of any worth persisted until the end of the East India Company's history. Between 1858 and 1860 literally tons of documents were sold off as waste paper, ironically coinciding with a growing awareness in other quarters of their value as historical material and the first efforts to calendar them as

State Papers. In 1860 when W. Noel Sainsbury, who calendared the State Papers East Indies, made enquiries about some missing letters from the Original Correspondence Series,it was discovered that Thomas Rundall, compiler of *Memorial of the Empire of Japan*, published by the Hakluyt Society in 1850, had, with the consent of the Court of Directors, taken a number of letters home with him to help him in the writing of his book, including important ones from Cocks and William Adams. The letters were traced within four days of Sainsbury's enquiries to Rundall's residence in Highgate; but five were missing, and after looking for them Rundall could not find them, and they remain lost.[10] It was probably as a result of similar laxity, far from malicious in intent, that other East India Company-related material, including Cocks's diary, found its way out of the records proper either into other collections or sadly into oblivion. The company's seemingly cavalier attitude towards its records is well illustrated by the use, or rather lack of use, that was made of them when it tried to restore direct trade with Japan, which especially in the second half of the seventeenth century, as Dr D. K. Bassett reminds us,[11] was central to the company's strategic thinking about its trade policy in the Far East and remained so until the end of the century when it finally set its sights on China as a more promising market.

In February 1626, the southern presidency at Batavia (present-day Jakarta, its location from 1620 to 1628 during a Dutch blockade of Bantam, its original site) wrote enthusiastically about the prospects for profitable trade in the Far East, including Japan. In a detailed report the following year the president, Henry Hawley, and his colleagues urged the Company to obtain letters patent from the king addressed to the Japanese emperor (that is the *shōgun* whom Europeans confused with the real emperor in Kyoto until the nineteenth century, assuming the latter to be a kind of pope) 'to countenance your first expedition' thither. Hawley claimed that 'this trade of Japan is the *summum bonum* of East India' and boasted that English cloth would sell well (he was confident of a turnover of 100,000 cloths a year because, white silk was passable in summer, in winter the Japanese had to wear 'ten coats one over the other') and could be traded for Japanese silver, then a major Japanese export. The assessment was based on information obtained from Japanese locally who would have been either resident at Batavia or members of *shuinsen* vessels trading from Japan.[12]

This was barely three years after the closure of the Hirado factory whose existence had shown that English cloth would not sell in any significant quantity. The assertion that the company should send its first expedition to Japan seems puzzling, especially as Hawley had signed the presidency's report on the closure of the factory in 1624.[13] This was the report that caused so many problems for Cocks's executors for it was on the basis of its allegations that the company held him responsible for the alleged failure at Hirado. Amnesia seems an unlikely explanation for these lapses. Perhaps what Hawley meant was 'your first ("renewed" understood) expedition with a chance of sucess.' Whatever the reason, there is no hint that a search of the presidency's records was made. In theory, copies of all 'out' correspondence and the originals of all 'in' letters to the presidency

32

should have been available, even if some of these may have been lost in the disastrous attempt to relocate the presidency in 1624. A more likely scenario is that, as with the company in London, papers were not kept systematically but used for immediate purposes, and if not considered important enough, stored away and running the risk of deteriorating in the tropical humidity. Under these circumstances, what survived, such as the journal of the master of the *Hoseander* (which had gone to Japan in August 1615) that turned up among the presidency's papers in 1664, was very much a matter of chance.[14]

The East India Company in London, where memories were a bit longer (helped no doubt by the fact that William Eaton, the Hirado factory's deputy during its last years, had arrived back in England after service in India and was questioned about the factory's affairs, and by the continuing dispute with Cocks's executors over his will)[15] did not take Hawley seriously. This did not stop Thomas Smethwick, a freeman of the company and an adventurer in the third joint stock, from suggesting to the Court in March 1632/3 that trade with Japan should be reestablished because the Japanese market for English cloth was vast and lucrative. He envisaged profits of 400% and claimed that his information was based on a study of company records which he submitted to the Court (what these were is unknown) and on the Hawley paper. Smethwick was a frequent critic of the company but, far from being simply 'a troublesome eccentric,' he enjoyed the backing of the Crown and, with almost gangster-like audacity, was attempting to extort money from the company in return for royal protection.

The Court gave Smethwick's proposals very short shrift, concluding that they were derived from the Hawley paper, which it dismissed as 'ridiculous and the thing impossible.' In its comments, the Court also drew on its own collective memory and most likely on papers from its own records, stating that it 'well-remembered the ill success (it) had upon (its) attempt at Japan, having not vented in 22 months above 32 cloathes, and in 5 yeares not above 165, and many of them by retayle.' Interestingly, a subsidiary reason for rejecting Smethwick's proposals was that the Court felt that a profitable trade with Japan could only be pursued if it was part of a triangular relationship with China (to obtain silk, much in demand in Japan) and South-East Asia (to send Japanese silver) which shows that the company was at last beginning to appreciate the trade flows of the region. Smethwick was not unduly put out by the rejection and advanced similar, if not the same, proposals in November 1635, in which the ghost of Hawley again hangs heavy. Once more the Court threw them out.[16]

Meanwhile, at the beginning of 1635, the southern presidency made some suggestions for possible trade with China and Japan in a wide-ranging report. There was a realisation of the need to see the Japan trade within its regional context, but there still remained a firm belief that English cloth could become the principal trading commodity. The report appears to indicate an awareness of the Hirado factory, but this is somewhat ambiguous. The following year in its reply the Court was not as scathing as it had been to Smethwick and, while it recalled the unsuccessful experience in Hirado, it showed that its detailed knowledge of these years was fading because it stated that the factory had lasted 'not lesse than 15 or 16 Yeares' (it had, in fact, lasted just over ten). The Court generously acknowledged that Coulson, the president, was not simply relying on local hearsay and harbour gossip, in contrast to Hawley (although many of the suggestions look like a rehash of Hawley's), and urged him to make further detailed enquiries and do some research to find out what European commodities could be sold in Japan and what could be exported from there.[17]

In December 1636 Coulson replied, saying that there was not much information to go on concerning the Japan trade because nobody resident at Bantam had been there or was acquainted with it.[18] In reality, he does not seem to have bothered himself very much to find out additional information (the *Hoseander's* journal which turned up in 1664 must have been around in 1636, which adds strength to the argument that, by this time, whatever papers about Japan had survived at the presidency had been stored away and forgotten about). There is no intimation that any effort had been made to appraise developments within Japan, by consulting the Dutch or overseas Japanese and Chinese, for there is no mention of the shogunal decrees restricting direct foreign trade by Japanese vessels.

During the 1650s the company's monopoly no longer went unchallenged and, reflecting the expansionist mood of the times, partly attributable to the fact that after being on the defensive from 1649 to 1651 the English republic felt confident enough to go on the offensive, proposals were made for a much fuller participation in the East Indies trade, including Japan.[19] In September 1658 the company, under the governorship of Maurice Thompson, decided to send a ship for Japan and one for China and preparations, including the procuration of a letter from the new protector, Richard Cromwell, to the Japanese and Chinese 'emperors' went ahead at full speed until they were abruptly cancelled on 3 December because of the threat of renewed fighting with the Dutch.[20]

There is little indication about the information on which the company based its decision. However, one thing is clear; there is no mention in the minutes of the Court looking into the Company's records. Quarles Browne, who was appointed head of the proposed Japan factory and had gained valuable experience in the East Indies as chief factor at Cambodia from 1651 to 1656, in addition to his service at Bantam, undoubtedly provided some information as well as enthusiasm. He was an able and perceptive man who would have made a worthy successor to Richard Cocks as an informant about Japan. In 1661 in a paper presented to the deputy governor, Sir Thomas Chamberlain, outlining prospects for trade in the Far East, he noted that in Cambodia the Japanese merchants were 'the noblest Merchants in those parts, free from baffleinge, constant in his (sic) bargaines and punctuall in his tymes for payments, a ffirme ffriend,' a reminder that contacts between British and Japanese continued even after the restructuring of Japan's diplomatic and commercial relations in the 1630s and early 1640s. More significantly, in September 1658 when the project was getting underway, the Court of Committees ordered that the company's agent at Amsterdam was to be instructed to find out what he could about the 'traffique and custom of Japon' and to obtain any other relevant information. There is also some evidence to suggest that the governor himself did his homework. In 1668 when the company was again seriously considering reopening direct trade with Japan, a special committee set up to investigate the matter heard from Captain Robert Bowen, who had been in Japan in 1622, that he had given the journal of his voyage thither (it should have been handed over to the company on his return from the voyage) to Maurice Thomson 'about eight years ago.' Since Bowen would have been fairly old at the time it would be unreasonable to pin him down to 1660.[21]

In 1663 Browne, who in May of that year had been appointed agent at Bantam, was given permission to attempt a voyage to Japan at his own cost.[22] The solo mission never took place but Browne certainly sparked off a renewed interest within the company about the prospects for a resumption of trade with Japan. In February 1664, the Court wrote to Bantam, sketching some general thoughts about the trade and asking Browne for his views, especially about the most appropriate form of address and language suitable for the 'emperor' of Japan and what presents would be most appreciated. The Court emphasised that, if at all possible, a letter from Charles II should be avoided because it did not want to trouble the monarch, and more importantly because they preferred to see themselves as a sovereign body, and be recognised as such, able to initiate and conduct trade by their own authority.[23] It is interesting to contrast this confidence with Hawley's belief in 1627 that the English had no grounds to fear the Dutch 'for it is the maxim of the Japanese that the English have a king and country of their own, while they imagine that the Hollanders live on the spoil and roam about with their wives and children.'[24]

Browne's reply made some very poignant recommendations, the most notable of which was the suggestion that a profitable trade with Japan could only be obtained if intermediate factories were set up either in Siam or Cambodia and at Tonkin, or where the Japanese procured most of their supplies of raw and wrought silk through Chinese and Dutch intermediaries. This trade had existed since the *shuinsen* days to which the company now began to pay more than just passing curiosity. Browne also said, and here his extensive local experience was invaluable, that, as for the letter to the Japanese 'emperor', a letter from Charles II was imperative. He concluded by apologising for not being able to furnish any information about the Hirado factory, declaring that no one present had any recollection of it and that the only written material he could find was the *Hoseander* journal.[25]

From around 1668 somewhat more systematic efforts were made to reopen the direct trade. One noticeable feature of these efforts, which culminated in the despatch of the voyage including the *Return*, is just how much had been forgotten both in London and in Bantam about the Hirado factory and how remarkably little was known about recent developments in Japan. Bantam was staggeringly ignorant of the original factory, believing that the Japanese were just waiting for the English to come back and reopen their old factory. It believed that the Japanese had rejected numerous Dutch overtures to purchase the factory and the island on which it was situated. The reason for this optimism is unknown as is Bantam's impression that the Hirado factory had itself been an island. This would seem to be a much garbled understanding of the reality of Deshima. Even more curious were the instructions issued at Bantam to the *Crown* and *Bantam* which were sent unsuccessfully for Japan in 1671. These instructions urged the supercargoes to make discreet inquiries about the Hirado factory in order to find out where it was located (presumably the site) and why it had been removed (whether in the sense of 'physically' or 'closed down' is unclear). There was also the bizarre expectation of finding some Scots and Irish to whom English cloth was to be given in the hope of stimulating demand for bulk purchases! The only really reliable information the instructions included was an awareness of the Japanese government's detestation of Roman Catholicism.[26]

The special committee set up in May 1668 to consider 'how a trade may be had and managed to Manila (that is the Philippines) Japan and other parts in the South Seas' took its task seriously and on 16 October decided to send 'for such persons as have served the Company in India & to consult with them what meanes are most effectual for procuring and opening a way of Commerce & traffique in those parts.' Those summoned included three captains who, in addition to their reminiscences, came up with a mixture of useful and inaccurate information about the commodities that would sell well in Japan. The committee also learned that 'Mr Eaton who was second at Japan is living and dwelleth at Highgate who may be able to give the Company full satisfacon as to the trade there, and of the civilitie of the people.' Unfortunately, he does not appear to have been summoned or even consulted but, historical curiosity apart, it is remarkable that the company was prepared to take seriously the memories of a man who must have been well over seventy by this time.[27]

One of the captains who appeared before the committee reported that he understood that when the English left Hirado they had left debts 'contracted by the last chiefe theire.' It transpired that this story was put about by the Dutch and it caused the company great consternation. The company was eventually able to establish that it had not left Japan with debts unpaid but that debts to the tune of 12,000 tais, or £2,400, were allegedly still owing to the company. It made this discovery by examining its own records, although it could not have done this very thoroughly or else it would have discovered that there was little chance of recovering the debts. The document which confirmed this was a narrative of 'transactions at our coming away' from Hirado which detailed the major transactions of the factory during its last months and mentions a debt of 12,821 tais, or £3,205/5/0, owing to the company.[28]

Another document was carried aboard the *Return*. This purported to be a copy of the original trading privileges granted to the company. In reality it was a copy of the Japanese version of the petition to the Japanese government for privileges, a mistake which was not discovered until the nineteenth century. The document had been published by Purchas and it is not known whether that carried aboard the *Return* was not in fact a copy made from Purchas.[29] A copy of the list of commodities that could be sold in Japan originally produced by Quarles Browne was also sent and the selection of European goods that was despatched was chosen by comparing the company's 'former proceedings in Japan with the particular commodities usually sent thither, and advising with some experienced herein.' What this seems to boil down to is recently acquired information especially what could be gleaned about the Dutch trade from the company's own factors in Asia.[30] There was no search of company records to learn from the mistakes of the past, nor to establish a clearer picture of the polity and society the company's servants would encounter in Japan. There was no recognition of the value of such an exercise anyway. The instructions to the supercargoes of the *Return* were very general: not to cause offence to the Japanese, especially by avoiding drunkenness and disorder, the sort of caveats that would have been emphasised anyway in relation to almost any trading destination even if the instructions are wrapped up in language that implies some familiarity, albeit superficial, with Japan.[31]

The mission of the *Return* was unsuccessful as is well known. The Dutch tipped off the Japanese authorities about Charles II's marriage to a Portuguese Catholic which quickly changed the amber-green light the English received from the Nagasaki officials into a bright red one from Edo. The Bantam agency tried to rationalise the rejection from a somewhat different angle. On 5 October 1674 it reported to London that the Dutch trade in Japan was very much circumscribed and suggested that the Japanese wanted 'to weary (the Dutch) out of the trade by degrees and not to forbid them at once. They have an old Prophecy that red-haired men (which they call all that have not black hair) will one time or other do their land an injury and from thence also some think we were not admitted to trade to Japan.'[32] However, the company persisted for some time after the rejection at Nagasaki in its efforts to obtain a foothold in Japan before focusing its attentions on China.

The company's seemingly casual attitude to its records did not prevent it from jealously guarding access to them. Both Hakluyt and Purchas were indebted to the company's first president, Sir Thomas Smythe, for making material available and, when Purchas applied for permission to consult documents in the company's possession in February 1622, he was permitted to do so on condition that he made notes about 'that which is proper to a history not prejudiciall to the Companie.' He also had to submit his notes for examination by the deputy governor before he could take them home. The company's jealousy was probably occasioned by fears of information falling into the wrong hands, competitors and critics, rather than by an interest in 'preserving their journals' as Sir William Foster rather oddly implies.[33]

Some of the material relating to Japan used by Purchas in his *Pilgrimes*, and which may have been copied from company originals, now only survives in that work. The circumstances which allowed the relatively easy transformation from manuscript to publication that had greatly assisted Hakluyt in his great undertaking were already altering by the time that Purchas took it upon himself to continue Hakluyt's work. Purchas commented that, after the establishment of joint stock voyages in 1613, access to East India Company material became much more difficult and in 1694 the editor of a collection of voyages to the South Seas mentioned that he could provide no information on recent voyages thither because he had not been able to see any journals relating to them.[34]

It was, of course, only in the nineteenth century that recognition of the historical value of the manuscript sources came about and that steps were taken to look after them and make them accessible. It was too late to do anything about the weeding out, or rather, given the volume of stuff thrown out, disafforestation, that had steadily taken place, but the transformation in attitude is nicely captured in a minute from Sir George Birdwood, curator of the India Museum, in 1875. Birdwood recalled that on his appointment, Colonel Bourne sent him a box he had received from Sir John Kaye, one of the defunct Company's servants, with a statement saying 'that it had been lying in his room beyond the memory of any one in the Political Department and was said to contain very important documents.' On opening the box, Birdwood found a box marked '15 pagodas' which contained two lumps of iron and forty parchments' 'all mixed together in great confusion.' The parchments related to the company's history and included commissions for commanders of fleets, a warrant issued under Cromwell's seal for payment of £50,000 to the company and one issued by the company for a loan to Charles II. Birdwood ordered that the parchments were not to be sent to the Museum after restoration work but were to be kept in the India Office commenting, 'they are not idle curiosities to be toyed about in Museums, but State Archives which should be reverently kept in the India Office itself.'[35]

The disregard and neglect of the Hirado records shows that, while the knowledge about Japan transmitted in the early seventeenth century, may have been relatively extensive, its diffusion in English society certainly was not. There is a yawning gap between what was known and what could have been known, and, of course, between what could have been known and what the *mentalité* of the people permitted them to know.

6

Russian Notions about Japan

S. I. VERBITSKV

In our day and age, the objective notions of peoples about each other are particularly important because to a considerable degree the development of good neighbourly relations between different countries depends on them. Views and stereotypes perceived by one people about another are formed over a long period of time, involving the most diverse factors, including sources of information, exchange of cultural values, personal contacts, and the character of inter-state relations. Soviet scientific writings devote considerable attention to this problem. Interesting works dealing with the evolution of Russian notions about Britain, Switzerland and Africa have recently been published.[1] At the same time, it should be pointed out that the very process of forming notions of one people about another is not quite clear. Discussions are still under way concerning the degree of reality of such ideas, the causes of the emergence and stability of different stereotypes.

The complicated and relatively slow process of 'acquaintance' of Russians with Japanese has been preconditioned by a number of circumstances. It should first be pointed out that, after the reign of Peter the Great, Russia's state interests were oriented towards western Europe. Due to direct contacts, research, publications and translations of European literature, Russian society had an opportunity to work out certain notions as regards Frenchmen, Englishmen, Germans and some other European peoples. There were some other obstacles along the way frustrating Russia and Japan from getting acquainted. These were primarily the considerable distance between Russia's cultural centres from Japan, and also the closed character of the Japanese state during the Tokugawa period, which hindered the setting up of inter-state relations and direct contacts between Russians and Japanese.

The process by which Russian ideas about Japan were formed can be subdivided into several periods. The first one lasts from the time of obtaining the first data about Japan up to the beginning of the nineteenth century. The second — it can be called the 'discovery of Japan' — is the first half of the nineteenth century. The third period is the latter half of the nineteenth century, which was marked by the establishment of inter-state relations between the two countries. And, finally, the fourth period is the beginning of the twentieth century, the period of the Russo-Japanese War which exerted a particular influence on the formation of Russian notions and stereotypes about Japan.

The first printed information about Japan appeared in Russia at the end of the seventeenth century, drawn from works by west European authors, information obtained by Russian explorers as well as information from the Chinese and other peoples of the Far East. The French edition of the book *Opisaniye Yaponii* by F. Karon, for example, was the first book about Japan. Apart from important data contained in this and other books by foreign authors, there were quite a few legends and delusions which were mainly concerned with the persecution of Christians in Japan.

The first book about Japan written by a Russian author, Professor Ivan Reikhel of Moscow University (1773), contained information on the geography, history, religion, customs and state system of Japan.[2] At the end of the eighteenth century information about Japan, though brief, was already included in the geography textbooks at that time. The Japanese themselves, including fishermen and merchants who were ship-wrecked and rescued by Russian sailors, constituted an important source of ideas within Russia about Japan. Their stories awakened among Russians interest in Japan. They laid the foundations for studying Japanese in Russia. The kind attitude taken towards Japanese who found themselves in trouble should also be pointed out: some of them established their second motherland in Russia, while others were granted an opportunity to return to Japan. Among the most colourful Japanese who happened to be in

Russia were Danbei, a shop assistant, and Kadayu, a merchant. Danbei was brought to Moscow in 1701 and, after a conversation with Peter the Great, became the first teacher of the Japanese language in Russia. Kadayu was the first Japanese to visit Petersburg in 1791. There he was received by Catherine II. The information obtained from him about Japan as well as his reminiscences about Russia, comprise one of the most interesting pages in the history of contacts between the Russian and the Japanese peoples.

The first half of the nineteenth century was the period of a true discovery of Japan by Russians. The journeys to Japan of embassies and expeditions headed by A. Laksman, N. P. Rezanov, V. Golovin, and E. Putyatin attracted the attention of Russian society at that time to Japan and her people. Diaries and descriptions of those travels were widely published in contemporary periodicals.[3] The embassy, headed by Admiral E. V. Putyatin, promoted the establishment of trade and inter-state relations between Russia and Japan. However, this expedition attracted considerable interest due to the participation of Ivan Goncharov — a prominent Russian writer who aptly described Japan and the Japanese during the period which preceded the Meiji revolution in his essays *Russians in Japan*. Later, these essays became part of his well-known book *Frigate Pallada*. Thus, it was precisely during the first half of the nineteenth century that the Russian public first obtained reliable information about Japan and its people with their specific history, peculiar culture and habits. It is worth noting that the works published during this period were friendly towards the Japanese. The authors tried to make out objectively what they had seen and, at the same time, pointed out that the possibilities of their acquiring a better understanding of the life of the Japanese people were limited.

The most significant influence on the perceptions of Russians about Japan in the latter half of the nineteenth century was exerted, first, by the establishment of inter-state relations between Russia and Japan, and, second, by internal developments in the political life of Japan connected with the incomplete Meiji revolution. Political developments in Japan became of interest to the Russian public and gave a considerable impetus to more profound studies of Japan in Russia.

The journals which reflected the opinion of democratic and liberal circles in Russia somewhat idealised the reforms during the Meiji period. Russian progressive intellectuals used the developments in Japan to advocate the need for bourgeois-democratic changes in Russia. For example, an article carried in the magazine *Otechestvennye Zapiski* compared the protracted 'progress' in Russia with the fast transformation in Japan, particularly in education and the creation of legislative bodies. Moreover, the article emphasised that Japan would be a success 'when all old departments supporting feudalism vanish and when the people realise the advantages of European civilisation.'[4]

N. Ya. Danilevsky, K. N. Leontiev and V. S. Solovyov — philosophers who belonged to the religious-conservative group — exerted a certain influence on Russian public thought during the second quarter of the nineteenth century. In their concepts of historical development,

Danilevsky and Leontiev already devoted considerable attention to the interaction between different cultures of the West and the East. They tried to substantiate the need for an alliance between Orthodox Russia and traditional civilisations of the east to give a common rebuff to the 'destructive liberal ideas of the West.'[5] V. S. Solovyov was the first to use the phrases 'yellow peril' and 'pan-Mongolism' as symbols of a real threat to Russia and to the whole Christian world.[6] These concepts, to a certain extent, served as the ideological basis for the need to consolidate Russia's positions in the Far East.

The latter half of the nineteenth century saw a number of works dealing with Japan's history, culture and religion. The most profound of these works were written by Russians who had taught in higher educational institutions in Japan. Of great interest is the work by L. I. Mechnikov, *Era prosvesheniya Yaponii. (Meiji).*[7] M. Watanabe, a Japanese historian, highly valued this work: 'The books by Mechnikov were written to refute the prejudices of the previous specialists in Japanese studies (who inclined to see Japan through the prism of China. -S. V.) and present Japan's domestic life as it was to European and Russian readers.' I. V. Kasatkin (Archbishop Nikolai) published an article on the establishment of Japanese feudalism on the eve of the Meiji revolution.[8] He also sent to Russia 'Letters from Japan' which were published in many periodicals.

Profound works about Japan were written by M. I. Venyukov,[9]A. I. Voyeykov and V. Ya. Kostilev. All this shows that this was the period during which Japanese studies emerged in Russia. Interest was growing in foreign books, including works by L. Hurn and P. Loti, which led to the creation in Russia of the stereotype of 'exotic Japan,' a country of *geisha,* chrysanthemums and *hara-kiri.*

Russo-Japanese inter-state relations were increasingly influencing the Russian public's perceptions about Japan. By and large, periodicals provided objective information about developments in Japan. However, as militant sentiments were escalating in Japan, particularly during the Sino-Japanese war and the seizure of South Korea, the official Russian publications, more often than not, regarded Japan as Russia's principal competitor in the Far East. Still, it should be acknowledged that, by the beginning of the Russo-Japanese War, the information about Japan and the Japanese was still rather limited in Russia. With the exception of the relatively narrow stratum of intellectuals, this information, even among the literate population, was confined to the data available from geography textbooks and some vague stereotypes. As a matter of fact, the Russian army did not know its adversary. An officer who took part in the war wrote that in the army the information about Japan was limited to the fact that this was a 'small country, whose history is of no interest. That was an enemy of whom Russia had never heard before, and it was no·use to disdain it or to be afraid of it. It was imperative, first and foremost, to get acquainted with it.'[10]

The authorities sought to rectify the situation. They promoted the publishing of the so-called cheap popular literature which praised to the sky the courage of the Russian warriors who could easily smash the small, weak but cunning and perfidious Japanese. At the beginning of the war

41

official propaganda managed to raise monarchic sentiments among a certain part of the population but after the military defeats it became ineffective. Hundreds of thousands of soldiers and sailors, former peasants, 'got acquainted' with the Japanese in the battles of Port-Arthur and Tsushima Island.

A new factor contributing to the formation of opinion about Japan and Russia emerged during the Russo-Japanese War. Social-democratic publications which exposed the unjust and predatory character of the war from both sides exerted certain influence on that process. It was precisely at this time that there appeared Lenin's works, *The Fall of Port-Arthur, The Defeat* and *On the Separate Peace Treaty,* which contained a profound Marxist analysis of the causes of tsarist Russia's defeat in her struggle with Japanese capitalism which was gaining in strength.

The sentiments of the Russian public as regards Japan and the Russo-Japanese War are aptly described in the reminiscences of academician N. I. Konrad: 'Everybody in Russia felt the bitterness of defeat and mourned the mass of officers and soldiers killed and maimed in the war, who selflessly fought for their fatherland which, as it was clear to everybody, was subjected to an attack by Japan ... At the same time there was no enmity towards the Japanese people.' If one tries to formulate the impact of the Russo-Japanese war on the evolution of views about Japan and the Japanese in Russia the following can be said: the sudden attack against Port Arthur and the fanaticism of the Japanese officers and men created stereotypes about the features of the Japanese character such as perfidy and cruelty. The soldiers who came back from the battle-fields of Manchuria brought such words as *samurai* and *banzai* which for a long time afterwards were associated with the notions of the 'Japanese' and 'Japan' in the eyes of ordinary people. Interest was growing among intellectuals in the national character of the Japanese and the phenomenon of the 'mysterious Asian soul.'

It should be pointed out at the same time that the Russo-Japanese War did not lead to chauvinistic psychosis and the formation of any stable negative views in relation to the Japanese people. The attitude towards war and Japan on the part of the Russian public was determined by the mounting revolutionary situation in Russia in 1904-5. After the war a more profound study of Japan began not only at Petersburg University and the Lazarev Institute in Moscow, but also at the Oriental Institute in Vladivostok. It was at this time that a group of gifted specialists in Japanese studies — linguists and historians — including V. M. Menderin, D. M. Pozdneyev, O. V. Pletner, Ye. G. Spalvin, and K. A. Kharnsky became known.

The views of ordinary Russian people about Japan, which were taking shape all through this long period, continued to exert a definite influence on the formation of public opinion in the USSR as regards Japan. For example, the first contacts with the Japanese and the descriptions of the travels during the first half of the nineteenth century were an important influence on the evolving perceptions of the Soviet people. Those works were reprinted many times and became the basis for fiction which is still popular among the young.[11] Japanese studies in Russia became the basis for the creation of the Soviet school of Japanese studies which has served as a most important source of knowledge for the Soviet public to get acquainted with different aspects of Japanese society, its culture, traditions, and state system.

However, the notions of the Russian people about Japan were primarily predetermined by the policy pursued by the Japanese ruling élite which regarded Soviet Russia as Japan's inveterate enemy. Japan's intervention in Siberia and the Far East between 1918 and 1922, the provocations of the Japanese military at the border, and the support given to Nazi Germany during World War II brought about a sharp increase in anti-Japanese sentiments among the Soviet people. During the pre-war period Japan and the Japanese were usually associated in the minds of the Soviet people with the words 'militarist' and 'samurai.'

The post-war period witnessed considerable changes in the views of the Soviet poeple about the Japanese and Japan. This was largely due to the sympathy felt for the Japanese who had lived through the hard years of US occupation and the tragedy of Hiroshima and Nagasaki. The declaration of an anti-war constitution and the massive struggle against nuclear weapons promoted the creation of an image of the 'peace-loving Japanese people.' The restoration and development of Japanese-Soviet inter-state relations and broader contacts between our countries in different spheres enabled the Soviet people to get a more detailed idea of the different aspects of life in modern Japan.

However, Soviet people somewhat changed their ideas about Japan in the 1980s. At present these views are of a dual character. On the one hand, the interest in different aspects of life of the Japanese people and in the technological progress in Japan continues to dominate. The Soviet public is still convinced of the peace-loving character of the Japanese people which experienced the tragedy of Hiroshima and Nagasaki. On the other hand, there is a view emerging which perceives Japan once again turning into a big military power and that nationalistic and great-power sentiments are becoming increasingly active among different strata of Japanese society. The propaganda campaigns staged in recent years and aimed at rehabilitating war criminals condemned by the Tokyo tribunal and extolling the 'heroes' of the Russo-Japanese war serve to whip up chauvinism and anti-Soviet moods among the Japanese public. The campaigns towards rehabilitating the war criminals who unleashed World War II are gathering momentum in Japan. Some developments connected with the first contacts between Russia and Japan and particularly the Russo-Japanese war are used to create a stereotype about Russia as an 'enemy-country.' Japan publishes a considerable amount of literature and produces movies which hail the 'heroes' of the Russo-Japanese War; the war is depicted as an example of 'unity between the state and the people in fierce fighting against the enemy.'

These facts demonstrate how tragic developments of the past can be used for the purpose of whipping up animosity amongst nations. In my opinion, historians should interpret complicated periods in the past relations between peoples in such a way as to help draw lessons for future generations, making them wiser and more far-sighted. All of us are interested in the views and perceptions of our two peoples about each other in order to promote a favourable political climate and strengthen good-neighbourly relations between our two countries and peoples.

7

The Shimonoseki Affair, 1863-1864

H. J. MOESHART

At the beginning of the 1860s the relations between the shogunal government at Edo, the *Bakufu*, and the Imperial Court at Kyōto were rather bad. Their opinions were mainly opposed over the question of the presence of the foreigners in Japan and the treaties signed with some nations. The court, supported by masses of *rōnin-samurai* who had left their clans, demanded the expulsion of all foreigners and the breaking off of all relations with the so-called treaty nations, namely Holland, the United States, Britain and France. The *Bakufu*, on the contrary, wanted to continue the relations and, with caution, to expand them.

In an endeavour to reach an agreement with the court, the *Bakufu* tried to make use of Chōshū, one of the large clans. Chōshū, situated on the most southern point of Honshū consisted of two provinces: Nagato and Suwō. Shimonoseki was one of the most important towns and alongside this town runs the strait connecting the ocean with the Inland Sea. Many western ships made use of this passage to avoid the longer way around Kyūshū.

The movement to unite court and *Bakufu* (in Japanese Kōbu gattai) found some support but, when one of the retainers of Mori Motonori, the daimyō of Chōshū (1839-1896), tried to convince the court that at that moment the expulsion of foreigners could not be undertaken, his master lost a lot of his supporters under the *rōnin*. Many of these turned to Satsuma, a large clan from the south of Kyūshū, where the daimyō, Shimazu Hisamitsu, had plans for reform of the *Bakufu* and wanted to restore relations with the court. These plans, however, did not go far enough to please the more hot-headed young *samurai* and *rōnin* and it was even necessary for him to use arms to restore order in his own clan.

One of the first results of the acceptance by the court of the Satsuma plan was the summons to the *Shōgun* to come to Kyōto. The officials of the *Bakufu* who had had something to do with the signing of the treaties were dismissed and some of them were even banned. The rule that the *daimyō* should have their wives and families live in Edo was revoked. Thousands of inhabitants left Edo as a result of this and the political centre moved from Edo to Kyōto.

Chōshū supported the *Kōbu gattai* but its enthusiasm had cooled a

44

bit as a result of these events; and the number of members of the clan that wanted to square the bill with the *Bakufu* formed a majority. A demonstration by the *rōnin* against the *Shōgun*, just before his arrival in Kyōto, resulted in a sharp reaction from the court. It was, however, Mōri who succeeded in averting punishment for them and as a consequence many of the *rōnin* flocked to Chōshū. In Kyōto the date was set for the expulsion of the foreigners: June 1863. The guardian of the *Shōgun*, Hitotsubashi Yoshinobu, was sent to Edo to close the ports. After a short time he had to report to the court by letter that it was impossible to execute his orders and that he retired in anticipation of some punishment.

On 24 June 1863, the Dutch Vice-Consul at Yokohama[1] received a letter from Ogasawara, stating the following:

'Herewith I inform you that I have been appointed with full powers to let you know that I have received orders from his majesty the Tycoon, who is now at Kyōto and has received such orders from the Mikado, to have all the opened ports closed and to remove all subjects of the Treaty Nations as our country does not want to entertain relations with them.'[2]

It was already clear to all concerned, except the Imperial court, that such an order could never be executed. Chōshū, however, went into action and opened fire on ships passing through the Strait of Shimonoseki. The first victim of this action was the *Pembroke*, a small steamer belonging to the American company of Walsh Hall.

The Dutch Consul-General, Dirk de Graeff van Polsbroek, was at that time at Nagasaki where he was taking over from his predecessor, De Wit. His return to Yokohama had been fixed for 10 July on board the navy corvette *Medusa*, commanded by De Casembroot. At a dinner-party at the house of Walsh Hall, who was the American Consul at Nagasaki, the news of the attack on the *Pembroke* was brought by the captain of that ship. It was received with much indignation and excitement from the guests. De Casembroot, according to the diary of De Graeff, stood up and said: 'Well, tomorrow I shall pass Shimonoseki and, if they fire on me, I shall give them hell!' This short speech was received with enormous enthusiasm from the audience and numerous toasts were drunk to the 'brave Dutch commander.'

Later that evening, on their way back to their lodgings at Deshima, De Graeff told De Casembroot that he had spoken too hastily since the decision which route to take was his on account of his higher rank. But, as none of them expected the Japanese to fire on the well-known Dutch flag, they decided to take the Shimonoseki passage. They asked the Dutch Consul, Bauduin, to provide a pilot for the Inland Sea. When the *Medusa* had almost left the Bay of Nagasaki on the morning of the 10th, she met the French despatch-boat *Kienchan*, which hove to and sent a boat to the *Medusa*. The commander of the *Kienchan*, Capitaine Lafon, came on board the *Medusa* and stated that his ship had also been the victim of the batteries at Shimonoseki.

The story of the *Kienchan* is told in detail in a letter from Weuve, the interpreter of the French consulate at Yokohama, who was on board the vessel. He describes how the *Kienchan* on its way from Yokohama to

Nagasaki had anchored opposite Shimonoseki for the night. In the early morning a small vessel with two Japanese officers on board came alongside and asked what nationality the *Kienchan* belonged to. After receiving the answer that she was French, the Japanese returned to shore. When Commander Lafon got under way, some shots were fired from a battery and at first it was thought by the French that they were practising. But, when the *Kienchan* passed in front of the city, a strong cross-fire was opened on the vessel from which she escaped unharmed. In order not to risk his ship, Commander Lafon took a channel only used by Japanese shipping in order to continue on his way to Nagasaki.[3]

After receiving this news, De Casembroot and De Graeff consulted with each other — the conversation being recorded in De Graeff's diary. In order to avoid the danger of Shimonoseki De Casembroot proposed to go around Kyūshu. De Graeff, however, was of the opinion that this was impossible after the public remarks made by De Casembroot — all the more so, in fact, because the news of his remarks was already being carried to Yokohama by the passenger steamer *Hellespont*. In the end, De Graeff gave written orders to the commander to proceed through the Strait of Shimonoseki. After this incident, relations between De Graeff and De Casembroot were never very good — De Graeff always avoiding the parties that De Camembroot organised each year to celebrate the *Medusa's* forcing of the Strait of Shimonoseki.

When darkness came that day, the ship anchored at Aishima, three miles from the entrance to the Strait. The practice of anchoring at night was observed by everyone because navigation in Japanese waters was still dangerous due to the lack of good maps. There were countless rocks and reefs which were not yet charted and there were no beacons or lighthouses. The next morning the *Medusa* entered the Strait and was greeted by a signal-gun from one of the batteries. Arriving opposite Shimonoseki, the ship was treated to a hail of bullets from three shore batteries and two Japanese ships. The *Medusa* unfurled the Dutch colours and returned the compliment paid to them shot for shot, as De Graeff wrote in his diary. The engagement with the batteries lasted one-and-a-half hours as the *Medusa* could not make much speed against the current running through the Strait with her weak engine. In the logbook one can find that in a quiet sea the ship steamed 11 miles in 8¼ hours. To travel long distances the sails were set and the screw hoisted clear of the water.

In the letter of Lieutenant Petrus Wittop Koning, written to his mother on the evening of the battle, one can find a first-class eye-witness report of the events of that day:

'... suddenly smoke rose from the shore and the first grenade pitched into the sea, close to us. Soon the two Japanese ships were firing and a second battery from the shore opened up. The order to open fire was given and after a few moments, when the Japanese ships appeared before the guns, the fire was opened and soon we exchanged shot for shot with the Japanese. One of the first shots wounded a sailor close to me in such a way that he died two hours later; that was not a pleasant sight but I had no time for such things. The commander went into the battery and the Japanese pilot, frightened by the sound of the bullets, ran away and dared not even to look over the bulwarks; the helmsman was crouching down at the wheel and no one navigated the ship at that time. I saw the ship was heading the wrong way, ran on the bridge and commanded the ship in the heat of the battle as I thought was best, taking care to choose my course in such a way as to give our guns ample opportunity to reach the Japanese. The reason for the commander's absence was that, arriving in the battery, he had been wounded by a splinter in the face. The wound was insignificant, now already it is no more visible. The men behaved well, even when some grenades exploded in the battery and a fire broke out. We were holed in 27 places. After the fight was over, we found in the hull four bullets of 16 pounds, two of 24 pounds and one of 32 pounds. The shrapnel we found from the grenades thrown at us, point to a calibre of at least 16 inches.'[4]

After leaving the Strait, the *Medusa* buried her four dead at sea and continued on to Yokohama. Before arriving there she met the *Sémiramis*, the French admiral's ship, going to Shimonoseki to seek revenge for the attack on the *Kienchan*. The admiral wanted to destroy the batteries and, if possible, to take a position on land from which it would be possible to keep the Strait open for western shipping. He was followed by the other French ship in Japanese waters, the *Tancrède*. Before them the American gunboat *Wyoming* had left for the Strait to avenge the attack on the *Pembroke*.

The population of Yokohama waited anxiously for news about these ships. On the one hand, it was feared that a successful attack would lead to war with Japan; on the other hand, it was felt that, if offences like these attacks went unpunished, it might lead to more violence against foreigners. The *Wyoming* was the first to return to Yokohama. She had lost five of her small crew, while seven were wounded. But she had a victory to announce: she had succeeded in crippling one of the Japanese ships with a shot into her boiler. The French admiral arrived later. The French had demolished one of the batteries and burnt a village. It had not been possible to take a position on shore.[5]

In Kyōto in the meantime, the supporters of *Kōbu gattai* tried to wrest power from the hands of the more radical parties, headed by Chōshū, Tosa and the *rōnin*. The court wanted to act more carefully and did not want to abolish the *Bakufu* completely as these groups wanted. Shimazu was called to Kyōto and a plan was made to subdue the extremists. Nakahara, a retainer of Satsuma, was to be sent to Chōshū with an army. But the lord of Satsuma needed his army at home, as he received a message in Kyōto that the British were preparing some action against Kagoshima. The reason for this action was the killing of a reckless Englishman, Richardson, the year before, at Namamugi on the·Tōkaido. Richardson, in the company of other foreigners, rode on horseback through the cortege of Shimazu Hisamitsu, though the others urged him to turn back. He was instantly killed by retainers of Shimazu. The British, for whom this accident came as the next in a series of fires and attacks, asked an indemnity of 100,000 pounds and another 25,000 pounds for the relations of Richardson. The 100,000 pounds had been paid by the *Bakufu*, but the

47

remaining 25,000 Satsuma had to pay herself. With the British admiral on his way to Kagoshima, the defense of Yokohama was in the hands of Admiral Jaures and, as the Dutch and the Americans had both one ship in Japanese waters, no action against Chōshū could be undertaken by the foreigners.[6]

Several letters from foreign diplomats to the *Bakufu* about the punishment of Chōshū went unanswered.[7] At a meeting of these representatives (Neale for Britain, De Graeff for Holland, Du Chesne de Bellecourt for France and Pruyn for the United States), it was decided to ask the naval commanders to go into action if the *Bakufu* did not undertake to punish the *daimyō* of Chōshū. The *Bakufu*, however, played for time and refused to discuss the matter. On 28 October 1863, De Graeff was informed by officials of the *Bakufu* that Ogasawara's letter had been revoked, and he was asked to return the letter to the Japanese authorities. As a compromise the Japanese proposed to close Yokohama, but to leave Nagasaki and Hakodate open. De Graeff asked to receive this message in writing to pass on to his government, but such a letter was never received by him.

In May 1864, the patience of the foreign representatives had worn out and a conference regarding Chōshū was held. As Mōri, the *daimyō* of Chōshū, had not stopped his attacks and did not let any ship pass his Strait, action by the foreign powers had become unavoidable. The Consuls sent a *Note Identique*[8] to the *Bakufu* in which they threatened to take action into their own hands if the *Bakufu* did not punish Chōshū. The return to Japan of two students, subjects of Chōshū, Itō Shunsuke and Inoue Bunda, prompted the British admiral, Sir Augustus Kuper, to try to reach an agreement with Mōri, by sending the students in a navy ship back to their homeland, at the same time making observations in the Strait.

De Graeff sent a letter to Mōri, carried by a Dutch officer on board the British ship.[9] In the letter he demands of Chōshū a salute of 21 guns for the flag of the *Medusa*, recognition of the unlawfulness of the attack by Chōshū and a declaration of regret. A reasonable indemnity in money was asked for the relatives of those killed in the action. Mōri answered that he was acting under orders of the Emperor and, though he was unable to fight the western powers, he could not change his ways without permission from the court. He intended to go to Kyōto to have a meeting with the Emperor and thought that this would take three months. He therefore begged the foreign powers to wait for his return. This message was brought back by Itō and Inoue, who had spoken to Mōri, but it had not been put into writing.

On 22 July the diplomats held another conference. Now it was decided that further waiting was not advantageous for the western powers and that the *Shōgun* was too weak to attack Chōshū. An ultimatum was sent to the *Bakufu*, expiring after twenty days. The power of the Treaty Nations had been growing steadily during the past months. The British fleet, already the largest, had grown further and soldiers had been brought over from Hong Kong. The French fleet was also enlarged and the Dutch now had four ships in Japanese waters. The Americans, plagued by the Civil War, had one ship in Japanese waters to guard against the coming of a ship of the southern party. On 16 August the navy commanders were asked to form an allied fleet under the command of the British admiral and force the Strait of Shimonoseki from the power of the *daimyō* of Chōshū. According to a letter of De Graeff, he had received secret information from a *Bakufu* official that such an action would have the consent of the *Shōgun*.

Just when all the preparations for the action had been finished, the message arrived that in France representatives of the *Bakufu* had managed to conclude a treaty with France, obliging the *Shōgun* to take action against Chōshū and reopen the Strait. However, as soon as the Japanese delegation arrived in Edo, they were all thrown in jail. One of the *Bakufu* officers remarked to De Graeff: 'it would have been better for them if they had drowned on their way home.' Ratification by the *Bakufu* of the treaty was out of the question. Now it was no longer necessary to delay the action and on 25 August the naval commanders received their orders: to destroy the batteries; if possible, to take a position on the strait and hold it in order to extract an indemnity for the cost of the operations; and, if possible, to open another port for trade. On the 28th the combined fleet sailed from Shimonoseki. It consisted of the British admiral's ship *Euryalus*, corvettes *Tartar*, *Barrosa*, *Perseus*, a two-decker, the *Conqueror*, paddle-wheel sloops *Argus*, *Leopard* and *Coquette* and the gunboat *Bouncer*. The French Navy contributed the admiral's ship *Sémiramis* and the corvettes *Tancrède* and *Dupleix*. The Royal Dutch Navy sent the *Metalen Kruis*, *Djambi* and *Medusa* and the paddle-wheel ship *Amsterdam* joined the fleet coming from Nagasaki. The Americans contributed one chartered steamer with one gun.

On 5 September, after passing the night in front of the Strait, the ships prepared for action and took up their positions[10]. The British admiral opened fire at ten minutes past four in the afternoon. The *Barrosa*, *Tartar*, *Djambi* and *Metalen Kruis* formed the so-called heavy squadron and took up position along the northern coast of Kyūshū at Tanoura where Chōshū also had erected batteries. The *Perseus*, *Medusa*, *Bouncer* and *Tancrède*, forming the light squadron steamed along the southern coast of Honshū, while the *Amsterdam* and *Argus* with their powerful engines were kept in reserve to tow off any ships that might run aground. The *Euryalus*, *Sémiramis*, *Conqueror* and the American *Takiang* anchored off the batteries of Maedamura, out of reach of the guns. Shortly after the *Euryalus* opened fire, the whole fleet was firing away at the batteries. A battery at Kushisaki was quickly silenced by the light squadron. The *Euryalus* fired at the enemy positions from a distance of 4500 metres. The *Sémiramis* with her large guns silenced another battery. The ships at the Tanoura side had to fight a long gun-battle until they got help from the light squadron. A little past five o'clock all firing stopped. A fire started in the Maedamura battery had reached a powder-house that went up with a loud bang, making it the third of that afternoon. Ernest Satow, who was on board the *Euryalus* commented on the fighting of the Japanese: 'it must be admitted that the Japanese fought well and with great persistence ....'[11] De Casembroot and Kingston of the *Perseus* landed with men of their ships and succeeded in silencing the guns in the Maedamura battery.

Early next morning, however, the Japanese opened fire again from

49

Maedamura. Once more the battery was silenced by fire from the ships. After this 1900 men were put ashore to destroy the batteries and take away the guns. Amidst guns founded in Edo, the men found wooden guns, good for one shot only. Several of them were lying ready for use on the parapet. At noon Itō Shunsuke arrived and stated that the *daimyō* of Chōshū, his master, admitted his defeat and that an envoy was on his way to negotiate. In the terms agreed upon it is stated that: foreign ships were to be treated in a friendly way and allowed to buy coal, water and food in Shimonoseki. New batteries were not to be erected, nor the old ones to be repaired, no guns mounted. Because the city of Shimonoseki had been spared, Chōshū had to pay a ransom of 3,000,000 dollars to be divided betwen the allied powers who had contributed to the naval force in the action.[12]

8

Towards a Comparative Study of the Emergence of the Press in Japan and China

ALBERT A. ALTMAN

As in other countries outside the West, a western-style press emerged in Japan and China during the nineteenth century. It was the fruit of contact between intruding westerners and Japanese and Chinese too weak to repel them. This contact suggested to some Japanese and Chinese that they might overcome the uninvited foreigner by borrowing elements of his culture to hold him at bay.

A comparison of the emergence of the press in Japan and China yields a number of generalisations that help to illuminate the history of journalism in each country. But the significance of such a comparison is not limited to the press alone. Since the press is only one of a number of modern institutions that took form at this time, its history can also cast light on the study of other aspects of modern Japanese and Chinese history. Not least, it places in context the mutual influence of the Japanese and Chinese press upon each other.

The western-style press is one of the elements borrowed, but, by the end of the first decade of the twentieth century, it had become naturalised and had entered the mainstream of Japanese and Chinese politics and culture. In neither country was the new press a carbon copy of western examples; and each was different from the other, having taken shape in response to different domestic and foreign problems. By this time, both the Japanese and Chinese press had acquired some of their characteristic features and were on the threshold of their next leap forward. The moment was particularly propitious for further development. Japan was reaping the harvest of the Meiji leadership's policies, but was also soon to face a host of problems — political, economic, social and cultural — which these same policies had spawned. China stood on the verge of the 1911 revolution that toppled the Manchu dynasty. The beginning of the second decade of this century, which is the eve of further significant change in both countries, also provides a parameter for this particular study.

The introduction of the western-style press into Japan and China in the mid-nineteenth century guaranteed that this model of journalism would be taken up and developed. Both Japan and China were on the edge of change and the press provided a new medium in print to those wishing to learn about the course of events and even to influence them.

In both countries, there already existed printed broadsheets which were often illustrated; these were commonly known as *kawaraban* in Japanese and called *xinwenshi* in Chinese (which in the Japanese pronunciation is *shinbunshi*, the term for 'newspaper' in the early Meiji period), which reported what journalists today call 'human interest stories.' These broadsheets had a popular appeal and lacked a serious treatment of news and issues which educated readers concerned with politics could later find in the western-style press. In Japan, this western-style press was a completely new departure, but not so in China. In the early eighteenth century, private publishers in Beijing had received permission to copy certain government documents and reprint them for sale. These publications appeared under a variety of names, but foreigners in China gave them all a single, and misleading, title, the *Peking Gazette* by which they are commonly known in western literature. From among the large number of documents made available daily, so large that no publisher could reprint them all, each publisher chose what seemed most likely to interest his subscribers. An analysis of the different publications would probably reveal a large measure of common content, because in the traditional Chinese political system the emperor was the supreme decision-maker and the most important documents were those reporting his decisions. Since they were often responses to memorials, the authorities also released the texts of the memorials and those, too, were reprinted. The authorities also released a report, a kind of 'court circular,' that provided details about whom the emperor had received at court and what places he had visited the day before; this report, too, was reprinted in the 'gazettes.'

No one concerned with politics could afford to ignore these 'gazettes' despite the fact that they did not carry the most important policy decisions. Even the western-style press in foreign languages and Chinese regularly exploited these publications for information and often reprinted entire issues day after day. Yet, their considerable merits notwithstanding, these publications could not satisfy readers who wanted more than the imperial point of view on domestic issues. The 'gazettes' also lacked any news of foreign countries or of commercial activities and economic change, particularly the strengthening economy of the treaty ports. News and

51

discussion of these and more, the reader could find in the western-style press.

Foreigners were the earliest pioneers of the western-style press in Japan and China, both in foreign languages and in the native language. Being foreigners, these pioneers lived at the fringe of Japanese and Chinese society. After Japan was opened to foreign settlement in mid-1859, Nagasaki was initially the sole port for foreign trade; and there Japan's first newspaper in any language, the *Nagasaki Shipping List and Advertiser,* was published on 21 June 1861. It was short-lived because the publisher, Albert W. Hansard, an English merchant, soon transferred his business to Yokohama where he started publishing another newspaper, *The Japan Herald,* from 23 November 1861. Hansard's move exemplifies the rise of Yokohama, at Nagasaki's expense, as the main port for foreign trade and it soon held the main concentration of foreigners.

A number of other foreign-language newspapers, all in English, appeared in Yokohama before the Restoration in January 1868. Only two Japanese-language newspapers had been published there before 1868. One was the *Kaigai shinbun,* published by Joseph Heco, a castaway who had reached the United States where he had been converted to Christianity and given American citizenship. The other newspaper was the *Bankoku shinbun,* published by the chaplain to the British legation, the Reverend Buckworth Bailey.

The Meiji Restoration had important consequences for the fledgling Japanese press. The main centre of journalism moved from the Yokohama foreign settlement to Edo, soon to become Tokyo, the new capital, thus putting the press at the very centre of Japanese politics. Concomitant with this geographical shift, the practice of journalism also moved out of predominantly foreign hands into those of Japanese who had been scholar-bureaucrats in the *Bakufu* employ, that is, men of *samurai* origin. Between the early spring and midsummer of 1868, while Japan was in the grip of the post-Restoration civil war, these men brought out at least 17 *shinbunshi* in Edo and two in Yokohama.

A little more than a year after the Restoration, another significant development took place in April 1869, when the Meiji government accorded legal existence to the press and put it in the service of the new regime. From this time on, the western-style press, in its Meiji adaptation, became an inseparable element of Meiji politics and society. But, following the government crisis of 1873 and the memorial for the establishment of a representative assembly in 1874, the press lost its official patronage and has ever since been a privately-owned enterprise. The present-day pattern of national, regional and local newspapers emerged in the first decade of the twentieth century (between the Sino-Japanese and Russo-Japanese wars). The major newspapers, which featured both domestic and foreign news, were then already large, capital-intensive enterprises, using the latest printing technology which enabled them to satisfy the demand of rising heterogeneous and still mainly urban circulations.

These changes are the hallmarks of the early stage of the Japanese adaptation of this foreign means of communication. The Chinese adaptation occurred under radically different circumstances. When the first newspapers were being published in Nagasaki and Yokohama in the early 1860s, a western-style press, in newspaper and magazine format, already had a forty-year-old history in China. It had emerged on the south-eastern fringe of China, which historically had been a place of commercial contact between Chinese and foreigners, where the centre of journalistic activity was the Macao-Canton area. China's first western-style newspaper was published in Macao in 1822, called, in the Portuguese-language, *A Abelha de China*. It was sponsored by the Macao authorities and was the organ of a political party, the Absolutists; its editor was the Superior of the local Dominican Order. The Catholic Church in Macao and the East India Company in Canton kept Protestant missionaries from taking up residence in the area. The missionaries, therefore, established a centre in Malacca where in 1816 an English missionary, William Milne, who was associated with the Anglo-Chinese College edited a monthly publication with a magazine format — the first western-style journal in Chinese — the *Chashisu meiyue tongjiquan*. Soon after, in 1827, Canton produced its first newspaper, the English-language *The Canton Register*.

As a result of the Opium War of 1840-2, Canton lost its position as the centre of journalistic activity. It was supplanted first by Hong Kong, which became a British colony, and then by Shanghai, which was opened as a treaty port. Hong Kong and other treaty ports, but particularly Shanghai, maintained their primacy in the field of journalism well into the twentieth century. The treaty ports with their extra-territorial rights were a visible symbol of the absence of Chinese sovereignty. In Japan, it had become legally impossible from 1875 onwards for a foreigner to publish a newspaper in Japanese, but in China, foreigners, as well as opponents of the regime, could publish newspapers and magazines in Chinese in the treaty ports under the protection of foreign law. The main centres of the Chinese press, therefore, were not under the control of Chinese law, not only on the mainland, but also in Tokyo, which early in the first decade of the twentieth century became a haven for Chinese revolutionaries and anti-Manchu elements.

In the early stage of the adaptation of the western model, there is also a difference in the social origins of the native pioneers. In 1868, the Japanese press moved into the hands of a *samurai*-derived élite. They were the editors, writers and publishers of the civil war press, of the newspapers that sprang up in Tokyo and the prefectures after the abolition of the feudal polity in 1871, of the press that came into being after 1873-4, concomitant with the blossoming of the people's rights (*jiyū minken*) movement and even, with few exceptions, of the press that emerged in the 1880s after the movement declined. Increasingly from this time, too, journalists became professionals.

In China, by contrast, the press moved into the hands of men without status, very likely of lower gentry-merchant background if the pattern of change in other areas of Chinese life is a guide. In the Chinese world, these men lacked the prestige that came with being officials or scholar-gentry; in the world of the treaty port, they lacked status because they were Chinese. In the terminology of sociologists, they were 'marginal men,' living and working at a point of contact between two worlds, but belonging

53

fully to neither. However, the reform movement of the late 1890s changed this by moving the Chinese-language press away from the periphery of Chinese society. A reform press sprang up in the treaty ports, but also moved inland, the classic example being the reform movement in Hunan province, where scholar-gentry and officials used the western-style press as a channel for spreading ideas for change. What had happened in Japan in 1868 when the western-style press became a political instrument of the *samurai* élite, now happened in China when the western-style press became a political instrument of officials and scholar-gentry.

But, by being absorbed into Chinese politics in this manner, the press became subject to new restraints. Unlike the press in Japan at this time, the reform-minded press in the provinces lacked a foundation in law for its operation. Its existence depended upon the protection of powerful patrons who shielded it from enemies and provided funds. But such protection also had its price; it exposed the press to control by these patrons and, when they withdraw their support, the press withered and died. Yet, despite its short existence, the provincial reform press bequeathed an important legacy to Chinese journalism: journalists (who were becoming professionals) and journalism had become respectable and had become (and was to remain) an integral part of Chinese politics.

In the decade between the end of the reform movement in the provinces and the 1911 revolution, the main centres of Chinese journalism remained beyond Chinese jurisdiction, notably in Hong Kong, Shanghai and for a while also in Tokyo which now had a large population of Chinese students. This was the decade during which the western-style press displaced the older *Peking Gazette*-type press. By providing a far wider and more varied coverage of news, both domestic and foreign, the western-style press appealed to a fast-growing and more heterogeneous urban readership. This decade, for example, saw the growth of a press appealing to special groups, such as newspapers and journals for women, and press written in vernacular or semi-vernacular, a style closer to the spoken language than that favoured by the press for more educated readers.

The *Peking Gazette*-type press also became obsolete when first provincial authorities and later the government in the capital, no longer depending on proxies, themselves began to issue periodical publications known as *guanbao (kanpō* in Japanese, from which the Chinese usage is probably borrowed) that reported information which the authorities wished to convey to the public.

The western-style press was now largely in private Chinese hands and was, with the adoption of western printing technology, becoming a capital-intensive enterprise as in Japan, although the many capital-starved, small and ephemeral newspapers and journals published by equally small and ephemeral groups, should not be overlooked. And finally, during this decade, too, the Qing government promulgated regulations, some of them based on Japanese precedents, aimed at bringing under control the press which increasingly was becoming an instrument for revolution and anti-government agitation.

9

Image of Japan in Foreign Newspapers Published in Japan Before the Meiji Restoration

OLAVI K. FÄLT

Images play an important rôle in the study of cultural interaction. It is through images that we learn about the creators of those images, those who examine them and the objects of these. In other words, an image may tell us as much about its creator as about the object of the image itself.[1] People's views of other people and other cultures are dependent on their own outlook on the world[2] and thus, by studying the westerners' image of Japan, we can also pick up traces of their own world-view.

The 1860s were a time when Japan was searching for her own identity, as it were, in an attempt to adapt to the challenge posed by western culture. This pressure was released in the form of violence and hatred of the West, on the one hand, and by a commitment on the part of the Tokugawa government, on the other, to the acquisition of western knowledge in order to strengthen Japan's position with respect to western culture.

From the time of the opening up of Japan in 1854, people outside had been following carefully the events that were taking place in that country[3] the best opportunities for which existed in Yokohama, which, since the opening of the city to foreigners in 1859, had been rapidly developing into a flourishing western community, largely based on trade. Many manifestations of western culture were on view there in the context of everyday life. It was a laboratory in which the Japanese could view this strange but fascinating culture in natural surroundings. One manifestation was the foreign-language press.[4]

The western press, the pioneer of which had been Albert W. Hansard with his *Nagasaki Shipping List and Advertiser*, which commenced publication on 22 June 1861, was precisely the forum which followed most closely the first steps taken by the Japanese on their new road, and the newspapers' articles about Japan, her development and her future prospects, created an image which was to have a lasting effect on relations between the Japanese and western cultures.

The early western press in Japan has survived only in a fragmented form and research on the topic has been very general in character up to now.[5] This present paper, which is based on research in progress into the rôle of the foreign-language press in the westernisation of Japan in the 1870s, makes use of the following material: The *Nagasaki Shipping List and Advertiser* for 1861, *The Japan Herald* 1861-62, *The Daily Japan Herald*

1864, *The Japan Times* 1865-66 and *Japan Punch* 1862-68, all except the first being published in Yokohama and the last being in the nature of a satirical magazine.

A general frame of reference for these new newspapers may be obtained from *The Japan Herald's* definition of its task as published in 1861, in which this was stated to be the satisfying of the rapidly-growing demand for information about Japan in England and other parts of the world. This was not concerned only with trade and social progress, but also included original information on this beautiful country and its fascinating inhabitants.[6] The starting-point was thus a highly constructive one. Indeed, it should be remembered that from the earliest information about Japan brought back by Marco Polo at the end of the thirteenth century, that country had generally been looked on in a favourable light in the West,[7] a situation which had not changed with the opening of Japan to outsiders in 1854, when it had merely become an object of exotic admiration.[8] The foreign image and general perceptions of Japan naturally gained in detail once more foreigners were able to visit the country; less favourable aspects also began to emerge.[9]

Westerners living in Japan were apt to come to the defence of Japan and the Japanese when unfavourable criticism was expressed, as the *Nagasaki Shipping List and Advertiser* did in 1861, when it attempted to refute the claims made by Bishop George Smith of Hong Kong[10] on his visit to the country in 1860 that the Japanese were one of the most licentious races in the world. On the contrary, it replied, the large cities of Japan were the most peaceful to be found anywhere:

' ...we have never been in any large city in which it is less prominently thrust under public gaze than it is in the large cities in Japan.'[11]

At that same time, it disputed the idea that there were a lot of drunks to be seen in the streets, or that Japan was a particularly corrupting place for young western men.[12]

Understandably, the articles in the newspapers also reflected the desires of the writers themselves, the members of the trading fraternity. The *Japan Herald* was of the opinion in late 1861 that the Japanese in general were against any increase in contacts with foreigners. (In fact, this opposition arose from the eastward expansion of western countries, which had forced the Tokugawa government to accept the notion of cooperation with the major powers.) The newspaper called upon other nations to be meticulous in honouring the agreements made with Japan and in exacting from her the privileges which had been promised; every concession made without a response from the Japanese was likely to shake their belief in the power and determination of other nations. The western residents evidently felt that any concessions would detract from their own commercial dealings, especially since they firmly believed in the trading opportunities offered by Japan.[13]

The westerners' impressions of the future of Japan, especially as one of the major commercial nations in the world, were highly optimistic, as expressed by the *Daily Japan Herald* in March 1864

'Among the most conclusive of the many evidences we have lately had of increasing confidence as to the probable great importance of

the position which will hereafter be assumed by this country in the great comitia of trading nations, one of the surest is the attraction it appears to have become to men of scientific attainments.'[14]
The *Japan Times*, which appeared for the first time on 8 September 1865, announced quite plainly that it would strive above all to serve the interests of the western trading fraternity and would discuss matters of trade in Japan in that light.[15] Concerning relations with the Japanese, it indicated that it would attempt to assure them that foreigners were not hankering after territorial power, but that they could learn from them not only the arts of war but also the arts of peace.[16] The paper believed that the Japanese would soon notice their errors once they had been pointed out and would alter their systems of administration, trade and finance to their advantage and that of the foreigners.[17]

This view was in line with the community's own commercial interests, but also incorporated hopes for a strengthening in the merchants' position in their dealings with the Japanese, since the purpose of the article was to promote the founding of a Japan Chamber of Commerce. It was the merchants themselves who were intending to point out errors, since underlying the article was a doctrine of economic liberalism which sought to break away from government control and the restrictions which it placed upon trade.

The general image of the Japanese at this stage was somewhat equivocal. They were referred to at one point as 'this primitive yet highly civilised people'[18] and, though the country was even referred to at times as 'the Paradise of the Pacific,' this did not mean that it was above criticism. What worried the *Japan Times* most was the inability of the Tokugawa government to fulfil its undertaking to facilitate trade by opening more harbours and otherwise creating more favourable conditions, an attitude which naturally fitted in very well with the newspaper's rôle as a guardian of the merchants' interests. It was also in favour of the western powers bringing pressure to bear upon Japan in this respect, regarding this as in no way unjust but merely an insistence on rights which had been promised. These demands should be met even if there was the danger of the existing governmental system collapsing, since the favourable consequences would be the development of the country's resources, an extension of trade and increased affluence for the Japanese people.[19]

This idea reflects the sincere belief held at that time in the happiness which could be conferred upon mankind by international trade and the right of the major European powers to world leadership. In fact, the *Japan Times* usually justified the reforms or amendments which it proposed in terms of the profit they would bring to the Japanese themselves, i.e. the people or the government,[20] and to the westerners, i.e. the foreign merchants.

The Japanese government, nevertheless, was not usually treated very kindly in the columns of the paper, a fact which was associated with the weakened position of the Tokugawa in the country. The Satsuma and Chōshū domains threatened their military supremacy, and the Emperor was becoming more of a uniting factor for forces opposed to the government, which also meant an increase in importance as far as foreign powers were concerned. This emerged in practical terms in November 1865, when the Emperor acceded to foreign demands and approved agreements made by the Tokugawa government regarding such matters as the opening up of Hyogo (Osaka) to trade from the beginning of 1868.[21]

The newspaper regarded the position of the Tokugawa government as a weak one, which did not give this family any greater right to power in the country than any other *daimyo*. Admittedly, this claim was conditional in the sense that if the Emperor had not agreed to ratify the agreements, the support of the western powers without any doubt, would have been on the side of the Tokugawa government, which had approved them, since the entry of Japan into the family of nations was looked on as a good and justifiable act on account of the enormous benefit it would confer upon the Japanese and indirectly upon the whole world. The country's political future was seen as a gloomy rather than a rosy one, since in the paper's opinion it lacked any real leadership, an obvious reference to the indeterminate relations between the Emperor and the Tokugawa shogunate.[22]

This gloomy view of Japan's future did not extend to the commercial sphere, however, where it was foreseen that she could become the Venice of the Pacific and a mediator between Europe and China, even though at that stage the country was regarded as backward[23] and the Japanese as rather primitive people.[24] With Japan occupying this new position of importance in the future, the writings of the Yokohama press were expected to carry much more weight, so that people would wait with great interest to hear its voice and listen attentively.[25]

The fact that the prophecies about Japan were not concerned only with the commercial interests of the western community but also with the newspapers' aspirations regarding their own status serves to demonstrate the extent to which the image projected of Japan arose very largely out of its creators' own interests and outlook on the world. The *Japan Times* did not make any attempt to deny that it had a clear viewpoint of its own, but even emphasised the fact and stressed its Englishness:

'We write in general — in an English newspaper, necessarily from an English point of view.'[26]

This still did not prevent the paper from praising the Japanese people, their friendliness to foreigners and their desire to learn as much from them as they were able to teach, particularly when compared with the Chinese, whose hostility was looked on as senseless and whose resistance to reform was viewed as complacent stupidity. This was again an opinion which fostered the interests of the western residents of Yokohama, since, alongside the enthusiasm shown by the Japanese, it also emphasised the frenzied activity going on in the young settlement itself.[27]

This does not mean that there was nothing in the Japanese to complain about. The inefficiency and untrustworthiness of Japanese servants was a particular source of dissatisfaction and, although westerners had come up against similar problems everywhere in the East, they seemed to be particularly accentuated here. The blame was not placed, however, on the Japanese whose own families were harmonious and homes clean and tidy, but on the westerners themselves, who (the paper said) should pay more attention to their servants' interests and their comfort and well-being, an attitude which would pay dividends, since the Japanese were not an ungrateful race like the Chinese.[28] Thus the 'golden land of Japan' tradition of Marco Polo lived on in the Yokohama press, which still insisted that Japan was in some way better than other non-western countries.

Although the *Japan Times* frequently painted a rosy picture of Japan's commercial prospects for the future, it had no fear that she would ever seriously compete with Britain, certainly not in the textile industry, because she had no home-produced raw materials or machines. This view was again in accordance with the commercial interests of the western community, as the article concerned was attempting to justify the lifting of the customs duty on wool and cotton. It claimed that their importation did not pose a threat to Japanese industry, as it was inconceivable that any industry could arise in that field, and there was no reason to charge duty on re-exports, i.e. the use of Japan as an intermediary.[29]

The *Japan Times* returned to the subject of the unstable internal situation, i.e. the limited power of the Tokugawa shogunate, in May 1866, calling for an agreement to be made between the Emperor and the confederate *daimyos*, the *de facto* rulers of Japan. This demand similarly arose from commercial interests, since it was feared that the situation might lead to a political crisis which could interfere with trade. Also the existing unstable conditions were such that trade could not be expected to achieve the same importance and status as it might otherwise have had.[30]

From the paper's point of view, Japan took a new step forward in May 1866, when the shogunate issued a decree permitting Japanese citizens to travel abroad. This was taken as an important sign of a liberal, pragmatic policy on the part of the government, and the paper believed that it would improve the reputation of the Japanese government in the civilised world and show that the country was moving forward in the march of the nations.[31] This decision inspired the paper to see in the Japanese many 'characteristics of the sovereign Aryan race,' and also raised the status of the shogunate in the paper's estimation. The complaint now was that it had proved impossible to find a person sufficiently competent to serve as *shōgun* so that he could have become the real leader of the country with support from the outside world. The paper saw the shogunate as attempting by means of this decree to establish the middle class as a buffer between itself and the aristocracy, which was threatening its position, and gave its readers to understand that it had nothing against the *shōgun*, but would even prefer to see him as the ruler of Japan rather than the Emperor, as the *shōgun* had looked with favour upon the expansion of contacts with the West. This permission to travel abroad was a blessing not only for Japan but indirectly for the whole world.[32]

This change in attitude as regards the shogunate shows once again how matters were viewed constantly from a western, or more precisely a British, angle. Britain dominated world trade and navigation, and this freedom of association naturally widened the opportunities for trade. Praise for Japan continued to pour from the pages of the newspaper. The Japanese were exalted as one of the oldest peoples on earth:

'The Japanese nation, in fact, has probably a better claim than any other race, save the Arab and the Jew, to call itself autochtone.'[33] and their development was regarded as having been spontaneous and original:

'...that the development of its character, the creation of its civilisation and the organisation of its polity have all been innate, spontaneous and original, without help from without in the form either of education, suggestion or comparison.'[35]

Referring to the astounding effects which the freedom to travel would have in Japan, the paper emphasised that the Japanese race should be valued very highly in ethnological terms:

'...the necessity of giving to the Japanese race its proper — and, as we think, an exceedingly high — ethnological position. The nations of the old world, more particularly the irresistible Anglo-Saxon-Scandinavian race, are too prone to underestimate orientals.'[35]

The Japanese were described as a noble race which had created a civilisation for itself, so that there was no cause for looking down on them. If the British treated them wrongly, they would be forsaking a unique opportunity to spread the principles of religious, political and commercial freedom of which they were so proud and the dissemination of which they regarded as their particular task. Linked with this hope was the expectation that one day Japan would become one of the major naval powers in the world, so that it was desirable that Britain should help to build up her fleet and then enter into a pact with her in the face of the Russian threat in the Pacific. The paper saw the opening up of Japan as one of the major achievements of the century, on account of which the promotion of her development should be a matter of duty and honour for all other civilised societies.[36]

Here we no longer have passing hints at common interests between Britain and Japan but a straightforward call for cooperation, in which the first to benefit would naturally be the English merchants in Japan, whose interests the *Japan Times* represented. In this way favourable impressions of Japan and high expectations for her future became firmly associated with British glory, liberalism and local commercial interests.

Japan Punch, which followed the development of Japan through the medium of its satirical cartoons, was sharp to take note of the rapid changes occurring there. Its first issue, in May 1862, contained under the headline 'First Impressions of Japan' a picture of a traditional Japanese woman with a child on her back.[37] The change which had taken place was well illustrated by a pair of pictures published in September 1865 with a traditional Japanese army officer and his assistant on one side and a corresponding pair in western military dress on the other, carrying the title 'Results of our intercourse with Japan.'[38] A similar spirit emerges in a cartoon of a young *samurai* accustomed to spending his time in a western club, who is dressed in western style except for his swords and has a cigar in one hand and a glass in the other. He announces, 'I like only civilisation!'[39]

Japan Punch was respectful towards the Tokugawa government, as may be seen from a cartoon referring to the reparations paid by the government for the opening of the straits of Shimonoseki, which had been blocked by the Chōshū domain. The caption reads 'Britannia bleedeth the Tycoon' i.e., great prince — a title used to refer to the *shōgun*), and Britannia is seen bleeding money from the arm of a handsome Japanese. The British lion is so ashamed that it has gone into hiding.[40]

Others pictured in fashionable western dress and smoking cigarettes include students of French and members of a western-style orchestra.[42] Studying French was obviously an elegant and stylish thing to do in Japan at that time, even to the point of ridicule, as another cartoon shows a group of well-dressed students with the caption 'Elegant and pleasing costumes of Japanese going to their French drill.'[43] The accent placed on the spread of French culture may well also reflect some measure of Franco-British competition for influence in Japan.

One good example of well-meaning satire based on the changes taking place in Japan which also provides an excellent picture of the reality of these changes, is a cartoon strip in which a traditional *samurai* represents the Japanese of yesterday, a set of bowlegged men in assorted western dress the Japanese of today and an elegant gentleman with a top hat and cane in his hand the Japanese of tomorrow.[45] Further expressions of these changes and a certain disbelief in their rationality were pictures, for example, of young Japanese dressed in ill-fitting western clothes, while another shows pupils from a western school with their top-hats and outfits that represented the latest thing in fashions.[46]

Such rapid changes could only be achieved at a price, as *Japan Punch* warned its readers late in 1867. The way of reform with all its modern machinery, ships, navies, armies, shipyards and lighthouses would lead the country into an abyss of debt.[47] When the Tokugawa shogunate eventually fell from power early in 1868, the magazine showed no surprise, but published a picture of a blindfolded Japanese collapsing under a burden of reforms as his stick broke. The comment beneath was 'No wonder!'[48]

The papers discussed above, as they themselves stated, represented the commercial interests of the western community, predominantly British, which had settled in Japan, and thus the image of that country projected by them reflects those same interests. The result was a generally favourable picture, support for British-Japanese cooperation and a belief in Japan's commercial prospects, which constituted the foundation for the future prosperity of the western residents themselves. *Japan Punch*, however, was also prepared to wave a warning finger at the Japanese, perhaps with the idea behind it that, since development in the West had required such a long period of time, time would also be needed elsewhere before a new culture could be absorbed satisfactorily. Above all, the image of Japan contained in the local western press represented a British view of the world which proclaimed the glory and hegemony of Britain, and in which economic liberalism, in the form of universal international trade, was seen as the key to happiness and success.

10

Japan and European Brinkmanship, 1895

IAN NISH

This paper is based on a historical speculation which emerged from my recent book on the origins of the Russo-Japanese war.[1] Japan challenged Russia in 1904 and achieved victory; why did she not try to challenge the European powers when they intervened in her war in China in 1895? On 17 April 1895, Japan signed the treaty of Shimonoseki with China, obtaining the cession of a large part of the Liaotung peninsula. On 23 April a coalition of three European countries under the lead of Russia intervened between the eastern belligerents and offered 'friendly advice' to Japan to return the whole of the ceded territory on the ground that it was a threat to China. Under persistent pressure, Japan eventually agreed to retrocede the territory in question to China in return for a supplementary indemnity. On the surface this was merely an instance of nineteenth-century Great Power diplomacy. But it still leaves unanswered the question why Japan, which had just proved herself in war, gave in to this kind of blackmail. It was out of character for her to do so; and it was to be out of line with her actions in 1904.

Presumably Russia, France and Germany were prepared to use force to get the Japanese to submit. The only kind of force that they could muster in east Asia was naval power. Though there were signs that Russia was sending troops to the East through Odessa, that was not likely to influence the outcome. The only effective naval strength that the coalition could rely on in the waters of north-east Asia was that of Russia. In the German far-eastern squadron there were seven vessels of war which the Kaiser offered to place under Russian command; in the French there were thirteen but they were mainly dispersed in the South China seas. So it was the much larger Russian fleet which would call the tune. It is necessary, therefore, to look at the comparative naval strengths of Russia and Japan in the area.

RUSSIAN NAVAL STRENGTH

At the start of the war the Russian squadron in the Pacific was relatively strong, consisting of 1st class cruisers (*Admiral Nakhimov, Admiral Kornilov, Runda*) 2nd class cruisers (*Ralboinik, Kruiser, Zabuyaka*), gunboats (*Manchuria, Bobr, Sivuch, Koreyets*) and three torpedo-boats. By the time of the crisis in April her Pacific squadron had been strengthened with the arrival from the Mediterranean of 1st class cruisers (*Emperor Nicolas I, Pamyats Azova, Vladimir Monomakh*), gunboats (*Gremyashii,*

Otvazhnii), mine-laying cruisers (*Vsadnik, Gaidamak*) and three torpedo-boats. The *Pamyats Azova* was the flagship of the commander-in-chief, Vice-admiral Tyrtov, while the *Emperor Nicolas I* was the flagship of his second-in-command, Rear-admiral Makarov. Though this amounted in itself to a formidable naval strength, various wild rumours circulating in Japan were adding greatly to the estimate of Russian strength in the area.[2]Information was reaching Japanese intelligence that four large transports had come out with reinforcements heading for Vladivostok and that six cruisers were on their way to Chinese waters. Moreover, Japanese intelligence had for some years past made it its business to survey the state of the Russian navy. Thus, Major (later General) Fukushima Yasumasa, who was to be renowned as 'the father of Japanese intelligence,' had during the course of his stay in Russia in 1892 observed not only Russian military developments but also her naval achievements.[3]

How was this armada of 1895 viewed by the Japanese? Let us remember that it was always in the background of the political protests of the three powers. The initial 'friendly advice' was threatening enough. But it has to be remembered that the Russian, French and German ministers called on Japan on consecutive days to expedite her reply. This was not, of course, a menace in itself since the diplomats' representations had been made in the friendly terms of diplomatic advice. It was the suspicions of naval activity underlying them that carried the menace. Japanese sources tell us of the apprehensions felt by the intelligence authorities: that it was the intention of Russia to make a joint naval demonstration at Kobe, all her ships in Japanese ports being placed on alert to set sail at 24 hours' notice with their boilers fed day and night; or that it was the intention to move the Russian fleet presumably to a point such as Tsushima where Japan's communications with her continental army could be cut off. In addition to the threat offered in her own coastal waters Japan was worried over developments at Vladivostok, where a state of siege had been declared and the port was gazetted as a war zone. 50,000 active-duty soldiers and reserves were summoned to service under the command of the governor-general of eastern Siberia. Reports told that torpedoes had been laid at the entrance to the port and the use of ice-breakers was keeping the harbour open to traffic.[4]

Of course, the Russian perception of all this was different from that of Japan and presents a much less menacing picture. Foreign Minister Lobanov told the British ambassador that all that was contemplated by the three powers was a joint naval demonstration and that the three allies were confident that no war-like activity would be required to bring Japan to her senses. Be that as it may, the Russian squadron under Admiral Tyrtov certainly scared the Japanese ministers by its tactics.

JAPAN'S NAVAL STRENGTH

On paper, Japan's overall naval strength was considerable. But her fleet had, of course, been in action for six to eight months and, though it had been overwhelmingly successful against the Chinese fleet, it had been thoroughly exhausted by the prolonged war. It had been fully stretched with its rôle of retaining command of the seas, assisting the army, supplying ports in the occupied territories etc.[5] Another problem which developed in 1895 was that the Tokyo government decided that, as part of Japan's peace terms, it would ask for the cession of Taiwan and the Pescadores islands. It had not been opportune to detach a fleet for this purpose earlier in the war so it had to be done at the tail-end when peace talks were about to begin. Thus it was that the Japanese squadron set sail for the south on 15 March, the very day that Li Hung-chang, the Chinese plenipotentiary, set off from Tientsin for negotiations in Japan. The expedition was under instructions to return to the north without delay in case a major campaign was needed for the capture of the Chinese capital. The Pescadores islands were seized on 23 March. Landings were not made on Taiwan, although rumours abounded there that Japan would take the island. Instead, Admiral Itō's squadron was gathered again at the Pescadores on 30 April and steamed for home waters. At daybreak on 5 May it reached its base of Sasebo from which it had set off seven weeks earlier. For the critical ten days of high tension when the ministers were considering the 'friendly advice' of the powers, the squadron had been absent.

The squadron had established naval ascendancy in the Taiwan Straits, set up a base in the Pescadores and undertaken surveys of the Taiwanese coastline. But it had not carried out the invasion because of the hostile outbreaks which it anticipated on the island and the uncertain attitude of the powers. It was understood that the squadron would have to go back to Taiwan in order to enforce the terms of the treaty of Shimonoseki. At the end of May Japanese troops landed on the island; and Li Ching-fong, the commissioner appointed to cede the island, formally made the transfer on 2 June aboard the Japanese flagship.

THE CRITICAL FORTNIGHT

It was on 23 April that Russia, Germany and France had offered their 'friendly advice.' Hayashi Tadasu, the deputy minister in Tokyo, reported it straightaway to Count Itō, the prime minister in Hiroshima, and to his senior, Mutsu Munemitsu, the foreign minister, who had been forced by ill-health to leave the councils of state in Hiroshima and proceed to Maiko near Kyoto for recuperation. From this remoteness, Mutsu, on 24 April, made the following surprising assessment of the crisis:

'It was thus incumbent on us to consider the extent to which our armed forces (who had scored victory upon brilliant victory) might be aroused and the morale of our subjects shaken by news of any governmental action which nullified one of the main features of the peace settlement. We might well be able to minimise hostile international reactions to the policy we adopted but I was far less certain of our ability to curb adverse reactions at home ... The moment urgently required us to reject the advice of the three powers *for the time being* and at the same time to enquire both as to the nature of their actual intentions and the disposition of our armed forces and citizenry towards retroceding Liaotung.'[6] (my emphasis)

In other words, the foreign minister was as much perturbed by possible internal reactions as by foreign pressure.

Meanwhile, after long deliberation on 24 April at an imperial conference, the joint military-civilian forum at Hiroshima, the ministers present concluded:

'Our expeditionary forces then stationed at Liaotung had drawn away our best troops, and our best ships had been dispatched to the Pescadores. In short, our military capabilities at home were virtually nil. Moreover, our fleet had been for almost a year, continuously involved in action, exhausting both its men and its supplies. In this situation, it would prove to be quite a hopeless task to take on even the Russian fleet, let alone the combined naval forces of the three intervening powers.'[7]

Between them Prime Minister, Itō, Army Minister, Yamagata, and Navy Minister, Saigō, favoured a policy of avoiding resistance to the European fleets and decided, therefore, on a conference of the powers. But Mutsu in Maiko argued against this, suggesting that Japan should first test the solidity of the Dreibund. It was readily apparent to him that, should the three powers immediately involved be strongly committed to intervening, Japan would have no alternative but to give in; but an international conference would be dangerous for Japan. One of the cabinet, Nomura, returned to Hiroshima on the evening of 25 April to report to the emperor on the cabinet's decision to defer to Mutsu's views.

As a preliminary to reaching a decision in cabinet, Prime Minister, Itō, referred the problem to the army and navy ministers and the chiefs of the General Staffs (sambō shuseki), the so- called gunji shunobu (military brains trust). The service ministers replied that,

' ...in present circumstances our armed services consist of crack troops but, in comparison with the three countries who are evenly matched and are among the leading powers in the world today, it is impossible for us to contemplate resistance or undertake a major struggle against them.'[8]

Such was the private thinking of the military leaders in Japan, who surrounded the emperor. On 26 April, Nomura obtained the emperor's approval for the Maiko decision and returned to Kyoto. Saigō as navy minister remained in Hiroshima with the emperor and then accompanied the imperial procession which left the war-time capital and reached Kyoto on 29 April in order to hold an imperial conference there. At this meeting, Japan, which, in the meantime, had tried to win the support of Britain, the United States or any major power and failed, in effect agreed to accept the 'friendly advice,' though it was a matter of days before she let it be known that she was prepared to yield more than part of the Liaotung peninsula.

In an important move, the war minister, General Yamagata, left Hiroshima for Port Arthur. This took place immediately after the emperor had sanctioned the Maiko decision; and Yamagata carried an imperial edict, relaying that decision to senior staff officers in the field. The cabinet was scared that the army was hostile, or would be hostile, to the policy adopted to deal with the triple intervention. In order to secure the acceptance of the generals at the front, it was essential for Yamagata to bear with him a mandate from the emperor.[9] The mission was not really intended to consult the army overseas but to soothe, pacify and appease any rebellious instincts there might be among army leaders of the expeditionary force who were understood to be in hawkish mood and, it was feared, might be ready to go it alone.

It was clearly to the advantage of the Japanese to play for time. Their navy was inconveniently dispersed; their army was mainly on the continent and in rebellious mood. Moreover, their leaders were awkwardly situated: the emperor and court were at Hiroshima, while some cabinet members were en route to Kyoto and a key figure was in Maiko. Their initial thought had been that, if Japan declined to accept and left the three powers with no alternative to using naval strength in the area, France would withdraw from the combination, Germany would not contribute anything to the operation, and Russia would be forced to have second thoughts. But one week of procrastination left Japan with the impression that France and Germany were as committed to punitive action as was Russia. By 3 May all Japan's counter-proposals had been turned down by the three European powers who appeared to be solid in their responses. The action taken by Russia in moving her whole fleet from Japanese ports left no doubt in the mind of the Japanese government that the threat offered by the powers could not be taken lightly.

On 4 May a meeting was convened at Mutsu's lodgings in Kyoto. It was attended by all cabinet ministers and senior members of the Supreme Command, who had travelled thither, including Itō, Finance Minister, Matsukata, Navy Minister, Saigō, Home Minister, Nomura, and the chief of the naval general staff, Admiral Kabayama. After a meeting that lasted the whole day, they agreed to tell the three powers in rather vague terms that they were accepting their advice. But, if this was intended as a policy of concessions to Europe, it was not a policy of concessions to China. The Chinese, finding that they had been successful in obtaining the return of their Liaotung territory, now sought to extend the cease-fire while delaying the exchange of ratifications. When the Japanese were adamantly opposed to this, they appealed to the three powers. But the three European countries applauded Japan's decision to hand back the peninsula and refused to support the new attitude of the Chinese. Accordingly, ratifications of the treaty of Shimonoseki were exchanged on 8 May at Chefoo on the northern coast of Shantung province amid a great display of naval might on Japan's part. It may be observed, however, that, on the day, the Russian fleet in Chefoo harbour consisted of the *Pamyat Azova*, the flag-ship of Vice-admiral Tyrtov, and the *Emperor Nicholas I*, the flag-ship of Rear-admiral Makarov, plus three iron-clads, two cruisers and five other smaller vessels.

The Japanese government let it be known that Japan's decision to climb down had been arrived at on the strong advice of the ministers of war and navy and that the emperor had taken the same view. On 10 May an imperial proclamation (*shōchoku*) explaining about the retrocession of Liaotung was issued, the emperor being persuaded to subscribe to it with the soldiers very much in mind. It was eventually published in the gazette and an imperial rescript to the army (*chokugo*) was published on 13 May.[10] In this way, the hostility of the three powers was appeased and the hostility of Japan's military forces soothed by imperial intervention.

As an historian, I do not propose to answer the hypothetical question with which I began this short essay. I can only speculate that, if Japan had called the bluff of the three powers, she might have got away with it and retained Liaotung. But it is very doubtful.

In retrospect, Japan did not do her utmost to reinforce her position. The possibility of a Dreibund intervention had existed from the early days of the war. When it came, it could not be described as a surprise to the Japanese leaders. Of course, there were many uncertainties about the countries that would constitute the 'interveners' and the form their activity would take. I suspect that, as the peace negotiations began, Japan thought she had got away with it. Nonetheless, Japan was surely incautious in sending a substantial force to the Pescadores and allowing it to stay for as long as seven weeks. Opinions must differ on whether their expedition was necessary in March 1895. Admittedly, Japan was in an unusual, not to say unique, situation in that Japan's treaty demands included the demand for a territory where there had been no fighting, namely Taiwan. It was natural that her leaders would want to show themselves in that region before the negotiations got under way. It may be relevant to add, however, that the army and navy ministers when they were asked for their advice during the Dreibund crisis did not mention the Pescadores force; they merely spoke of the exhaustion of their services. Was this an admission that they had made a strategic mistake?[11]

When we come to examine the European brinkmanship, there are also uncertainties. Certainly Russia had amassed a sizeable naval force in the area and had bases there. France and Germany were camp-followers; and it is doubtful what they would have contributed if naval action had materialised. On the surface, the three-power front remained solid; but there was an element of posturing since they knew of Japan's naval weakness and of their own strong bargaining position. If we place the spotlight on Russia, it is doubtful whether Admiral Tyrtov had full authority to act. One presumes he had; his manoeuvres suggest so. On the other hand, St Petersburg may not have regarded it in these terms. Perhaps optimistic, as Russia was to be in 1904, she may have felt in 1895 that preparations for a naval demonstration would suffice to scare the Japanese. It may be that Russia, like her two partners, breathed a sigh of relief when Japan climbed down, because their east-Asian squadrons were unproven. Certainly there would seem to be some support for this when we look at the exchange of ratifications at Chefoo when there was a remarkable change from their previous support for the Chinese.

A final word about the marvellous Japanese source for the Sino-Japanese war, Mutsu Munemitsu's *Kenkenroku*. Judged by international standards, it is a fascinating book on diplomatic history. It has dominated several generations of interpretations on the Japanese side. But it has its limitations, one of which is its treatment of the Dreibund. The book suggests that all events of the crisis had their focus in Maiko. But this was not so. While the crisis was eventually solved diplomatically, the outcome depended on a delicate military-naval assessment of the strategic balance in east Asia. This was a matter which had to be left to the *Dai-hon'ei*

(Imperial Headquarters) which for much of the crisis, especially its early days, was in Hiroshima.[12] In this it was the naval and military leaders who had to have the final say.

11

The Debate Over Japanese Capitalism

NINI JENSEN

I am not the first person to point out that a tradition for Marxist studies is widespread in Japanese academia. Nor am I the first to note that, since the Second World War, the attention so far accorded this tradition in the English-language literature on Japan has been relatively limited.

This paper, therefore, is meant as an introduction to the so-called Debate over Japanese Capitalism - *Nihon Shihonshugi Ronsō*. The Debate took place in Japan in the 1920s and 1930s between the Rōnōha and the Kōzaha, the Labour-Farmer Faction and the Lecture Faction respectively. It analysed the historical period roughly from the first half of the 1800s to the end of the 1930s. The themes discussed in the debate were initially closely related to theses elaborated by the Comintern on Japan for the Japanese Communist Party, which was officially established on 15 July, 1922, and recognised as a branch of the Comintern at the end of that year. So, before entering into a presentation of the contributions to the debate itself, I shall briefly mention the so-called 27-, 31- and 32-Theses, which, although not the only theses on Japan, are considered the central theses.

The revolutionary strategy prescribed by the 27-Theses was a two-stage revolution: a bourgeois-democratic revolution with a tendency to grow rapidly into a proletarian one. The 27-Theses viewed the Meiji Restoration as opening the road to capitalist development, while seeing the political power as remaining in the hands of feudal elements: big landlords, the military clique and the Imperial Household. The period after the First World War was characterised by an increase in capitalist development and, furthermore, an increase in the relative strength and political significance of the bourgeoisie. Through pointing to feudal elements at the state level and the seriousness of the peasant question, the principal arguments for the bourgeois-democratic revolution were given. The rapid development into a proletarian revolution was explained by referring to the high level of capital concentration.

In 1931, however, a change in strategy was announced: the coming revolution in Japan was now seen as a proletarian revolution involving extensive bourgeois-democratic tasks. The line of argument now based itself on a view that considered the Meiji Restoration as a bourgeois revolution — 'no matter how incomplete.' The 31-Theses consequently stressed the development of capitalism and, though semi-feudal exploitation could be used to describe relations in agriculture, the Theses found that the agrarian proletariat had undergone a steady increase in recent years. Also the Emperor System which was earlier described mainly for its feudal proportions was now considered to be an instrument of oppression and exploitation of the ruling classes led by the financial oligarchy. The 31-Theses were rather compromising for the Japan Communist Party (JCP) and, although I cannot go into details here, the change in strategy ought to be seen against the background of factional disagreements in the CPSU and with changes in Comintern policies. I am primarily thinking of the tendency to view the relative stabilisation of capitalism as a thing of the past and to connect the worldwide crisis with a worldwide revolutionary upswing in the years following the 6th World Conference of 1928.

While the 32-Theses have likewise been linked to factional disagreements, a major reason for a new revision of the Theses can be seen in the Mukden Incident of September 1931, which caused an increased scare of an impending invasion in the USSR. The new Theses implied a return to the conception of a two-stage revolution and, compared to the 27-Theses, were much more emphatic in stressing the feudal side of Japanese capitalism, particularly stressing the fight against the Emperor System.

I shall now turn to the contributions chosen to represent the Debate. I shall discuss the contributions under the heading of themes rather than splitting the Debate up into many sub-debates, hoping that this can be done without too much confusion and that the selection will not appear too subjectively narrow.

The first theme on the agrarian structure also includes strategic conclusions drawn by some of the authors since the first part of the Debate was closely related to strategy. Inomata Tsunao, who had been a member of the Communist Party before going to jail in 1923, did not join the party after he came out of jail in January 1927. In September he finished writing an article in which he meant to criticise the views expounded in the journal *Marxism* regarding the fight against absolutism. The article was called 'The Political Position of the Bourgeoisie in Contemporary Japan' and was published in *Taiyō* in November 1927 after being turned down by *Marxism*. According to Inomata, capitalist development had proceeded quite rapidly following the Meiji Restoration. After the First World War the part of production controlled by the bourgeoisie had became quantitatively and qualitatively superior.

Parallel to this process was the bourgeoisie's conquest of political power through the establishment of party cabinets. The landlords, although holding a majority in the early political parties had not held real power, this had been in the hands of the bureaucracy and the military clique. And the landlords alongside the political parties challenging this political power had gradually undergone what Inomata called 'embourgeoisement.' Regionally, however, landlord power was still strong *vis-à-vis* the masses of small peasants and tenants. The peasant movement was rapidly uniting with the urban proletarian movement, basically made possible by a semi-proletarianisation of the peasantry.

The strategic conclusion Inomata drew was an interim culmination in a bourgeois revolution, a revolution led by the proletariat and directed against the bourgeoisie, which was too reactionary to put bourgeois demands on the agenda, not because it feared losing absolutist support, but rather because it feared the struggle of the masses.

This was written in November. By December Inomata's strategic thinking had changed into a one-stage revolution. This was in the first issue of a new magazine, *Rōnō*. Another article in *Rōnō* worth mentioning as another representative exposition of *'Rōnōha'* arguments was: 'Towards a United Political Front!,' written by Yamakawa Hitoshi, a veteran on the left wing and a supporter of the dissolution of the JCP in 1923-4. According to Yamakawa, the lower *samurai* who had been the main actors in the Meiji Restoration had based themselves on the economic basis of the still weak bourgeoisie and through protective measures favoured the development of capitalism. The establishment of the bourgeoisie's political power had been realised some 50 years later without any serious confrontations with the landlords since these had undergone embourgeoisement. In the transition from capitalism to the new society, the proletariat in alliance with mainly poor peasants, semi-proletarianised tenants and the lower level petty-bourgeoisie would have to fight the bourgeoisie. Here Yamakawa advocated the formation of a United Front party.

Noro Eitarō had been Inomata's assistant at the Institute of Investigation of Industrial Workers and in his graduation theses 'The History of the Development of Japanese Capitalism' published in January and June 1927 had been quite close to the views of Yamakawa and Inomata. The Meiji Restoration was seen as a social transformation, by which the capitalists and capitalist landlords achieved a ruling position. The Land Tax Revision Act had replaced feudal land-ownership with capitalist land-ownership. But the management of agriculture was carried out as a feudal small-scale enterprise. The coming revolution was proletarian.

It is not possible here to deal in detail with the fluctuations in Noro's strategic thinking and the modifications in his view of agricultural relations that this entailed. In any event the reading of the 27-Theses made Noro undertake certain revisions in his 'The Historical Conditions of the Development of Japanese Capitalism.' While still expressing a view inclined towards a proletarian revolution, his discussion of the agrarian structure now stressed the two sides, that is, both the feudal and the capitalist side of the landlord, while viewing the state as the highest landlord in its capacity as receiver of the land tax.

In his critique of the Inomata article mentioned above and published in April 1929 ('Criticising Inomata Tsunao's Work: The Political Position of the Bourgeoisie in Contemporary Japan'), the strategy was in complete accordance with the 27-Theses. While concentrating his attention on 'the hidden basis of the political form,' that is, the direct relation between owners of the means of production and the direct producers (using Marx as reference), Noro pointed to agriculture: in other words small land-holding peasants and the relationship between tenant and landlord. Noro died in jail in 1934, but before this in April 1931 a group of scholars under his leadership had planned the publication of 'Lectures on the History of the Development of Japanese Capitalism', published from May 1932 to August 1933. The planning of this publication started around the publication of the 31-Theses, when the strategic discussions had more or less died down. Although the participants were not limited to those later identified as Kōzaha scholars, this was the publication from which Kōzaha got its name.

The next person to be mentioned is Kushida Tamizō, an economist who was also involved with the magazine *Rōnō* and who worked at the Ohara Research Institute for Social Problems. Mentioning him here is because of his article 'On the Special Character of the Japanese Tenant Rent' (June 1931) which was an attempt at a theoretical clarification of rent from the economic standpoint. Kushida mentioned two characteristics of the tenant rent that made some people view it as a feudal rent, based on extra-economic coercion. One was the fact that the tenant rent was paid in kind, the other that it was remarkably high.

Regarding the first characteristic, capitalist commodity production, according to Kushida, predominated in Japan. The Japanese peasant household was integrated in commodity and money circulation for its reproduction and the tenant rent, although paid in kind, was in the peasant's mind calculated according to the market price. It could thus not be viewed outside capitalist commodity distribution, and Kushida concluded that it was ideally monetarised. The high rate of tenant rent was seen as being dependent upon three factors: the growth of the forces of production of land, the rise in land prices and the demand for tenant lands. The first two conditions the tenant rent shared with capitalist ground rent. But tenancy was a kind of family production that could not be compared with capitalist agriculture and the two features held in common by the tenant and capitalist rents could not explain the high rate of tenant rent.

On the background of Japan's land shortage where demand on tenant land outran supply, Kushida chose to explain the high rate in terms of the supply and demand for tenant land. In short, Kushida concluded that, because the tenant rent was not applied totally to capitalist laws, the rent was to be seen as transitory or pre-capitalist, while it had a tendency to grow into a capitalist.

Finally, let us consider Yamada Moritarō and his *Analysis of Japanese Capitalism*, published as a book in 1934, although most of it had appeared already in 'Lectures on the History of the Development of Japanese Capitalism.' The book is considered one of the most important Kōzaha contributions and is well known for its difficult dense academic style, not unrelated to an attempt to avoid censorship, which had grown increasingly strict after the Mukden Incident. It was Yamada's intention to analyse the basis of Japanese capitalism in terms of the reproduction process, thereby revealing what he called 'the fundamental structural conditions and prospective of Japanese capitalism.'

Yamada saw the Meiji Restoration as a compromise with 'pure

feudalism' and it became central for him to determine the character of landed property in order to determine the basis of Japanese capitalism. In other words, the Land Tax Revision Act did not signal the introduction of bourgeois landed property, but a 'semi-feudal landed property with a semi-serf, parasitic landlord character.' 'Semi-serf small-scale peasant cultivation,' therefore, constituted one of the two pillars of 'extremely hard labour in Japan.' The other one was semi-serf-like wage labour in industry (paid at a sub-colonial level) which was centred around what Yamada called the 'military key-industries.' The establishment of industrial capital in Japan took place roughly between the Sino-Japanese and the Russo-Japanese wars, indicating a transition simultaneously to imperialism and the formation of finance capital, a process that determined the military, semi-serf character of Japanese capitalism. The basis of Japanese capitalism, defined as the semi-feudal landownership — semi-serf small-scale cultivation through the mutual relation to this 'military, semi-serf power' had so far been guaranteed a structurally unchanged reproduction.

For good reasons Yamada was far from explicit regarding revolutionary strategy. But, by defining the basis of capitalism on the above lines he had essentially presented an argument for the necessity of a bourgeois revolution. Yamada's book became the source of further controversy, adding several supporters and several critics of his work to the Debate.

The next theme is concerned with the different views that were presented of the Emperor System or rather absolutism. In the nature of things, this was mainly a Kōzaha concern, since for the Rōnōha the Meiji Restoration was essentially a bourgeois revolution. Paradoxically, the writer we are going to deal with first is Inomata on account of his views concerning absolutism in the article mentioned above. Meant as a critique of views that wanted to ensure that the coming revolution was aimed against absolutism, Inomata did not deny the existence of absolutism as such. He recognised the existence of its institutional manifestations in, for example, Sumitsuin, Sambōhonbu and Iakujōsō, but he particularly wanted to stress the survival of absolutism in the form of ideology. The essential point for Inomata was that the manifestations of absolutism existed without any material class basis.

Turning now to people associated with Kōzaha, we shall discuss Hattori Shisō and Hirano Yoshitarō. Hattori was one of the contributors to the 'Lectures' series though he was not a member of the JCP. His views on absolutism before the war were primarily expressed in 'The History of the Meiji Restoration' (1928) and 'Absolutism' also from 1928. In Hattori's opinion, the development of capitalism in Bakumatsu Japan was limited compared to Europe and, although some forms of manufacturing had begun, handicraft production was still dominant. The opening of the ports in 1858 did not lead to a growth of industrial production. Instead, Japan began to import cheap industrial goods from abroad. Under these conditions a resistance to the *Bakufu* was built up that resulted in the Meiji Restoration. This Hattori saw as a change from a pure feudal state system to absolutism, feudalism's last political form. This was a state form that Hattori on the economic level associated with the development of manufacture.

The absolutist state so formed was quickly replaced by the bourgeois revolution 'from above.' This happened as early as 1871 with several civil laws initiated by the government, like the emancipation of Eta, abolition of restrictions on the sale of land, The Land Tax Revision Act etc. The revolution 'from below' started in 1874 with the request for a popularly elected parliament by the Popular Rights Movement. However, this movement was put down and with the promulgation of the constitution in 1889 and the establishment of the parliament in 1890 'pseudo-constitutionalism' was introduced. In Hattori's opinion, this could best be described as Bonapartism, a form of the modern capitalist state.

The other Kōzaha contributor to the clarification of the character of the state following the Meiji Restoration was Hirano Yoshitarō who, together with Yamada, is considered to be one of the later Kōzaha scholars. His views regarding absolutism is taken from two articles, the first of which is called 'The Form of Political Control in the Meiji Restoration' published in the 'Lectures' series in 1934 and the other 'The Political Form of Primitive Accumulation of Capital in Western Europe' published in *Science of History* (1934). In Hirano's opinion, an absolutist state was formed following the Meiji Restoration. In the tradition of Yamada (and Noro for that matter in his critique of Inomata), Hirano focused his attention on the relation between the direct producers for the identification of the material basis of absolutism and defined this as the semi-feudal serf system.

Contrary to Hattori, however, who associated absolutism with the development of manufacturing production, Hirano above all pointed to absolutism as the lever for primitive accumulation of capital. Merchant capital was considered absolutism's initial political support, while manufacturing production was regarded as only secondary, subordinated to the expansions and contractions of merchant capital. The overall result was Japanese capitalism's decay and deformation. Rather than seeing this structure as having undergone any basic change, Hirano pointed to the establishment of absolutism with the constitution of 1889 and, through reference to the semi-serf basis and the consequent deformation of capitalism, Hirano saw no possibility for transforming absolutism into either Bonapartism or constitutional monarchy.

Finally, there is the theme of manufacturing production in the Bakumatsu period which, compared to the other themes presented here, takes on the character of a debate in a more explicit sense. I should also note that, in view of the times in which it took place, this shows the Debate moving in a direction more likely to avoid censorship.

After having stated the need to criticise the tendency to underrate manufacturing production in a Tokugawa period in relation to handicraft production, small-scale peasant production and peasant household home industry in a publication in the 'Lectures' series in February 1933, Hattori later in the year expanded his views and declared the Bakumatsu period to be 'a genuine manufacturing period' in the sense used in *Das Kapital*. This was in the article 'Problems Regarding the History of the Restoration from a Methodological Standpoint.' (*Science of History*, April-June 1933).

Hattori's exposition was meant as a critique of both Rono and Kōzaha views including his own in 'The History of the Meiji Restoration.'

Tsuchiya Takao's critique was also directed against Hattori in 'The Manufactures of the Tokugawa Period' (Reconstruction, Sept. 1933.) Tsuchiya believed it possible in Hattori's work to distinguish three forms of capitalist production preceding 'the system of machinery:' 1) handicraft production (where the master used hired labourers); 2) capitalist household labour; and 3) manufacturing. In order to determine when one was dominant in relation to another, each (according to Tsuchiya) had to be carefully studied. Despite his respect for Hattori as a theoretician, it was Tsuchiya's opinion that Hattori had used too few examples of manufacturing production to argue convincingly for the existence of 'a genuine manufacturing period.' Tsuchiya's own analysis of manufacturing production, e.g. textile, brewing, refining of magnetic sand and wax production, although more numerous than Hattori's examples, could not move him to accept the latter's conclusions. His reservations were attributable, for instance, to an 'unusually high frequency of home industry' in textile production; and regarding the production of magnetic sand and wax, which was under the control and management of feudal lords, Tsuchiya felt it was difficult to determine the exact character of the production.

Hattori's response to Tsuchiya had a strong flavour of the theoretician arguing against the empiricist. Hattori had already emphasised that manufacturing production in 'the genuine manufacturing period' did not penetrate the whole of social production; and he now criticised Tsuchiya for what he believed to be a misleading separation of capitalist household labour from manufacturing. For Hattori it was not a question of 'either — or' and, on the basis of Lenin, he claimed that 'the manufacturing period ... (could) be imagined with difficulty .. without the distribution of home work.'

Rejecting Tsuchiya's 'reservations' regarding the character of wax and magnetic sand production, Hattori claimed that one ought not to focus on the control as such, but rather on the form of exploitation. As long as this was what could be called de facto wage labour, it did not matter if the person in control had the status of being a feudal lord, in relation to the labourers he was a capitalist. Hattori felt compelled to mention that capitalist relations were generally dressed in feudal clothing at the stage of manufacturing.

The contributions that followed before this part of the Debate faded away temporarily in 1934 did not add anything new to the pattern outlined here. Tsuchiya, for instance, pursued the study of textile manufacturing and Hattori, apart from defining more closely the extension of the manufacturing period as stretching over a period of 50 to 75 years from before the opening of the ports until the beginning of the 1890s also dealt with the theoretical problem of how to decide what he called 'the determining historical pre-requisite' of the manufacturing period pointing to 'primitive accumulation' and, in the same vein, identified the home market as 'the general precipitating moment' for primitive accumulation.

So much about the contributions to the Debate which came to an end with the arrests first in July 1936 when Yamada and Hirano were arrested and then in December 1937 when Yamakawa and Inomata were among those arrested.

In conclusion, I mentioned earlier that this study had grown out of the observation of a gap in Japanese historiography presented in the English-language literature and a consequent wish to fill at least part of this gap. In order to do this, I had set my eyes on the Debate over Japanese Capitalism, which is central in the development of the social sciences and the formation of Marxism in Japan prior to World War II. The Debate, moreover, functions as an important background for studies of, for example, the Meiji Restoration, the Emperor System, Japanese Capitalism and the landlord system etc, undertaken in the post-war period. But, apart from more quantitative considerations, there is also a need in a more qualitative sense to come up with a reevaluation of the Debate, since the evaluation so far accorded it has functioned as the basis for more or less neglecting it. This in my opinion is far from justified.

In the nature of things this is not the place for a detailed discussion of the merits and demerits of the Debate. The Debate grew out of disagreement over the applicability of the Comintern Theses to the Japanese situation: while Kōzaha proponents basically accepted Comintern authority and most of the time a two-stage revolution, Rōnōha argued for a one-stage revolution. During the course of time the Debate became more academic and detached and the initial disagreement developed into some more or less sharply drawn theoretical confrontations — although one must admit at times the difficulty in pin-pointing clearly-defined differences. Over all, Kōzaha ought to be seen as a more homogenous group than Rōnōha.

On the whole, one can criticise the Debate for evolving into a form of philological trench warfare where 'ammunition' consisted of the 'correct' scriptures retrieved from the classics of Marxism, visible, for instance, in the confrontation between Tsuchiya and Hattori. One could point out a 'freezing' of the Debate into a confrontation between the level of production and the level of circulation, visible in Yamada and Hattori on the one hand and Kushida and Tsuchiya on the other. One could point to signs of 'economism' or 'mechanical materialism' in, for example, Yamada and Hirano. Theoretically speaking, the Debate is not able to contribute much that is new. This is not very surprising if one takes into consideration that 50 to 60 years of further research have been undertaken since then. However, if this evaluation alone remains it becomes very much one of hindsight. What has been done so far is to focus too blindly on Marxist jargon combined with an insensitivity to the curtailing influence that censorship and oppression had on the unfolding of the Debate. In other words, it is also important to evaluate the Debate against the background of the historical context in which it took place, keeping in mind that this does not turn into an excuse for its shortcomings.

Since the Theses on Japan were, to a large extent, marked by factional disagreements in the CPSU and also bore the imprint of interpretations that had originally been applied to Russian and European history, the critique of the Theses came to establish itself as an important alternative to the Comintern interpretations, which were in many ways inadequate.

In its own historical context, the Debate ought to be seen as quite a remarkable contribution to the analysis of Japanese history from the beginning of the 1800s to the 1930s. First of all, in a general sense the Debate signals new research strategies and topics in relation to Japanese history compared to interpretations that had been presented until then. Taking the censorship and oppression in Japanese society at the time into consideration only reinforced this evaluation. The Debate stands comparison with later Debates with related research topics, like, for example, the now classic 1950s discussion of transition from feudalism to capitalism in Europe, but also the later discussion of under-development, between A. G. Frank and Ernesto La-Clau.

Elucidation of the Debate could be of value in a clarification of obscurities regarding the Debate on the part of western scholars who have recently attempted related studies of this period in Japanese history, such as Perry Anderson and Jon Halliday; but an elucidation could also acquaint a western audience with the special Japanese Marxist jargon used in the few translations available in this tradition.

12

Satō Naotake's Mission to Rome in 1940

VALDO FERRETTI

From September 1939 to June 1940 Japan and Italy shared a similar position in respect to the conflict which broke out in Europe. With the German invasion of Poland and later when war was declared on Germany by England and France, both countries announced their neutrality. An interesting, even if secondary, event which emerged from this state of affairs was the mission headed by former Foreign Minister, Satō Naotake, who came to Italy in the spring of 1940. In this paper I shall endeavour to shed some light on this visit, relying on a still almost unsearched file in the Historical Archives of the Japanese Foreign Ministry. But some preliminary observations seem to be necessary in order to introduce its contents.

In 1936 and 1937 Rome and Berlin had signed with Japan the Anti-Comintern agreements, officially meant to check the Bolshevik threat. Thereafter, in extended discussions which lasted from the summer of 1938 to that of 1939, negotiations aiming to strengthen the treaties had taken place. Moreover, the Italo-German 'Pact of Steel' was concluded in May 1939, though Japan had not yet agreed on a final text with her European partners. On the eve of the Nazi-Soviet protocol of August 1939, the Tokyo Government decided to drop the matter.

In the summer and autumn of 1937 a neutrality and consultation treaty *à deux* had also been discussed with Italy, but at the last moment, because of lack of enthusiasm in the Japanese Foreign Office, it had been replaced by an oral promise of neutrality given by the Japanese Ambassador in Rome, Hotta Masaaki. In this connection, between 1937 and 1938, a series of initiatives were being pursued with the purpose of improving and enlarging the sphere of collaboration between the two countries. In late autumn 1937 Baron Okura Kishichirō, the president of the Japanese Association for Italian Studies, paid an official visit to Rome which was reciprocated by a fascist party delegation, whose chief was Marquis Giacomo Paulucci de Calboli, himself the President of the *Societa degli Amici del Giappone,* a cultural association sponsored by the Italian Government.[1] He was warmly welcomed and it is possible, in spite of the scanty evidence in the Italian and Japanese documents, that political themes were touched on by Paulucci during his visit. Apart from the propagandistic purposes of this initiative, however, one of his tasks was to study a traditional field of Italian interests, i.e. investments and foreign trade concerning Manchukuo and Japanese-occupied China. Once back in Rome, the ambassador mentioned in the final words of his long report the chances of developing trade between the Italian colonies in East Africa and Japan but, at the same time, laid much more emphasis on the hindrances being suffered because of protectionist views still held by Tokyo.[2] Paulucci sailed back on 6 April 1938; and shortly after another mission led by Senator Ettore Conti went to Japan and continued its journey to the Asian continent with the strictly economic purpose of reaching an agreement with the puppet government of Emperor Pu-yi in Manchukuo.

Economic policies developed by Rome in east Asia since the beginning of the thirties were twofold, being directed both to improving exports of heavy industrial items like buses, trucks and planes, and to compensating for the balance of payments deficit she was suffering from trading with the two far-eastern states, whose main exports consisted of agricultural goods like mulberry, silk and oil-seeds.[3] In 1935 the *Ministero delle Corporazioni,* which administered economic matters, had opposed the idea of commercial rapprochement with Japan, claiming that the Rising Sun's attitudes were far less promising than those of Nanking,[4] but by 1937 Italy had taken a pro-Japanese stance and relations with Chiang Kai-shek's government deteriorated. In this way, following the path of Paulucci's propagandistic and cultural work, it was Conti's wish to attempt to open the Manchurian market, which was controlled by Japan, to increased Italian trade. The result was a commercial agreement signed on 20 August 1938, which fulfilled most of Rome's expectations and brought the value of global exchange to 170 million liras. Negotiations, however, had been far from easy. The Japanese Foreign Ministry and Hsinking proved to be hard bargainers. The former feared value disbursements and both of them, according to Conti's reports, were trying not to grant Rome the terms already enjoyed by Germany and Japan herself in Manchuria. Talks were about to be dropped; and a friendship treaty seemed likely to be the only meagre success that could be foreseen, when, thanks to the intervention of the military attaché in Rome, Arisue Seizō and, on his initiative, of the Army Ministry in Tokyo, the *Gaimushō* and consequently Hsinking were persuaded to relent. Ultimately a trade convention with Rome was signed.[5]

By September 1939 German-Japanese relations were in deadlock. When war began in Europe, two matters were still open to new possible settlements: a political rapprochement, insofar as a neutrality pact of some sort might be of interest to both sides, and the topic of Italian interests in China which had been left untouched by the treaty of 1938. Both of them had been restudied in Tokyo early in 1939 and on 22 March a final document was produced by the second European Office of the *Gaimushō*.[6] Events on the continent, it was said, made it expedient not only to confirm Italian interests in China, but also to make a gesture so as to ameliorate political relations between the two countries. Past negotiations intended to strengthen the Anti-Comintern pact were reviewed and it was explained that the need for a common attitude was suggested by the economic consequences of the war between Britain and Germany, towards which both Italy and Japan were neutral. The worsening of relations with the USA, the office went on, was not to be feared, as a gesture towards Italy would not lead to aggressive military agreements likely to hurt public opinion there, and also because it seemed as if Italy were trying to improve her relations with Washington.

Hints to the United States and to Britain are worth some attention. Both Rome and Tokyo experienced some diplomatic friction with Britain early in 1940 (on Japan's side, for instance, the famous *Asama Maru* incident) on the ground of application of Sea War Law, while the mission to Rome of the American Under-Secretary of State, Sumner Welles, in March led some people to believe that a kind of alignment between Rome and Washington was possible.[7] The office judged much more important, however, the Soviet side of the matter. As both countries had spheres of action bordering on the USSR (Italy in the Balkans) and Italo-German relations had been shaken the year before, collaboration between Rome and Tokyo could prove itself to be useful *vis-à-vis* Russia. In addition to that, though no explanation was given, by acting jointly over the Soviet Union, the two countries were said to be able to exert influence in London as well.

As to the contents of the gesture, it was added that the draft of a neutrality and consultation agreement might be prepared in future, as by March 1940 it was not considered certain whether the Italians would be willing to sign it. The decision finally taken was to send to Rome a mission as an official answer to those of Conti and Paulucci, and Ambassador Satō Naotake was appointed as its chief.

The above project, however, was also debated outside the Foreign Ministry, because the Italy and France Bureau of the Army Ministry suggested going beyond the *Gaimushō* proposals and produced on 1 April a draft of a neutrality treaty to be presented. In 1937 the Army General Affairs Bureau, led by the influential Lieutenant-General, Isogai Rensuke, had supported a similar scheme;[8] and now the *Rikugunshō* wanted to stick to the original idea. An agreement in five articles was outlined,[9] to last as long as the war in Europe, aiming to protect the contracting parties as neutrals and open to other states. Should one of them enter the war, the other would not be obliged to follow it; but, if one of them should decide to take part in the war because its interests as a neutral were being damaged, the other would back it by economic and political means (quoting Article 3 of the draft: *Nichi-I ryōkoku no uchi ippō chūritsukoku no kanri kigai ni yori sansen suru ni itaritaru bahai hoka no ippō wa shūshi koiteki taidō o iji shi keizaiteki narabi seijiteki enjō o atafu*). The army intervention, however, probably only annoyed the Foreign Ministry as Satō did not appear to take it into account during his journey at all.

Not only did the military scheme run contrary to the March memoranda but also the ambassador himself was a well-known opponent of the army, even if some contemporary Japanese historians refuse to enlist him in the so-called *Shinōbeiha* (pro-Europe-America faction) and consider Satō as an isolated heir of Motono Ichirō.[10] At any rate, we may assume that he belonged to the mildest *Gaimushō* wing, which strongly pleaded for negotiated solutions of pending disagreements with both the Anglo-Saxon countries and Russia. His nonchalance towards the military in 1940, therefore, is not difficult to grasp.[11]

During his journey he landed in Naples, travelled to Rome where he met the Duce and his foreign minister, and then continued his official visit to northern Italy. The result of the mission was an exchange of engagements touching on reciprocal support, protection as far as possible of Italian interests and Rome's attitude to Japan in China. A short joint communiqué abridged the contents of the meeting with Ciano.[12] Mussolini's declaration of war on Britain and France on 10 June, however, deprived the mission of its sense. In Tokyo it was decided to keep Japan's neutrality in the new phase of the war and to renounce any possibility of a political treaty with Italy, which could hurt the USA while continuing at the same time to foster friendship with her.[13] Satō, however, went on with his travels to Germany as a sort of personal envoy of Foreign Minister, Arita Hachirō.[14] The latter intended to keep the door open to the Axis powers, while trying to come to terms with Britain and America. This was a delicate game, easy to be disrupted, and hence intended to make clear the carefully-weighted attitude which Tokyo was taking on the eve of Satō's mission. It is likely to be considered as one of the last attempts on Japan's part which was inspired by traditionalist views on the balance of power in Europe.

13

The Kwanggaeto Stele Inscription

J. Y. KIM

The monument of King Kwanggaeto (AD 391-413) was erected in AD 414 by his son and successor, the 20th king of the Koguryo Kingdom,

Changsu. The inscription of the stele was held to be a valuable document illustrating the achievements of Koreans — in north-eastern Asia under King Kwanggaeto's authority. Eight years after its discovery, in 1884, Sakawa Kageaki, a captain of the Japanese Imperial Army, brought back to Japan a good reproduction of the rubbing of the stele inscription. For Japan, it had great importance because the character *Wo* is repeated nine times — Wo being a term which also designated 'Japan'; — its importance also derived from the fact that the period of the king's reign corresponds in one part to details of Wo activities in the south of the Korean peninsula, according to Japanese ancient records. Japanese and Korean scholars have laid claim to differing readings and interpretations of the inscription.

For the past century, Japanese scholars have maintained their officially-established interpretation of the inscription whereby Japan crushed both the Paekche and Silla kingdoms, bringing them under her control in AD 391; Japan attacked the actual boundaries of Pyung-Yang, by the river Han, where the Japanese and Koguryo met in battle; and Mimana was a colony of the Yamato kingdom. By introducing their interpretation as a source of Japan's historiography, Japanese scholars unanimously conclude that Japan, by the end of the fourth century AD, had established its colonial authority in the south Korean peninsula in such states as Paekche, Silla and Mimana.

Contrary to this view, Korean scholars claim that it was Koguryo which destroyed Paekche, Wo or Silla; some part of the inscription was falsified by the men of the Japanese Imperial Army at the end of the nineteenth century, a view approved by Korean scholars in 1973 as an officially-established theory; and Mimana (in Korean 'Imna') was not controlled by the Yamato kingdom, and the inscription does not confirm the Japanese scholars' assertion. Korean scholars have concluded that the interpretation of Japanese scholars, based on the questionable Japanese Imperial historiography, was mistaken. Hence the enduring controversy between Japanese and Korean scholars appears to stem from misreading and misinterpreting the inscription.

It is necessary to point out the mistakes committed by the Japanese and Korean scholars; how western scholars were misled into repeating the assertions of Japanese scholars; and what the inscription really says by way of a revised interpretation.

On the four sides of the monument is engraved an inscription describing the glorious achievements of the deceased king. This inscription consists of 43 vertical columns of 41 characters each, with the exception of the last column which has 40 characters, thus forming altogether a total of 1762 characters. Among all the textual characters, 202 are completely defaced or only partly legible. Thus, there are gaps which make it difficult to understand or see where the sentences stop. Additional problems in reading the inscription are that the surface of the stele has been affected by a long period of atmospheric erosion which has left many of the characters unclear. For Korean scholars the reading of the inscription should have been carried out exclusively with the help of rubbings or informed scholarly publications, since the site of the stele is located in Manchuria in the territory of the Peoples' Republic of China with which the Republic of Korea has not yet concluded any diplomatic relations. Furthermore, one is faced with other difficulties when reading this inscription. 'When a rubbing is made,' Professor B. Szczesniak remarks, 'the artisans endeavour to obtain the clearest and most complete reproductions' or 'the over-zealous workers fill in and complete defaced or weatherbeaten strokes of characters of monuments.'[1] It is difficult, therefore, to understand the precise meaning of the original inscription.

The inscription of the monument can be divided into five parts.[2] The findings of my research are here based mainly on the third part of the inscription which has provoked the principal points of controversy in the interpretations of Japanese and Korean scholars. The third part of the inscription (sentences 19 to 72) is composed of 881 characters, including 183 illegible characters. It illustrates the glorious deeds of the deceased king and his victorious war against the neighbours beginning in AD 395. This part is the core of the inscription, because it expounds the state of relations between Koguryo and its neighbouring kingdoms in the South Korean peninsula — Paekche, Silla and Kaya (Kara), and also with Wai.

The results of my examination of the stele inscription so far bear the following fruits. Firstly, Sentences 26 to 28 constitute an introduction to the king's exploits in the south Korean peninsula from 396 to 407 AD. Secondly, it was King Kwanggaeto who crossed the sea and crushed Paekche in 396 and also in 407, Wai during 400 to 404 and Anra during 400 to 403. Thirdly, the Wai who came to the south-eastern Korean peninsula in AD 391, during 399 to 404 and probably in 407 were clearly specified in the inscription. However, the eight years of Wai raids cannot be interpreted in the sense that one scholar has advanced, namely that the inscription describes the victories of Koguryo over invading Wa (Wai) armies in a series of engagements lasting from 391 to 404. It is clear from this that Koguryo and the Wa were competing for dominance over both Paekche and Silla.[3] Fourthly, the inscription neither records nor specifies the fact that Wai armies came to Pyung-Yang and near the Han and Taedong rivers. Fifthly, the operational territory of King Kwanggaeto's southward expansion policy was strictly limited to the south Korean peninsula. Sixthly, the inscription does not mention Mimana as a colony of the Yamato Kingdom, either as a military base or as the territory occupied by Wai. Furthermore, the inscription does not give a clue which would lead to the allusion that Japan had established her authority in Korea in such states as Paekche, Silla and Mimana.

The funeral stele of King Kwanggaeto of the Koguryo Kingdom is a precious record, and the monument itself is a work of art-material for historians and archaeologists. It is a testimony to the grandeur of modern Korea's ancestors and their actions in Manchuria during the fourth and fifth centuries AD. Because of the stele's intrinsic merits, visits have been strictly limited and even the taking of photographs was forbidden until the middle of 1984. It stands in Chian, which is in Kirin province, not far from the Yalu river, protected by a surrounding wall and is completely isolated, waiting until its true meaning, as was originally expressed by the erector, will be revealed.

14

Buryoku shori:
The Japanese take over
French Indo-China
9 March 1945

LOUIS ALLEN

The Japanese *coup de force* of 9 March 1945, in what was then French Indo-China and is now Vietnam, Cambodia and Laos, is an event whose importance varies depending on which national historiography produces the accounts. For French historians, it is an episode in the conflict between an almost triumphant de Gaulle and the remnants of the Vichy régime, part of the debate between resistance and collaboration which has been pursued since 1940 and shows no sign of slackening off. For the Japanese, it is part of that history of the war in South-East Asia which illustrates (or puts in doubt) their claim to be the liberators of the native peoples of the area from their old colonial masters. For the United States, it is merely a preparatory chapter, often ignored, in histories of what to them is the vastly more significant conflict of the 1960s and 1970s. For the British, finally, it symbolises the increasing divergence between their aims in the war in Asia and those of their American allies.

The French Governor General, Admiral Jean Decoux, and his staff unhesitatingly blame an ill-trained and utterly insecure Resistance for upsetting the Japanese and thereby provoking the *coup de force*.[1] Certainly de Gaulle himself preferred that French Indo-China should be taken from Japanese hands by force rather than diplomacy, in order to re-establish the French presence in an unquestionable manner; even if this involved heavy sacrifices on the part of the local population.[2] On the other hand, even though a Japanese journalist then in Saigon appears to confirm Decoux's analysis,[3] a symposium of scholars, administrators and soldiers with experience in Indo-China came to the conclusion in 1981 that the effect of the Resistance in French Indo-China upon Japanese actions was nil.[4]

But it is not simply a question of arbitrating between two diametrically opposed positions in French historiography. There is also an abundantly

82

documented Japanese case, which shows that the Japanese had planned the possibility of a *buryoku shori*, or *coup de force*, long before there was any real resistance among the French population in Indo-China, at least on any considerable scale. From November 1942, the month of the Allied landings in French North Africa, the Japanese began to wonder for how long stability could be preserved in Indo-China, which had been for two years a most important base for operations in South-East Asia and the Pacific. Japanese reactions were far from monolithic. There were sharp differences between the three levels of military command: Imperial General Headquarters in Tokyo, Southern Area Army in Singapore (later in Manila, and finally in Saigon), and the local garrison headquarters in Saigon. Views in the Japanese Foreign Office also differed. It was the Foreign Minister, Shigemitsu, who urged upon the Army the use of force. He considered Decoux's régime, and its predecessors, to be violently reactionary in relation to independence movements, and he was aware of the paradoxical status of Japan as supporter of a European régime when much of her war-time propaganda had been to show herself as the liberator of East Asia from the European colonial past.[5] The Japanese ambassador to Decoux, Yoshizawa Kenkichi, had been foreign minister in the past and was regarded by Decoux as a cultivated diplomat of the old school, sympathetic to European cultural traditions. In fact, on a number of occasions, Yoshizawa pressed the Gaimushō to do something positive on behalf of Annamite independence, and pressed these views home with the War Ministry, with whom he had discussions early in 1944, and also in telegrams to the Greater East Asia Ministry, three days after the Normandy landings. The Army showed a layer-cake reaction at the centre, both Tojo and Lt-General Umezu indicated that a policy of maintaining absolute tranquillity in Indo-China should be maintained. Tojo saw no reason to attempt to separate Indo-China from the mother country, France, when he put forward his 'Principles for the Conduct of Political Strategy in Great East Asia' *(Dai Tōa Seiryaku Shidō Taikō)* at a Liaison Conference on 21 May 1943.[6] The local garrison at first seemed to accept this view, but was later won over to the contrary view, expressed by various staff officers, at Southern Area Army.

Late in 1944, there were two significant changes at local level, both military and diplomatic. Yoshizawa left Saigon for good on 21 October 1944, and was succeeded by Matsumoto Shunichi, who had been Vice-Minister for Foreign Affairs. Decoux disliked him. The Japanese army official history describes him as a 'young and impetuous diplomat' *(shinshin kiei)*[7] but Decoux is less euphemistic. He found Matsumoto coarse-fibred, blunt, lacking in subtlety.[8] Yet it was Matsumoto who, having asked for a sight of the plans for a *coup*, expressed himself in hostile terms. No doubt the reason was partly professional pride: the rôle of the Foreign Office in Indo-China would be diminished by a local military take-over. He signalled the Foreign Office and the Greater East Asia Ministry that a *coup* was inexpedient, and that the setting up of military government in place of the French administration would do great harm and no advantage would be gained from it. More, Japan should not interfere in Indo-China's internal policy. It was a stance the military did not permit him to maintain.

In October 1944, the garrison commander, Lt-General Machijiri, fell sick, and was replaced by the army commander on the island of Timor, Lt-General Tsuchihashi Yûitsu, who had spent three periods as military attaché in France and had been appointed to Saigon to ensure smooth relations with Decoux and the French Army. On the way from Timor to Saigon, he called on the GOC-in-C 16 Army in Java (Harada) and the GOC-in-C 7 Area Army in Singapore (Doihara). Both indicated their anxiety: if he could not secure the situation in Indo-China, the entire supply base for the Southern Army would be disturbed.

Tsuchihashi left Saigon for Hanoi on 18 December 1944, to inspect 21 Division and to use the opportunity to have talks with Decoux, Gautier, and the French commander-in-chief, Lt-General Aymé. His talks with Decoux on 29 December left him in no doubt that, if there were an allied invasion, Decoux had no intention of defending Indo-China against it, in collaboration with Japan. He saw no purpose even in discussing defence problems with Tsuchihashi. When it came to Aymé's turn, Tsuchihashi was blunt. If the Americans landed, and the Chinese moved in from the north, would the French fight alongside the Japanese, in accordance with the mutual defence agreement? Aymé looked perplexed (*kanwaku*) and said he could only answer after consultation. Whether the French would actually strike at the Japanese in the event of such an invasion remained unclear, Tsuchihashi noted; *he* would be glad if they would simply make no move either way, hostile or cooperative, but even that seemed hard to expect. When he got back, he made a note on how weak the security of the *coup de force* was. Code-named at that time 'Operation *M*', the term seemed on everybody's lips, and it was likely it had leaked to the French. To tighten security, he changed the designation to 'Operation *M*' on 17 January 1945, had the secrecy of the ciphers checked, and ordered his troops to watch their conversation in bars and cafés.

Much of his command was nominal. It was no longer termed a garrison army, but had been put on an operational footing as 38 Army, with two divisions (21 and 37) under command, and two independent mixed brigades (34 and 70). 2 Division arrived from Burma on 24 February, and he had also been allocated part of 4 Division and 22 Division. But the figures were deceptive: 21 Division was complete, but 37 was at half-strength; 2 Division had one infantry regiment, and 22 Division was still involved in operations in China, though nominally in his order of battle. His total forces numbered 40,000, distributed over an area larger than Japan. French forces numbered over twice this figure. 20,000 troops and 70,000 native troops were divided into three commands: North (45,000 in Tonkin), Centre (10,000 in Annam and Laos), and South (35,000 in Cambodia and Cochin-China); with 5,000 men in auxiliary security units. Tsuchihashi knew, though, that these forces were not well equipped for modern warfare, had only rifles and mountain guns, and were inadequately trained. Their morale was not high.

This paper is not concerned with the negotiations for increasing the financial allocation to the Japanese occupation forces or the negotiations for the rice supply agreement which were to be carried out between Matsumoto and Decoux. Whatever Matsumoto's views about the desirability of a *coup de force*, he naturally cooperated with the Japanese army when the time came. It was agreed that he should present the Japanese ultimatum to Decoux, using the financial discussions as a pretext, and indicting 9 pm (10 pm Japanese time) as the time limit for a reply, after which he would withdraw to 38 Army GHQ, where the reply should reach him. To ensure that there should be no difficulty in the reply being delivered, a copy of the street name and number of the Japanese Army GHQ was handed over to the Governor-General, an action which must seem the height of absurdity, were it not for the even more absurd situation which occurred later.

The signing of the rice supply agreement was to be concluded by 6 pm (7 pm Japanese time). Matsumoto was then to present the ultimatum and withdraw, after a preliminary discussion on military expenditure. This discussion began at 6.30 pm (7.30 pm Japanese time), starting with the situation in Europe. Decoux took pleasure in pointing out to Matsumoto that he considered Germany was on the brink of surrender, but Matsumoto's mind was elsewhere. 'He seemed to me,' Decoux later recalled, 'preoccupied, jumpy, a rare thing for an Asiatic. He made one or two fleeting observations, without any apparent logical connexion, rather incoherently.'[9] Matsumoto asked Decoux if he were in touch with the French Government in Paris, and Decoux replied that he was not (this was not strictly true, of course). Decoux was acting on the basis of a delegation of powers from the previous French government (ie, Vichy). They discussed de Gaulle's wish to see Indo-China return to 'the French community' and the intention to concede a more liberal régime to the native peoples, both perfectly natural desires, Decoux observed. Matsumoto was behaving more and more awkwardly, and Decoux suspected he was trying to gain time. But for what?

At 7 pm exactly, in Decoux's phrase, Matsumoto 'unmasked his batteries.'[10] He presented a memorandum, the terms of which, in the eventuality of an American invasion, put French forces in Indo-China under Japanese command, together with all rail and maritime transport and all communications, external and internal. A reply from the Governor-General was expected by 9 pm (10 pm Japanese time). Decoux promptly summoned his diplomatic adviser, de Boisanger, and vehemently protested against the memorandum in his presence. When Matsumoto brutally hinted what might happen to the 40,000 Frenchmen living in Indo-China if the demands were not met and Japan had to resort to force, Decoux hotly answered that Japan would be responsible before world opinion if they were subject to reprisals (a vain threat, as it turned out: the Japanese forces in many instances behaved with the brutality for which they had already acquired an unenviable and durable reputation in East Asia).

Boisanger temporised, suggesting that in the two-hour interval some compromise solution might be reached. Decoux thought Boisanger was trying to gain time to alert the French military commands, but in fact Boisanger had already managed to do this. When Decoux summoned him, he had been waiting in a nearby room with Decoux's *directeur de cabinet*, Aurillac. Realising from the language of the memorandum that relations with Japan were at breaking-point, Boisanger slipped back to Aurillac and told him to alert all military commanders immediately. He then returned to Decoux, who by 8.15 pm (9.15 pm Japanese time) had had enough of Matsumoto and asked him to withdraw. After conferring with General Delsuc, in command of the Cochin-China Division, and Admiral Bérenger, in command of French naval forces, Decoux drew up a note. The terms of the note accepted that, in the event of an invasion, Japanese forces should take control of all operations, but added that Decoux could make no dispositions about the status of the French forces under Japanese command without consultation with his commanders. French forces would not engage in hostile activities against the Japanese, unless the latter attacked them.

The memorandum was ready by 9.15 pm (10.15 pm Japanese time). Decoux learned that the Japanese had already cut the roads between Saigon and Cholon, that the Government-General was surrounded, and that Frenchmen had already been arrested and molested. The Commissioner-General for Franco-Japanese relations, Captain Robin of the French Navy, was told to carry the reply to the Japanese.

It is at this point that farce takes over. Captain Robin lost his way. The *shōgai-bu* (Japanese Army Liaison Office) telephoned Japanese Army GHQ to say Robin had called there and asked to be taken or directed to Army GHQ. The distance between the two was a stone's throw or, as Tsuchihashi put it, the distance between eye and nose *(me to hana no kyori)*. Robin should have been there almost immediately. The group at 38 Army GHQ, which included Lt-General Numata, Terauchi's chief of staff from Southern Army, waited for fifteen minutes. Tsuchihashi had originally said he would give the Governor-General five minutes' grace, out of, as he ironically put it, *bushi no nasake*, the compassion of one *samurai* for another.

The phone rang. Southern Army GHQ reported to Tsuchihashi that fighting had already broken out between French and Japanese in Hanoi. The time was 9.18 pm (10.18 pm Japanese time). If Decoux's answer were a rejection, then it did not matter if some hotheaded or nervous commander had jumped the gun. On the other hand, if Decoux had accepted the Japanese ultimatum, it would look as if Tsuchihashi had lost control of his subordinate formations. To avert this, Tsuchihashi called for Kawamura and his Chief Staff Officer Operations. 'Give the operation order now,' he ordered. The French envoy was apparently on his way, Kawamura interposed. Should they not wait a little while longer? Tsuchihashi refused, and gave verbal orders to start the *coup de force* at once. The time was exactly 9.21 pm (10.21 pm Japanese time) and the Chief Staff (Operations) went to the Signals Room and ordered the signal to be made: 7 7 7. The three figures meant that the Governor-General had rejected the Japanese demands and that units were to begin operations immediately. Signalling ceased at 9.23 pm (10.23 pm Japanese time). At 9.25 pm (10.25 pm Japanese time), Tsuchihashi saw Captain Robin being ushered into the presence of Ambassador Matsumoto. In no time at all, he heard Matsumoto shout, *Kore wa akiraka ni kyozetsu da!* (This is clearly a rejection!).[11] Whether it was a rejection or not had ceased to matter. In the conventional Japanese phrase, the arrow had already left the bow.

86

If we analyse those few minutes in 38 Army GHQ, what happened was quite contrary to what had been planned. The nature of Decoux's reply was supposed to be determined by Tsuchihashi and Matsumoto jointly. In the event, it was Matsumoto who, without consulting Tsuchihashi, declared the reply to be a rejection. And, in any case, the Army commander had given the order for the operations to start, on his own initiative, at a time when he did not know whether Decoux had rejected the Japanese demands or not. As Boisanger says, 'before the Japanese ambassador declared to Captain Robin that he considered the note from Admiral Decoux to be a rejection, we knew that his request for an interview "to raise again the subject of military expenditure" had been nothing but a trap, and that the surprise attack on our troops had been prepared in minute detail and probably long beforehand by the Japanese command.'[12]

Indeed it had. So long beforehand that speculations among French historians on the responsibility of the Resistance movement in Indo-China for the unleashing of the *buryoku shori* are wide of the mark. The change of mood in the French population was, no doubt a factor in Japanese thinking; so, too, was the uncooperative reception of Tsuchihashi by Decoux, Gautier and Aymé in December 1944. But it seems likely that, whatever their views of the effectiveness of French collaboration with an eventual American landing, the Japanese Army would have taken over Indo-China anyway.[13]

There is one final bitter paradox: the *buryoku shori* was conceived as a riposte to the danger of a US landing after a Japanese defeat in the Philippines. But Manila fell in February 1945, and American strategic thinking had already begun to range much further north. No question of a side-sweep at the continent of Asia, whether on the shores of French Indo-China, or China. The US forces were now aimed directly at Okinawa and the Japanese islands themselves. The *coup de force* took place against a danger that had already ceased to exist.

One thing becomes very evident from a study of 9 March 1945: the importance of the rôle of clandestine agencies. Inevitably, in a war which involves resistance activities and guerrilla fighting, the supply of these forces falls into the hands of secret or semi-secret agencies. In theory, they should be neutral suppliers. In fact, they rapidly become politicised. Three of these are involved in the 9 March affair: on the allied side, Force 136 (the equivalent in the Far East of Special Operations Executive in Europe), and the American Office of Stragetic Services; on the Japanese side, the various *kikan* or organisations which operated in French Indo-China staffed by graduates of the Nakano School, in particular the unit known as A Kikan, or An Butai (A being the first syllable — and character — for 'A', the Japanese form of the name Annam).

As French Indo-China was outside the operational boundaries of South-East Asia Command until August 1945, the clandestine forces operating under Mountbatten had, or should have had, no part to play. In fact, since the Free French had begun to operate from Ceylon and Calcutta as well as from Kunming in Nationalist China, and were dependent on the RAF for transport and on South-East Command for supplies,

Mountbatten was naturally involved in any operation which was likely to be mounted by any French resistance movement inside Indo-China. It was, for instance, an RAF plane which flew 'Colonel Passy' (André de Wavrin), de Gaulle's head of clandestine organisations, to the then little known airfield of Dien Bien Phu to make contact with resistance figures in Indo-China.

The rôle of the OSS was quite different. In French Indo-China, as in Burma, as in Thailand, the OSS was ordered to keep itself distinct from the activities of the colonial and imperialist powers. This was not a question of operational convenience. Edmond Taylor, the former *Chicago Tribune* correspondent in Paris, who was recruited by Colonel Donovan into the OSS, and spent several years in South-East Asia, puts the matter quite simply:

> 'The longer we stayed in the theatre, the more OSS became permeated with the suspicion and disapproval of western imperialism which characterised the new generation of Old China Hands in the State Department. In South-East Asia as in China, United States policy, it seemed, was to dissociate ourselves as often as possible from the imperial aims of our colonialist allies while vigorously asserting on occasion our claim to enjoy equally with them the commercial — and implicitly the strategic — rewards of colonialism, in the measure that the institution survived our disapproval. It was not always an easy policy to uphold, especially within the framework of a wartime alliance, but OSS did its best.'[14]

The policy was not autonomous. It was a faithful reflection of the policy of General Wedemeyer, US commander in the China Theatre after October 1944, and of the US President himself. Roosevelt's views on the French and their rôle in Indo-China was gauchely Francophobe, and quite well-known. He intended to do all in his power to prevent the French regaining their former position in Indo-China. So the French found themselves with an enemy who intended to extrude them from France's largest and most valuable overseas possession, and also with an ally whose policy coincided exactly with the enemy's. On French Indo-China, Roosevelt and Japanese Imperial General Headquarters were — almost — at one.

The end product of these views has recently been examined in some detail by a USAF colonel who decided to research the background of the Vietnam war in which he had played a combatant part.[15] Not only was the intervention of the OSS crucial in preventing de Gaulle's government putting its officials into Indo-China; the attempts to supply the French resistance to the Japanese in Indo-China during and after Operation *Mei* were frustrated by General Wedemeyer's contention that Mountbatten's South-East Asia Command, which wished to help the French, had no operational standing in French Indo-China, which lay in the China Theatre and that, as US Commander in that Theatre and Chiang Kai-shek's Chief of Staff in succession to General Stilwell, he had no intention of allowing Mountbatten's forces to supply the French. Much of this has been know for a long time, of course, and Dunn dots the i's and crosses the t's with interviews with Wedemeyer, Patti, Pierre Messmer, Massu, and so on.

But Colonel Dunn also refers to two RAF Liberators being shot down not by Japanese fighter planes but by aircraft under Wedemeyer's command, for intruding on French Indo-China airspace while bringing in relief supplies to the French.[16]

On the Japanese side, the clandestine activities of most interest are those of the Nakano School graduates, particularly Captain Kaneko, head of the small unit called '*An*' or '*Yasu*' Organisation. Its function was to stimulate and encourage local Annamite liberation movements against the French. An organisation had been constituted at first from the China Expeditionary Force and sent by it into French Indo-China. It was therefore regarded somewhat askance as an interloper by the Supreme Commander, Southern Regions, General (later Field-Marshal) Terauchi, whose headquarters had been transferred to Saigon from September 1944. The Japanese garrison army in Indo-China had asked for reinforcements, and the kind of reinforcements it received are of interest: 100 Kempei were sent in, and the Kempei Colonel, Hayashi Hidezumi, was transferred to the staff of the garrison army (later 38 Army when put on an operational footing), a clear indication that the Japanese realised that the main effort of Operation *Mei* would be in terms of maintaining civil order and organising counter-agent activity. (There must be a wealth of information on this matter in the French military archives, since Hayashi was held by the French authorities from 28 October 1946 until 20 May 1950, the date on which he left Indo-China for Japan. Unlike the interrogations of Hayashi carried out in later years by the Kido Nikki Kenkyūkai, which concern Hayashi's activities in Shanghai in the 1930s and which are available in print, the interrogations he underwent in Saigon have never, as far as I know, seen the light of day, and it would be interesting to learn of their whereabouts.)

To return to Captain Kaneko. On the night of 9 March 1945, he was in Hue, dressed as usual in Vietnamese clothing. With him were a number of war correspondents who seem to have been momentarily incorporated into *An* Organisation, Maruyama of the *Asahi Shimbun,* Tominaga of the Taiwan *Nichi-Nichi Shimbun,* and the army interpreter, Sanō Yūji. They foregathered at the house of the Japanese consul, Urabe, to await news from Saigon. The Japanese were vastly outnumbered in Hue. The French 10th Regiment, about 4,000 strong, was charged with the defence of the Imperial Palace, and there were also two companies of police squads and a motor transport company. By the military agreement between Japanese and French, the Japanese were limited to less than 100 men, a platoon for the protection of the Consulate, and, if a clash occurred between French and Japanese, the Japanese were likely to be massacred out of hand. But 190 Independent Infantry Battalion of 34 Independent Mixed Brigade (Iku Group, stationed in Da Nang) had moved just to the north of Hue on the pretext of manoeuvres and were to rush the city as and when the signal came from Saigon.

Given the French numerical superiority, Kaneko decided to use subterfuge. The function of *An* Organisation was to give support to the Emperor, Bao Dai, nephew of the exiled Prince Cuong De. Bao Dai was under house arrest in the Imperial Palace at Hue. He was to be approached by the Japanese and to declare the independence of the Empire of Annam from the French. The risk was that he might be removed by the French army, in which case the Japanese plan would misfire. It was vital to put Bao Dai on the Japanese side, which meant freeing him first, and Kaneko was in charge of this operation. He chose a group from his organisation, the day before Operation *Mei*, to hide in the palace grounds and open the gates to Japanese troops. They entered the palace in the evening on the pretext of sight-seeing, hid in a bamboo grove, dashed out on the agreed signal — the ringing of a bell from the watch-tower at 10 o'clock — took the keys from the sentries and waited for the arrival of Japanese troops.

The Japanese army order to begin operations was given at 10.25 (Japanese time), and an assault on the French army barracks began at once. Kaneko, accompanied by an interpreter, Katano, penetrated into the palace grounds once the gates had been opened by his squad, and used a sampan to move along the inner moat to where the Emperor Bao Dai's sleeping quarters were. But the boatman was dismayed by the gunfire. The resistance of the French troops guarding the palace had proved unexpectedly fierce and a real battle was raging. So Kaneko was forced to go on foot round the palace wall. Major Kawai, in command of the Japanese infantry who had seized the watch-tower, asked Kaneko to investigate what seemed like a couple of prominent Annamese. They had been apprehended, but Kawai was not sure who or what they were. The couple were sitting in a large luxurious car, and appeared to be people of some standing. Instinctively, Kaneko guessed this was the emperor Bao Dai and his consort.

'What the Japanese Army is doing now,' he told the young emperor, 'is a battle for the independence and freedom of Annam. You have no need to be on your guard. The long history of Annam as a colony of the French is at an end. Tomorrow begins the bright future of Annam for the Annamese. Please be reassured.' Bao Dai was overcome with emotion, as Kaneko remembers it, and said to him, weeping as he did no, 'I will never forget what you have said. After the war is over, I want to go to Japan and grasp the hand of the Japanese in friendship. Today is a unique day, for me and for my country.' Similar approaches took place elsewhere. The Japanese 2nd Division had been ordered to 'protect' the young king of Cambodia, Sihanouk, and General Manaki, the GOC, had Phnom Penh ringed with road-blocks to ensure the king did not escape. Sihanouk had not put in an appearance on 10 March, and on the 11th, he was discovered in the palace grounds disguised as a monk. Taking along the Japanese consul, Takashima, as interpreter, Manaki's chief of staff, Colonel Kinoshita, explained that the Japanese purpose was to disarm the French, and they had no objectives in Cambodia other than that the king should take over the government. Sihanouk declared Cambodia's independence on 13 March.[17]

Things did not go so well for the Japanese in Laos. The Japanese consul, Watanabe Taemi, did not arrive in Luang Prabang and the royal palace before the 20 March, given the poor communications between Laos and the rest of Indo-China. He told the king, Sisavang-Vong, that the Japanese had taken over administration from the French and had disarmed the French forces. The king, who was past sixty, did not speak French very well, and had suffered a great deal when part of Laos was transferred to Siam as a result of the Japanese mediation in the Franco-Siamese war of 1940. But he was a great friend of France, had negotiated a fresh protectorate agreement with Admiral Decoux some years before, and had travelled to Hanoi to visit him. He did not bow to the inevitable until two Japanese infantry battelions arrived in Luang Prabang on 7 April. He proclaimed Laos independent the next day.

Japan had done to the French what she had done to the British three years before. By planting the Japanese flag over Singapore she had brought British rule to an end. There would be an attempt to establish the old régime, as in Burma, but the forces Japan had liberated would ensure that it would never succeed in implanting itself again. Japan had replaced French rule in Indo-China by that of the local monarchies, supported by her army. But it was the actor in the wings who eventually profited most from the Japanese intervention: 'It was,' writes Colonel Dunn, 'one of the major reasons for the ultimate success of the Communists.'[18] Dunn's comment does not imply a direct causality as far as the Japanese *buryoku shori* is concerned. He is thinking chiefly of the effect of the action of the OSS, which in turn was only rendered possible because of the impotence of the French, and that in turn had been brought about by the Japanese: 'It is one of the assertions of this work,' he maintains, 'that Ho's recognition of the political immaturity of his OSS colleagues, and the manner in which the Communists were able to manipulate the anti-colonialism of the US officers, was a major factor in their eventual triumph.'[19]

The Japanese would have been content with monarchical form of independence for Indo-China, just as in Burma some of them favoured those few Thakins who would have supported a modified form of a restored Burmese monarchy. But those Thakins ultimately had no effect on the policies of the Anti-Fascist People's Freedom League (AFPFL), just as, in Vietnam, the monarchical structures admitted to national independence by the Japanese coup did not survive the war with the returning French.[20]

Japan had done to the French what she had done to the British three years before. By planting the Japanese flag over Singapore she had brought British rule to an end. There would be an attempt to establish the old régime, as in Burma, but the forces Japan had liberated would ensure that it would never succeed in implanting itself again. Japan had replaced French rule in Indo-China by that of the local monarchies, supported by her army. But it was the actor in the wings who eventually profited most from the Japanese intervention: 'It was,' writes Colonel Dunn, 'one of the major reasons for the ultimate success of the Communists.'[18]Dunn's comment does not imply a direct causality as far as the Japanese *buryoku shori* is concerned. He is thinking chiefly of the effect of the action of the OSS, which in turn was only rendered possible because of the impotence of the French, and that in turn had been brought about by the Japanese: 'It is one of the assertions of this work,' he maintains, 'that Ho's recognition of the political immaturity of his OSS colleagues, and the manner in which the Communists were able to manipulate the anti-colonialism of the US officers, was a major factor in their eventual triumph.'[19]

The Japanese would have been content with a monarchical form of independence for Indo-China, just as in Burma some of them favoured those few Thakins who would have supported a modified form of a restored Burmese monarchy. But those Thakins ultimately had no effect on the policies of the Anti-Fascist People's Freedom League (AFPFL), just as, in Vietnam, the monarchical structures admitted to national independence by the Japanese coup did not survive the war with the returning French.[20]

15

Controversial Problems of Japan's Post-War History in the Works of Soviet Historians

I. A. LATYSHEV

In this paper I would like to consider certain problems of Japan's post-war history which have given rise to discussion both among Soviet historians and our academic colleagues abroad. My main purpose is to give a general outline of how these problems have been treated by Soviet Japanologists (of which, unfortunately, our academic colleagues abroad know little) paying special attention to the points on which the majority of Soviet scholars agree and the points of their disagreement with Japanese historians and scholars engaged in Japanese studies in other countries.

Though forty years have elapsed since Japan's surrender, the starting point of her post-war history, Soviet students of Japan continue to show a considerable interest in the period 1945-52, i.e. the period of the allied military occupation of Japan. The interest is not accidental, since it was during this period that the basis of the contemporary development of Japan was laid and the Japanese social organisation acquired the forms which continue today. It was a time when truly historic changes took place in the life of Japanese society and had an impact which can be compared only with that of the Meiji reforms.

It should be noted, however, that such an understanding of the significance of the post-war transformation in Japan was not always the case among Soviet historians: in the late 1940s and the early 1950s, the writings of Soviet scholars on Japan contained very reserved and even sceptical assessments of the transformation going on in the country.[1]

In articles and books published at that time in our country, the chief concern was to do with the obstacles which hindered the consistent demilitarisation and democratisation of Japan demanded by the peace-loving world public opinion. Justly criticising the American occupation authorities for their unwillingness to do away with the foundations of monopoly power and the imperial system, Soviet students of Japan, carried away by polemics with those who idealised MacArthur's reforms,[2] sometimes underestimated the scale and significance of the changes occurring in Japan, independently of the will of the MacArthur military administration, under the pressure of international and Japanese democratic public opinion. But by the mid-1950s this one-sided approach was overcome in the course of a number of discussions and the events of the first post-war years received an all-round and objective elucidation.[3] Thus, for instance, in the *History of Japan, 1945-1975*, a major collective work by Soviet Japanese historians, reforms of the period of occupation are described in the following way: 'Reforms of that period delivered a serious blow to the feudal legacy in the country. Formerly a military and feudal absolutist monarchy, Japan became a constitutional monarchy, a state of socio-political nature similar to the developed capitalist countries of the West.'[4]

The understanding of the fundamental causes of the transformations in post-war Japan is of paramount importance for the study of the reforms of that period. One can see in the American writings on Japan, especially in the immediate post-war years, many categorical statements that the reforms were undertaken due to pressure from above — of the occupation authorities — and were wholly inspired by the American military command under General MacArthur who expressed the will of the American Government.[5] Though a superficial approach could make this version seem plausible, it is rejected in the Soviet scholars' works as incorrect. According to our researchers who base their opinion on an all-round analysis of the international situation and events in Japan at that time, the directives on the reforms were worked out by the American occupation authorities not because of the goodwill of MacArthur or Truman but contrary to their desires, under pressure from outside — the pressure of world democratic forces and the revived democratic forces of Japan.

This may be said, in particular, about Japan's new Constitution, the draft of which had been hastily prepared by MacArthur's headquarters only because the American Commander-in-Chief wanted to be ahead of the Far Eastern Commission whose proposals might have been too radical to suit the US Administration.[6] Incorporation in the Constitution of Article 9 and some other democratic provisions was a forced concession to the demands of the world democratic public opinion, made by the MacArthur administration in order to achieve the main goal — to preserve the monarchy as the corner-stone of Japan's state system.[7] The above-mentioned collective *History of Japan, 1945-1975* contains a conclusion that, 'the struggle of the working people, alongside the pressure of the world democratic public opinion, the Soviet Union in the first place, influenced the scale and level of the post-war democratic transformations and forced the ruling circles of Japan and the United States to make serious concessions because of fear of greater social upheavals.'[8]

From this point of view, the study and assessment of the situation and developments in Japan in 1945-7 were quite important to Soviet scholars. The lack of necessary information prevented them from properly appreciating the significance of these developments in the first post-war decade. But in subsequent years a retrospective analysis prompted them to reach the conclusion that at that time a revolutionary situation actually existed in Japan. This situation was brought about by economic chaos and mass famine, by the discontent of the masses with the policies of the ruling circles, by the confusion at the summit of Japanese society and by a tempestuous and spontaneous growth of the working class and Communist movements. It was the moment in the history of Japanese society, when we can use V. I. Lenin's formula: 'the lower classes rejected the old system and the upper strata were unable to live in the old way.'[9] In other words, it was the moment when the country found itself in the grip of a national crisis, and the discontent of the masses reached the 'boiling point.'

Demonstrations of hungry people in front of the Diet and Imperial Palace in May 1946 and the general political strike of the Japanese proletariat scheduled for 1 February 1947, but prohibited by MacArthur's Headquarters, were the climax of these events. But for the intervention of the American authorities, coming to the defence of the existing régime, the revolutionary explosion in Japan would have brought about changes in the life of Japanese society more radical than those which actually occurred. As regards the evaluation of the latter, the opinion of Soviet Japanologist, Ya. S. Pevzner, that the changes were 'similar to those which are characteristic of the radical bourgeois democratic revolution,'[10] seems to me quite justified.

In many works by foreign scholars, American in the first place, the democratic transformations implemented in Japan in the post-war period have been described as a step towards the so-called 'modernisation' of Japanese society. What is meant by 'modernisation' here is a long historical process starting with the collapse of the Shogunate and the reforming activities of the Japanese Government in the Meiji period. Soviet students of Japan do not share this concept and use the term 'modernisation' in their works very seldom and give it a meaning different from that of American scholars (we use it mainly when we speak of Japan's technological progress).

Why do we not accept the term 'modernisation?' Firstly, because this theory arbitrarily presents the capitalist system and the western bourgeois culture as standard models of world progress and world culture. The advocates of this theory define the extent of the 'modernisation' of Japan and other countries by the conformity, in the final account, of Japan's development to the norms of material and intellectual life of the capitalist countries of the West.[11] Other ways of development of the economy, state system and culture, including those of the countries of the Socialist world, are ignored in this theory or treated as an anomaly. The fallacy of this view is nowadays quite striking.[12]

Secondly, this term is used to negate the Marxist classification of the history of mankind as passing through the stages of such socio-economic formations as feudalism, capitalism, socialism etc. The advocates of this term strive to ignore the class nature of the state at different stages of the development of society. Such factors of social development as the class struggle, the working class movement and the confrontation of two world systems do not exist for them. Being quite uncertain and amorphous, this term introduces confusion into a clear scientific understanding of human history.

Thirdly, the notion of 'modernisation' as applied to the post-war history of Japan, over-simplifies the picture: complex signals of struggle, taking place during the twenty years since the surrender between the forces of reaction and progress, do not receive the necessary analysis and elucidation from the adherents of the theory of modernisation and, as a result, the reader gets too superficial and rosy a picture of the Japanese state policies.

At the same time, Soviet scholars cannot but take an interest in the question of how far the transformations that have taken place have changed the intellectual and cultural lives of the Japanese people. It would be interesting, in particular, to find out whether or not the administrative imposition, with the help of the mass-media, of various elements of the so-called 'western way of life' resulted in organic changes in everyday life, in the characteristics and way of thinking of the Japanese, in the erosion of the national identity which makes the East differ from the West, one nation from another, and which is an attractive field of study for an orientalist. Quite a lot of discussion dealt with this problem in the Soviet Union. The majority of our orientalists tend to believe that it is impossible to deny the influence of the western bourgeois culture on the mind and way of life of the Japanese, but at the same time it should not be exaggerated.[13] Alongside the American influence, the ideology of the common Japanese was greatly influenced during the same period by the world of socialism. As a result, the intellectual life of Japan today resembles something like a puff-pastry: most different ideologies are intermittent. One may find there the integral elements of the traditional national world outlook (the Confucian ethics, Shintoist and Buddhist dogmas, precepts of the *samurai* code of honour, *bushido*, specific attitude to the norms of human relationships expressed in the almost untranslatable notions of *giri kankei*, *haragei* etc.), and elements of American ideology (for instance, *maihomushugi*), and, at the same time, embryos of a new world outlook characteristic of the representatives of a socialist society (atheism, intolerance towards exploitation of man by man, proletarian internationalism, anti-war sentiments etc.).

Differences in the ideology of various strata of the population are determined in contemporary Japan's real life mainly by the class and social status of the individuals. Thus, traditional ideology prevails among peasants while businessmen and the bureaucracy are the main champions of the western way of life. As far as progressive Marxist ideology is concerned, its adherents are found among the working intelligentsia and the representatives of the advanced strata of the Japanese working class. It is impossible to draw a sharp dividing line here but, as regards the majority of the Japanese people, their world outlook and approach to life demonstrate the elements of all three. Nevertheless, from our point of view, the growth in the popularity of democratic and Communist ideas has become in the post-war decades the most important factor in the intellectual development of Japanese society, which has found reflection, for example, in the increase in the membership of the Japanese Communist Party and its mass support.

The publication in 1981 in the Soviet Union of *Studies in the History of Japan's Communist Party After World War II, 1945-1961* by Prof. I. I. Kovalenko, testifies to the great attention paid by Soviet historians of Japan to this problem. Doing justice to the stubbornness and achievements of Japanese Communists, fighting for the transformation of Japan's social structure on a democratic basis against the American-Japanese reaction, the author writes that 'despite mistakes and drawbacks, the activities of the Japanese Communist Party in the first years after the war won it a prominent place in the life of Japanese people. The party has become an acknowledged leader of the working class and has won the love and respect of the working people of Japan. The Party has emerged, steeled and enriched by the valuable experience of struggle for building a new Japan out of many class battles that were waged during these years.'[14]

The book describes with bitterness and regret the circumstances behind the 1950 split in the ranks of Japanese Communists which, in the conditions of repression by American occupation authorities, resulted in a serious weakening of the Party's influence among the masses.[15] Such important events in the history of the democratic movement in Japan as the 6th National Conference of the Japanese Communist Party, where the unity of its ranks was restored, as well as the 7th and 8th Congresses of the Party were positively evaluated in the book. 'The 8th Congress,' writes I. I. Kovalenko, 'played a tremendously important rôle in the development of the Communist movement in Japan. The programme adopted by it showed the Japanese Communists and the entire people the road to progress, a correct course for the struggle for genuine national independence, peace, democracy and socialism. The Congress contributed to further political, ideological and organisational strengthening of the Communist Party and laid the organisational and theoretical foundations of a mass vanguard party.'[16]

The San Francisco peace treaty which was signed in September 1951 and became operative on 28 April 1952, was an important landmark in Japan's post-war history. The treaty has received much attention in works by Soviet historians of Japan. But as regards its evaluation, our scholars seriously disagree with historians in Japan and the US who tend to regard this separate peace treaty and the 'Security Treaty' signed simultaneously as diplomatic acts meeting the national interests of the Japanese people.[17] The majority of our researchers share the views of those of their Japanese colleagues who criticise these documents and see in them a means of subjecting Japanese foreign policy to the military strategic course of the American government and maintaining Japan's economic, political and military dependence on the US.[18]

On the other hand, as our historians believe, the ruling circles of Japan, and the Japanese monopolistic oligarchy in the first place, have gained much from the signing of the treaty, using it and the Security Treaty to strengthen their economic and political positions in the world.[19] Japan's dependence on the US, confirmed by the San Francisco peace treaty, the 'Security Treaty' and the so-called Administrative agreement, is not regarded in Soviet historians' works as a permanent and unchangeable factor in Japan's post-war history. The majority of us tend to believe that during the 1950s and 1960s the extent of Japan's economic and political dependence on the US gradually diminished as Japanese imperialism was rehabilitated and increased its strength. On this issue Soviet students of Japan are in agreement with those Japanese scholars who regard the San Francisco treaty as a historical landmark, the starting-point for the ruling circles of Japan to restore their independence lost as a result of World War II.[20] The 1950s and 1960s were the period of a slow, cautious, highly contradictory and at the same time steadfast, restoration by Japanese imperialism of its own foreign policy. The doves of the Hatoyama government aimed at the restoration of diplomatic relations with the Soviet Union and other socialist countries, despite the cool and suspicious US stance, and were, in the Soviet historians' opinion, an important landmark in that direction.[21]

Beginning with the second half of the 1950s, Japan's foreign policy, as distinct from that of the preceding years, was determined, in the opinion of Soviet historians, not only by the American interests, but also by the interests of the Japanese monopolies, which, however, considered it advisable and profitable to continue military cooperation with the United States. The 1960 revision of the Japanese-American Security Treaty was, therefore, regarded by our scholars not as the result of a one-sided US military dictate, but as the outcome of a deal between the ruling circles of the two countries which was in the interests of the Japanese side, too.[22] They regarded the Security Treaty signed in January 1960 by the Kishi government as a military alliance of Japan with the United States hostile to the cause of peace. 'The new treaty,' notes the *History of Japan, 1945-1975,* 'is a military alliance of two imperialist states in which Japan, though remaining the weaker partner, obtained the right to determine its rôle and the extent of its participation in the US military strategy in the Far East. Therefore, Japan's responsibility for any actions of American armed forces in her territory has grown considerably.'[23]

On the other hand, works by Soviet historians attach great importance to the unprecedented mass protest of the Japanese public against the revision of the Security Treaty, its struggle for the annulment of the treaty and for a transition to a neutral peaceful policy, which shook the country in 1960 and resulted in the cancellation of US President Eisenhower's visit and the resignation of the Kishi cabinet. These mass actions are regarded by Soviet students of Japan as a vivid manifestation of the Japanese people's desire for peace and disagreement with the policies of the ruling circles, a manifestation of the potential militant energy which has been instilled in the Japanese people by the entire preceding course of events both inside and outside the country. At the same time, the 1960 events revealed, in the opinion of Soviet scholars, the weak side of the contemporary democratic movement in Japan: lack of sufficient unity of the progressive opposition and the inability of some contingents of the democratic camp to find, in the 1960s and 1970s, the road to a stable and lasting unification of forces on the basis of a united national democratic front.

97

It should be noted, in this connection, that Soviet historians, in the course of the post-war years, invariably paid great attention to the problem of the unity of the working class and democratic movements. Showing sympathy with the desire of the Japanese democratic forces to achieve unity in their ranks, Soviet scholars, at the same time, have not evaded a critical analysis of the causes of the split in the Japanese working class movement and the failure of the leaders of the Communist and Socialist Parties to act together to consolidate their position in the Diet and to overthrow the power of the ruling Liberal-Democratic Party. Analysis of this kind may be found, for instance, in the annual reviews of the internal political life of Japan, published in the Annual, *Japan*, featuring papers by leading Soviet students of that country. Much space was given to this problem in the books and papers by such Soviet researchers of the history of Japan's social and political life as I. I. Kovalenko, P. P. Topekha, V. A. Khlynov, A. I. Senatorov, G. I. Podpalova, I. K. Derzhavin, Yu. D. Kuznetsov and many others. They see the major cause of the disunity of the Japanese democratic movement in the divisive policies of the leaders of the rightist social democracy, in the anti-Communist prejudices existing in the Socialist party, the trade-unions and the progressive intelligentsia, prejudices intentionally fanned by the conservative ruling circles and the bourgeois mass media.

Especially active in attempts to prevent the unity of the democratic forces are such 'middle way' parties as the Democratic Socialist Party and Komeitō. 'Adhering to the ideology of anti-Communism,' writes I. I. Kovalenko, 'these parties chose the unsavoury rôle of the executors of the plans of the Japanese and American reaction in splitting the leftist forces.'[24] Not a small rôle in deepening the split in the Japanese democratic movement was played in the 1960s and 1970s by the interference in Japan's domestic affairs of Maoists who strove to impose on Japanese communists and socialists, extremist leftist and adventurous slogans. The smack of Maoism, for instance, was quite apparent in the mass student riots of 1969. One of the most painful and sad effects of the split in the democratic camp was the 1960s and 70s disunity of the peace movement, so strong in the 1950s, resulting in a considerable weakening of the movement, and its ability to influence the policy of the ruling circles.

The 1970s is treated by Soviet historians as a new stage in the development of Japanese-American relations characterised by an aggravation of imperialist contradictions, most vividly manifested in the so-called 'trade war.' But, pointing out the aggravation of Japanese-American contradictions, Soviet historians have continued to take notice in their works of the consolidation and expansion of business links between the monopolies of the two countries, their mutual interest in the preservation of the world capitalist system, in hindering all revolutionary processes undermining this system. It was on this basis that Japan's military cooperation with the US, gradually becoming a serious threat to peace and security in the Far East, was strengthened during the 1960s and 70s. Problems of Japanese foreign policy were most extensively discussed in D. V. Petrov's *Japan in World Politics*, which has been translated into Japanese.[25]

I would like also to touch upon another controversial problem of Japan's post-war development, the problem of the revival of Japanese militarism. This problem has been the subject of extensive and heated discussions throughout the entire post-war period not only in the Soviet Union, but also in Japan and the US, treated quite differently in the works of students of Japan. Many Japanese and American scholars are of the view that all foundations of militarism in Japan have been liquidated and that the peace-loving public has no grounds to fear the revival of Japanese militarism.[26] At the same time, there are many scholars in Japan who maintain that Japanese militarism has been revived and strengthened, and not independently, but under US auspices.[27] There have been quite a number of discussions on the subject among Soviet students of Japan, too, though in principle most agree with those Japanese scholars who consider the policy of steady military build-up in Japan as a movement towards the revival of Japanese militarism.[28] The points of view of our historians are, however, rather different as regards the periodisation of the stages in this process and the estimation of the extent of the militarisation of the country at various political moments, the strength of the militarisation trend in the 1950-60s and the present-day prospects of its development. There are so many opinions on the subject which are at the same time so close to each other, that, not to be inaccurate, I shall confine myself only to the statement of my own point of view.

I believe that, though post-war Japan cannot be called a militarist state, still throughout the 1960s and 70s militaristic trends became more and more pronounced in the policies of the Japanese ruling circles, the rôle of the armed forces in Japan's state policy grew, and the Japanese military-industrial potential was becoming a more and more weighty factor in foreign policy calculations of the Japanese ruling circles. Thus, ground has been laid for the revival of militarism. These trends became more apparent in 1982-3 in the policies of the Nakasone Cabinet, openly declaring its intention to transform the country into an 'unsinkable aircraft carrier'.

At the same time, there are now, in contrast to the pre-war years, real forces in Japan able to curb the attempts of the advocates of militarism to speed up the implementation of their far-reaching plan. The resistance of the peace forces of the country to the manoeuvres of the advocates of Japan's re-militarisation has been throughout the post-war years a strong obstacle to the attempts to revise the Constitution and introduce conscription. In this Soviet historians are unanimous, though we have different opinions about the strength and effectiveness of the influence of the Japanese peace-loving public on the government.

The problem of the revival of Japanese militarism is, in effect, a problem of the struggle between the reactionary and progressive forces of Japanese society which has been going on in the post-war period and has not yet entered its decisive stage. Recently, the advocates of militarism were able to score certain gains, but their adversaries certainly have the scope to continue the struggle and to change the course of events in their favour.

While internal political questions were the pivot of developments in Japan in the first post-war decade (workers' and communist movements,

99

the constitutional problem, inter-party clashes etc.), while in the second decade (1956-65) the focus of attention shifted to the foreign policy problems (restoration of relations with the socialist countries, revision of the 'Security Treaty' with the United States, 'normalisation' of relations with South Korea), in 1965-80 problems of an economic and social nature became important. This prompted historians studying that period to go into problems usually studied by economists and sociologists. In parallel with the economists, historians have to look, among other things, for the causes of the rapid economic development of Japan in the 1960s which greatly influenced various aspects of Japanese life. We, Soviet historians of Japan, try to find answers to these questions jointly with our colleagues — Soviet economists, studying Japan,[29] who in their works stress the circumstances explaining the lasting economic boom in Japan in the 1960s. Most important among these was a high rate of monopoly exploitation of the labour of Japanese workers, of the toiling masses and, due to this, a high rate of capital formation.

But economic issues are important to historians from the point of view of their social, political and psychological implications. Evaluating these implications, we do not always agree with the conclusions of those foreign scholars who tend to identify the growth of GNP with the improvement of living standards of the entire population of the country. As regards this question, we rather agree with those Japanese economists and publicists who in their works write about a substantial gap between the rates of Japanese economic development and the living standards of the bulk of the Japanese population, i.e. the working masses of the country. It has been stressed in Soviet literature that the rise in wages of the Japanese working people during the 1960s and 70s was by no means due to the goodwill of the employers — rather that wages were raised contrary to the employers' wishes, under the strongest pressure from the trade unions including their famous annual 'spring and autumn offensives.'[30]

On the other hand, Soviet academics, in their books and papers, consider the negative phenomena accompanying the economic boom: excessive intensification of workers' labour, inflation, the rise of consumer goods prices, land speculation, pollution of the environment, housing crises, transportation difficulties, low level of social security etc. Only taking into account these negative consequences of the 'forced economic growth' *(keizai kōdō seichō)*, one can understand why, for instance, in the 1960s and 70s there were so many manifestations of discontent in the country, be they strikes of the proletariat or other social and political conflicts. Soviet students of Japan believe that only a scientific Marxist analysis of the class essence of the policy of Japan's ruling circles may provide a sound explanation for all these phenomena of Japan's social life and politics. The policy expressing the interests of the upper strata of Japanese society, the monopolies, has conflicted throughout the past decades with the interests of the broad masses of the Japanese population, the working masses of the country. Frequent and acute conflicts, occurring in connection with this policy in Japan's political life, confirm the legitimacy of such a view.

Our publications on the history of post-war Japan reject as groundless and politically biased the attempts by some American and Japanese scholars to describe Japan's experience of economic development as a 'miracle,' enhancing the prestige of the capitalist system opposing socialism.[31] History shows that there are no miracles and that the long economic crisis into which the Japanese economy plunged in 1974-5 has been a clear testimony to the fact that the laws of capitalist development apply to Japan, too, that she is also not insured against economic slumps, mass unemployment and other manifestations of the viciousness of the capitalist system, disastrous for the working masses.

In conclusion, a few words about the views of Soviet-Japan specialists on the history of Soviet-Japanese relations after their normalisation as a result of the signing in Moscow by the two governments of the Joint Declaration of 19 October 1956. This event has been discussed in detail both in general studies of Japan's post-war foreign policy and in specialised works, including the book by L. N. Kutakov, *The History of Soviet-Japanese Diplomatic Relations* (Moscow, 1962); a collection of papers *Establishment of Soviet-Japanese Diplomatic Relations, 1925-1975*, edited by S. I. Verbitsky and I. I. Kovalenko; *The Soviet-Japanese Economic Relations* by M. I. Krupianko (Moscow, 1982), V. N. Berezin's *Course of Good-Neighbourliness and Cooperation and Its Enemies* (Moscow, 1977) and others.

The most common feature of the opinions expressed by Soviet historians as regards the development of Soviet-Japanese relations is perhaps that all of them envisage a possibility and an objective necessity of improvement and strengthening of business-like cooperation and close good-neighbourly contacts between both countries. Soviet scholars, in their books and papers have positively assessed such events, in particular, the signing in 1957 of the Soviet-Japanese Trade Treaty or of a number of important agreements on cooperation in the development of the natural resources of Siberia and the Far East in the late 1960s and early 1970s, or the bilateral Summit talks in Moscow in October 1973, resulting in the signing of a Joint Declaration. Stressing the usefulness of Soviet-Japanese good-neighbourliness, the authors of the book *The USSR — Japan* write, *inter alia:* 'Historical experience shows that improvement of relations between our countries led to relaxation of tension in the Far East, to the enhancement of Japan's international prestige. And, vice versa, any attempts on the part of Japanese reactionary forces and their allies to put obstacles in this way resulted in the increase of tension in the Far East, a decline of Japan's international prestige.[32]

In this context, studies by Soviet historians of Japan never fail to condemn, criticise and expose all the steps of the Japanese ruling circles as well as the governmental circles of the US, aimed at bringing about a deterioration of Soviet-Japanese relations and to undermine the good-neighbourly links between our two countries. It was in this context that the Japanese-American Security Treaty revised in 1960 with a clear intention to be made an instrument of the Pentagon's anti-Soviet strategy, has been sternly criticised in Soviet studies. It is in this context that the signing by Japan in 1978 of the so-called 'Japan-China Treaty of Peace and Friendship,' containing the notorious provision of the two countries opposing 'hegemonism' and aimed, as it has been frankly admitted in Beijing, against the Soviet Union, received a negative evaluation in the publications of Soviet historians and political scientists. Denouncing the political rapprochement of Japan and the PRC on an anti-Soviet basis, Soviet historians at the same time emphasise the necessity of a defente in the Far East and of measures to strengthen mutual trust between the countries of the region.

The latest publications of our scholars analysing Soviet-Japanese relations in the late 1970s — early 1980s express regret about the fact that Japan is going further down the path of an anti-Soviet policy and show the incompatibility of such actions of the Japanese Government as joining the so-called 'sanctions' against the Soviet Union, or fanning a nationalistic and clearly hopeless campaign in Japan for the 'return' of the so-called 'northern territories,' with the cause of strengthening peace in the Far East and of Soviet-Japanese good-neighbourly relations. Rejecting in their works the unfounded and illegitimate territorial claims of the Japanese politicians against the Soviet Union, Soviet researchers strive to explain to their readers that there is no other way to good-neighbourly relations and friendship between the Soviet and Japanese peoples than the way of recognition of, and respect for, the boundaries established as the outcome of World War II, of active development of many-sided and mutually-advantageous contacts between the two countries.

16

Remarks on the Approach to Japanese Public Opinion Research on Defence-Related Questions

PETER GETREUER

When I started to develop an interest in Japanese public opinion on defence-related questions, one of the first things to do was, of course, to go through the various bibliographies in search of related books and articles. Rather quickly I began to realise, however, that studies which dealt in detail with public opinion and defence were indeed rare. One of the few writers who did publish a considerable number of such works was the late Douglas H. Mendel Jr. Out of his long personal experience in this field, he evaluated Japanese public opinion research very favourably. His expertness seemed to me to be most convincing. He had served in the Morale Division of the United States Strategic Bombing Survey (Mendel 1959: 326), thereby actively taking part in the first scientific opinion research in Japan in 1945 (Mendel 1975: 151). He then studied survey research in the Survey Research Centre at the University of Michigan (Mendel 1959: 326), before he became one of the most distinguished and productive writers on Japanese public opinion, especially on foreign policy and defence issues.

He held the view that any doubts concerning the scientific value of survey research in Japan should be dispelled (Mendel 1961, 3). The applied methods were comparable, in his opinion, to those of the best United States survey organisations (Mendel 1961: 3 f.). He even considered 'the quantity and quality of Japanese surveys the best in Asia, if not the world' (Mendel 1966: 2; Mendel 1971: 522).

During the analysis of Mendel's writings, one has to realise, however, that he does not elaborate much on the rôle and meaning of public opinion in Japan. He just held the view that public opinion on a general level had assumed a large rôle in post-war Japan. Mendel referred to the Occupation reforms, democratic ideals and promises of the conservative government to follow public opinion (Mendel 1966: 1). He conceded, however, that the influence of mass public opinion on the formulation of defence policy was limited. But he obviously still regarded it of some importance, stressing that Japanese cabinet members had always insisted on the necessity of a domestic consensus on national defence (Mendel 1975: 149 f.). To come to the point, in a nation in which democratic institutions were moulded by the American Occupation, public opinion could not be ignored (Mendel 1975: 175).

Holding this somewhat dogmatic but still rather vague position, Mendel dealt in relatively great detail with public opinion surveys' results *per se*. He thereby provided valuable descriptions of the behaviour of Japanese people in answering questions on defence from the early 1950s to the first half of the 70s. Mendel's analyses and interpretations, however, do not provide a critical investigation of the surveys and their results. Perhaps, he was too convinced of their quality and the functioning of American-moulded democratic institutions.

In Japan, the high esteem of public opinion and public opinion research seems to correspond perfectly with the favourable scientific evaluation by Professor Mendel. Perhaps the most striking evidence of that high esteem is the vast number of opinion surveys conducted by various institutions. On quite a regular basis in the main daily newspapers, one finds quite detailed reports (often two to four pages long) on public opinion surveys.

Quite often also, the headline is devoted to their main conclusions. The three big daily newspapers all have their own opinion research organisations, as does NHK, whereas the news agencies are closely affiliated to major research companies. Is it imaginable that they would all bear the considerable costs of such polling activities without regarding the results as important? And what about the government? Governmental bodies not only conduct a great many of their own surveys, but the Prime Minister's Office also regularly publishes a rather detailed 'Yearbook of public opinion research.' This provides various kinds of research data on even the most obscure topics. In addition, the Prime Minister's Office publishes a monthly magazine, which is entirely devoted to up-to-date research reports by the various survey institutions. To me, this seems to be an almost excessive preoccupation with the significance ascribed to public opinion.

Corresponding to these surveys, are numerous books and articles which deal in one way or the other with their results. This statement, of course, applies also to the topic of defence. But it is not only politicians, journalists and 'critics' who often refer in their articles to survey results. Many Japanese and western scholars also do not seem to hesitate to use the outcome of opinion surveys extensively on defence-related questions to support their arguments. The crucial question, however, is: should they hesitate?

If one believes the American political scientist, Donald Hellmann, they definitely should hesitate. Hellmann, a distinguished writer on Japanese politics, took up a much more critical point of view then Mendel. (I refer to Hellmann, because he is one of the few writers to consider this question. Despite the fact that his views stem from the early 1970s, they still represent the best critical appraisal. Most of the other authors who have dealt with survey results have just evaded the problem.) In Hellmann's view, public opinion surveys reflect only 'opinions held by the public,' since they were mere descriptions of people's opinions. He distinguishes these 'opinions held by the public' from 'effective public opinion' whose effectiveness he sees in two ways, as either 'mass mood' or 'articulate opinion.' Hellmann stresses how important it is to recognise that mass mood does have influence on the general aims of foreign policy and on those very few decisions which are dramatic as well as far-reaching, e.g. decisions in the face of the immediate danger of war. To a not clearly manifested mass mood, which is the usual case in most of the issues concerning foreign policy and defence, he ascribes, however, only unclear and indirect influence (Hellmann 1969: 7 ff.). Hence, he regards it as far more important to concentrate attention on 'articulate opinion' at the top of the opinion pyramid, i.e. on those who regularly express opinions on the nation's security policy (Hellmann 1972: 162).

However, Hellmann not only minimises the importance of 'mass opinion' as a determinant or significant influence on Japanese defence policy, he also casts serious doubts on the surveys and their results. In his view, there were clear but only rarely observed limitations on accepting these polls' results at face value. He came to the following devastating conclusions:

— polls in Japan had given distorted profiles of opinions held by the public; — issues tended to be approached with either excessive simplicity or complexity; — responses to such questions provided insight into little more than reactions to proddings on matters that the questioner saw as important.

Furthermore, he found fault with the way in which the survey questions were framed and he located a strong bias relating to abstract notions of peace. Taking these shortcomings into consideration as well as the public's low level of general knowledge of, and interest in, defence matters, Hellmann even doubted the very meaning of detailed surveys regarding the issues of security and peace. His argument finally culminated in the warning: 'The use of the results of such polls, except on the most general level of analysis, is extremely hazardous' (Hellmann 1972: 161). As a practical consequence, he simply turned down any careful scrutiny of opinion polls as 'premature,' until there was far more evidence of a dramatically-intensified concern for defence questions among the public at large (Hellmann 1972: 162).

Thus Hellmann holds a very different view from Mendel. The only obvious agreement between these two basic approaches regarding defence-related questions is the fact that both authors consider the influence of mass opinion on the formulation of defence policy to be minimal. But who is right? Mendel, with his favourable evaluation of Japanese opinion research and his rather uncritical description of the results, or Hellmann, with his approach which leads to a de-facto refusal to deal with the results in detail?

Let me set out my own views on the relevance of Japanese public opinion research regarding defence. My assessment derives from a secondary analysis of defence-related questions from more than a hundred nationwide Japanese public opinion surveys. I would say that one has to agree with Hellmann when he criticises serious defects in the surveys. I traced questions with suggestive wording and unbalanced response options. Frequently, the importance of the framing of the questions within the survey was completely neglected. I also encountered cases of unnecessary changes in different polls conducted by one and the same survey organisation, changes which, of course, impaired their effects on the comparability of the results, etc.

I cannot, however, agree with Hellmann's generalisations. The evidence of these shortcomings might be sufficient to reject Mendel's idea of Japanese public opinion research as perhaps the best in the world. It might even be sufficient to suppose a general inclination towards a rather light-hearted way of handling the very sensitive instrument of public opinion research. Nevertheless, it is definitely not sufficient to disqualify the research on defence issues as a whole. There is a sufficient number of surveys which definitely do allow the reader to draw reasonable conclusions. Even Hellmann points out that fact by conceding the results' use 'at a most general level,' whatever that may be. What really has to be done, in my view, is to carefully scrutinise and interpret the results.

But there is also a kind of light-heartedness at the presentation level of the surveys' results. At best, the data are presented in fairly detailed reports, which is the case with the few surveys on defence and the SDF, conducted by the Prime Minister's Office and some of the NHK's polls. But even here, the results tend to be presented at face value without any substantial comment, even on the purely statistical significance of the data. Generally speaking, systematic and detailed breakdowns of the results from the mass media's surveys are not available. Occasionally, newspapers and news agencies offer some additional details which can serve as a valuable source for otherwise unavailable data. Sometimes, however, the presentation is misleading: the fact that the statistical error grows with the decreasing size of the polled sub-group, is usually completely ignored.

The term 'statistical error' is rarely ever mentioned in a newspaper's report on surveys' results. Accordingly, the sub-group-results in question are sometimes simply irrelevant. But problems also arise when up-to-date results are compared with those of older surveys by the same sponsor, even if the wording of the questions was identical. The framing of the questions, however, was often completely different — but any qualifying comment is usually not provided. Hence, after some careful scrutiny, quite a few of the seemingly significant developments in public opinion turn out to be not interpretable in this sense.

In my view, the improper and sometimes really careless presentation and interpretation of survey results pose a far bigger problem than the shortcomings of the polls themselves. Critical comments on research- and presentation-practices are extremely rare in Japan. Too many scholars or writers who might be expected to have enough professional knowledge to know about the sensitivity of this research method just use selected results which fit their arguments and obviously ignore others which do not. Hellmann is correct in pointing out the limits in taking poll results at face value. But such a limit does not necessarily mean that the information-output from such a question is reduced too. It just requires a careful scrutiny of the circumstances under which the results were achieved, and then a careful drawing of the proper interpretative conclusions. Nobody is forced to take results at face value! The frequent abuse of the results, however, has to be blamed, at least partly, also on the sponsors of the surveys. Many of them neither apply the necessary care in presenting the results nor point out the limits of interpretation. It might be suspected that a careful presentation of a poll's results is regarded as counter-productive for some of the aims of opinion research.

I assume three main reasons for the high esteem of public opinion research in Japan:

1) public opinion research in Japan has developed under strong US influence and is regarded as a token of western democratic thinking; 2) political motives, as opinion research serves as a valuable tool for the calculation of political risks and necessities in policy-making as well as a source for political argument and PR activities; 3) commercial motives, either directly with information as a product to be sold, or by way of the necessities of competition.

In my view, these three factors do not imply the absolute necessity of presenting and publicly interpreting the results in a scientifically correct way. My suspicion that a proper scientific basis for handling the data might even be regarded as counter-productive, especially applies to some of the political and commercial motives. I refer, on the one hand, to the idea of using opinion survey results as a source for political arguments and PR-activities and on the other hand, the aim of marketing like any other product, since a proper presentation and interpretation could undermine the attractiveness of the data extruded.

To sum up: in spite (or perhaps I should say because) of all these shortcomings, public opinion research in Japan is held in high esteem which in turn leads to the production of great quantities of research data on defence-related questions. Such data are, in some respects, problematic.

The biggest problem in my opinion, however, lies in the light-hearted and sometimes careless presentation of these results and in the way they are used or abused by some politicians, journalists, critics and even scholars. Too many of them seem to regard public opinion surveys as some kind of supermarket, where they can easily help themselves with data which fit their arguments and objectives.

But how to deal with these research data? Neither of the approaches by Mendel and Hellmann seems to me to be convincing, nor do any of the other ways Japanese public opinion research on defence has been dealt with up to now. Taking into consideration this situation, I have chosen a basically historical approach. What I am actually trying to do in my thesis is to give a thorough description of Japanese public opinion on defence issues, as it is manifested in opinion poll results. I try to achieve this by taking into account all available defence-related results from nationwide Japanese surveys, conducted between April 1972 and March 1983. By comparing all the comparable results, by contrasting the not comparable outcomes, and by analysing the differences in results due to different wording, framing etc., my aim is to produce some reasonable and well-founded interpretative statements on the development and characteristics of the Japanese public regarding defence. My aim is not, however, to give a rather uncritical report on the surveys' results, as Mendel did, but to deal critically with the circumstances under which the results were achieved. Since any interpretation is to some extent a subjective matter and, since it is not possible to consider every single result in detail, I think it is essential to provide also a comprehensive documentation of all the polls' results which have been the basis of my analysis.

Secondly, there is the basic concept of public opinion which underlies my study. It differs from the concept which most of the writers who have dealt with public opinion on defence have used up to now, including Mendel and especially Hellmann. I refer to a concept, which the German communication-scientist Elisabeth Noelle-Neumann calls the *Elitekonzept* of public opinion. Public opinion in this way is primarily understood as actual or potential pressure on the government (Noelle-Neumann 1982: vi). This concept makes it relatively easy for Hellmann, for example, to turn down as premature any careful scrutiny of opinion polls, since he assumes only vague and indirect influence on the formulation of defence-policy.

There is, however, also another aspect of public opinion, an aspect which includes the factor which Edward Ross in 1898 called 'social control:' it is the so-called *Integrationskonzept* of Noelle-Neumann. These two concepts do not differ that much, as far as the relation between public opinion and government is concerned. The main difference lies in the relation between public opinion and the individual (Noelle-Neumann 1982: vi f.). This is, of course, not the place to elaborate on this theoretical concept. I want to stress, however, as important features, the integrative function of public opinion and the increasing pressure for conformity when there is more need for it, i.e. in times of crisis or social danger. This pressure is determined by the threat of isolation, which serves as the actual driving force of public opinion processes and which itself derives from a value-laden, moralistic, often irrational element which is an indispensable part of any public opinion process (Noelle-Neumann 1982: xi *et passim*).

In my view, this aspect of public opinion has so far been more or less neglected in Japanese studies. But I regard it as really important especially because matters of peace and war, of defence and country are heavily value-laden, with moralistic and irrational factors playing a considerable rôle. Hence, it can be assumed, that the pressure for integration exerted by public opinion on the individual would rise dramatically in the case of events which are perceived as dangerous for society. Therefore, a careful scrutiny of the behaviour of Japanese people in answering defence-related questions seems to me to be important, despite the still low knowledge of, and interest in, defence matters of the average Japanese and despite the various shortcomings of opinion research. The results of such a study, I believe, could contribute to a better evaluation of possible developments in Japan in the event of a serious future crisis.

SECTION 2:
Sociology
Anthropology

17

Work-Groups in a Japanese Enterprise

KURUMI SUGITA

This paper represents a simple attempt to initiate study in this vast field of research using data collected during research on Company X which is one of the largest Japanese firms in the field of electric and electronic instruments.

When I started research, the first thing which struck me was the collective functions of the work-group which consists of about ten people, excluding those on the assembly lines involving some 50 to 70 people; the work group is above all a unit of organisation, whose responsibility and relative autonomy are recognised institutionally. As is well known, the functioning of companies is not based on jobs but on the work-group where the nature of jobs stays ambiguous and where each person goes beyond the limit of his duty to help others and to complete the work collectively.

The work-group is also a social reality experienced in a very complex way. People are very concerned with interpersonal relations and the sociability of the group. They organise various activities after hours; they get together to welcome new members or to hold farewell parties; they organise excursions, trips, sports competitions, etc.; they drink together after work, and so forth, in order to reinforce the sense of unity. This is a very brief description, more a caricature of work-groups. However, when one examines this phenomenon of the collectivity of labour more closely, one notices that there exist variations and even cases where there is a complete absence of this phenomenon. For example, collective functions and representations are very strong among final-assembly groups in heavy machinery, whereas collective practices are almost non-existent among certain groups of designers or those working on assembly lines, although here the ideology of collectivity persists. As for groups of researchers, we observe neither collective practices nor representations.

The examination of these variants has led me to identify certain factors which may influence the constitution or development of collective practices and representations.

1) Responsibility has to be attributed collectively to the group. The only exception to this rule was the case of work-groups composed of researchers at laboratories. These groups are organisational units; responsibility is not attributed to the group, but individually to each researcher. They do not have a collective aim. Of course, they exchange ideas and consult each other when necessary, but in principle each person works for himself. It is rather the emulation between the researchers than their cooperation which is exalted here. These researchers are notorious for their individualistic attitude to life, and it is very rare that they spend

their leisure time together. Other examples which have a fairly weak collective responsibility are certain groups of designers and white-collar workers. The designers show characteristics more or less similar to the researchers, calling themselves 'lone wolves' with a certain sarcasm and pride, having relatively few relations both with co-members of their group or with people outside their group. On the other hand, certain white-collar workers especially those in the service sectors (material supply, production planning, etc.) present quite different characteristics. Very often they work with individual responsibility. To accomplish their task, they do not work with co-members of their group, but with blue-collar workers who need their service. When I posed the question concerning the famous 'wa', the workers in service sectors immediately referred to their relations with assembly-line workers, whereas others spoke of the solidarity of their work-group. This weak internal structure of groups in service sectors with their centrifugal relations with outsiders contrasts with the in-group solidarity of production groups which is accompanied by segmentary relations with outside groups.

2) The higher the degree of cooperation in the group, the stronger the collective functions and representations are. In the case of final assembly groups for heavy machines such as large generators, synchronic cooperation and rotation of posts characterise work organisation. Besides their individual qualifications, workers insist on their collective qualifications, that is to say, their skill as a group. Among these groups, group unity and solidarity are considered an indispensable condition of production. A lot of activities are organised outside of the work place and the members of the group spend a great deal of leisure-time together.

3) If skill plays an important rôle in the accomplishment of tasks attributed to a group, this favours the collective ideology. In the case of groups working with machine-tools, 3 or 4 years are necessary to execute the work with dexterity and 10 years to develop the flair with which one can spot a defect at first sight. It is here that the pride of skilled artisans subsists. Since work itself does not exalt the unity of the group, the necessity of solidarity or good human relations is expressed in a different way. It is mutual aid between independent workers and the atmosphere of the place of work which are valued. Activities outside of work are less frequent, but remain intense. Nevertheless, group solidarity is stronger among the final assembly groups mentioned above. One could say, therefore that cooperation plays a more important role than skill in the exaltation of collective functions and representations.

4) Egalitarian relations and homogeneity of status favour group unity. When there are many workers from sub-contractors, seasonal workers, part-timers or regular workers sent from other groups (or even other factories or plants) to participate in the work of the group for a certain period of time or when severe hierarchical relations exist inside the group, group solidarity deteriorates.

5) Individuals have to stay at the same place of work for a sufficiently long time, so that stable social relations can be forged within the group. In general, the mobility of blue-collar workers is lower than that of white-collars. Thus, we observe stronger group solidarity among blue-collar

workers. On the other hand, mobility is very high among non-regular workers and regular workers who are sent from other groups as reinforcements. They usually leave after 3 or 6 months. In the case of light instrument assembly lines where there are many non-regular workers, it is very difficult to establish stable social relations, and what we often observe are rifts between regular and non-regular workers.

6) A group should not consist of more than about 10 people. In the case of light instrument assembly lines, the size of a group varies from between 50 and 70 people who are regrouped in small sub-groups of similar status.

7) A group must have sufficiently large institutionally recognised autonomy. The position of group chief is significant in this sense. For workers the ideal image of a group chief is, among other things, as a person who can defend the autonomy of the group *vis-a-vis* the management. A chief who is completely submissive to the influence of management and who seeks to apply instructions which appear absurd to the workers will be despised and meet with their hostility. However, such resistance by workers will take the form not of a direct expulsion of the chief but rather of a deterioration of group productivity.

8) Group responsibility goes together with group autonomy and necessitates an abundant supply of information. A relatively free circulation of information is facilitated by the context of permanent employment and fixed salary which reduce the resistance of workers against modifications in general.

9) Group solidarity is also related to the predominance of local considerations over general ones. For example, the international competition of professional education constitutes a consideration of cosmopolitan character, valid in all the social groups concerned. On the other hand, at a local level, it is the utility of an individual for a specific group which is taken into account. Among the groups where we observe strong solidarity, the local considerations predominate, and the general considerations are undervalued.

10) There often exists a conflict between the social relationship established inside the group and that in which the members of the group participate outside the company. For group solidarity, it is important that the first should have priority over the second: this is often the case for large firms like Company X. However, from time to time, we can find rare cases where the relationship outside the company prevails over that inside. For example, in the case of a factory which I studied, many workers are actually also farmers, and undertake agricultural activities parallel to their work in the factory. For them, relations inside their village communities are of more importance than those in the company which has only a temporary existence as seen from the view point of the history of the village community. For chiefs of groups and managers who come from other plants and who are used to the predominance of company values, this attitude may appear to be very shocking.

The fact that the degree of the collective functions and representations or even their existence depend on these factors shows that cultural elements cannot by themselves explain this phenomenon. It is rather the organisation of labour within the framework of the socio-economic and technological evolution of society which plays the major rôle in the formation of representations of labour, integrating both cultural and traditional factors.

We will be able to see matters more clearly if we take the historical process of constituting the work-group into account. In fact, the collective functions and representations we observe are recent phenomena. The work-group, not as a simple organisational unit but as a bearer of these functions and representations, was constituted towards the second half of the 1960s. In the case of Company X, what played a decisive rôle was the introduction of the 'Measured Daywork Plan' in 1967-8, conceived by an American company with which Company X had a technical cooperation arrangement. This plan permits control of the performance of the individual, the group, section, etc., for a given period of time. Control is maintained on a time-standard basis, but the individual's performance does not affect his wage. The introduction of the 'Measured Daywork Plan' was designed to resolve the various problems caused by the system of payment on the old basis of the time standard by the establishment of a more 'scientific' basis for performance control.

The new 'Measured Daywork Plan' reduced competition and conflict between the workers. As individual performances did not influence the wage any more, they did not fight each other to obtain more profitable tasks and they did not hide their skill any longer. Thus skill and know-how became accessible to all workers. Moreover, the control of performance on a collective basis created the foundation for exaltation of the group. These bases probably already existed in the case of the price system for collective jobs which preceded the 'Measured Daywork Plan,' but it is only in the second half of the 1960s that we observe the ideological exaltation of the solidarity of the work-group. Quality control developed, founding itself upon the collective functions thus established and on the new representations which accompanied them. Thus, the introduction of the 'Measured Daywork Plan' has contributed to the constitution of work-groups, although this was not the original aim of management.

The formation of work-groups is also accompanied by the transformation of certain representations of labour and social relations. For example, technical know-how does not play as important a rôle as before. This corresponds, of course, to the technological developments which have reduced the rôle of individual skill. In place of know-how, it is assiduity, sincerity and the capacity to cooperate with others which are now esteemed.

Relations between the senior and junior workers have become less hierarchical. This is related to the breakdown of the status of the technical know-how, mentioned above. Before this, it was dormitory life which had played an important part in the creation of the senior-junior relationship, especially for young workers who entered the company at 15 years of age. But the dormitory system for boys of this age was abolished in 1982. In fact, only a very small number of people start working at the age of 15 these days. At present, all recruits live in dormitories during their training period: but it is relations between fellow-recruits which are created rather than the hierarchical relations between senior and junior.

In the ideology of the workers at Company X, the work-group is a necessary condition of production in the same way as machines, tools and the organisation of the work process *stricto sensu* are. In this context, social relations inside the work-group appear, not as a consequence of the necessities of labour, but as a condition of the realisation of labour. The place occupied by the work-group in representations is related to the real functions of the group in the division of labour and cooperation. It is important to note here that these functions and the work-group representations cannot be regarded as premises. They are historical products and have been formed through the concrete modality of the realisation of labour, as a conjunction of diverse effects, and not as a result of the explicit intentions of the company.

18

Modern Times for Ama-Divers

RUTH LINHART

At least at first sight the *ama*-divers have stepped over the strict borders that have been set for women in nearly all cultures of the world. As the German ethnologist, Klaus E. Muller, in his detailed book about the *Ethnology of the gender-conflict* says, women universally were placed throughout history in the inner part (*Binnenbereich*) of society — with the familial fire-place in the centre, within the hut, the tent or the house.[1] In Japan, to mention only one little example, the word *kanai* (my wife) provides evidence of this division of the world, which allows men to have a view above the far horizon but forces women to be content with a glimpse at their own narrow neighbourhood. Everywhere in the world, as Muller states, even in the very highly developed cultures of Greece, Rome and the modern European cultures, this division was defended by the argument that nature or even god(s) want it like that[2] — because these arguments are hard to oppose.

The *ama-* divers contradict this female stereotype and therefore have been an amazing phenomenon to people outside the fishing and diving communities until today. One must not be surprised, therefore, that their real existence and life-style differ to a great extent, from that of romanticised legend and the visions that many men have. There is the romantic pearl-diver, who no longer exists outside the tourist centres; there is the beautiful *ama* of the *ukiyoe*, who is often shown as a seductive water-nymph, offering her shell to some prince. Also men are irritated when thinking about the strong *ama* women that *ama* are reported to be. *Ama* divers are exotic also in Japan. Tourists in Mie-prefecture get to know them as slim girls, feeding fish in aquariums or playing with dolphins in amusement-parks. In pearl-breeding-centres like Kashikojima visitors can take souvenir photos in front of pasteboard *ama*. At such times you see them in their white *isogi*, a dress they rarely wear in reality today. By the way, the *ama* dress of the Shima-region in Central Japan, shows the history of growing prudishness: before Showa *ama* only wore a *koshimaki* (loincloth) and a *tenugui* (towel) around their hair; from that time onwards they added a blouse, then trousers and for about ten years proper diving-dresses they called 'wet-suits'. In the real-life situation of Katada, a diving and fishing village in Shima, Mie-prefecture, where I was in 1978 and again in 1983 where I spent a longer time in an *ama* household, I encountered *ama* as hard-working middle-aged women. Their working places are the reefs under the blue surface of the sea to which the object of their work, the *awabi* (abalone), cling.

Sendo or *tamae* are the names given to the men who own the boats in which the *ama* go out for work. There are three different kinds of boat-diving in Katada: *ipponbiki* or *ippaibune*, *haikara* and *okedo*. In the first type of boat one *ama* goes out with one boat-man, usually her husband. She dives to the farthest and deepest points. The second type carries three to five *ama* and *okedo* means that one boat-man takes with him, five to seven *ama* who dive not very far from the coast. The *ama* share their income with these boat-men, *okedo-ama* give him 15%, *haikara-ama* 25% and *ipponbiki-ama* 50%, unless he is her husband.

The second type of diving work involves swimming out to sea without a boat. These *ama* are called *kachido-ama*, and they are content to work in more shallow grounds. Diving time is strictly limited from March to 14 September; there are also strict rules governing the daily diving time: in spring one hour in the morning and during the warmer period up to two hours in the afternoon. The objects of the *ama* work are *awabi* (abalone), *sazae* (snails) and *uni* (sea-urchins). After work the *ama* bring their daily harvest to the *awabi* market. After that the best part of the day begins — they rest in the *ama*-hut, washing, changing dresses, warming up, all activities that are necessary for withstanding the coldness of the water next day.

*   *   *

I would now like to consider the changes that modern times have brought to *ama* work. First, let me begin by reproducing an official statement issued by an official of the women's section of the fishing corporation of Katada in 1983:[3]

'In earlier times it might have been that *ama* could not lead an economically safe life, but today the men are all working somewhere nearby. Thus, the husbands of today's *ama* — as the *ama* are diving only one season and are at home in winter — are not lazy men.'

Fifty years ago in 1933, an old *ama* of Kuuzaki told Segawa Kyoko, who published a famous *ama* monograph in 1955:

'In my village only the wives of the priest, the doctor and the teachers do not dive. People think that it is a pity for them, that they cannot dive, even if their husbands die. Here is one place where women can surpass men. Village women can bring up their children when their husbands die, whereas it would be a serious problem if a man became a widower. I think in town women have decided not to work. Here is a region where women dive in the sea and rush to their fields, where women work hard and take care of their men.'[4]

These two statements indicates that men worked less in the past than today. Also the position of women seems to have changed: the old woman before the Second World War sees herself economically independent, not so the woman, who was young after the Second World War and is now in her fifties.

But, before we delve further into the problem of social status of men and women, let us have a look at the changes in *ama* work that I was able to discover in Katada in 1983. That *ama* work has greatly changed, *ama* confirmed daily in their conversation.[5] Many changes have been for the better from the standpoint of convenience, security and health of the *ama*, though not necessarily for the sea and fruits of the sea. I have already mentioned the dress: the rubber diving-dress called 'wet-suit' that Katada-*ama* have worn since 1976 keeps the body warm and protects it from sharp reefs and encounters with sea-creatures. At the same time, the fishing corporation decided on limiting diving time. The reason for this was that with the new warmer and safer diving-suits a lot of women found themselves able to dive for longer periods of time, even in cold water. Without time-limitation this would have led to a rapid exhaustion of *awabi*. But the *ama* do not like the time limits, because it puts even more stress on their work than before. They dive without snorkel and oxygen, as they only have about one minute for diving, looking for *awabi*, cutting the *awabi* from the cliffs and coming up again. Now, as I have already mentioned, they may dive one hour in the morning and one hour in the afternoon in spring and two hours twice a day in summer. This does not give them enough time for recuperation between. It is like piece-work in a factory, the time-pressure is enormous. Similarly, as in a factory there is also strict control of each dive exercised by a harbour-representative. Another change is the shortening of the diving season as a whole. In earlier years diving began soon after the New Year celebrations.

The *sendō* have changed to motor-boats since the fifties. They also no longer have to pull out the *ama* by their own strength but do this with the help of an *'enjin.'* Medical care has improved and *ama* are no longer required to dive until the day of childbirth. Electricity and water were installed in many *ama-goya* (*ama-*) huts and the *ama-goya* which in former times were built with wood and bamboo and had straw-thatched roofs,[6] are now made with corrugated iron. The living standards in the former poor fishing-villages have improved to a degree which the *ama* of 1933 could not possibly have imagined. Every family has at least one car, a boat, of course a telephone, a room-cooler etc. Katada, whose inhabitants often fled from local poverty to America in the Meiji- and Taishō-eras, has joined the prosperity of post-war Japan. Yet, along with such improvements, the old traditions and mutual solidarity seem to have become weaker and the whole *ama* profession is in danger. There are 120

116

ama in Katada. *Kachido-ama*, who do not need as much skill and training as a boat-*ama*, have increased in number and boat *ama*, the so-called *puronoama* (professional *ama*) have decreased, so that the number of *ama* in a boat has become smaller and the harvest richer. But in spite of this the daughters of the *ama* do not want, and their parents do not urge them, to take up *ama* work after school as the now older *ama* did in their young days. The young girls go to school until they are 18, then work, get married and have children. Whereas the old *ama* continued diving in spite of marriage and children, the young people are also following the prevailing trends of post-war Japan. In 1983 there was no mother diving whose child was younger than two years and could visit a nursery or a kindergarten.

* * *

We return to the (for me) crucial question, whether modern times have brought changes in the position of men and women in the diving community of Katada. It is generally believed that *ama* are strong women with a much higher status in their community and family than middle-class Japanese women. This assumption may be based on statements like the following of Iwata Junichi, who published a book about the *ama* of Shima in 1939. He wrote:

> 'Women have from old times been the sovereigns over production. Although you hear from fishermen: "In such and such a village many wives are deciding things but in our village men are the boss," in reality the *ama* always have the power and the men could only be called their assistants.'[7]

In addition, Iwata describes how the women not only dive but do all the house-work and upbringing of children as well and, unlike their husbands, have not a minute of leisure. Iwata concludes that this responsibility brings women self-confidence! I quoted also the old woman of 1933 who laid stress on her economic independence (in case her husband died) but at the same time mentioned hard work as a kind of price for this.

Segawa Kyoko herself during her visits to *ama* communities recognised the high valuation accorded to *ama* work, but also noted that this by no means implied female dominance in the family and the community. She saw that women had to give their boat-men a surprisingly high percentage of their income and that they had troubles with mothers-in-law and boatmen if they did not fulfil their high expectations. Segawa, in the introduction of her *ama* monograph, tells how 'A hard-working daughter was courted from all sides because a *man* through the work of such a wife could become rich after twenty years, buy a ship and a house and even try to be successful in *awabi*-dealing.' Men appreciated in women their working capability and self-confidence, quite contrary to urban conditions, Segawa continues.

Literature about the *ama* profession and also statements of older *ama* in Katada seem to indicate that women in *ama* communities gained prestige, first, through their work and only second because of their capability for childbirth, which in most societies is the main reason for respecting women. What is still unanswered is the question whether *ama* in the past did really

117

step over that border of 'the inner part of the society' and managed to cross the circle of that 'knowledge in boundaries' (*Wissen in Grenzen*)[8] which women are allowed to adopt in most societies. Of course, from a feminist point of view one hopes for a society that could serve as a model for more female participation and equal treatment. But I am afraid that even in the former *ama* communities the patriarchal norms and values regulated society.

Ama had, and have, a highly specialised knowledge about diving. But did this knowledge bring them influence outside their narrow *ama* world, outside their boats and huts? It seems that, even inside their *ama* world, where they did a typical if female collecting task, they were not free to decide for themselves; rather, they were controlled by men and other women from morning to night. Also the good income they earned was spent mainly by their husbands on leisure and other pursuits. It is a question which still has to be answered by further research whether they were independent persons deciding issues for themselves or were dominated by their husbands, their sons and their mothers-in-law, who internalised the aims of a patriarchal society.

At the present time, Katada men clearly represent the responsibility, control and formal sanctions towards the outside world.[9] The means of production belong to men; men occupy the main offices in the mighty fishing corporations. No doubt, in the past *ama* won the respect of the community because the community was dependent on their work. Segawa heard in 1952 from the people of Hekurajima:

'At the time of the Japanese-style boats women were respected. Now everywhere the income of women is some degrees lower than that of the men. *Awabi*-diving can no longer support a household.'[10]

Also in Katada female income is no longer the main source of income for a family and *ama* work is no longer the only work that women can find in the village.

Bearing in mind that further research is planned, what preliminary conclusions can be drawn? The German sociologist, Helge Press, stated in a famous phrase that 'Women are guest workers in a male society.'[11] This does not seem to have been true for *ama* in the past but it has become reality today. *Ama* in former times at least did not have to doubt the necessity of their work. Although today many more Japanese women, middle-class women, work and have to work in order to sustain the industry of the country and to afford their high living standards, the attitude towards *ama* work seems to have changed. All working women are today beset with a certain feeling of guilt towards their husbands but mainly towards their children. This feeling of guilt, by the way, enables men to approach women as a convenient labour-reserve.

The very western normative image of the professional housewife and mother has, through television and education, reached even the remotest *ama* villages and is diminishing the prestige of the professional *ama*. *Ama* work seems to be on its way to becoming a hobby (as the wife of the head of the fishing corporation called her *ama* work). Or it becomes part-time work for those financially not as well off that they can afford not to work at all. Therefore, whereas in 1983 *ama* were still proud to be divers and to earn a lot of money, not one of their daughters wanted to follow in the foot-steps of her mother.

There seems to be a danger to the *ama* profession not only because of the growing pollution, technical developments and international trade, which brings *awabi* cheaper from far away countries to the Japanese gourmet than from his own shores. But also modern patriarchalism is endangering the basis of professional *ama* work.

19

Gender-rôle Socialisation, Achievement Motivation and Occupational Choice Among Professional Women and Housewives in Japan

E. MOUER-BORNER

In this research the extent to which reference groups, rôle models, demographic factors and other influences on the socialisation process shape the achievement motivation and career aspirations of university-educated women in Japan was examined. Attention was also given to the effect of marriage on women contemplating professional careers. Between 1978 and 1980, thirty women in three professions (law, academia, and the public service) and thirty housewives (selected as university classmates of the professional respondents) were randomly selected from alumnae directories and interviewed. The women were cohorts aged between 31 and 44. Subsequently, an extensive questionnaire survey was sent through the post and returned by 385 cohorts with similar education and occupational backgrounds.

The research findings may be summarised as follows: Attitudes of parents figured importantly in the educational and career aspirations of both types of women. Parents of both types were highly educated and the occupational backgrounds of the mothers differed little. Among housewives, fathers were more likely to have been employed in business occupations, while among professionals a correlation existed between fathers' and respondents' career occupations. Parental attitudes and respondents' career choices were also correlated, with parents of housewives more likely to oppose such aspirations while those of professionals were supportive.

A critical event in the lives of most women is marriage. The study clearly indicated that there is a continuation of patriarchial values in the post-war period. While spouses of the professional respondents were perceived on the whole as being more supportive, other marital factors such as type of marriage (*miai* or *renai*), age at marriage, marriage differentials between spouses, household composition and the number of children also differentiated the samples.

In addition to the attitudes of significant others and the above-mentioned situational and demographic factors, the rôle of change happenings or life crises cannot be dismissed as motivation factors accounting for the way professional women conceptualised their careers. Most of the life crises, many of which were experienced during or immediately after the war, were directly related to career choice, were twice as likely to be experienced by the professional women (40%) as by the housewives (19%).

Although most of the housewives in the study attributed their educational attainment to factors which related to the sweeping changes in the Constitution, they also felt constrained in setting their occupational goals by the restrictive values of parents, spouses and employers. At the same time, less fortuitous events or life crises provided professionals with the motivation to achieve professional careers, which were largely regarded as providing a more equitable work environment than most other options available to women. While housewives experienced fewer life crises, the majority nevertheless had had career aspirations. A range of factors, including their choices of spouse, combined to work against their pursuing the career to which they had aspired.

20

Self-assessment and Consciousness of Housewives: A Case Study on Women in Nagano and Shizuoka

ULRIKE JALALI-ROMANOVSKY

In my paper I want to present the results of a questionnaire which was distributed among women of Nagano and Shizuoka in 1982. My aim was to find out the degree of identification and satisfaction of women with the rôle of a housewife, and how the women questioned assess their rôle in society and their position in relation to their husbands. Emphasis is laid on the comparison between the different age groups and between persons with different educational backgrounds, as to whether they show some obvious variations in their attidudes.

SOCIAL POSITION OF HOUSEWIVES IN GENERAL

Before I start to present my data I want to outline some ideas about the term 'housewife'. First of all, who is to be called housewife? This word seems to characterise an attribute a woman attains when she gets married. So it would be the same as using the expression 'I have become a housewife' instead of saying 'I have got married'.

The housewife *per se* does not belong to a certain social rank, but is more or less affiliated to one person, her husband, who determines her social position and even her behaviour outside the house. As the wife of a manager, she is expected to behave differently from the wife of a labourer.

How is the social position of an occupational married woman determined? First, one must not forget that, in spite of all social changes, the educational level of men and women is still unequal, and the expectations of rôle behaviour differ for each sex. Therefore, even in the case where a woman's educational or professional status is higher than that of her husband, she will not be able to change his social position for the better. Also, both sexes commonly look for a partner of their own class, so that the problem just mentioned is quite rare.

My sample shows clearly that the professional activity of women is regarded as of secondary importance by society, and therefore, the husband's assistance in the household is kept to a minimum.

SOME PERSONAL DATA OF HOUSEWIVES EXAMINED

As mentioned before, I confine my examination to married women regardless of whether they are full-time housewives or working housewives. Only 171 out of 214 women from Nagano and 162 out of 197 women from Shizuoka fulfilled this qualification.

Age   Checking the general attributes like age, education, place of living, etc., several outstanding differences between both groups become evident. Concerning age, one can find an over-representation of women in their fifties in the Nagano group (56.1%) whereas there is a lack of twenty-year-olds and only a small number of thirty- (4.7%) and seventy-year-olds (1.2%). This produces an average age of 49. Shizuoka, on the other hand, shows a fair preponderance of forty-year-olds (50.6%) and a very few aged twenty (4.3%) and sixty(3.1%). The average age here comes to 39.6.

Place of residence and size of household   Almost 90% of the Shizuoka group were from urban areas, whereas approximately half of the Nagano women came from rural areas. Most of the latter (3/4) are living in one- or two-generation-households; three generations in one household mostly consist of the parents, a child, the daughter- (or son-) in-law and grandchildren; in the case of the elder co-inhabitants it is — first of all — not the husband's parents (or mother) as might be expected, but the wife's parents or mother. The opposite may be said for the situation in Shizuoka: every tenth family lives together with members of the older generation, in most cases with the husband's parents. In my sample, 80%

of the women aged 60 are living separated from their children (in Nagano: 63.3%).

Education   60% of all women in Nagano and Shizuoka are senior high school graduates; 20% in Nagano reached junior high school level, and less than 10% junior college or university level, whereas 20% of the Shizuoka women attended junior college and one out of seven even attended university.

To clarify the terms used in my sample, persons with only 4-6 years of education are generally called junior high school graduates, up to 12 years senior high school graduates, those with one or two more years junior college graduates, and those with more than 15 years of education university graduates. The 20 and 30-year-olds, that is, the generation educated after World War II, have found conditions to be much better than those of the older women. So it is not surprising to find a steadily increasing number of university graduates among the younger groups.

Quite different is the situation for men: there are only 34.6% (Shizuoka) to 38% (Nagano) senior high school graduates. Surprisingly high is the rate of junior high school graduates in Nagano (27.5%). In comparison with 25.1% university graduates in Nagano, the rate of men who had attended university in Shizuoka is twice as high (50.6%). Worth mentioning is the fact that about 16% of the women in Nagano in my sample surpass their spouses so far as the educational level is concerned.

Working situation after school   After finishing school, most of the women started to work for a couple of years. In Shizuoka, there are three or four principal jobs to choose from: more than 50% of the girls were working in offices, while about 22% worked mainly as teachers or nurses. In Nagano, on the contrary, we find a high proportion working as farmers, and with similar numbers working in offices or in jobs involving special training, such as pharmacists, teachers, kindergarten teachers, and the like.

Subdivided into age groups, one comes to understand that the younger generation are to a high degree tied to office jobs; and the question arises whether women cannot get other kinds of work easily nowadays or whether they expect themselves to work for just a few years and get 'quick money'. With a higher educational level the attitude towards choice of work changes considerably: while junior and senior high school graduates are mostly found in offices, junior college and university graduates prefer to work in more qualified professions.

Like the husbands, there is a similar occupational break-down for women at work: a rich variety of jobs in Nagano stands in contrast to a concentration on the *kanrishoku* and *jimushoku* and a smaller group of jobs with special professional training.

Asked the reason for quitting their jobs, 4 out of 5 women in Nagano gave marriage as the explanation, but only 1 out of 2 women in Shizuoka did so. However, a surprisingly high number of Nagano women have continued to work, even if they have children. For example, all of the women in their thirties, without exception, are at work. They stand in obvious contrast to the Shizuoka women in the same age-group of whom about 75% belong to the group of full-time housewives. The same can be said for all of the twenty-year-olds.

Social contacts After marriage, a woman often faces a situation entirely different from before: having quit her job and maybe expecting her first child, she has to get used to her new rôle as housewife and mother, and she has to come into contact with her new neighbours. They will remain the most important people around her, and so it is not surprising that in an average of 70% of the women, regardless of age, they have most frequent contacts with their neighbours. In the thirties and forties age group, the parents of one's children's friends also become important. In addition, many Nagano-women meet their colleagues from their working place, and are active (mostly starting at the age of fifty) in consumer organisations and women's groups and participate in hobby clubs. Shizuoka-women, however, do not show that much interesst; they seem to be more isolated, rarely being seen in groups similar to Nagano women. The only exception is the local Parent-Teachers Association.

SELF-ASSESSMENT OF THE HOUSEWIVES

This leads us to the question of self-assessment of housewives. How do they estimate their own position, their rôles as housewives and mothers, and what do they expect? Since I cannot draw up a complete image of them, I want to highlight a few characteristic facts. For instance: do housewives still accept the traditional sex rôles, and what does occupation mean to them? If they go to work, do they expect their husbands to help at home?

Satisfaction with the role of a housewife On the whole, the women surveyed seem to be more or less satisfied with their rôle as housewives. This attitude even increases with age (especially from the age of fifty). But not with women of a higher educational level. Apparently, a university degree makes it more dfficult to identify with this rôle. On the contrary, junior college graduates show a remarkably high degree of satisfaction. Therefore, one can understand that attending a junior college (commonly called 'bride school') is taken as the appropriate preparation for marriage, whereas university students seem to accord occupation approximately the same rank as the rôle of a housewife.

Abilities for running a household and for occupation The attitude taken towards the question whether a housewife has to have more ability than an average woman in a profession verifies this trend. For instance, in Nagano almost 2/3 of the junior college graduates gave priority to a housewife's abilities, but 50% of the university graduates did not agree with them. On the other hand, in Shizuoka graduates from junior college showed a more neutral attitude; they obviously gave preference to neither of these rôles. It is a surprising fact that the university graduates from Shizuoka attach more importance to housework than to occupational work. The reason for this is not easy to find. Maybe these women were disappointed by the situation on the labour market and decided to devote themselves more to the rôle of a housewife and mother where they try to apply all their energy and abilities.

In Nagano, 2/3 of all full-time housewives assert that the traditional rôle of women demands more abilities than the average occupational work.

On the contrary, one in three working women denies it entirely. Here, the tension between the non-working and working group is obviously strong. It is difficult to say whether the answer given expresses the wish to work because housework alone is too boring and makes no use of many other areas of a woman's ability, or because the persons concerned need a kind of excuse for their decision to give preference to an occupation instead of being a perfect housewife and mother. In this context, age does not play an important part in either regional group.

The decision for profession or full-time housework   A conflict may in many cases arise out of the necessity for women to decide what is more important in one stage of their lives: the rôle of mother and housewife or the occupational one. Women are generally aware of the big responsibility of child-rearing; on the other hand, they may value highly the jobs they have and wish to continue with them. Then it can happen that some of them quit their jobs in favour of their children but feel dissatisfied and begin to develop resentment against their rôle as housewives. In this case it seems logical that they should deny the importance of being mother and housewife at all.

Education also seems to exert a strong influence on the decision whether to work outside the house or not. Compared with junior and senior high school graduates, university and junior college students reveal a stronger inclination to work outside the house.

Attitudes towards the traditional division of labour   In my sample, about 50% of both groups give priority to the tasks of the traditional female rôle, ie, of housewife and mother, and around 40% regard an occupation as important as household duties. Subdividing into age groups the trend is for the younger generation to give equal importance to job and housekeeping, whereas older persons think their place is or should be at home. The comparison between the thirty-year-old women of Nagano and Shizuoka who are regarded as being most involved in child-rearing over the question of compatibility of job and housework makes regional differences evident: while 75% of the Nagano women concerned find — at least theoretically — both the rôles of a housewife and mother, and occupation equally important, they in fact all have jobs — one out of three is even fully employed. I am unable to say how many women have to work because their families need their financial support. In Shizuoka, on the contrary, most of the women in their thirties do not only theoretically give preference to the rôle of a housewife and mother but also practically: 2/3 of them do not have any job.

The strongest opposition to division of labour among sexes comes from the groups of women aged twenty (85%) and thirty (50-60%). Yet, starting with the forties, one can notice a steadily increasing rate of traditionalists. Generally speaking, the consciousness of women has changed and has made professional activities a fixed part of most females' lives. When they are only housewife and mother, they are no longer satisfied with it as their sole rôle.

Relationship to the husband   But the bare statement by women not to accept the traditional division of labour among sexes, does not automatically mean that women can or do expect their husbands to share the responsibilities for household chores and child-rearing with them. Female occupation has in many cases brought only one-sided changes in female consciousness and daily schedule but has not affected a man's life much.

Asked about their spouses' opinion concerning occupational activities of mothers, the answers given show men's tendency to accept more and more their wives' paid work but at the same time not to offer much more help at home. For example, wives with full-time jobs are not offered more support from their husbands than women who are full-time housewives. Although most wives approve of their spouses' occasional help at home they are not satisfied with the rarely exercised rôle as fathers and want them to devote themselves much more to their children. It may be a sign of the awareness of women not to expect that habits, so deeply-rooted in Japanese society, could change within one generation but only to hope for change some day. For example, 65-80% of those questioned want boys also to take classes in home economics at school.

Concerning finances and the question of who decides how the money has to be spent, the wife is responsible for it, in 23.4% (Nagano) against 34.6% (Shizuoka) of all cases, while 24.0% (Nagano) against 15.4% (Shizuoka) of all husbands are the decision-makers. 31.6% (Nagano) to 41.4% (Shizuoka) of the couples decide after discussing with each other or have their own responsibilities defined.

It may be of interest to investigate whether and to what extent women have a feeling of inferiority to their husbands, and which factors could be decisive. This question is relevant only to full-time housewives since women with occupations can find some recognition in their jobs quite apart from housework. In general, about 3/4 of all full-time housewives do not feel inferior to their spouses, whereas 1/4 of them have this feeling sometimes or even often. Differences by age are hardly evident, although persons aged twenty seem to have the biggest problem in identifying themselves with the rôle of a housewife. Also, educational background and former occupation cannot give any explanation for the question why women feel inferior to their husbands (besides the main reason for the different socialisation of both sexes in a man-dominated society, which may lay the foundation for women to feel inferior to men). Looking at the husbands' professions, some slight differences become evident. So it is the labourer's wife who values her work equally with that of her spouse's (100%), followed by the wives of men in jobs with special professional training (82.4%), farmers and shopkeepers (80%). The strongest feeling of inferiority is found among wives of employees of trading companies, retired people and those with freelance jobs (in this group only 66.7% of the wives do not feel inferior).

Another reason can be found in the question as to who has mainly to decide about spending money. If it is up to the wife, she shows much more self-consciousness and therefore less feeling of inferiority to her husband (79.7%) than women who have to leave the main decisions to their spouses (only 61.4% do not feel inferior). In cases where both women and men are equally competent, 81.4% of wives do not complain about inferiority.

21

Hospitalisation of the Mentally Ill in Japan

INGRID KARGL

Though this topic may seem a rather specialised one, the sociological approach is amply justified by the social importance of psychiatry. Mental hospitals as well as psychiatry as a medical science have come under severe criticism over the past two decades and, as it became a sociological issue, feminists, too, have begun to concern themselves with psychiatry.

Quite a number of works have tried to establish whether women psychiatric patients are discriminated against; there have been studies trying to discover whether some diagnoses are to be considered 'female' diagnoses or whether the pathogenesis may be traced back to the specific position of women in society. However, there are very few statistical data to show if there really exists a difference between male and female in-patients or if possible differences are simply due to outside factors like differences in the age structure or in diagnosis.

If such data are scarce in the West, it is safe to say that in Japan they are virtually non-existent. In 1983 I conducted a prevalence survey in four mental hospitals in Kumamoto prefecture, Kyushu, with special consideration for possible sex differences. Before I present my results, let me make some general observations on the nature of Japanese psychiatry as there are hardly any books or even articles on the subject in western languages.

JAPANESE PSYCHIATRIC HOSPITALS AND THE MENTAL HYGIENE LAW

Japanese psychiatry closely resembles the European discipline, which is not very surprising since Japan took over western, especially German, medicine in the late nineteenth century. This is not to say, however, that mental diseases were not recognised or treated before that time. I do not want to go into historical details — suffice it to say that the Japanese did recognise psychiatric disorders and commonly attributed them to being possessed by animals or spirits. Among scholars, concepts of the more sophisticated Chinese medicine were prevalent and from the sixteenth century onwards European medicine was also studied. Treatment centres tended to be of a place-of-pilgrimage type; later on they were attached to temples. After the Meiji Restoration medicine, too, underwent a change. Japan 'imported' German psychiatry, which continues to dominate even today, although ideas of the American school have found some acceptability.

One of the dominating personalities in the field of psychiatry, Dr Shuzo Kure, took stock of the facilities for the treatment of mentally ill persons after returning to Japan from studies in Europe in 1901. He realised that there was an enormous need for psychiatric hospital beds, which appear to have been synonymous with psychiatric treatment. The state, though recognising the necessity, did not have the money to assuage the needs. In this dilemma, the government decided to tolerate and, after the Second World War, to encourage the establishment of psychiatric hospitals as private enterprises. Consequently, quite a number of hospitals were built and soon private beds dominated. They still do so today, even though under the present law they are considered to be only subsidiary.

According to the Japanese Ministry of Health and Welfare[1] there were 1,570 mental hospitals with an average of 200 beds in Japan in 1983. The Japanese Association of Psychiatric Hospitals counted 1,079 members with an average 240 beds in the same year. This means that almost seventy per cent of the mental hospitals and eighty per cent of the psychiatric hospital beds are private. Also, compared to Europe or the United States, mental hospitals in Japan are mostly rather small.

Admission into psychiatric hospitals may either be voluntary or compulsory, provisions being much the same as in most western countries. However, it may also be semi-compulsory. This form of admission, *doi nyuin*, provides for a patient's hospitalisation with the consent of the person responsible for his care, regardless of the patient's will. Now, 'person responsible for the care of the mentally disordered person,' *hogogimusha*, does not mean a legally appointed guardian, but usually only a near relative. For example, if a husband considers his wife (or *vice versa*, of course) mentally disturbed and in need of hospital treatment and, if the head of the mental health facility shares this opinion, the said wife may be committed to the hospital. It is not necessary to go through any formal procedures. A court is called in only in cases where two or more relatives are eligible or where the nearest relative refuses to act. The family court then has to appoint a suitable person. In my survey, this type of admission accounted for 85 per cent of the patients. 'Voluntary' admissions are practically non-existent, since the hospitals, 'considering the peculiarities of mental disorders' (as they put it), prefer to obtain the consent of a relative even when it is the patient himself who asks to be admitted.

Patients committed in accordance with the Mental Hygiene Law (that is, compulsory admission or *sochi nyuin*) are treated at public expense. For this reason, compulsory commitment is widely used as a means of alleviating the financial burdens of hospitalisation for patients in economically straitened circumstances. In Kumamoto, three-quarters of the compulsory admissions are estimated to be due to financial reasons, only one quarter of the patients show symptoms corresponding to the legal requirements for compulsory admission.

PATIENTS IN FOUR PRIVATE MENTAL HOSPITALS IN KUMAMOTO PREFECTURE

This is the framework in which my research took place. In the four mental hospitals I included all patients hospitalised at a given day, 765 persons, 44 per cent of whom were female; emphasis was to be laid on non-organic diseases, that is, on schizophrenia, manic-depressive psychosis or neurosis. Because of the enormous proportion of schizophrenia - 67 per cent of the female and 73 per cent of the male patients were labelled schizophrenic — I decided to concentrate exclusively on this diagnosis.

I investigated the age, marital status, parents and school record; the duration of stay, number of hospitalisations, type of commitment and insurance; the reason of hospitalisation, visits, outings and holidays and the willingness ('acceptance') of the family to accept the patient after his discharge. Next, I tried to find out whether differences between the sexes could be observed. Using the chi-square test, I ascertained that some differences were highly significant, but even then results still supported the hypothesis of a discrimination against women. Finally, I established correlations between the different factors, amongst which age as well as length of hospitalisation and acceptance proved to influence, or be influenced by, most of the other factors. These three factors are so closely entwined that it is impossible to say which one is the determinative one. I will return to this point later on.

I will not give a summary of my results, omitting all mention of levels of significance or graphs — the detailed analysis is presented in my dissertation:[2]

How do male and female patients differ in their social background and in their hospitalisation record? The social background on the whole is certainly less favourable for female patients. The average woman patient — I will call her Keiko-san — left school at the age of fifteen, was 28 years old when admitted for the first time into a mental hospital (two years older than Kazuo-san, her male counterpart) and is now 45.6 years of age, four years older than Kazuo-san. She has no family, since she is single and her parents are already dead. Kazuo-san is not married either, but at least his parents are still alive. Also, Kazuo-san has graduated from high school. Female patients dominate the age brackets over fifty years, whereas male patients are over-represented in those under forty. One of the consequences of higher age is that fewer female patients still have one or both parents alive. The majority of the patients, sixty per cent of the women and eighty per cent of the men are single. Women's age at the time of their first admission being higher, and their marriage age being lower, it is only natural that more female patients should be married. This disadvantage on the part of men, however, is more than compensated for by the greater number of female divorcees or widows.

Keiko-san's career as a mental patient is characterised by a longer period of stay: her present admission took place ten years ago, Kazuo-san's only eight-and-a-half years ago; and by slightly more re-admissions (3.7 as compared to Kazuo-san's 3.5). When combined with her longer average duration of stay, she has spent more time in psychiatric hospitals, which difference cannot be entirely explained by her higher age. The difference in the type of commitment is slight: it is remarkable that more women are committed on a compulsory basis although far fewer displayed violent behaviour. Again, since fewer women draw on an insurance that covers all costs of the treatment, it is unreasonable to assume them to be in financially more straitened circumstances than men. (As I have mentioned before, compulsory admission is often used as a means to alleviate the financial strain on less well-off patients).

To show the implications of these differences, it is necessary to consider the correlations between the different factors. Concerning correlations, the two important questions are: in what way does the social background influence the hospitalisation, and the other, perhaps more important one: how does the hospitalisation influence the social life of the patient? Firstly, what is the influence of the social background of a patient on his or her hospitalisation record, especially on the length of stay? Three factors - all of them setting women at a disadvantage - are of major importance:

a) the higher the education the shorter the stay; b) if one parent, or preferably both parents, is alive, the patient remains in hospital for a shorter period; c) the older the patient is, the greater the number of admissions and the longer the stay.

However, age presents something of a vicious circle: the longer the stay, the older the patient. The older the patient, the bigger the likelihood of his parents' being dead. Patients without parents are far less willingly accepted by their family (if, indeed, they have one). A bad acceptance again results in a longer hospitalisation and consequently in the higher age of the patient.

Curiously enough, the reason for hospitalisation seems to have no influence on any other factor, either on the type of commitment or on the acceptance. In other words, a tendency to assault does not necessarily lead to compulsory admission, and a patient who has, say, threatened to stab his mother is not significantly less welcome to his family than one who has been staying in bed all day.

On the other hand how does hospitalisation influence the social life of the patient?

a) The school record is apparently independent of the hospital career. Patients whose first admission to a mental hospital took place early in life usually continue school and the overwhelming majority is hospitalised at an age when they would have at least entered high school, had they so wished;

b) Certainly marital status depends on age. Patients whose first admission took place at a later time in life are more often married or divorced or widowed;

c) The family life is of course influenced by the length of hospitalisation, since parents die as the patients grow older. This, together with the initially higher age of women, explains why far fewer female patients still have parents.

Family acceptance is highly correlated to age and to the parents being alive or not. As I have pointed out, there is something of a vicious circle and so, acceptance in turn influences, and is influenced by, age as well as the length of stay. Patients with good acceptance remain a shorter period in hospital. Married persons have the best, widowed and divorced the worst acceptance. Needless to say, patients with at least one parent alive have a better acceptance than those without parents. In this respect again, women are handicapped. 57 per cent of the male, but only 43 per cent of the female patients will find a home after being discharged. Not welcome or altogether without a home were 31 per cent of the women and 25 per cent of the men. The family seems to be the mainstay of a patient's social life during his confinement as well as after discharge. Visits received and holidays taken (which usually means spending a night at home) depend on relatives who are willing to care for the patient.

The contact of patients with the outside depends on age and family as well as on their career as a psychiatric patient. Outings, for example, are more generously granted to younger and male patients, especially if their admission is not a compulsory one. Keiko-san receives more visits, but Kazuo-san has better opportunities to leave the hospital, even overnight. Holidays and outings depend on age and on whether the parents are alive, on acceptance by the family and on the length of hospitalisation. It is not therefore surprising that more than half of the male, but less than half of the female, patients were able to enjoy a vacation.

To conclude, the better integrated a person is in his personal surroundings, in particular in his family, and the higher his status is in society, the shorter will be his stay in hospital. Hospitalisation, especially if the average length is nine years as in my survey, must be considered a severely disruptive factor, one that disintegrates the patient from his or her social environment.

Women are generally less well integrated in their families as well as having a lower status in society as evinced by the educational level. This results in a more unfavourable career as patient which in turn impairs their social integration. Even where equal conditions prevail, for example, even in the same age brackets or in case of patients with good acceptance, female patients tend to be hospitalised longer and rehospitalised more often. Also, in their communication with the outside world — outings, holidays and, most important of all, acceptance by the family — women find themselves in a more disadvantageous position. That is to say, even when one or both parents are alive, women are less welcome within their families.

To condense the outcome of my research in one sentence: Schizophrenic women in mental hospitals are discriminated against (if such a severe expression may be used) and the differences are not simply due to outside factors such as age or diagnosis. Women not only have to put up with social circumstances that exercise a negative influence on their careers as psychiatric patients, independently of their age, marital status, or parents they also have to put up with longer as well as more frequent hospitalisations and with worse acceptance. To find out the reason for their higher age and the 'discrimination' in the course of their psychiatric careers would be the next step.

22

Shinkyo — A Japanese Commune: An Interpretation of Social Action as Performance

MICHAEL SHACKLETON

Shinkyo lies on the edge of the village of Kasama, on the outskirts of the town of Haibara, on the eastern side of Nara prefecture and on the very edge of the Asuka plain, close to the Kintetsu line to Ise. There is a book called *Sensei and His People*, which is a translation by David Plath of most of a book containing the reminiscences about Shinkyo by the wife of its main figure, Ozaki Sensei. She has been part of the Shinkyo commune since the very beginning. The book takes the story to 1965.

To the eyes of a visitor, Shinkyo is very clearly flourishing. The buildings are neat and modern. Inside, every room is very well equipped including underfloor heating. There are now about 210 permanent members and so the kitchens, dining rooms and other communal areas are quite large. At times, they have to cater for large numbers of guests: for example, at the autumn Shinkyo festival, which I attended in 1984 and 1985, there were about 500 people who sat down to lunch together.

The clothing of members is quite ordinary and functional, though like everything else in Shinkyo it is very clean. By comparison, there is a real glorification in expensive gadgetry that has a communal function — such as a giant TV and the latest kind of juke-box for dances. At the end of July 1985, Shinkyo invested in the Rolls Royce of Japanese cars, a Nissan Sovereign, such as only the Imperial Family, company presidents and the like tend to use. Shinkyo clearly likes to impress visitors, of whom there is an increasing number. There is a growing amount of publicity about Shinkyo. In September 1984, Shinkyo was graced with a visit by the Crown Prince and his wife, and this visit was followed up a month later with an invitation for the main figures to talk with them again for they were staying in the area. One of the reception rooms at Shinkyo was specially decorated and equipped for the royal visit, and is now shown off to visitors.

Shinkyo started just before the last war, and its history thus spans almost 50 years. For the members the central figure is, and has always been, Ozaki Sensei. The story of Shinkyo is essentially the story of his own life. He is now 85 and remarkably healthy, apart from a limp that can be dated back to over-exertion on the Shinkyo Sports Day, almost 30 years ago. It is upon Ozaki Sensei that writings about Shinkyo seem to

131

concentrate. I, too, am interested in him and in the nature of his 'leadership;' but at the same time a study of leadership must also embrace a study of what it means to be a follower.

The founder members of Shinkyo were all members of Tenri-kyo, as were nearly all the other 70-odd families that made up Kasama. Ozaki indeed was a Tenri missionary in Osaka. He was not, however, anything like orthodox, and was clearly opposed to the way in which the Tenri establishment supported itself with donations from the membership. Instead of living off such grants, Ozaki preferred to work as a labourer, so that his Tenri uniform was often quite dirty, with the two-fold result that most other Tenri missionaries and members seemed ashamed to associate with him and also that his mission did not grow very much, no doubt because it failed to look at all prosperous and because Ozaki was also working. On the other hand, Ozaki felt he was only applying the basic principles of Tenri-kyo, in accordance with the teachings of its founder, Ooyasama, who had herself lived a life of poverty and preached against the kind of covetousness that Ozaki found himself seeing increasingly in the Tenri church of his youth.

Eventually, in 1934, Ozaki felt obliged to destroy the Kamidana in his own household and persuaded others to do likewise. This caused quite a lot of trouble, not surprisingly, since it also occasioned Ozaki's permanent return to the village, for he could no longer serve as a missionary in Osaka. The head of the leading family of the village began to feel his position threatened. The result was '*mura-hachibu*' — ostracism by the villagers. But Ozaki had the support of three other families, two from Kasama and one from his parish in Osaka. Given such bad beginnings, it has clearly been a long uphill battle to Shinkyo's current position of prosperity and national recognition, so that for example it could merit a visit by the Crown Prince.

In 1943, Shinkyo, with a membership of about 60, decided to move to Manchuria, to join one of the many cooperatives that the Japanese government was establishing there. At the end of the war, Ozaki and Sugihara, who is now his wife, were fortunately in Japan, albeit incarcerated in detention, but most of the others were not so lucky and suffered a lot before returning to Japan. Shinkyo's land in Kasama had largely been rented out. As a result, most was lost to tenants because of the Land Reform pushed through under the Occupation. After a lot of difficulties, however, they were able to start making *tatami* mats, and quite soon had the largest *tatami* factory in Japan. In the early 70s, they opted instead to make *fusuma* (sliding screens) and to grow *shiitake* (a special kind of mushroom). About the same time, they also made an even bigger decision and set up a school for mentally-retarded children. Later on, however, they gave this school to the local authorities, and set up Shinkyo as a home for mentally-retarded adults. These now number about 150, and thus comprise a sizeable part of the total membership, given above as 210.

Local relations have also been improving. 'Mura hachibu' disappeared after the war and Ozaki even served as chairman of the local town council for three years (1958-60). Yet Shinkyo remains visibly set apart from the rest of Kasama, although several of the villagers come to work at Shinkyo during the day, and Shinkyo, because of its size, has become a significant market for local produce. The ten or so residents' children eligible for school or kindergarten attend local institutions and sometimes bring friends home. Several members of Shinkyo are also active on the PTA committees. Shinkyo, therefore, whilst it is distinctive, is very much part of local life.

There are over 100 'communes' in Japan, but Shinkyo considers itself unique for having arisen 'naturally' (*shizen*). By this it meant that sharing their resources and living as a single household seemed the only way in which they might survive, without bending to the will of the village 'bully' — the head of the leading family. Older members do not voice any greater founding ideology except their anger and indignation at the behaviour of this man, and their refusal to give in.

Moreover, since their expulsion from Tenri-kyo, there has never been any direct association with religion of any kind, except for the veneration of the Emperor that was general before the end of the war. Although the photos of deceased members line the walls of the main room of their house which alone of the original buildings survived as a memorial to their past endeavours, there is no Butsudan (just as there is no Kamidana) and, when they die, the bodies of members are donated to the service of medicine. Individual members may honour family tombs, and groups sometimes visit temples and shrines etc., for example, at New Year, but there is no correlation with religious 'belief.' Shinkyo members find temples and shrines interesting and enjoyable places to visit. But they do not find in religion, or ideas about the kami-sama, any other kind of significant resource, save of course that it is through religion that they distinguish themselves from Tenri-kyo and organised religion, and also from the locality since they do not take part in local shrine festivals. During the war, Shinkyo, it is true, funded the construction of two imperial shrines for local schools, at truly colossal expense, but this relates to a fascinating duel with the other villagers and the local authorities to establish Shinkyo's respectability. Despite the somewhat misleading sound of their name, the characters for Shinkyo have no connecton with those which are used for 'Shinkyo-shukyo' (New Religions or Protestantism).

One effect is that the cult which 'communes' have attracted has largely passed Shinkyo by (although it is nonetheless listed in directories of 'communes'). There is no Tolstoyan ideology, no folk crafts, and since the end of the war virtually no farmland either. Members hitherto do not generally seem to have felt the lack of these, and the explanation is regularly given that Shinkyo has grown 'naturally.' If we realise how much there was a radical tendency within traditional village life (for example, the extent of peasant protest, the rise of a moral movement such as Tenri-kyo, and even the keen interest displayed in many country areas to tender advice to the Emperor for the new constitution of the Meiji Era), it does seem reasonable that no new radical philosophy was needed. We should also remember that Shinkyo is also rather unusual among other communes in that Ozaki Sensei founded it within the home community where he had lived since childhood, and it was after all local circumstances that led to its foundation.

In fact, rather than laying claim unnecessarily to its being a revolutionary commune, I would argue that Shinkyo seems to have capitalised successfully on accepting the ways of the world. Financially successful, and mustering almost 200 votes, it is much cultivated by local businessmen and political figures. It can feel strongly buttressed by local interests. Consequently, it is not dependent on popular support or on a band of followers outside the bounds of Shinkyo itself.

Nevertheless, Shinkyo has now been in existence for almost 50 years. As older members die or leave and new members join from outside, there is concern that it will lose its way. Officals at Tenri-kyo have forecast to me that it will disintegrate upon Ozaki's death. It is clear that living at Shinkyo the members realise the danger and indeed that it is partly recognition of this danger that unites them together. This is turn reinforces the spirit of needing to survive that has characterised Shinkyo throughout its history and has shaped a common style and ethos. Altruism developed because it was necessary for Shinkyo to survive. Sugihara talks about how mothers stopped treating their own children any better than the other children, to the extent that children slept with different mothers. But this practice disappeared long ago. Altruism has become part of Shinkyo's ethos, but it is no longer necessary for survival, to combat threats from without. The dangers seem to be greater within. Although it was always true that the survival of Shinkyo depended upon the strength of the bonds between the members so that if these bonds were strong, Shinkyo could survive against almost any odds, the threats from without that gave meaning to these bonds have all but disappeared. Shinkyo is still essentially a group of families that share their resources together, under the shadow of Ozaki Sensei, but doing this has required a continual search for new ways to make a living and find a cause to keep them together.

Thus, whereas it might be tempting to explain much of Shinkyo's present situation in terms of its history and to frame this history in terms of a grand philosophy such as 'Self Help' or 'Communal Living,' this is to neglect the fact that Shinkyo is, and has always been, intensely pragmatic, and very consciously so. Historical processes and ideological principles are not totally absent. For example, it is clearly significant that the founders of Shinkyo were 'middle farmers' — they had the resources to succeed, albeit with difficulty, whereas the majority of farmers simply could never have done so since they did not own enough land and were at the mercy of the big *oya-bun* of the village, as his tenants, whereas Shinkyo by contrast could take great pleasure in defying him. As for ideology, the pre-war period abounded in idealism of all kinds. But Shinkyo did not wish to be associated with any particular ideological movement, especially a political one such as Communism or a religious one such as Tenri-kyo, although much of the teaching of communal living and social service derived from them.

It would be misleading, therefore, to discuss Shinkyo simply in terms of 'social forces,' if by this we mean external and autonomous influences that have shaped the development of Shinkyo. If we accept that Shinkyo members are well aware of what they are doing, then can we not see them constantly manipulating and exploiting events, both intended and unintended, and thereby at the same time expressing and developing

134

dramatic themes and rôles to suit different situations — 'social texts' concerning a real life 'soap opera,' the history of Shinkyo.

I cite as a classic example the decision to become a home for the mentally retarded. It can be interpreted either as due to a wish to establish a model for a caring community, or as a response to the memory of the slander and felt prejudices of the local community and Tenri-kyo generally. (For example, Ozaki Sensei had had a mentally-retarded and physically-handicapped daughter who died young. Many Tenri-kyo members seem to have blamed her tragedy upon Ozaki's failure to conform to Tenri orthodoxy.) Alternatively, the dependency of the mentally-retarded members upon Shinkyo strengthens the bonds between members and creates a strong focus so that Shinkyo will survive even after Ozaki and the last founding figures have passed on. Moreover, the decision created a lot of new jobs, for example, nursing and social therapy and of course extra administrative responsibilities. Thus, younger members can usefully stay at Shinkyo and use their educational qualifications rather than leave to follow a career outside. Furthermore, the move ensures a very regular income for Shinkyo — it receives about ¥100,000 per head per month for the mentally-retarded members, so that the profit margin of Shinkyo's own products — mainly *fusuma* and *shiitake* — need not be very high, which again gives it an edge *vis-à-vis* competitors, and consequently extra security. (In Britain there would be strong opposition from unions, if a similar scheme were operated there.) In addition, there will be many other reasons, not least the fact that Ozaki Sensei was very keen on the idea, and keeping him happy is also a very important aspect of Shinkyo. In other words, Shinkyo members need not think the same as each other, and each, for example, would evaluate differently the changeover to being a home for the mentally retarded. But it is emblematic of what I call Shinkyo's 'pragmatic' approach — Shinkyo members may call it 'natural' — that a communal policy is chosen that can satisfy everybody and inspire them to work even harder for each other and keep Ozaki Sensei happy.

23

Japanese Burakumin: Civil Rights Policies in the Post-war Era

JOHN B. CORNELL

Japan's efforts to deal with the phenomenon of outcastes from the beginning of the Restoration onwards, have presented a singularly thorny obstacle when it comes to formulating national policy. Clearly, it is difficult to make appropriate policy unless one knows the dimensions of the phenomenon. Critically important to discerning the nature and scope of the problem are its sociological and demographic variables — what is the size of the minority population and how are they distributed? Still more elusive are questions concerning economic conditions, social organisation, human relations, and psycho-cultural predispositions.

Demographic issues have proved to be singularly intractable to empirical measurement. Many attempts to confirm the actual number of burakumin have been made. In general, succeeding enumerations have brought forth ever larger totals, yet this trend may be due to improving census methods. The range is from around 443,000 in the 1880s to some 1.13 million in 1973 (note that pre- and early post-war counts, in fact, gave even higher figures). None of the results has come close to the 'magic number' of 3 million claimed by *kaiho* partisans. A fair guess is that the minority total of the Japanese population is between 1-2 per cent[1].

The most reliable study to date is that done in 1963 by Isomura. Like all official studies of the minority since the 1920s, the Tsomura study also bases its count on burakumin identifying the buraku communities. Nor have these censuses taken account systematically of burakumin mobility, including those severing links with the buraku. Furthermore, counts since the late 1950s have had to deal with a somewhat altered enumeration unit: for purposes of implementing its post-war anti-discrimination policy (styled *dowa* 'integration'), the government replaced the ghetto-like buraku communities with 'integration districts' (*dowa chiku*), a larger jurisdiction encompassing an area containing a customarily and traditionally recognised buraku ghetto as well as neighbouring ordinary (*ippan*) communities. A chiku so designated usually contains a substantial proportion of ippan residents, who do not identify with the minority[2]. As a result, researchers must isolate the burakumin percentage of the chiku's total population, which can prove difficult.

This redrawing of local ghetto units (*dowa chiku*) points up a sociological dilemma; is residence in a recognised buraku (ghetto) sufficient reason to assume that residents are burakumin? In the light of field experience, I am inclined to believe that a buraku may often contain a leavening of people who identify as ippan, persons who move in by reason of 'intercaste' marriage (*dowa-kon*), availability of low-cost housing, convenience to employment, etc. Since the most reliable basis for determining minority status today is self-identification, headcounting outcastes has become an increasingly tricky business.

The second dimension of the problem has to do with discovering and defining the nature of the buraku community. In kaiho rhetoric, the claimed 'magic number' of buraku in Japan is 6000. None of the modern census counts of ghetto numbers has come near this figure. The first modern census of 1920 found about 5000, however, successive census numbers have declined to a range of 3,500-4000[3]. I believe it is futile to strive for objective perfection in measuring this scale of the phenomenon.

The important thing is to look at distribution in terms of geographic patterning of buraku (*dowa chiku*). Thus, densities are notoriously high in the Keihanshin region, the Kinki in general, and the littoral zone of the Inland Sea, but few or none (reported) in Tohoku, south-west Kyushu, and Hokkaido[4]. More than 70 per cent are in two regions, Kinki and

Chugoku, both by the Inland Sea.

Until the post-war period, relatively little attention was paid to the dynamics of determining caste status using the ghetto as salient lead. For the most part, ethnographic studies and reports concerning discrimination cases in the media refer to the ghetto as the major source of information or referrent in tracking down an individual's identity or as the focal feature mediating burakumin-ippan relations. One outcome of current public policy, achieved only in scattered instances, I believe, is to obliterate the buraku, dispersing its inhabitants to other districts having no relation to outcasteism. It seems generally correct to say that connection with a ghetto, whether as resident or point of origin, is a prime clue to discovering identity. Since the household registers (koseki) were closed to outside inspection in the 1970s (finally, in 1976), a flurry of reports have surfaced concerning underground publications known as 'buraku lists', which are said to provide valuable details about thousands of buraku[5]. They appear to be intended to replace access to koseki, now forbidden. Connection to the ghetto through public registers is one illustration of why association with the buraku, once acquired, is so difficult to lose and easy to use for discriminatory purposes.

The prevailing view is that the existence — and persistence — of segregated buraku is the single most intransigently visible symbol of caste difference today. It is the one tangible feature which can be readily studied. This perception is reducible to a 'minority image' in ippan minds. The image can be visualised in terms of a sub-culture embodying many negative earmarks of caste 'character.' Odd behaviour, gossip alleging such behaviour, 'funny' occupations, family strife, crime, philandering, hard-nosed shrewdness in business, etc. tend to be noticed outside and embedded in the melange of traits which comprise the 'image.' The image factor is less apparent now than it was, however, less scurrilous now it remains in place and sometimes comes out in confidential chats with ippan informants. The record of the main direction of public policy over at least six decades shows that the public aim has been to facilitate assimilation (dowa) by bringing about conditions of life and instilling competences required to operate in an open, equal-opportunity society. Obliteration of buraku communities, although the indirect effect of dowa programmes on occasion, has never been a credible goal of government, nor has it been broached in kaiho polemics.

POST-WAR DOWA POLICY AND KAIHO ACTIVISM

Soon after the war's end in 1945, Suiheisha elements began reorganising again. The society had for all practical purposes disbanded in 1942 in support of the war effort. The Occupation triggered a flurry of political revival and realignment. 'Emancipation' soon reappeared as a national issue. The new 'democratic' Constitution stressing equal privileges of citizenship and the principle of absolute non-discrimination, promulgated in 1946, instilled fresh vigour into the movement. The pre-war Suiheisha and Yuwa organisations' leadership joined forces to create the nucleus of what became the Buraku Liberation League (Buraku Kaiho Domei). This

137

body took a more positive approach to calling public and government attention to the abuses of discrimination (*sabetsu*). A rising tide of protest against instances of discrimination accompanied renewal of kaiho militancy.

During the 1950s, leaders of the kaiho movement became divided as one faction supported the government's premise that the burakumin's plight does not stem from intentionally discriminatory economic policies, from capitalist exploitation. At base, it was a philosophical split. The one side, parading under the slogan 'let the sleeping child lie' (*neta ko o okosu na*), favoured the gradualist approach to solving the problem. The opposite wing adhered to the view that the then dominant faction in the Kaiho Domei was only interested in lifting the burden of economic oppression from the burakumin proletariat — that is, those minority members still identifying with the buraku community[6].

The implication of the latter contention is that genuine emancipation is impossible unless *all* burakumin are liberated together (later this position was extended to include other oppressed groups, women, Koreans, Ainu, even the physically handicapped). The soft-line position — let the sleeping child lie — came in the 1960s to stand in opposition to the radical opposition, who wanted collective and total elimination of difference as the sole acceptable solution. The split widened until in 1972, the Communist ideologues in the movement broke with the Kaiho Domei to establish a rival organisation, the *Buraku Kaiho Domei Zenkoku Seijoka Rengokai* (Buraku Liberation League National Normalising Liaison Association=known by the acronym *Zenkairen*). This splinter body is dedicated to the proposition that capitalist exploitation is the prime cause of the problem, that its ideology is the pristine Kaiho Domei ideology, and that the Kaiho Domei solution is a deviation from the line pursued from Suiheisha beginnings[7].

In the 1960s, in response to kaiho-inspired pressure the government created the Dowa Taisaku Shingikai (Integration Policy Commission), which commissioned another full-dress study, the 1965 Isomura report. At length, the fruit of this compact between the movement and the state was the Law for Special Measures to Implement Integration Policy (*Dowa taisaku jigyo tokubetsu sochiho*) enacted in 1969. The law was to be in force for ten years (until 1979). Its provisions are very sweeping and ambitious, touching on the spectrum of evils in society which the Kaiho Domei's 1960 demand for public remedy underscored and the 1965 Commission report declared critically urgent. Its underlying aim was to enforce the civil rights guarantees contained in the post-war Constitution, and as well it echoed the larger concerns of the universal human rights declaration. In broad terms, its programme entailed creating a series of agencies within the ministerial branches of state, and at prefectural and local levels, to develop and manage the grand array of dowa (integrationist) programme the law was to spawn. Funding for this immense, coordinated effort was to come from the national budget (two-thirds) and from local budgets (one-third) with the national government guaranteeing loan for specific projects. In general, it focused on economic and material conditions of life affecting burakumin, housing, health, employment, etc. But it also addressed the items in the minority's bill of complaints concerning public ignorance of the problem and the hardships the dead hand of status ideology imposes on burakumin. Furthermore, in the context of job opportunities, it sanctioned the right of minority members to preferential treatment over ordinary (ippan) citizens[8]. The possible effect on ordinary citizens of entitling burakumin to privileged treatment under law has been recognised both by thoughtful burakumin and the government. The possibility of provoking 'reverse discrimination' (*gyaku sabetsu*) is raised by the minority intelligentsia in particular with the caveat that in the process of implementing special dowa projects the danger is that privileged treatment may reawaken discriminatory feelings towards the buraku in neighbouring ippan areas (wherein the largesse of material benefits accruing to minority residents of the chiku would be all too evident to the ippan neighbours, who do not share equally in such bounty). For this reason, they point out, some buraku may be reluctant to accept these 'gifts' fearing that it will reignite tensions of *sabetsu*[9]

One clear measure of the force of the dowa 'special measures' is the rapidly rising totals budgeted for the programme after 1969, nearly doubling in the first year, then rising steadily thereafter. Money committed to various programmes related to employment alone went up almost 10 times in the 1969-1980 period. The amounts devoted to public works, housing, etc., were more than 30 times higher in 1980 than 1969. Even these numbers do not reflect the stipulated contributions to each project by prefectural and local governments, which should make the figures still more impressive[10]. In sum, judged by growth of public subsidies alone, the undertaking is of breathtaking scale. Yet it remains to be seen how salutary its impact on the problem has been.

In 1978, at the urging of interested bodies, prominently the Kaiho Domei, the law was extended for an additional three years until 1982. Then it was given five more years of life, to 1987. In 1985 the kaiho movement is agitating for replacement of the present fixed-term legislation with a permanent act, which incorporates articles similar to the 1969 law but argues that the government's ratification of the international covenant on human rights (1979) adds justification for making permanent integrationist (dowa) machinery now in being (Buraku Liberation News 1985). This is in line with arguments used in seeking extension of the present law in 1978 and 1982: long-term undertakings begun under the current act are as yet in mid-course; because the reality of discrimination is that it is deeply rooted, final solutions cannot be achieved within this narrow allotment of years[11].

THE CASE OF TOMIHARA-MATSUZAKI IN OKAYAMA

I turn to consider the case of an outcaste buraku in Okayama city I originally studied in 1957-58 and again in 1980-81. This buraku is well-known in Okayama and is one of the largest such communities in the prefecture. Situated in an area of ancient settlement, it was some 30 years ago a hamlet community of Yokoi village, therefore nominally in a rural district. However, since Yokoi was a close-in suburb of Okayama city —

the chief urban centre of the ancient Kibi plain — the economic character of the area in the 1950s was equally about farming and wagework, as it remains today.

Through a process of administrative annexation, the old village finally merged with the city on its doorstep in 1971. This would not be very interesting information, were it not that the presence of a buraku ghetto in Yokoi had much to do with preventing the merger of Yokoi to the city when it was first proposed in the 1950s and was the sentiment of the ippan villagers. The buraku leadership, staunch Kaiho Domei people, feared annexation with Okayama would force poor outcaste families off a former military reservation they had taken over as squatters to till for food. The matter simmered for some years until a hostile Matsuzaki delegation confronted village officials threatening violence unless the planned union was rejected. It was, and the village then merged with another non-urban jurisdiction in 1959.

The annexation struggle of the 1950s is an isolated episode in minority-majority relations in this area. However, with firm establishment of democratic self-awareness in Japan after the war, the burakumin of Yokoi realised that when their vital interests were at stake they were heavily outnumbered by ippan voters. Annexation would further dangerously dilute their political power. So they resisted. The 1959 decision to combine with the adjacent autonomous jurisdiction Tsudata town (*cho*) entailed some weakening of Matsuzaki's power but much less than joining Okayama.

By 1971, a few years after the special measures law came in force, Tsudata town — and Matsuzaki — became part of Okayama. By this time the law's provisions were fully operational at the grassroots level of government. Okayama city had had an 'integration policy office' with a dowa projects budget since 1969, the amount rising steadily through 1980 (Outline of Dowa Policy Programme 1980). There seems to have been no minority resistance to annexation this time, since with the promise of the new law and a special agency set up to oversee the dowa programme, burakumin voting power was a far less important political concern than in the days of the village. I will return to examine some aspects of procedures developed to distribute dowa taisaku funds to eligible communities below.

Let me now examine the economic and material conditions of Matsuzaki residents and what forces have been responsible for changes since the late 1950s. With respect to economic circumstances, the buraku was not very different from ippan communities in the immediate vicinity. While the ecology of the area was from ancient times apparently suitable for paddy rice, in the modern period before the war fruit orchards became the most important feature of agriculture. Since the war, hothouse grape production has flourished replacing peaches and pears as the primary farm crop. Matsuzaki farmers did not get into this line of farming until 1946 but, having done so, they dedicated themselves to it so energetically that the quality control and distribution cooperative — the Kanetomi, which they dominate — is today instantly recognised all over Japan for the superiority of its fruit. Even in the 1950s, the level of involvement of burakumin in agriculture was greater than in adjacent ippan hamlets.

140

Occupation-instigated economic and social reform triggered radical realignment of relationships in agriculture. The traditional independent 'peasant' households of Matsuzaki, numbering about 10, continued to comprise the upper class core group of the community. Their houses clustered together in the central neighbourhood. They seem to have comprised the community core since late Edo times.

Before the war, most burakumin active in agriculture here were tenants, many working land owned by landlords in the nearby ippan hamlet, Tomihara-hommura. Tomihara-hommura landowners often took pity on their poor Matsuzaki tenants, providing them charity in time of need. The Land Reform, however, drastically reversed this relationship. Burakumin tenants now became owners of the land they tilled. The reform triggered emergence of a growing number of enthusiastic farmers in the buraku, who now armed with land of their own, set to analysing how best to use this new capital. Led by scions of the old core 'peasant' households, a number of them organised a 'good farming society,' which included some ippan individuals. This society had no direct ameliorating effect on buraku-ippan relations for its members were only concerned with the narrow purpose of increasing agricultural productivity, otherwise they did not socialise. By 1958, 60-70 households were full-time farmers, a dramatic change since pre-war days. Most of this increase represents the success of hothouse grape growing. In the 1980s, the profitable alliance between burakumin and ippan growers continues in the grape producer cooperative; as in the 1950s, the burakumin are still the dominant group outnumbering their ippan colleagues 4 to 1.

What has occurred in Japanese agriculture since three decades ago is that more and more owners of farmland have become part-timers, working for stable wages off the farm most of the time but farming at weekends and during holidays. The same pattern occurs in our area, salaried workers tending their crops in free time only. This is possible because the variety of farm machinery allows the owner to minimise time and labour input by relying on machines to do the work. In Matsuzaki, alone in its area, farm machinery is owned collectively and used individually. Money for acquiring these machines and for their storage has come from programmes under the special measure law. Since farm machines are soon obsolete, such subsidies seem to provide a distinct edge to farmers in Matsuzaki over their ippan neighbours. They have enhanced the value of farmland and encouraged the owners' commitment to work their land themselves in their free time.

It is difficult to assess the effect of the law on grape-growers, who require ever-increasing amounts of capital to buy state-of-the-art equipment. Most appear to resort to borrowing capital for this investment. In the old days after the war, when money was scarce, growers also borrowed heavily but without the benefit of subsidised interest rates. Then, in order to keep up loan payments they sent family members out to day-wage work or peddling. The difference now is that growers are able to keep up with their obligations, even without outside income between harvests. Loan terms now are relatively easy because of guaranteed loan provisions of the law.

141

But what of the majority of Matsuzaki households who may grow crops only to meet domestic needs or not at all? We have no accurate statistical breakdown of current occupations, but there were some 233 households in the buraku in 1980-81, of which only slightly over 100 claimed to be in farming, that is, about 55 per cent were not involved in cultivation. The picture of non-agricultural work in the buraku appears to be about as complex as in the 1950s, when peddling and construction labour defined the main categories of non-farm employment. In all then, there were 76 distinct occupations found in our survey. Among this diversity flower-selling and goldfish peddling were the most lowly and humiliating even to the people doing them. Now, flower-selling has shrunk almost to zero and peddling goldfish has vanished. This spectrum of non-farming, wage-labour jobs is the source of livelihood of the economically marginal stratum in the buraku. Among them, a large number are young couples living in low-cost public housing constructed by the city under the dowa projects programme. They work as truck-drivers, shop clerks, waitresses, sales persons, construction workers (even 30 years ago, very common among young males), sanitary workers, temporary factory labour, and so on. Such work seems to have no permanency, no fringe benefits, and tends to be fragile in that these workers switch jobs often. The difference now is that for this element of the workforce job opportunities seem to be abundant and real unemployment low, yet it continues to be unstable and frequently untenured.

The dowa reforms since the late 1960s aside, most of the improvement in conditions of life among the poor and the young seem to be attributable to rising prosperity in the region and nation, not to any direct effect of the 1969 law. It is difficult to determine what are causes of an effect. In any event, for perhaps 60 per cent or more of Matsuzaki people who work, the buraku is a 'bedtown,' more so than it was in the 1950s. But unlike nearby ippan communities, it is a bedtown not just for its long-term residents but for people who move in in order to be close to the Okayama job market. In Matsuzaki, I found a continuous influx of outsiders — some clearly not burakumin — but, in contrast to outsiders moving into neighbouring ippan communities, they were allowed to settle freely in the buraku community without physical segregation. Buraku informants have stressed the openness of the community to outsiders of whatever status. The buraku appears to have offered haven to the economically disadvantaged seeking to find improved work opportunities.

Urbanisation has accelerated since that time. Annexation in 1971 simply hastened a process already well under way. Visible evidence of this transformation is now abundant. Its main features include a major highway through the heart of Tsudaka; traffic jams this roadway and small manufacturing and retail businesses line most of its length (in Tsudaka); four modern residential developments (*danchi*) in the zone nearest the inner city — one so sizable that it accounts for almost half the population of Tsudaka. A splendid golf-course/country club stands atop a hill above one of the old ippan communities, and a new international airport and a dual-lane freeway running parallel to the present inadequate highway are projected for the next few years. New construction is found everywhere.

Of this, the most impressive is modernisation of housing using new-fangled design and materials.

The few surviving delapidated houses are rarely occupied. Some houses are truly grand and proudly display the ornate touches seen in the most affluent districts of Okayama. Most of this renewal seems attributable to the increased general level of income coupled with the decline in unemployment and the opportunity for regular work. This radical change seen in private sector housing is reflected in ippan areas too, but it is in the public sector that the dramatic difference appears. Ippan hamlets have not received the special government subsidies granted to the buraku.

Let me try and highlight the key elements in the puzzling differential treatment. First, in the urbanisation process there has existed since 1948 a formal code of urban planning, a system of zoning intended to shelter rural areas enfolded into crowded city jurisdictions. With annexation by Okayama, the previously autonomous Tsudaka town came under the zoning regulations of the city. Two kinds of zoning restrictions were applied to Tsudaka: one, the 'suburban zone' (*shigaika*) designation was given to an area fringing the national highway; another, the 'intermediate zone' (*choseika*) to the rest of Tsudaka beyond a specified distance from the highway. By and large, the latter zoning restriction meant that the traditional hamlet areas could not be developed for non-traditional purposes without approval by a special referendum of the long-time residents — who have a stake in maintaining the traditional economy (agriculture) and the integrity of their community. Thus, both ippan communities around Matsuzaki as well as the buraku remain essentially intact and farmland, which is valuable to outside developers, is inviolate. Matsuzaki, influenced by its kaiho leadership, has firmly resisted leasing unused community-owned hillsides (unlike its ippan neighbours). Moreover, because of its greater involvement in farming, the large expanse of wetfields lying before the settlement and the dryfields on closer-in rises, allowing alternative development of these spaces has never been raised. Indeed, the city's zoning regulations not only serve to stabilise all hamlets, both ippan and burakumin but also tend to have a special effect on Matsuzaki. They are a valuable instrument for preserving the buraku's physical and economic integrity. However, they also reinforce buraku solidarity against the spread of politically unsettling, diluting elements from ippan-dominated society. Also, the zoning shelter seems to contribute to persistence of the hoary attitudes, sentiments vis-a-vis buraku people within neighbouring ippan communities. I found in my 1980s fieldwork that ippan neighbours were far more reticent in expressing these feelings openly than in the 1950s. It is considered inappropriate, if not downright dangerous, to do so. One ippan informant wryly observed that on a 10-point scale Matsuzaki was 3 and we ordinary people (ippan) were 10. Now, it is exactly the reverse. The burakumin are the well-to-do, in a position to do us favours, whereas they used to be struggling to get along and we did them favours.

As remarked above, the buraku has specially benefitted from public bounties in the past decade. The community has also profited from various programmes designed to uplift citizens generally, particularly those connected to agriculture. But they have the extra edge of the 'law.' In

Matsuzaki, the neighbourhood hall is the focal institution in exacting the privileges provided by the law. Morever, the existence of Matsuzaki in this area of the city qualifies it as a dowa chiku. Neighbouring ippan hamlets, such as Tomihara-hommura and Oiwa, are within this chiku and in principle can avail themselves of the services it provides. But in practice its patrons are nearly all burakumin.

Administration of the law's provisions reaches into a broad range of national budgets in addition to funds specifically earmarked for dowa projects. Indeed, it appears that in Matsuzaki the greater part of this dowa largesse is from sources not designated for dowa purposes per se. Each year there is a special dowa programme priority in the city, which is worked out by negotiation among various interested parties. For example, paving roads one year, building childen's playgrounds another. Decisions on allocating dowa money to each buraku (dowa chiku) in the city involves lengthy politicking (the standard term for it is 'undo'=campaigning) by buraku chiefs. Each representative presents his demands to the city's dowa office, then demands of all are subjected to scrutiny by interested pressure groups, and finally they are negotiated and sifted out between officers of the two major kaiho political organisations, the Kaiho Domei and the Zenkairen.

The head of the Matsuzaki neighbourhood hall is one of the local buraku chiefs presenting these initial demands. He is away from his office most of the time and his absences are always explained by saying he is off doing 'undo.' The key inputs, at least in Okayama, come from the minority's own spokesmen and kaiho élites. The results of 25 or more years of government efforts to eradicate the causes of discrimination seem to be that the complex called outcasteism has become the pawn of emergent factional streams of vested political interests by which the civil rights struggle has been corrupted.

Finally, the formerly solid Matsuzaki community has been rent asunder by the contest between two opposing wings created by the kaiho schism of the early 1970s. They are engaged in a bitter internecine struggle in Okayama. Matsuzaki is divided down the middle between these two factional organisations: the Zenkairen of the neighbourhood hall on one side and the Kaiho Domei on the other. The neighbourhood hall operation is paid for by the city's dowa projects budget while the Kaiho Domei is lodged in a separate building built and supported by the Domei's own resources. For various historical reasons involving personalities, prestige and loyalty, the Zenkairen is officially in charge in Matsuzaki. Yet, with about equal constituent support, neither is able to win unchallenged supremacy in the community. This situation engenders extraordinary tensions among residents. When partisans of the two sides attend the same meeting, it is alleged, they storm at each other in vitriolic language or, otherwise, cut the other side in stony silence.

The situation is shocking as compared to the 1950s, when all were ostensibly united behind the community's Kaiho Domei leadership against their ippan neighbours. A sharp, emotionally-charged line could then be drawn between burakumin and ippan people. Now, the main line of tension and partisan cleavage is *within* the buraku rather than between it and the outside. It is usually explained that a profound philosophical chasm exists between the adversary groups. But this ideological dichotomy is not so neatly described at this basic level. One suspects that the rivalry has as much to do with things material as with ideology. The special measures law has in this case provided those in the position of leading cadre with the resources to reinforce and maintain their power. When I innocently suggested that a promising course for solving the problem might be to dissolve the buraku as a distinct (and different) community entity in the Tsudaka landscape, the elderly leader of the Zenkairen ruling faction responded by declaring passionately that that would never happen so long as he lives, not in another 30 years!

To conclude, the proposal to make permanent the main features of the current law threatens to institutionalise the problem by institutionalising the dowa administrative formulas it has mandated, giving the problem the resources to persist but without a foreseeable final solution. As administered, the law — and presumably its future extensions — nurtures the segregated community, which is the locus of case inequality and the focus of sabetsu.

A new policy thrust within the framework of the law is being attempted: giving greater attention to informing and enlightening the public about the nature of the problem of discrimination. While still premature, the results of this 1980s emphasis on airing ideological and attitudinal roots of ostracism of burakumin are not in the main encouraging. People object to being told about an ideology of discrimination which has little meaning in their daily lives, even less so in their children's when they are forced to attend day-long workshops built into the school curriculum.

It is absolutely the case that eradication of discrimination vis-a-vis the burakumin is a long-term undertaking. To institutionalise the machinery of dowa administration, which is now proposed for 1987, carries the risk that in the long run it will serve more to keep the problem alive than to kill it.

24

A Legal Solution to the Buraku Problem?

IAN NEARY

Suggestions that the Buraku problem might be solved by legislation have been around since the 1920s but the origins of the present set of proposals go back no further than the early 1980s. In 1981 when the Buraku Liberation League (hereinafter BLL) was urging the government to revise and extend the lifetime of the Law on Special Measures for Dowa Improvement Projects (hereinafter the Special Measures Law - SML), there was mention of a need for a 'basic law' but the notion does not seem to have been developed very far.[1] Over the next few years, however, the idea takes on a clearer shape so that by 1984, with only three years before the revised SML was due to expire, the central committee of the BLL established a committee to frame a Basic Law on Buraku Liberation. Seminars and consultations were held throughout the rest of 1984 and a report drawn up which was published in January 1985. On 14 May, the proposed legislation was formally announced at a meeting held in the New Otani Hotel in Tokyo and it is the hope of the BLL that it will pass through the Diet in time to replace the current SML when it expires on 31 March 1987.

In this paper I intend to describe some aspects of the legislation proposed by the committee and consider some of the responses to the proposals both from within and without the Buraku liberation movement.

Before looking at the specific proposals, it may be useful to describe what a basic law is. Several such laws were passed in the late 1960s — for example, the Basic Law on Pollution Policy, (1967), the Basic Law on Consumer Protection (1968) and the Basic Law on Policy towards the Mentally and Physically Disabled (1970). They relate to issues considered to be of fundamental importance which require the special attention of, and coordinated activity by, a number of government organs and other sections of society. The laws clarify the broad aims of government policy for the guidance of all those involved. The 'basic law' is envisaged as a central column around which more specific policies may be developed by either central or local government. Such laws make the agencies of government aware of their constitutional obligations at the same time as providing a legal framework for their activities.

One might have thought, however, that the Dowa Commission report of 1965 and the Special Measures Law of 1969 were tantamount to a Basic Law. The former had, after all, set out a statement of basic principles and overall aims and the latter provided an administrative structure which could encourage and supervise specific projects which would improve Buraku living standards. Moreover, the central authorities have, albeit reluctantly, restricted access to the *koseki* and similar documents which have made it more difficult to ascertain an individual's status background.

However, although everyone would accept that the implementation of innumerable projects to improve housing and roads and to ensure access to health and educational facilities have eliminated the worst aspects of the abject poverty in which Burakumin used to live, there is equally no doubt that more remains to be done. In some more rural areas, improvement projects have not yet been fully implemented. In Japan as a whole only 75% of the major construction projects have been completed and the completion rates for other projects lag behind even this.[3] Some legal provision, therefore, needs to be made so that at least the existing improvement projects can be finished off.

One of the basic premises of the 1965 Dowa Commission report was that discrimination was closely related to the abject poverty which surrounded Buraku: improve their living conditions and the prejudice against Burakumin would disappear. Prejudice in a society is difficult to assess. But there is still plenty of evidence which suggests that, despite material improvements, prejudice remains rife among the general public. This manifests itself as overt discrimination, particularly at times of employment and engagement. It is true that the constitution and other laws have established that such discrimination should not be tolerated, but the citizen has little legal redress because there is no law, civil or criminal, which specifically addresses the problem of discrimination.

The 1965 report also recognised the importance of changing attitudes in the majority population towards Burakumin. This would be achieved in a number of ways but mainly via the implementation of Dowa education in schools and policies to enhance a better appreciation of the issue in society at large. Unfortunately, this aspect of the report has been largely ignored. With a few exceptions Dowa education is only to be found in areas where there is an active BLL group. In prefectures where there are very few Buraku communities Dowa education scarcely exists at all. And, even where the Burakumin population form a substantial sector of the community there have been very few attempts to dispel prejudices from the minds of the general public.

So, although it is now twenty years since the Dowa report was issued, there remains much to be done. If no law is introduced to replace the SML in 1987, there will be some improvement projects left incomplete. More significantly though, if no new legislation emerges the government would be indicating that, in its opinion, the problem has been solved, there is no more that it can do. Most observers would argue that this is not the case and in their report the members of the special committee argue that an opportunity now arises for the government to enact a comprehensive piece of legislation which will not only permit the completion of those improvement projects which remain but also provide a legal framework for the constitutionally guaranteed civil rights. Attention must continue to be directed to improvement of material conditions — the 'hardware'— but at the same time government must ensure that 'software' is also made available, that Burakumin have full social equality.

As published in May 1985, the proposed law consists of 14 sections. Without going through each of these, some comments on the character of the proposal may be useful. Firstly, in Article 1 and in several other places, there are statements of the importance of the issue and explanations of the overall objectives of the policy. It will be noticed that the main points of reference for the bill are the rights of Japanese citizens as defined in the constitution; in particular the articles contained in Chapter III on the Rights and Duties of the People. Secondly, provision is made in Article 9 for the continuation of various projects to improve the material conditions in Buraku (Dowa) areas. Thirdly, specific mention is made of the government's obligation to attempt to influence the opinions of the majority population; 'to diffuse and promote knowledge concerning Buraku discrimination problems and to spread and enhance ideas about human rights.....' (Article 5, see also 4 and 6). Fourthly, a commitment is given to take measures 'to prevent discrimination incidents from occurring'

(Article 7). This, it is anticipated, will require further legislation about which more in a moment. Finally, the government is obliged to establish a Buraku Liberation Council, submit annual reports to the Diet on the progress of measures being taken and survey conditions in the Buraku every five years (Articles 11 - 14).

Much of the literature which has been produced by way of explanation of the bill argues that it is just an attempt to realise in full the recommendations made in the Dowa report. Both documents emphasise the need for a series of measures which, taken together, will provide a global solution to the problem. Dowa improvement projects, education policy and access to family records are brought into the scope of one piece of legislation which would, if accepted, lead to the coordination of policy in the future. Moreover, the law links the Buraku issue not only to the Japanese constitution but also to the concept of human rights which has attracted increasing attention in international law too.

The problem, then, is defined in a way in which it ceases to be an isolated domestic issue. But perhaps the most important difference is that there is no time limit placed on the validity of the act. Previous acts have been restricted to a duration of five or ten years within which it was assumed the problem could be resolved. The BLL has argued that this has demonstrated the government's lack of appreciation of the Buraku problem. If passed, this act will ensure that the Buraku issue is regularly considered by the Diet, presumably for as long as Buraku discrimination continues to exist.

THE LAW TO CONTROL DISCRIMINATION

The committee which sat during 1984 went slightly beyond its brief and in its report discussed the provisions of both a Basic Law and a law which would make discrimination illegal. Such a law is foreshadowed in Article 7 of the Basic Law and the relation between these two proposals is likened to the relation between the Basic Law on Pollution and subsequent legislation which dealt with specific aspects of pollution control. At the present time Japanese law does, in various ways address the problem of Buraku discrimination albeit indirectly. Labour legislation, for example, forbids discrimination at the workplace and the constitution in Article 14 declares '...there shall be no discrimination in political economic or social relations because of race, creed, sex, social status or family origin.' But the labour legislation does not cover the recruitment process and cases which invoke the constitution tend to be lengthy, expensive and their outcome shrouded in uncertainty. What is required, it is argued, is legislation which creates a system which can effectively control discrimination and provide procedures for the redress of those who are victims of it.

Under the proposed law pernicious (*aku shitsu*) acts of discrimination because of race, nationality or disability would become illegal. Discrimination between individuals, groups or resulting from 'personal surveys' (*mimoto chosa*) would not be punishable by criminal law but victims would need to pursue redress at civil law. In cases of incitement to violence or racial hatred and in cases of discrimination, though, the state would be able to bring prosecutions. Even in these cases, it is proposed that Human Rights committees be established in each prefecture to bring together all the interested parties so as to resolve the issue prior to prosecution. The decisions of such a body would be subject to review by a central body and, though it would not have the same powers as a formal court, its decisions would be as binding as (say) those of labour standards inspectors on matters of factory safety. Persistent offenders would be punished by, for example, the revocation of the appropriate license(s) in the case of an investigation agency or, in the last resort, by fines and/or imprisonment.[4]

Inspiration for these recommendations would seem to come from a number of quarters. There is the clear influence of such international agreements as the 'International Convention on the Elimination of All Forms of Racial Discrimination.' The discussions of various aspects of the law also cite the examples of quasi-judicial bodies which have been established in Canada and the UK to conciliate in cases of alleged discrimination. No doubt, too, that those who formulate these proposals have had to take into account the Japanese reluctance to resort to formal legal machinery to resolve social problems. And, related to this, it is clear that the radicals of the BLL wish to avoid further strengthening the power of the state and prefer that, where possible, bodies composed of informed citizens independent of central government deal with the bulk of the complaints. But, having said all this, it is not yet clear whether the BLL is going to proceed with demands for such an act. For the moment at least, it would appear that they are going to concentrate their efforts on guiding their proposed 'Basic Law' through the Diet onto the statute books. This will establish a framework in which the 'Control Law' can later play a rôle. As those involved in the campaign accept, legal controls will work best with the support of public opinion as well as being a way of changing public opinion.[6]

REACTION TO THE PROPOSALS

The Japan Socialist Party (JSP), even before the special committee report was published, announced its support for the legislative proposals. By December 1984, it was already clear what the recommendations of the committee would be and in the JSP draft plan for 1985 which was published on 26 December, they promised to support the bill within the Diet.[7]

Meanwhile, the Communist Party of Japan (CPJ) and its affiliate, the Zenkairen, will have nothing to do with these proposals. Their analysis of the problem proceeds from quite different premises which it is not possible to examine here in any detail. Simply put, however, they argue that discrimination will disappear as the capitalist system develops. In fact, they argue that prejudice and discrimination no longer exist in virulent forms and quote figures which suggest that a majority of Burakumin have had no direct experience of discrimination. To introduce a law or indeed any new set of regulations which would interpose state power between the two sectors of the community will only harm the normalisation of relations between Burakumin and non-Burakumin.[8]

Still, the Zenkairen does recognise that some improvement projects remain incomplete. Where it is clear that a project cannot be completed before 1987, it will be necessary to assess how much time and money is required to finish the project and ensure that there is sufficient for this purpose. But the aim is to reduce and finally end Burakumin dependence on SML funds as soon as possible. The Zenkairen has argued for some time that the way the projects are operated serves merely to perpetuate communal division and contribute to working-class weakness. Rather than create new laws, they suggest that discrimination will disappear more quickly if Burakumin cease to receive special treatment. Moreover, where improved facilities have been provided such as housing, schools or community centres, they should be made available to all in the neighbourhood who might benefit from them rather than their use being restricted to individuals who can demonstrate descent from feudal outcasts.[9]

In fact, the CPJ has refused to have anything to do with proposals to regulate discrimination. When, earlier this year, the Osaka prefectural assembly voted on a series of bye-laws which would prohibit 'personal investigations' by detective agencies, they were supported by representatives of all the parties except those in the CPJ.[10]

As yet, I have come across no formal statements of opinion from leaders of the Dowa movement. Usually, they have supported the LDP government policy with little criticism. But recently they have spoken in favour of taking a broader approach than that of simply organising improvement projects. Instead, they would like to see policies based on notions of human rights which are aimed at the country as a whole.[11] More recently, one of the leaders has expressed his personal approval of the proposals.[12]

Perhaps most interesting are the criticisms of the proposals which have come from within the BLL itself. Lack of space prevents detailed discussion; but let me take as an example an article recently published by Inoue Kiyoshi.[13] His remarks are centred around four criticisms of the proposals. *Firstly,* though it is entitled the 'Basic Law for Buraku Liberation', in the component articles no reference is made to Burakumin but rather there appears the euphemistic 'residents connected with Dowa areas.' This is an abandonment of the pride demonstrated by the earlier leaders of the movement and typical of the spirit of the new law. *Secondly,* he suggests that, although much is made of new emphasis on 'human rights' and the need to solve the 'software' problems, the key section of the bill is article nine which removes all time limits on the improvement projects. This, above all else, is what the movement's leaders are working for. *Thirdly,* he points out that the bill makes no mention of 'the right to denounce discrimination' — a point that requires a little elaboration. The 'denunciation struggle' — *kyudan toso* — has been the focal activity of the Buraku Liberation movement in both its pre-war and post-war manifestations. It is not the sole activity of the groups in the movement any more than negotiations with management or strikes are the sole activity of labour unions. But just as industrial action is that part of a union's activities which involves and directly affects all its members so are local and national *kyudan toso* the rallying point for the BLL groups. It can take many forms. A minor incident might be resolved by a simple but sincere verbal apology. More serious and complex cases will require long negotiation and more time-consuming demonstrations of the sincerity of those accused of discrimination.[14] The essential point is that the protest is carried out by Burakumin who themselves confront the discriminator.

Kyudan toso is regarded as an educational process. *Firstly*, in the sense that, through their direct involvement in such campaigns, the rank and file Burakumin become conscious of the nature of the prejudice and discrimination which oppresses them and the relationship of this to the oppression of the monopoly capitalist class system. *Secondly*, the organisation of such campaigns contributes to the maintenance of Buraku solidarity and the morale of the BLL groups. *Thirdly*, a successful campaign also educates the discriminator who, as a result of the activities of Burakumin, is brought to realise the error of his or her ways. Whatever the BLL may have achieved for Burakumin by virtue of its campaign and negotiations for improvement money, the lifeblood of the movement has been its involvement in these protest activities. If organs of the state interfere with this process or if a new semi-formal network for conflict resolution is established, *kyudan toso* will no longer have a rôle. Critics such as Inoue are worried that not only will the BLL lose its sense of purpose but impersonal legal or semi-legal procedures will tend to increase the mistrust of those involved in an incident rather than remove it. This brings us to the last of Inoue's criticisms which is that the law will encourage Burakumin to rely on the state to solve their problems rather than seek a solution for themselves. Already the BLL is involved in the administration of the SML; if these measures are passed, it will become even more subservient to the demands of an increasingly powerful Japanese state. It is not clear how much support these views have within the BLL but it seems fair to say that a significant minority within the organisation is worried about the effect the passage of this law will have on the movement and Burakumin in general.

PROSPECTS FOR THE PROPOSALS

The success or otherwise of the campaign in support of this Basic Law will be judged by what legislation, if any, comes into operation on 1 April 1987, the day after the present SML expires. What is the likelihood of these proposals finding their way onto the statute book?

International legal trends point in the direction of adopting such a law. Over the past two decades several western countries have adopted legislation that has provided a legal framework for the control of discrimination and the reduction of prejudice. Moreover, there is pressure for Japan to adopt some kind of legislation in order to bring her in line with such international law as the International Convention on the Elimination of All Forms of Racial Discrimination. Nevertheless, through the SML and reform of the *koseki* regulations, the government has demonstrated its intention to improve the lot of Burakumin. The case for the Basic Law is that it tidies up the legislative structure and makes a clear statement of intent that Buraku discrimination will not be tolerated in Japanese society.

Domestic political considerations are more likely to determine in the end what becomes law. The support of the JSP and probably all the other opposition parties apart from the CPJ is significant but guarantees little. That some of the leadership of the Dowa movement have expressed interest in the proposals and that the chairman of the committee supporting the proposals is the chief priest of a branch of the Honganji temple,[15] indicates that the bill may attract support from across the political spectrum. But there are no signs yet that the ruling LDP will accept the proposals as they are. Indeed, the proposals for a control law represent a challenge to government policy which hitherto has tried to contain the various demands for social equality from such groups as working women, Burakumin and Koreans by trying to keep the issues separate. The effect of coordinated demands from a number of groups for a law which would make discrimination of many kinds illegal might be to diffuse norms of social equality throughout Japanese society which could have unforeseen consequences.

Perhaps the greatest danger is that the government will elect to introduce some legislation whose content will be anodyne but worthless or even counter-productive. Recent legislation to ensure equality of opportunity between the sexes has been criticised by women's groups for its lack of teeth. A Basic Law on Human Rights is currently under consideration which might be put forward as an alternative to the BLL proposals. This might reaffirm some principles already in the constitution but it is unlikely that it would contain provision for the extension of the improvement projects or commit the government to a regular review of conditions in Buraku communities. It is unlikely that such an act would produce real benefits for Burakumin.

Paradoxically, the best reason for the LDP to adopt the BLL proposals is that in the medium- to long-term to do so will weaken what is probably the best-organised left-wing pressure group in Japanese society. And, moreover, one that provides considerable support for the JSP, the largest opposition party. It would not be the first time that the LDP adopted a proposal which originated in the opposition and still claimed credit for it.

25

Japan's Returnee Children: Some Initial Observations

ROGER J. GOODMAN

Though it is perhaps slightly unusual, I would like to start by explaining the title of this paper. Since it will, I trust, become clear later why I have chosen the phrase I have for the first part, it is on the second portion that I need to make a brief comment. While I was in Japan in 1984 completing my fieldwork, I prepared a paper which covered the basic points most essential for an understanding of the problems concerning returnee children in Japan. It was my original intention to reproduce that paper here but, as I prepared myself to do so, I was rather surprised to discover that my views had modified considerably in the short time between the completion of my fieldwork in Japan and my return to England. Briefly stated, I discovered how I had, to a certain extent, projected the over-idealised view of my own country and some of the frustrations of my fieldwork experience on to a rather negative view of Japanese society. This is, of course, because I am a returnee myself, and in my final thesis I hope to be able to incorporate this element of my own experience as a returnee into an understanding of the Japanese case. For the moment, I must insist that I only intend here to make some general preliminary observations about the returnee children in Japan, in the hope that these might add a new perspective to a much-discussed topic.

First of all, I must explain who is referred to by the word *kikokushijo*, as returnee children are known in Japanese. These are Japanese children who, because of their parents' work, have received some or all of their education overseas and then returned to Japan. According to Japanese Ministry of Education statistics there were nearly ten thousand *kikokushijo* in the single year of 1984. It must be understood that these children range from, say, fifteen-year-olds who have spent all their life in America and speak no Japanese at all, to five-year-olds who have attended a Japanese kindergarden in Seoul for eight months or who know no language and no individuals but Japanese. It is the simple fact of having lived outside Japan for longer than a few months and then returned which defines a child as a returnee.

The interest in returnees in Japan is enormous. Indeed, it would hardly be an exaggeration to suggest that the topic has become something of an obsession. A never-ending stream of newspaper and popular magazine articles is produced on the subject. As for books, so many have been written that it is possible to find in certain bookshops whole sections devoted to the topic. So many researchers are working on the matter that, as an anthropologist, I became as interested in the community of researchers as in the children themselves. In terms of money, every year billions of yen are being spent, in some form or other, on the returnee children. In this paper, however, the two main questions to which I address myself (under the general rubvic of communication) are the following: (1) What is the image or message being put across about these children, and (2) Why is it being put across?

THE IMAGE OF RETURNEE CHILDREN IN JAPAN

It seems to have become almost *de rigueur* for any book on Japanese society to mention, if only in passing, and to 'prove' any number of different points, the negative attitude of stay-at-home Japanese towards those who return from overseas. Profesor Ohnuki-Tierney, for example, in her latest, well-received book writes:

'There are 'marginal outsiders,' however, towards whom the Japanese feel ambivalent or downright negative....(For) example..the *han japa* (half-Japanese; *japa* from English "Japanese"), who are the children of Japanese parents whose work required the children to be reared in a foreign country.'

Critics of Japan, such as the British-based Minority Rights Group, suggest that perhaps returnee children should be seen as victims of Japanese society, comparable to *burakumin,* Ainu, Okinawans and Japanese Koreans.[4] Even such staunch supporters of Japan as Vogel in *Japan as Number One*[5] and Reischauer in *The Japanese*[6] feel compelled to comment on this negative attitude as one that Japan can ill-afford as the country is drawn increasingly into the international arena. Personally, I prefer to summarise this attitude towards returnees as *different* from other Japanese: this permits recourse to the concept of positive discrimination, something which has, in fact, become institutionalised in recent years and which actually favours the returnees (particularly in university entrance) while reinforcing their difference from other Japanese children.

Many theories, of course, have been put forward for the causes of this discrimination. At its very simplest, the argument goes something like this: as a homogeneous island people with a long period of seclusion (*sakoku jidai*) and a unique culture and language which, to be mastered, require constant attention from birth, it is natural that the Japanese have an innate sense of suspicion towards anything coming from without. More subtle interpretations, however, are also offered. For example, I recently attended, along with about two hundred others, a conference in Fukuoka[7] where the causes for returnees' differences were discussed from a number of different viewpoints. I trust, through the following summary that I do not, through oversimplification, do an injustice to any of the arguments I heard put forward by those present. A linguist propounded the theory that the foreign language ability of returnee children necessarily detracted from their ability to speak Japanese. Since it is essential to be able to speak Japanese to be Japanese, then the lack of the former strongly militates against the latter. An educational sociologist suggested that, since education was the key to providing a position in Japanese society, the fact that these children were educationally deficient (in a Japanese school sense) meant that they could not participate fully in Japanese society. An anthropologist described Japaneseness, or at least its perception, as pure Japanese blood, Japanese language, Japanese cultural skills, thereby appearing to suggest, if only implicitly, some kind of Japanese national mathematical formula whereby the Japanese age of a returnee can be calculated by the real age minus the number of years lived abroad. A psychologist put forward the concept of 'identity-crises,' which can leave returnees unable to function normally while they anguish over whether they are Japanese or something else. A psychiatrist claimed that his research had led him to the discovery that the special nature of their psyche makes Japanese particularly liable to breakdowns when they go overseas and when they return again. Such breakdowns he terms *futekiobyo*, or non-adaptation disease.

There is truth, I have no doubt, in some, if not all, of the above arguments which attempt to explain discrimination against returnee children. Nevertheless, they are far from the whole story. In anthropological terms these models are both functionalist and static. Why does there continue to be such fascination with returnees? Why is there so little apparent attempt to see the returnees in a positive light? Is it not possible that the work which purports to explain the discrimination towards returnees might not actually be maintaining or even boosting it? As an additional perspective to the arguments presented above, I would like to offer a more dynamic model of the causes of discrimination towards returning children.

TOWARDS A DYNAMIC MODEL TO EXPLAIN THE NEGATIVE
PERCEPTION OF KIKOKUSHIJO

It is important to point out that one reason for the sudden interest in the returnee children has been the fact that their parents form a very powerful group in Japanese society. Diplomats, businessmen, academics and other professionals are statistically far more likely to take their children on overseas postings than blue-collar workers; and it is almost certain that it was the combined complaints of this élite group in the mid 1970s which led to the formation of an official policy for the returnee children.[9] The main gist of their complaint was that, while they (the parents) were serving their country by working abroad, their children were being handicapped by being unable to compete equally with other students on their return to the education race in Japan.

With the government forced to act on the issue of returnee children, there arose essentially two distinct schools of thought about the most appropriate policy. One of these, known as the *kokusaiha*, or the Internationalist Faction, argued that the returnee children would be the potential future leaders of Japan as the country was drawn increasingly into the international world, and that they should, therefore, be treated almost as national treasures for their multilingual and multicultural skills. The second school of thought, known as the *kokunaiha*, or the Integrationist Faction, argued alternatively that, since these children had received their

155

education overseas, they could not be considered representatives of Japan until they had properly learnt, as individuals themselves, what it really meant to be Japanese.

It has clearly been on the basis of the second school of thought that educational policy for returnee children has been established. The view has been taken that returnee children, far from being an asset to Japan, are more to be pitied for their lack of ability in Japanese society and their need of help to readjust to it. This view has become institutionalised in the way returnee children are officially discussed. One group, for example, the International Children's Bunko Association (*Kokusai Jido Bunko Kyokai*) argues that the characters (which independently stand for child [*shi*] and woman [*jo*] chosen to express the word 'children' in the phrase 'returnee children' suggest, if only subliminally, the idea that there is something weak and helpless about such children, especially with the emphasis on the rightness of masculinity in Japan. Indeed, they have taken as one of their main aims the elimination of this word (*shijo*) from official usage.[9] Secondly, it has become official policy and thereby common practice to refer to the 'Returnee Children Problem' (*kikokushijo mondai*). This also creates the impression that these children either have or are some kind of problem. Thirdly, when discussing returnee children in connection with other children who have not been overseas, it is common practice to refer to the latter as 'normal students' (*ippansei*), with the connotation that the returnees are somehow something else.

In a more concrete sense, the Government has set up several different types of institution to aid the reassimilation of returnee children. Perhaps the most interesting of these are the Government-sponsored research institutes. The main research into returnee children is carried out at Tokyo, Tokyo Gakugei, Kyoto, ICU and Tsukuba universities. With perhaps as many as fifty researchers altogether in the field, what is so striking is that, virtually without exception, every one of them works within the same accepted framework that the returnee children have a problem and that they, as researchers, are best employed by 'scientifically' measuring that problem so that proper guidance and curricula can be set up for alleviating it. Great effort is taken to ensure the so-called 'scientific' validity of this research, the best example perhaps being an enormous survey project carried out from Kyoto University to plot graphs of average times for individual adjustment considering several variables of overseas experience.[10] It is, therefore, particularly noteworthy and even surprising that only two of all the pieces of research which I have seen have examined the returnee children in direct comparison with children who have not been overseas.[11] The question of whether the problems which the returnees have might actually be those not just of a returnee but of any adolescent, any schoolchild, even any Japanese has quite simply been ignored. The philosophical and political basis upon which the research rests has been left quite unexplored and there is no consideration of the possibility that, for example, what is taken as the problem of the returnee child might actually be an indictment of the education system in Japan.

The Advice Centres (*sodan senta*) are a second type of quasi-official organisation set up to deal with the returnee children. There are at present three of these and they work within the same philosophical framework as do the researchers. If anything, their view that the returnee children are badly in need of help is rather more extreme. Considering the nature of their work, this is not surprising: were the children not in need of help then there would be no need for these centres. Indeed, a consultation in these places is sometimes, by the advisers themselves, described as a diagnosis (*shindan* — the same word as used by the medical profession in Japan). It is on the basis of this 'diagnosis' of the serious nature (*jusho*) or not so serious nature (*keisho*) of the individual child's returnee sickness, that parents, normally mothers, are advised in which school most appropriately to attempt to enter their children.

These schools are a third type of institution which the Government has set up. There are now around ninety schools which operate under a category generally known as *ukeireko*, or Reception Schools, which cater, though not exclusively, to the education of children returning from abroad. Indeed, my main fieldwork has been to examine the way these schools work and it is interesting that very largely the teachers operate within the same conceptual framework as has been set up by the Government, then presented as scientific proof by the scientists and disseminated as 'fact' by the mass media. For example, teachers frequently complain that the returnee children talk too much in class; ask too many questions; do not discipline themselves well enough to the task at hand; are poor at working cooperatively; do not understand the nuances of Japanese language and communication processes; are far behind in their educational skills and, generally, because of their difference from 'normal students' (*ippansei*), have trouble fitting back into society and, more specifically, into the school system. Significantly, often when something happens of a negative nature with a returnee child, a direct correlation is made with that child's overseas experience: a returnee who gets into trouble does so *because* he is a returnee; a returnee who has psychological problems coping with school has those problems *because* she is a returnee, and so on. On the other hand, when returnees do well, the fact of their overseas experience is rarely mentioned. In short, the teachers feel that they are there to help these children and not in any sense to learn from them.

Another institution which the government has set up for such children is the network of overseas Japanese schools, of which there are presently 78 operating on a full-time, and a further 102 on a part-time (generally Saturday morning), basis. These schools almost entirely ignore the locale in which they are placed. They try to compete as efficiently as possible with the same level schools in Japan and generally act to insulate the children against any outside culture, thereby ensuring their smooth reintegration on their return to Japan. Therefore, it is not uncommon to find children who have spent four or five years in (say) Taiwan, South Korea or Indonesia and who are all but totally ignorant of the languages and cultures of those places.

As I have attempted to show, the view that returnees are handicapped, even sick, is one that is being constantly reinforced and propagated throughout the media in Japan. I feel that this is not simply a spontaneous reaction to the sudden growth in the number of such children but that there may be several groups who have a vested interest, of which they may not even be fully aware, in these children being perceived in such a way.

First, there are the teachers who, when they refer to the problems from which the returnee children are supposed to be suffering, may actually indirectly be talking about their own problems in dealing with this kind of student. Returnee students, particularly those who have been in western schools, know that the teacher is not always right; they know that the Japanese-style of teacher-centred lesson is not the only way of learning; their foreign language ability is often far superior to that of many Japanese foreign language teachers. Even in such traditional Japanese strengths as science and mathematics, though they are probably poorer at the application, they may understand the theory better than some of the teachers. Japanese teachers are poorly trained to cope with such a new kind of student. Not only do they generally have to deal with up to fifty students in a single class, but it must also be remembered that teaching practice in Japan lasts generally only two weeks, of which the first is devoted to observation and the second consists of a mere eight practice lessons. If one remembers, therefore, that teachers are not accustomed to having their knowledge nor their judgement questioned, and especially not in class in front of others, it is not so surprising that they are apt to label students who indulge in such practices as disruptive or, if they are returnees, as having trouble readapting to Japan. When considered in the same context also, it is easier to understand why an over-stretched, harassed teacher might want to label a westernised and highly-individualistic returnee as suffering from an 'identity problem.'[13] Indeed, in the school where I undertook my main fieldwork, a special system of group education had been instituted in some classes, though not exclusively for the returnees, as a way of educating notions of cooperativeness rather than individualism.

At a second level, the education authorities in Japan may be aware that the returnee children, because of their experience of other education systems, offer an implicit, and sometimes explicit, criticism of some of the widely-accepted inherent weaknesses of the Japanese education system. Although they are themselves aware of many of these weaknesses, the authorities seem determined that it is they who should be responsible for exactly where and how change is wrought in the system. This attitude can also be seen in the politicking of the recently formed Provisional Council on Educational Reform (*Rinji Kyoiku Shingi-kai*). In short, the education authorities, by declaring the children and not the system at fault and in need of help, are able to deflect and reduce the potential power of these children to produce change in the system from within.

At a third, and even deeper, level there appears to be the feeling in some quarters that the attitudes and actions of the returnee children constitute a real threat to accepted concepts of 'Japanese Identity'[14] and thereby the very core of Japanese economic success. The perceived individualism of the returnees is thought to clash with Japanese group values; their supposed free-thinking with Japanese harmony; their dilettantism with Japanese diligence and single-mindedness. In this light, it might be interesting to note, if only in passing, that on the seventeen-member Policy Board on Returnee Children, which was created ten years ago, there sat senior representatives of Japan Air Lines, Japan National Railways, Mitsui Bussan, The Japan Economic Journal (*Nihon Keizai Shimbun*), The Japan Foreign Trade Council, Inc. (*Nihon Boeki-kai*) and the Japanese External Trade Organisation (JETRO) (*Nihon Boeki Shinko-kai.*)[15]

By way of conclusion, I must once again emphasise that I have had space in this paper to present only a very partial view of an extremely ramified and complex subject. I am painfully aware of having ignored historical, institutional and cultural factors which are essential for a full understanding of the position of returnees in Japanese society. What I have attempted to do, however, is to try and outline an extra perspective which should be incorporated into the debate and which has, until now, been virtually untouched. While not trying to suggest that any individual is trying consciously to denigrate the returnee children for whatever machiavellian reasons, it does seem to be the case that educationalists, teachers, economic leaders and even returnee parents are unconsciously reacting within the framework of their own accepted beliefs in the special nature of Japanese society, when they propose that the returnee children are not real Japanese until they have been properly reassimilated into Japanese society. Whatever the reasons, the way the returnees are perceived officially is, in effect, a statement of where and how the boundaries of what it means to be Japanese are drawn today.

26

Respect, Solidarity or Contempt? Politeness and Communication in Modern Japan

JOY HENDRY

A mode of communication in Japanese which potentially lends itself to considerable social analysis is the collection of speech forms nowadays subsumed under the category of *keigo*. There are various ways in which the subject could be approached, and the present paper represents some reflections on the possibilities rather than a set of definitive conclusions.

Although the politeness formulae and honorific styles indicated by the term *keigo* are by no means exclusive to Japanese,[1] they are, as linguistic forms, particularly well developed in Japanese, and Japanese writers on the subject are prone to assign them the role of giving some special quality to the language. In one manual which purports to show how to use *keigo* without shame, it is described as a 'precious beauty' (*kichona utsukushisa*), and the 'essence' or 'cream' (*sui*) of Japanese.[2] Elsewhere, *keigo* is said to give Japanese a lyrical quality, expressive of feelings (*jojoteki*), which is contrasted with the strength of logic in European languages, and without which it is felt that Japanese would lose its charm (*miryoku*).[3]

Keigo is also described as difficult and complicated, the source of worry to Japanese[4] and, on the cover of one book on the subject, the ability to use *keigo* is described as a 'weapon of self-defence in social life.'[5] However, the author of another manual encourages readers in his preface by noting that even foreigners with little language training have recently become quite competent at *keigo*, which is simply a natural way of showing concern and care for people[6]. A common argument centres around whether or not *keigo* is disappearing and, if so, whether it should be preserved. The importance of *keigo* relative to other aspects of the language is perhaps indicated in the way it was chosen as the first subject to be considered in a series on language commissioned by the Ministry of Education for the promotion of language education.[7]

In the book which resulted it is suggested that some of the power of expression symbolised in other cultures by gestures and facial expressions is in Japanese made up for by *keigo* to the list of elements which comprise theories of Japaneseness known as '*Nihonjinron.*' Befu has recently argued that the proliferation of such theories helps to rescue Japanese from a crisis in cultural identity created by continual westernisation and internationalisation in modern Japan.[9] If Befu's argument is sound, then one level of communication in the use of *keigo* would be to demonstrate a degree of Japaneseness, which could be threatened by too much westernisation and international experience.

It is probably true that those Japanese least concerned about the use of *keigo* are those unlikely to feel threatened in this way. The farmers and other country residents with whom I have worked in provincial and rural Japan are proud of their sometimes rather traditional customs, but express few worries about their use of polite language. They use their local polite forms without much self-conscious analysis and, for the most part, honorific language is confined to ceremonial occasions. It is also true that Japanese who have lived abroad for any length of time and, in particular those who spend their formative years abroad, express dissatisfaction with their own ability to use *keigo* properly. Indeed, some long-time Japanese residents in Britain prefer to communicate with each other in English, precisely because of their lack of confidence about the appropriateness of Japanese forms of address with each other.

Recently, I was involved in the selection of Japanese (female) employees for a British company in Japan, when the most suitable candidates for the job were expected to have a combination of traditional Japanese charm and an ability to use English well. Out of over 300 applicants, it was only just possible to choose the fourteen individuals required, mainly because those with a good enough command of English had usually lost the Japanese charm. The Japanese personnel manager was responsible for the final word on this 'charm,' and his interviews all dwelt for some time on the methods of upbringing (*shitsuke*) of the candidates involved. Those who had lived for many years abroad were often rejected out of hand as too westernised but, among them, those whose mothers had spent time training their daughters in the use of polite language were sometimes able to overcome this drawback.

The question arises, then, of what it is that comprises an ability to use *keigo*. A person who has lived abroad probably cannot fail to pick up some of the gestures and facial expressions being used around them, indeed an acquisition of fluency in another language would be unconvincing without these non-verbal clues. However, in a situation, such as that described, this must evidently not be to the detriment of depth of communication in Japanese. What, then, are some of these levels of communication, and how is the social vulnerability to be perceived if one has holes in this 'weapon of self-defence?'

Obviously, there is the dimension of respect and hierarchy. As the word indicates, in the use of the sub-category of *sonkeigo*, one is at the simplest level communicating a degree of respect for the addressee by choosing a deferential form. This may be reinforced by the use of *kenjogo* or humble language in reference to oneself. Between persons of limited acquaintance the communication may go no further than this, and it may indicate nothing more than the appropriate form of address in a given situation, whether any real respect is felt or not. Thus might a shop assistant speak to a customer, and bystanders would have no trouble in understanding the message. Relative age is said to be an important criterion for choosing respectful forms and, other things being equal, a younger person would be likely to show some degree of respect for an older one in this way. Again, this level of communication is clear to an outsider.

Within an organisation with a fixed hierarchy, such as a large company or a university, employees and colleagues may regularly use respect forms for their superiors as a matter of course. An outsider could probably guess at relative relations by listening to some of the exchanges but, as a rule, members of one enterprise will humble themselves collectively in reference to the outsider, so that the sale of simple deference or respect is now from the inside out. Here, one may be expressing a solidarity with one's colleagues which will say virtually nothing about relations between them, except that they belong to the same organisation.

Within such an organisation, people working together may use variations in usage regularly to express relative closeness or distance, changes in mood, or perhaps approval or disapproval of particular actions. In such cases, the choice of more deferential terms than usual may indicate a certain coolness, or even outright contempt, for someone or their actions. In a discussion amongst university teachers reported in the previously mentioned language series book on *keigo*, one professor reports that he would feel made fun of if his students were to be too polite to him.[10] At this level communication becomes more subtle, and is probably not readily accessible to the understanding of outsiders.

In the wider world, exchanges between women, in particular, may often be apparently reciprocal in deferentiality. According to a series of interviews I carried out amongst Japanese women living temporarily in Oxford, an important factor with women whose ages do not vary by more than ten years or so is the adjustment of one's language to a level appropriate for each particular addressee. Thus, in order to be friendly, one may gradually modify an extreme politeness of approach if one finds that the respondent is less adept than oneself. In any case, as women become closer, they may well signal their intimacy by dropping some of the deferentiality. Conversely, a return to politer language than previously is again a sure way of applying brakes if one feels someone is becoming too familiar. All this may be apparent only to the two people involved in the relationship, and the depth of understanding of the bystander is probably proportional to their own social proximity to the parties concerned.

Communication between women using *keigo* is also interesting because their language, more than men's, is often liberally punctuated with two other sub-categories of the species, namely *teineigo* and *bikago*, 'polite language' and 'beautification language' respectively. These forms adorn the language generally, as well as making statements about the relationships between conversants. In skilful usage of these forms an individual may communicate to the world at large something about their background and personality. Equally, a dearth of such forms in perhaps a career woman's speech may indicate a rejection of the feminine associations they imply.

Solidarity may here be expressed in a mutual ability to manipulate the various speech forms available. Women of a particular sort of upbringing are conversant with an extremely polite form of language which they may nevertheless use rather informally to indicate intimacy within the social group. Members of such groups assert that these skills are virtually impossible to acquire later in life, so that considerable trouble is taken to impart such skills to their children. The family is said to be the most important influence in this respect, but kindergartens, schools and even universities are also sometimes characterised by the kind of language in current use within their walls.

Theoretically, a high degree of skill involves the ability to switch between various forms so that communication is always maintained at a level appropriate to the circumstances, but one's style of speech is always subject to assessment by others. Some may regard the extremely polite forms as affected, whereas those who use the polite forms are quick to notice when people are trying unsuccessfully to join their ranks. Many Japanese people will readily discuss the way in which *keigo* is misused these days. Some talk of mistakes which are commonly made, others decry what they regard as an unnecessary superfluity of honorific 'o's at the beginning of words. Even quite young people will complain that youths are barely able to use *keigo* at all, whereas students I have interviewed describe with some fervour the importance of using polite language with their seniors.

These statements about the language of others would seem to be full of potential social implications. For one thing, they could indicate the existence and boundaries of Japan's version of social and generational classes. There might be an English bias operating here, but they seem to be remarkably similar to statements in Britain about the language of others,

162

and in particular about people who try to cross those boundaries. At a horizontal level people communicate solidarity in a sharing of abilities, but more interesting perhaps is the contempt they communicate in reference to the inabilities or superability of members of differing groups. As in Britain, it may prove to be very difficult to isolate groups, but this is something which still needs to be investigated.

My opening remarks about *keigo* in general, however, indicate some of the efforts made to maintain a clear boundary between Japan and the outside world. The boundary is evidently threatened by foreigners speaking Japanese, as Miller and others have discussed,[11] and by native Japanese who lose some of their linguistic skills. The intricacies and rapidly changing nature of *keigo* make it an ideal barometer for assessing the language of people who stop too far outside the boundary, but there is evidently much more at stake.

Those who lose their communication skills in this respect, who allow their personal weapon of self-defence to become too dilapidated, are in grave danger of finding themselves outsiders in the world to which they return. One hypothesis which seems to be emerging here, therefore, is that the level of understanding is related to social distance. One needs to maintain close relationships in order to reach the deepest level of understanding of the communication around one, in order to maintain a sense of belonging and solidarity within one's own social class. Otherwise one will find oneself, like the foreign commentators who have come in for so much criticism recently surrounded only by harmonious superficiality.

Perhaps I have exaggerated the case to make the point. For, if the argument is carried to its logical conclusion, we foreign observers may well abandon our efforts immediately. Fortunately, however, the boundary is a perceptual one, part of the rife mythology of Japaneseness which has already been discussed numerous times before. In Befu's words, '*Nihonron* as an ideology ultimately belongs to the realm of *tatemae*.'[12] *Keigo* is closely related to *tatemae* but, as one moves away from the sophisticated boundaries of internationalised Japan, *tatemae*, too, becomes less important, as I have already noted that *keigo* does.

Unfortunately, I fear that the writer who was quoted above as having noted the competence in *keigo* of foreigners with little language training was merely trying to encourage the faint-hearted Japanese reader. All Japanese, and most foreigners too, know how little Japanese a foreigner needs to speak to elicit praise from a native. From my experience so far, and in view of the persistence of this perceptual boundary, the investigation of *keigo* would seem to be an area where the participant observer would do well to concentrate on the observation, for too much participation is highly likely to cloud the issues!

27

The Religious Nature of Popular Confucianism in Japan

JAN VAN BREMEN

In the 1970s my research was largely focused on a popular form of Neo-confucianism in contemporary Japan and on the historical antecedents and background of its practices and beliefs. I studied popular strains of Wang Yang-ming doctrine, introduced in Japan in the period of transition accompanying the establishment of Tokugawa rule and consolidated and developed since then. I should like to offer a word of explanation as to why I studied the subject and then discuss matters of method and theory in my research and in the study of ideational realms in society and culture.

A prominent reason is the neglect and the scarcity of detailed discussion about the covert but continuing influence of Confucianism in modern Japan and in a number of other countries in East Asia. As a social philosophy, popular Wang Yang-ming doctrine plays an intriguing part in society as a moral imperative and leverage for social action and rebellion. Another impulse is the need to come to terms with ideational and indeed religious influences in modern societies. The combination of philosophical and religious knowledge and inspiration with social and personal action together with a notion of social order, make it of interest and relevance to study.

Given the variety of sources of information and inspiration in interaction with concepts and models in anthropology and in my research, I raise the problem of method and theory in my study of the popular exponents of the doctrine. One issue is the small number of adherents. The followers and practitioners of this powerful and consequential creed are, and have been, small in number. This is true for the masters of the Great as well as the exponents of the Folk Tradition. Yet the influence of both has been considerable and far reaching and includes the covert forms and dissemination which I made the object of my investigation, together with the religious nature of the creed.

There is a problem in working with a number of disciplines other than anthropology (in my case intellectual history) and in covering a very broad period of time and space and specific realms within them in order to obtain the relevant background knowledge. The amalgamation of sources and kinds of information which I drew upon for answers to my questions, was not really problematic. I should make the point, however, that Wang Yang-ming philosophy and guidelines for practical living are a complex creed with considerable interpretations and variations. It has an extensive history and combines Confucian, Buddhist and Taoist influences together with local and individual input.

Questions of method and epistemology have been constant issues in anthropology, not least in the past twenty years. It is not surprising, perhaps, that they have the attention of several of us here who are studying ideational phenomena and their translation into social action and collective representations. In order to discuss the features and methods of the research which I conducted, I shall list the main areas from which I obtained data and discuss some of the implications. I divide my data into three categories: data obtained directly from a small number of informants and primary sources; data obtained from popular works; and data obtained from secondary sources. The data obtained from informants centre on the small number I had access to and raise questions of interpretation and representation; but they enable the researcher to gain access to the living creed as it is lived and to those who are living it. There are similar problems with respect to popular works. The issues with secondary sources centre on the use of research produced by, and for, other disciplines and purposes and concern the aid they can give, or fail to give, to the problems and questions I need answering. .... '*autour de l'ethnographie se développe toute une littérature apparemment théorique, avec son jargon et ses hypothèses. De quoi s'agit-il vraiment?*'[1]

What is religion and how does one study it? The questions are closely interrelated. The concept of my first mentor, Jan van Baals, becomes clearer in the titles of his two latest major books, *Symbols for Communication* (1971) and *Man's Quest for Partnership* (1981). 'Communication' is the theme selected: and for Van Baal religion and communication are inherently linked. What one takes religion to be then partly goes together with how one studies it and what of it. I take religion for a 'social fact' and a dimension of consciousness and action. In order to study popular Wang Yang-ming exponents in contemporary Japan and to grasp the phenomena, I took as my basic research exponents those exposed by C. Wright Mills: 'Social science deals with problems of *biography*, of *history*, and their intersections within *social structures...*' [my emphasis].[2] In order to make an exploratory description and analysis of these realms, I used data I could gather first-hand from informants and primary sources, popular works and secondary sources. In addition to data, I needed conceptual aids and theoretical orientations, which I derived primarily from anthropology and history. The method was partly a matter of strategies borrowed and partly a question of considering methodological implications of uncontrolled research moments. In this paper, I pay attention to both of these.

To state my case, it is helpful to make a brief excursion into the work of a few anthropologists who study religion and state what anthropology is as they see it at the moment. In the widely used textbook, Roger Keesing in a paragraph called 'Modes of Anthropological Understanding: Theory, Interpretation, and Science,' summarises the work of anthropologists that bears closely upon the theme of this meeting and the topic of my presentation:

'Anthropologists have been less preoccupied with being scientific than many of their colleagues in psychology, sociology and political science, and by and large this has

165

probably been a blessing. Anthropologists have had to struggle with problems of communications as they have worked across gulfs of cultural differences. Being unable to use tests, questionnaires, polls, experiments, and the like, in human communities where they were guests and where western instruments of "objectivity" were inappropriate, *anthropologists have fallen back on human powers to learn, understand and communicate.* They have avoided many of the devices that spuriously objectify human encounters because they simply could not use them. [my emphasis].[3]

I find this statement consoling after the struggle with other opinions, particularly those that hold that anthropology should be a science.

In a society such as Japan, the abilities listed by Keesing are no less required of a fieldworker than of an anthropologist working in a non-literate society. In addition, research in societies with a long historical tradition, urges one to make contact with other disciplines, in my case particularly intellectual and social history and literature. I find an interpretative anthropology, in a holistic and comparative approach, important and beneficial, particularly for the study of religion. As a programmatic statement of anthropology, I value R. Needham's inaugural lecture: Needham stressed the idea that anthropology is not a science (the criterion being the use of mathematics) and said:

'Our intellectual congeners.... include philosophy, classics, philology, history (especially social history, the history of ideas, art history), theology..., and other non-mathematical kinds of study.'

and added

'... the social anthropologist must ideally be eclectic to the extreme in his range of interests, perpetually alert to points of instructive contact, and the variety of matters that he may find relevant to a particular study in his own field is quite unpredictable.'[4]

This indicates the position of anthropology *vis-à-vis* other disciplines and, important to us, Japanese studies or Japanology.

Another moment of recognition is the exposition on method given by Sherry Ortner in a recent study. It is important to note that she holds a similar view of anthropology to the ones advocated here. To make that clear, I quote the opening paragraph of the first chapter ('Introduction: some notes on ritual') of her study, Sherpas through their rituals:

'One may envision the task of an ethnography as opening a culture to readers, unfolding it, revealing it, providing not only a sense of surface form and rhythm, but also a sense of inner connections and interactions. If this is one's vision of the task, certain ways of launching upon it will be more powerful and effective than others. One could of course begin with the standard categories — kinship, economy, politics, religion — yet this approach is problematic, not only because the categories are externally imposed but because they are undynamic. They do not carry one into an experience of the interconnections that must be at the heart of the discussion.'[5]

What I recognise as well is a common interest in, as Ortner puts it, 'sources and forces of meaning.' How to arrive at the 'sources and forces of meaning' in a culture and how to report about them? Ortner used two privileged approaches, the 'representative anecdote or event' and the 'cultural performances,' in particular rituals. She remarks that there are more, namely 'key texts' and 'key symbols.' The idea is that one can study a culture and particularly the 'sources and forces of meaning,' through 'formal statements' and 'moments of greatest self-display.' Ortner believes that symbolic elements can be used as leads or guides to explore 'problematic structures, relationships and ideas of a culture.'[6] Clearly, these notions do not go undisputed in anthropology. Yet ritual is of much importance in the establishment of social order and is a manipulation of consciousness, of, by and for the actors.

The methodological issues discussed here have a venerable history in anthropology. An early treatise about the question was published by Bronislaw Malinowski in 1916 as 'Some general statements concerning the sociology of belief,'[7] Others have sparingly left their reflections, e.g. Paul Radin who in 1956 added the essay 'Methods of approach' to the second edition of *Primitive man as a philosopher.*[8]

At present, the work of Dan Sperber is of interest. I use the term 'interpretative anthropology' with more ease since reading his work. Sperber's intellectual congeners are G. Balandier and, in particular, R. Needham. In Sperber's work the problems identified by B. Malinowski — problems that every fieldworker and particularly so the anthropologist who studies religion, is confronted with anew — have been brought closer to clarity and solution. Malinowski's 1916 essay is an attempt to state and clarify the heuristics and hermeneutics of ethnography and ethnology (ethnography and anthropology in Sperber's usage), description, analysis and explanation or at least insight. Malinowski approached the problem by recognising two or perhaps three dimensions — much like Sperber. Data obtained from individual informants Malinowski called 'one-dimensional.' The anthropologist, however, aims also at the 'collective' and 'social' dimensions or levels. The question is how the two or three levels are to be linked and interrelated. In my study I used the term 'genre ethnography' for the ethnography of adepts of the Wang Yang-ming persuasions in Japan, in particular with respect to the portrayal of living informants.[9]

The term is appropriate in two ways as glimpses of life and moments and as stylised representations that give the particular and unique a collective dimension. To elucidate and retain the *ukiyo-e* simile — and one could take Brassai's photographs or George Gros's drawings — Utamaro's pictures of courtesans both represent unique persons and their activities as well as a class of persons and their habitual activities.

Sperber in the essay *Ethnographie interprétative et anthropologie theorique* has noted the dynamics of this process in the recurring patterns found in the construction of ethnographies. Taking Evans-Pritchard's *Nuer religion* as a case and example, he notes the following procedure.[10] The ethnographer gives a particular case or event (*l'anecdote*), which is then interpreted and explained (*la glose*) and finally made representative of a class of similar cases and occurences (*la generalisation*). The three levels or dimensions are joined by terms '*interpretive et synthetic*' moving from the specific to the general, from closeness to empirical reality to conceptual abstractions. Anthropology in Sperber's view is concerned not so much with theory as with interpretation. The sources from which that flows are recordings of field data and documents '*heterodites*'. The instrument of '*intuition*' seems to replace theory when beliefs are the object of study. The result is a monograph or treatise or, as Sperber calls them. '*representations semi-propositionnelles.*'[11]

You may well feel that, instead of offering clarification, I have added to the difficulties of studying ideation in complex societies. Nevertheless, I believe that I have outlined some of the methodological dimensions in the study of belief systems and action in Japan and literate societies. I have endeavoured to highlight some of the epistemological foundations that underlie anthropological studies of beliefs systems such as my own, in an attempt to construct better and more adequate representations of social and cultural realities.

28

Evolution of the Ideological Structure of Nationalism in Modern Japan

B. V. POSPELOV

The ideological structure of Japanese nationalism at the first stage of its evolution at the end of the nineteenth century was marked by the *wakon-yosai* formula, the first component of which stands for 'Japanese spirit' or 'spirit of Yamato' and the second one for 'western science and technology.' The notion of 'Japanese spirit,' however, became the principal goal with the idea of western technology, which had just started reaching Japan, becoming subordinate to this objective but also a way of reinforcing it. 'Japanese spirit' is a very broad notion. The ideologists of the ruling élite interpreted it as a world outlook (*Weltanschauung*), largely religious in character, relying on a mythological base. Besides, it covered political, moral and ethical dogmata, mostly echoing Confucianism. 'Japanese spirit,' therefore, readily penetrated all these categories and laid the foundation of the ideology of Japanism.

As a result of the support given by the ruling circles, the initial formula of the ideological structure of Japanese nationalism *wakon-yosai* (i.e. one which upheld the priority of traditional spiritual values against the background of spreading western science and technology), was retained and even strengthened at the turn of the twentieth century. The Meiji government managed to preserve various national, social, ideological and political institutions, which had evolved during the feudal period to suppress a mass democratic movement for 'freedom and popular rights,' and impose a barrier on progressive ideas. A dramatic turnover in the ideological policy of the Japanese state towards nationalism coincided with the transition of Japanese capitalism and imperialism. In foreign policy the new line of Japan's ruling élite climaxed in the Sino-Japanese war of 1894-5 and, particularly, in the Russo-Japanese war of 1904-5. Japan's victory in the 1904-5 war greatly contributed to the consolidation of nationalist ideas.

During the following years the ideological practices of the Japanese ruling class developed, mainly along already established lines. The 1920s and 30s, however, the period of preparing for, and unleashing, the Second World War, were particularly noted for the 'Japanese spirit' as the ideological backbone of the imperial régime. This 'spirit' was more than ever interpreted as a supreme manifestation of man's essence. In contrast to it, western civilisation was regarded as something second-rate, that was penetrated with 'rationalism' and 'materialism' and unworthy of imitation. At the same time, the idea of the uniqueness of Japan's state and political systems developed and nationalist intolerance for everything foreign took root. Japanese nationalism of that period took the form of racist chauvinism.

As for the attitude of the Japanese leadership towards western science and technology, the blame of western spiritual culture did not prevent Japanese zaibatsu from borrowing and using them in the interests of their economic strategy, aimed at war preparations. In other words, the interests of the Japanese bourgeoisie took the course of extreme nationalism and xenophobia. Nationalism, contrasted to western industrialism, was just an ideological instrument used to draw Japanese public into the orbit of militarist ideological influence.

Social, political and ideological processes, which swept Japan after 1945, greatly altered both the ideological situation in the country and nationalism's inner structure. The defeat of Japanese militarism in the Second World War torpedoed the ideological doctrines, relying on primacy of 'Japanese spirit.' Progressive spiritual values acquired greater importance in the country. Democratic ideas became widespread; internationalist ideology took root. Its champions sought to adapt to the Japanese soil universal elements of western culture. In the post-war years Japan saw, actually for the first time in her history, the formation of an ideological counter-structure which successfully opposed itself to the nationalist system of Japanism. The teaching of Marxism-Leninism has always been a major element of this counter-structure. All this weakened the ideological basis of nationalism.

But this situation did not last long. With the restored positions of Japanese monopolies and the accelerated economic advance of the country which by mid-60s had reached the level of industrialised western states, nationalist views enjoyed a period of renaissance. The correlation of elements and the very content of the traditional wakon-yosai ideological formula started changing.

In the context of drastically weakened traditionalist conservative spiritual systems the leadership followed several lines trying to consolidate the ideological basis of the existing political régime. On the one hand, it resorted to building up the significance of the old political and ideological institutions which had to a great extent lost their influence on mass-consciousness due to post-war democratic transformation. This trend revealed itself, in particular, in revitalising the emperor cult and the entire system of rituals and ceremonies connected with his worship. In other words, the ruling circles attempted to revive under new conditions ideological phenomena, some of which had been part and parcel of the 'Japanese spirit.'

But this ideological process did not amount to the simple reproduction of the old as under altered historical conditions the ideological functions of these phenomena acquired a different shade. Whereas the establishment had earlier raised them, despite their mythological origin, to the level of a world outlook, against the new background the rôle of the doctrines was played down: after the unmasking of the true content of the ideological concepts that had underpinned the imperial system they could no longer lay claim to performing in full measure their old functions. They were regarded as moral and ethical notions and national symbols designed mostly to affect man's emotions.

On the other hand, the Japanese leadership started adapting pre-war socio-political concepts to the new situation, claiming that they were scientific and 'unbiased' in describing Japan's social structure and purposefully stressing its 'uniqueness' and 'inimitability.' To these concepts belonged *inter alia* the 'theory of Japanese culture,' the 'theory of the Japanese essence' and similar theories. These processes parallelled development of some other phenomena which were even more important for their insights into the changes in the structure of nationalist ideology in the 60s and 70s.

The ruling élite decided to ideologise Japan's economic, scientific and technical strides. The category of 'western technology,' *yosai*, was contrasted with that of 'Japanese technology,' *wasai*. This popular notion meant the entire complex of contributors to technical progress and economic advance of Japanese capitalism. Instead of being analysed within the framework of the general system of universal features inherent in economic activity, they were interpreted as unique, exclusively Japanese principles of social relations, labour organisation and management of enterprises. A big propaganda build-up was given to the idea that exclusiveness of the Japanese nation and the very 'Japanese spirit' were manifest in Japan's technical and economic achievements rather than in its spiritual qualities. By analogy with the *wakon-yosai* formula ('Japanese spirit — western technology'), Japan's ideology started practising the formula *wakon-wasai* ('Japanese spirit — Japanese technology').

Ideological practices of American propaganda contributed to the growth and dissemination of new nationalist ideas in Japan. Washington chose the dual tactics of ideological pressure on Japan. On the one hand, the USA built up its direct ideological penetration into all spheres of social life. Some American theorists even tried to suggest historically the inevitable americanisation of Japan, arguing that it will 'do Japan a world of good' to assimilate the American way of life and American methods of economic management. All this gave birth to the feeling in the Japanese mass consciousness that it was necessary to beat off the increased American ideological pressure. This growing feeling, concentrated on the past and reviving reactionary traditionalist outlook, took the form of protest against the adverse effects of western-style industrialisation.

Such ideological processes, going on in Japan, made the United States complement the tactics of Japan's open americanisation with the ideological line oriented towards backing up the established trend to revive traditional Japanese institutions and, actually, encouraging nationalist ideas. The so-called theory of Japan's 'modernisation,' worked out by American ideologists at the beginning of 1960s on the basis of technological and economic strides of Japanese capitalism was meant to meet these at first sight incompatible, but actually closely interrelated, targets.

This theory distorted the true essence of socio-economic processes developed in Japan, and failed to identify the real source of its rapid socio-economic growth. It masked the genuine character of its industrialisation and concentrated on praising Japanese capitalism for its 'ability' to adapt itself to the needs of industrial development. Some authors of this theory started setting Japan as a model for all Asian countries and connected its advance with the future of humanity.

However, the 'modernisation theory', relying on distorted facts from Japanese history, fully met the interests of its ruling circles. Japanese leadership started crying from the house-tops that western-style modernisation 'was doing the country a world of good.' But the actual situation, and especially the socio-economic conditions resulting from the end of the next stage of industrial development in the 1960s, was far from the cheerful picture painted by official propaganda and the American authors of the 'modernisation theory.' The social effects of rapid economic development turned out to be destructive for Japanese society. Modernisation was accompanied by the transformation of many aspects of Japan's public and social systems. The unlimited use of scientific and technological breakthroughs stepped up the urbanisation process and aggravated ecological problems. Simultaneously, urbanisation affected the nature of public consciousness, encouraging growth of consumers' psychology and accumulating anti-humanistic features in the system of public relations. The country saw discontent with the established situation and a broader movement of protest against the policy of rapid economic growth pursued by the government.

Against this background the Japanese ruling class had to resort to ideological manoeuvres. Its ideologists admitted the adverse effects of modernisation. This confession relied on opposing the western development pattern to the Japanese national system or social relations and production organisation. Thus, Japanese nationalism acknowledged the formula *wakon-wasai* (Japanese spirit — Japanese technology). This is proved by the ideological doctrine, formulated some years ago by the Japanese government. In 1979 a special Committee for Studying Policy was set up under the Ohira cabinet. In 1980 the Committee published a number of reports, approved by the cabinet, which advanced a complex of measures to be taken in response to socio-economic and ideological processes entailing accelerated economic growth.

This doctrine is characterised by the following features:

1) Its initial ideological premise is deeper criticism of the western-style modernisation process; it notes the appearance of 'many difficult problems'

171

in industrial societies that 'have reached a high level of development' *inter alia* in Japan.

2) The adverse effects of the modernisation process in Japan are put down to specific social forms and methods of production organisation that came to Japan from the West rather than for structural reasons. The authors of the doctrine try to prove that the western origin of industrial relations adopted in Japan are the source of the difficulties accompanying industrialisation.

3) The doctrine proclaims Japanese national institutions and traditionalist behavourist motives as an alternative to western social forms and spiritual values, established in the country in the process of modernisation. It particularly stresses their specifics and uniqueness.

4) To prove this 'uniqueness' its authors use both traditional ideological and philosophical categories and comparatively new concepts which take in notions and ideas largely identical to those of the pre-war sociological concepts. They were best expressed in the 'theory of the essence of Japanese culture' which is the ideological foundation of the entire doctrine.

In contrast to the western-style modernisation epoch, the doctrine proclaims the advent of Japan's 'epoch of culture.' Its authors assert that it will be noted for the birth of a society embodying the Japanese national ideal of social relations which differs in principle from the western one and will render it possible to overcome drawbacks inherent in European and American capitalism. The new doctrine of the Japanese ruling class advances a large-scale programme of socio-economic and political measures, relying on Japanese-style economic and social practices, as an alternative to the modernisation process based on the American development pattern with its adverse effects on Japanese society.

Thus, the transformation of Japanese nationalism means, besides restoring categories and notions of the pre-war period, imparting to it some new elements, contributing to the use of Japan's rapid economic advance to meet ideological objectives. The ideological formula of the pre-war Japanese bourgeois nationalism made up of *wakon-yosai* (Japanese spirit — western technology) is now being replaced by a modern formula of nationalist ideology, expressed in *wakon-wasai* (Japanese spirit — Japanese technology.) The Japanese ruling class had gone so far in advocating this nationalist thesis that its propaganda is ever more clearly noted by an attempt to proclaim the Japanese model of industrialisation, allegedly capable of improving the entire western society, and to replace the European and American model by it.

As if developing and deepening this notion of Japanese leadership which is a challenge to European and American types of capitalism, the cultural fund of the Suntory Company held an international symposium in Osaka with the theme of 'Will Japan become a model for the world?' The very title of the symposium eloquently proves what ideas are now hovering in the heads of the rulers of this oriental country longing for the leadership of the western world. The symposium demonstrated the greater ambitions of the Japanese ruling élite to become the technological leaders in the capitalist camp. Actually, all the Japanese participants at the symposium openly said that the Japanese type of industrialisation could, and should, become an alternative to its western model. It was even stressed that 'Japan was truer to modernisation principles than the West,' that it 'had overturned the usual ideas of modern economics of the conditions, necessary for successful completion of the modernisation process' and it 'had latent energy to become the model for world development,' etc.[1]

It has been noted above that the 'theory of Japanese modernisation' was an important ideological stimulus, contributing to the growth of Japanese nationalism in the 1960s. Some western theorists even now stick to propaganda and the use of experience, accumulated by Japanese monopolies in the socio-economic field, including the idea of a Japanese modernisation model.[2] But their ideology plays into the hands of Japanese nationalists. Nationalism of the Japanese ruling class which is even more refined now and which is backed up by Japan's economic strides grows in momentum. Accompanied by the militarisation of the country, it has become a factor, destabilising the international situation in the Asian and Pacific region. Experience proves that nationalism has always promoted the unleashing of wars, has been a powerful instrument of population indoctrination with ideas of hatred and disdain for other nations.

Today, in the context of the increased danger of greater destructive rôle of negative factors in international relations, capable of torpedoing the very basis of man's existence, our most pressing objective is to counteract any tendencies which promote weakening of relations in the world community instead of their strengthening. We believe that scholars of the world should objectively analyse processes, developing in Japan inter alia in the domain of social relations and should give an unbiassed assessment of her economic achievements. Progressive Japanese scholars have made a tangible contribution to the research on problems entailing Japan's rapid economic growth. Their scientific and public work has promoted the identification of the negative effects of strengthened nationalist tendencies in the country. This trend in their scientific work should, without fail, be backed up by scholars, specialising in Japanese studies, from all over the world. It should be supported by all those who are genuinely interested in making Japan play an ever more constructive rôle in world affairs as a peace-loving democratic state which has critically reviewed the experience of its pre-war policies when nationalism and militarism laid the foundation of its state ideology.

29

Research Problems Experienced by a Foreigner in Japan While Using Macro-Sociological Research Data Collection Techniques

V. SAUNDERS

This paper is essentially an anthropological one, based on observations made while collecting data for a macro-sociological study of Japan's social stratification system. The study itself is in part an empirical study of some of Nakane's theories[1] on Japanese society but worded to fit into a sociological framework and using research methodology similar to a study done by Laumann[2] in 1966 on the American social stratification system. Data was collected by the use of a questionnaire survey from a representative sample of urban Japanese employees, according to gender, industry, age and occupation, from people living in Kanagawa prefecture in 1985.

As I was compiling my questionnaire and later interviewing people, I recorded incidents which happened as well as impressions as they, too, seemed to me to be rather enlightening as regards the structure of Japanese society. Some such incidents seemed to clarify matters which had not been empirically investigated previously, or they supported or refuted already published literature. Moreover, some helped me to understand why certain problems arose or existed as I was trying to collect data.

I suppose there are always going to be some research problems in a cross-cultural setting no matter how detailed the enquiry, or how experienced the researcher. However, to someone who was not only doing proper fieldwork for the first time, but who opted to use a method previously undocumented by foreign researchers in Japan, the initial problems were many. Gradually, with experience, many problems were deleted. They arose in part because such matters had not been documented previously, but also because there are misconceptions which some western social scientists have about what is happening in Japan today, particularly in regard to literacy and education. For example, on 12 February 1985, I attended a lecture[3] in a series organised by the College Women's Association of Japan, at which Professor James Abbeglen was speaking. During the course of the lecture not only did Abbeglen give testament to the notion of a very high literacy rate in Japan, but also to the notion that the Japanese have an average IQ of 111 compared with the average European and American IQ of 100. This seems to have been a comment made as the result of a 1982 study done by a non-Japanese psychologist. Again there is Vogel's book which describes Japan as number one.[4] These are but two examples of some current but unrealistic attitudes of western academics.

The Japanese government also helps to perpetuate the myth of a very high literacy rate by publishing misleading data. Thus, the current view in the West is that Japan has a literacy rate of something like 95%. What does not seem to be realised is that this much-touted figure is in fact a statistic about the number of students who enrol in schools each year. Hence, it is not a statistic about literacy at all since many students do not turn up to school, and there is no guarantee that those students who actually remain in the classroom are going to learn anyway. At the moment, therefore, there appears to be no statistic available which is based on actual measurement of literacy in Japan. Moreover, the Japanese government touts this statistic rather more for the benefit of the Japanese themselves than to mislead foreigners.

Consequently, I believe that the Japanese can be masters of deception when it pleases them to be so, and that reality in Japan is often quite different from what many westerners and Japanese believe. This is an opinion shared by Sugimoto and Mouer[5] and expressed in an article called *Japanese Society: Stereotypes and Reality*, where they state: 'the view of Japanese society as an integrated whole tends to serve the interests of the ruling class. A climate favourable to the governing elements in Japan is fostered both by (1) the general impression that there is little conflict among the various groupings comprising Japanese society or that everyone in Japan is living in a harmonious state of prosperity and (2) by the way in which paradoxes are explained as part of an exotic culture alien to the rest of the world.' I will return later in this paper to the point that this deception is geared towards the lower class Japanese in particular as much as it is towards foreigners.

This problem appears to be fuelled by western gullibility. I would have thought that, in reference to IQ tests in particular, past experience among social psychologists and anthropologists researching race relations in particular ought to indicate clearly that claims of either superiority or inferiority on the basis of national groups are of rather dubious reliability. In the past such claims have eventually proven to be measuring various aspects of social phenomena rather than general intelligence.[6]

I began to complete the final draft of my questionnaire after I arrived in Japan and discovered that in all the published questionnaires used by Japanese academics which I had read,[7] *keigo* (honorifics) had been extensively used. I had, however, used none so I began to incorporate honorifics into the questonnaire. During this period I encountered the verb *nasaru* (to do) for the first time. As I lived far from Tokyo and wanted instant assistance, I went next door to enquire of a Japanese neighbour how to use this verb. This visit was to prove rather educational. My neighbour, Mr Takahashi, was a businessman in his mid-40s and a university graduate. I assumed, therefore, that he ought to be familiar with honorific use. Mr Takahashi did not mind assisting, but assumed a very firm attitude with the foreign female. He told me in Japanese (but

175

drawing a diagram in his notebook and using English written words in order that no misunderstanding could occur) that *nasaru* was used only to indicate the future tense of the verb *suru* (to do). *Suru* was only used to indicate present and past actions. *Nasaru* was not an honorific verb at all as the foreigner had mistakenly thought. I was told this kindly but rather firmly and authoritatively. After all he implied, he was Japanese and he knew his own language far better than any foreigner. A few days later, I came across the verb *nasaru* in another questionnaire and it was obvious from the context that *nasaru* is indeed an honorific verb and only an honorific verb. It is not indicative of tense at all and is used in exactly the same way as *suru*. Mr Takahashi was incorrect in his assumptions about the use of *nasaru*. It then occurred to me that, if such a 'middle class' man as Mr Takahashi was not familiar with the honorific system, how many Japanese who were less educated than he do not use, cannot use and do not understand highly honorific language. In other words, the extensive use of honorifics in a questionnaire in Japanese would in all probability reduce the reliability of that questionnaire. Hence the reliability of questionnaires which have used honorifics must be questioned.

That many Japanese do not understand and do not use honorifics was borne out by my experiences later with blue-collar workers in particular, especially among the groups of bus drivers and the groups of skilled and semi-skilled workers employed in a car manufacturing factory. Although I had gone through and deleted many of the honorifics from the questionnaire, it was left in the neutral polite form, that is the -*masu* verb ending form. However, many men appeared to have difficulty in understanding the questionnaire and my Japanese. It appeared that roughly one third could not understand. This problem disappeared immediately I changed to the use of plain forms of speech. I also noticed that among themselves these men only used plain speech, and I can only conclude from my experiences among them that many Japanese blue-collar workers do not understand even so-called 'neutral' polite forms of the language, let alone highly honorific speech.

Another incident occurred with which I was inadvertently involved. One afternoon I attended a Japanese family birthday party. Gathered in the small kitchen-dining room of a friend's home was a group of Japanese women plus myself. These women consisted of the hostess, Iuko, Iuko's two elder sisters-in-law, and four of Iuko's friends. We all had children at the party. The oldest woman in the group, Mitsuu, also had the highest status among the Japanese women as her husband was a diplomat. Moreover, Iuko and her four friends were about ten years younger than Mitsuu, so on two counts, that of seniority and that of her husband's occupation, she was accorded highest status in the group.

It was the first time I had seen Mitsuu with such a group of women although I have known her for many years. At first, her use of language had me puzzled, until I suddenly realised what was happening. When she spoke to her younger sister, Ritsuko, and myself, she used plain forms of speech — that is speech totally devoid of honorifics and language which is theoretically reserved for family members, close friends or when an adult is speaking to a child. When she spoke to any of the four younger women, she, quite dramatically it seemed to me, changed her pattern of speech. She used extremely honorific language, which, I had always been told in language classes, is used to elevate the status of the listener. Thus Mitsuu used *gozonji* (to show), *irassharu* (to come, go, exist), *nasaru* (to do), and *gozaru* (to have), plus the two honorific prefixes *o* and *go*. In reference to herself she used *itadaku* (to receive humbly), and *morau* (to receive honorably) in reference to the younger women and their families. Again she used *ageru* (to give honorably) in reference to the other women.

Theoretically, all this ought to have placed Mitsuu's status as being lower than that of the other women, and with Mitsuu's sister, Ritsuko, and myself as having even lower status still. However, in actual practice, the effect was the opposite. The four women appeared cowed by Mitsuu's language. Their body language clearly indicated that Mitsuu's status was decidedly higher than their own. Moreover, Mitsuu's body language also indicated in a pleasant, albeit firm, manner that she had highest status of all the Japanese women present. The use of plain language to younger sister, sister-in-law and myself was in order to define a group boundary, that of the family (I am generally regarded as Mitsuu's fictive younger sister). In this particular situation the use of highly honorific language, which theoretically ought to have lowered Mitsuu's status, was actually used to maintain social distance. Moreover, it was quite clear that the extensive use of honorifics served as a *status reducing* phenomenon from the point of view of the visitors. They, too, used *keigo* in response to Mitsuu's example, but among themselves, they used neutral polite forms of speech, and reserved *keigo* for addressing Mitsuu. Again, in language classes in the past, I have been told that honorifics ideally promote individual humility. However, in the incident related, status was clearly raised by the use of honorifics. It was used to make a listener feel outside a group, thereby maintaining social distance, and instead emphasising the speaker's higher status.

A second incident occurred which appears to corroborate my hypothesis that *keigo* can be used to maintain social distance. One day, I went to the city library to obtain some statistics. As usual, I presented my *meishi* (business card) to the first person I met inside the door. He passed it on to his superior officer who came to assist. This person began speaking using highly honorific language, but obviously leaving it to me as the person with the higher status to select the level of honorifics to be used. I made it clear to him that I understood what he had said, including his choice of honorifics, but chose to use neutral polite language and get down to business. He responded in kind, dropping the honorifics and also using neutral polite language and got on with the business concerned. At first, I wondered what effect such a stance on my part would have. Would I be considered to be lowering my status, I wondered, to the extent that it would invite disrespect in particular. But in this instance, the opposite effect was obtained. It appeared to make for an easier working relationship. If anything, the civil servant concerned became more cooperative and positive in his efforts to find the requested information. This appears to confirm my hypothesis that honorifics are often used by people of higher status to maintain their status and thus to maintain the *status quo* currently in existence in Japan. Moreover, it seems to me that what is often taught in language classes, in English-speaking countries at least, is, in fact, 'middle class' Japanese or language used by high-status, well-educated people. If one is going to do research among blue-collar workers, in order to understand and be understood, it is necessary to be able to use very plain speech totally devoid of honorifics. It appears, therefore, that only by using such speech will a researcher be able to gain the confidence of many working-class people and thus obtain information about what is genuinely the case as distinct from what some Japanese would like foreigners to believe is the case. In addition, there is more than likely a relationship between social class and language. However, there has been no research done on this topic as far as I can determine. It is therefore apparent that there is a great need for socio-linguistic research on the relationship between language and social class in Japan.

A further problem relating to language existed as I found when I began using the questionnaire, but whether it is a cultural difference or indicative of the level of education, it is difficult to tell precisely and is possibly some of both. The final draft of the questionnaire was corrected by a native speaker of Japanese, a woman in her mid-50s and an experienced teacher at a language school. She informed me that, in her opinion, all the language in use in the questionnaire with the exception of one word on the final page, ought to be understood by everybody who was at least a high-school graduate. However, even with this word, the context ought to make the meaning clear. Nonetheless, I found that this was an optimistic view of either general knowledge of Japanese or level of education. There were several words in the questionnaire which were not understood by the majority of people who completed it. Such words as *oshutosan* (father-in-law), *kanrinin* (administrator), *sedai* (generation), *hikoshiki* (informal), *jotai* (attitudes) and *kachi* (values) are some of the vocabulary which proved difficult. As a result of comments made by a group of civil servants, I developed a standard set of oral instructions to go with the questionnaire. It became standard practice in each interview to provide a definition for each of these words which had proved to be a problem in the initial or two subsequent interviews, one with a group of planners in a construction company, and one with a group of sales-people in a department store.

I must confess to being rather surprised at the general ignorance of what seemed to me to be elementary vocabulary, by people who were university graduates. In spite of Japan's 'examination hell' there appear to be many people who graduate from university with a level of competence in their own language which leaves much to be desired. Although over 40% of the population these days enter some form of tertiary education, my observation of many university graduates leads me to query the standards of university education in particular. I heard one comment by a man in his mid-30s that he graduated in 'cross country skiing.' Although the remark was a facetious one, the implication behind the remark was that he spent as much time doing cross country skiing as he did serious academic work. I have also heard remarks made about two-year university graduates not having the time to attend classes in the first year because they are so busy becoming used to university life and joining clubs. Nor do they have much time in the second year because they are too busy preparing for graduation and employment. Although these comments are anecdotal, there are Japanese academics also who have been critical of the education system. One example of such an academic is Morishima,[8] who has this to say:

'At the undergraduate level the lower level graduates of the national universities are probably worse in quality than British graduates, but it may be said that overall the quality of Japanese national university graduates is not substantially lower than that of British graduates. The quality of private universities, however, is inordinately difficult to assess. The top level private universities have many students comparable to those in top national universities but there are some utterly irresponsible private universities. Moreover, it is extraordinarily easy to graduate at Japanese universities. I don't know whether the average quality of undergraduates at private universities is comparable to that of British students who have received an HND or far lower. Likewise, there is also no way of knowing whether the quality of junior colleges and technical school graduates can be equated to that of recipients of the ordinary national diploma.'

Unfortunately, my questionnaire did not distinguish between different types of tertiary education, so I cannot say whether the respondents were from national or private universities or both.

Morishima's statements are substantiated by Sodei,[9] who is currently a professor at Ochanomizu Women's University in Tokyo. Sodei spoke at another lecture on 18 February 1985 on the topic of women in Japan. During the course of the lecture, Sodei recounted how last year she was voted the most severe professor on campus. It seems that the basis for this value judgement was that she expected her students to work for their grades, an expectation not shared by her male colleagues who had the habit of giving all women students 'A' passes, regardless of what academic standard each might have achieved. Apparently the rationale behind this grade allocation was that women will leave and marry. If they have 'A' passes, it will help them to get better husbands. Although this situation occurred in a women's university, it seems to me to be indicative to a certain extent of more general attitudes towards education in Japan, particularly at tertiary level, where it appears that not a great deal is expected of students in the way of work, as Morishima has also recounted.

My comments have been largely geared to university graduates due to the fact that I went to Japan expecting university graduates to behave like British or Australian university graduates in terms of education and literacy, but found that this was an unreal expectation. Moreover, I expected most Japanese people to have a higher literacy rate than it has become apparent that they have. It seems, however, that it is likely that many Japanese people themselves in higher socio-economic groups have little idea of what the level of literacy and education is like for those lower down the socio-economic scale. In addition, there is probably a difference between what happens in Tokyo, which is the largest urban area in Japan and no doubt the most sophisticated and cosmopolitan area, and what happens in the rest of Japan. This was one of the reasons why I chose to do research outside the Tokyo area, as I am of the opinion that what happens in Tokyo is most likely not a representative sample of what happens elsewhere. But much sociological research in the past has been done in the Tokyo area, and this could be one of the reasons behind some western academics having such an optimistic view of the level of education in Japan.

In addition to language and literacy problems, there were several cultural phenomena which caused concern. One cultural factor in particular which I found influencing the responses of some people was that of *amae*[16] (dependency). It appeared that the further down the socio-economic scale one went, the more likely it was that one encountered dependency. Thus there was no apparent evidence of dependency among the group of civil servants, or a group of scientists employed in a research institute attached to a vegetable oil company.

The lowest socio-economic group which I interviewed and the one in which *amae* was quite apparent was in a group of foremen employed by a construction company. I interviewed these men in a building on a construction site north of the city. It was the most unsuccessful of all interviews attempted. The company had been founded by the current owner's father and was run by his younger brother who was also company president. I was taken by car to the site in the evening after work, and the interview was done prior to a foreman's meeting. The men arrived sporadically, and the president handed around the questionnaires. I began my usual spiel, pausing after each question for feedback and, as usual, asking *wakarimasuka* (do you understand), to which there was never any reply, unlike in other groups I had interviewed. I suspected they did not, but the president replied *wakata yo* (understood, emphatic). As the president was quite emphatic, I could but continue to the end to avoid loss of face on his part.

After the theoretical completion of the questionnaire and before the formal meeting began, I circulated among the men, relating to them on a one-to-one basis. I found that, under such circumstances, they were prepared to ask questions. The results were even worse than I had anticipated. Some had not even started the questionnaire, and needed advice as to how to put a ring around each answer before they would even start. They needed to ask questions about the most minute detail before they had the courage to record an answer. I repeated to each individual as I thought necessary information which I had already imparted to the group as a whole. I read over people's shoulders and pointed out omissions in information as they went. I spent considerable time during the foreman's meeting further assisting those who requested it before collecting the responses. However, as I read the responses during the remainder of the meeting, it was obvious that they would not do. There was too much information omitted in spite of the personalised attention. In particular, detailed information about occupation which was essential to the success of the research was omitted. Where I had requested information about occupation often there was the reply 'construction industry,' in spite of the fact that there were other questions about industry too, or it was simply left blank. I ended by discarding nine of the ten completed questionnaires. Ironically, the only one which I kept was that of the president — he was the only one who had understood how to complete the questionnaire.

In addition, the style of relationships in this company was moulded on the old patron — client system. The men gave unquestioning obedience in return for job security. Many were farmers for the warmer months of the year and construction workers for the rest of the year and hence were only temporarily employed, but on a permanent basis. The president informed me that most had never had another job. It was apparent that some were only semi-literate, but in the occupation of both farmer and construction worker literacy was not necessary.

A further cultural problem I discovered concerned a fear of foreigners. I believe that this was one of the reasons why I had problems with people in the retail trade and finance industries in particular. Amongst department stores a 70% refusal to cooperate rate was obtained. This compares with an overall cooperation rate of 60%. Only two department stores cooperated and one of those involved two months of negotiating and only on condition that I handed the questionnaire to the personnel manager who, in turn, would hand them out to employees for completion at home. This I was very reluctant to do as it would not permit feedback about any problems which might have been encountered. However, I eventually agreed and was able to collect the responses the day before I left the country. In a few companies I visited, although I was permitted to actually interview employees there was a manager present. Sometimes these managers interfered, more out of a desire to assist than to prevent the acquisition of information. However, once a manager interfered I felt that I was less likely to get genuine feedback from employees as they were far more in awe of officials than they were of me. It was always a relief when I was put in a room with a group of employees and left to myself to conduct the interview as I discovered that under such circumstances I was able to build a good rapport with people and obtain the feedback that I felt was so necessary. I was then able to determine for myself if there were any genuine problems in completing the questions amongst that particular occupational group and deal with anything that arose.

Some of the problems I encountered related to social change. For example, I discovered that the word *shinyu* (intimate friend) still appeared to have significance for older people and well educated younger people. However, for young blue-collar workers in particular, the word had little significance, and in fact some did not know its meaning. Thus, for lower socio-economic groups it became necessary to incorporate a definition of this word into my oral instructions. To many of these people there was no such person as an intimate friend. There were only one's colleagues at work and perhaps the occasional acquaintance in a bar. Most of these men lived in a dormitory, and this obviously had a restricting affect on social life. This was particularly so in view of the fact that the company has an enterprise union, so many do not even meet blue-collar workers from other companies.

In order to place these issues into perspective, I would like to relate them to an article written by Odaka[11] called 'The Middle Classes in Japan.' In this article Odaka discusses several issues, including among others, the superficial homogeneity of modern Japanese society and working-class

181

consciousness. He eventually concludes that people whose status is *lower* than middle class in Japan account for 60% of the population. He describes the two lowest classes as an 'intermediate stratum' and a 'lower class,' the intermediate stratum being 32% and the lower class accounting for 28% of the population. He draws a model picture of the Japanese class structure with the uppermost 3% forming a steeple and with the other four classes forming a base beneath this steeple.

Before going to Japan I had read Odaka's article with interest, thinking that the past twenty-five years must have seen improvements for those at the bottom of the stratification hierarchy in particular. However, after eight months in Japan, having visited twenty-nine different companies and organisations, and having personally interviewed over 200 people in a variety of industries and occupations ranging from the construction industry to government employees, from semi-skilled workers to top professional people, all of whom lived in an urban area located less than a hundred kilometres from Tokyo, the impression I am left with is that the picture for 1985 is that it is much the same as it was in 1960. That is, the situation of those at the bottom *vis à vis* the rest of society has not improved.

The more I see of Japanese society, in fact, the more I cannot help but agree with people such as Steven, 1983,[12] and Ohashi, 1971,[13] that in Japan there is an élite class, the members of which have a vested interest in maintaining their own status at the top of the stratification system. It is maintained at the expense of those at the bottom of the scale whose relative buying power is increasing little if at all, and whose real political and economic power is far more limited than among their western counterparts. Regrettably however, it seems that those at the bottom are oblivious to what is going on. They appear to be cossetted in some ways by the all-embracing life-style of the large company so that they are lulled into a false sense of security. It appears to me that by complying with petty demands of employees, managerial personnel cause blue-collar workers in particular to become passive servants of society. Most workers appear not to be aware of their own frustrations. After work men 'play' while drinking alcohol in various forms. It seems to be that in this way they drown their feelings and frustrations, and their level of social consciousness is thus made to remain low. Such people are then oblivious to the fact that they are being exploited and repressed. Moreover, by continuing to have enterprise unions and by continuously voting the Liberal Democratic Party (which is, in fact, a conservative party) back into power, they are upholding the *status quo* which involves their own continued repression.

Having been so critical, nonetheless I cannot go as far as Steven who believes there is a crisis in Japanese society. I have seen nothing at all to indicate that a crisis exists and suggest that the workers at the bottom of the hierarchy are unaware of their plight. Today they have a basic education, food, housing and clothing. Unemployment is only 2.4%. Standards are higher than they have ever been in Japan's long history, even if some of the houses are made of corrugated iron and some people can only read a few of the 1800 essential Chinese ideographs, and can only

182

afford to eat chicken but not beef. This is still more than their forebears had. Having never had more personal freedom or a higher standard of housing and education, and having an inward-turning disposition, the Japanese worker of today is not aware of what he is missing. No doubt this situation will continue until the Japanese worker begins to look outward, to take advantage of his compulsory education and to learn about other societies. Until he does so, it is to be doubted that there will be any awareness that his lot in life is less than in other parts of the developed world. And it is even more doubtful that those at the top of the hierarchy are going to inform him.

CEWJ—M

SECTION 3:
Theatre
Music
The Arts

30

Let's Dance a Dance — Song Texts for Basic Instruction in Shamisen Music

PETER ACKERMANN

If we glance through a history of *shamisen* music (the music for the three-stringed lute with a cat-skin body and struck with a large plectrum held in the right hand), we will find exhaustive reference to the great musical traditions of the *kabuki* theatre, or to the intricate art of accompanying the narrator in the puppet theatre, or to the elegant, lyric songs performed in the context of chamber music. However, hardly anything is said about the fact that, before the development of these great forms of art known as *nagauta, jōruri* and *jiuta*, the *shamisen* was used to accompany haphazard 'concoctions of primitive little verses;' as a rule, historical surveys make an effort to point out that it was not long before those somewhat crude early compositional attempts were replaced by proper pieces with sensible texts.

In this paper I want to focus precisely on these 'crude early compositional attempts' consisting of concoctions of all sorts of little verses sung to the tune of the *shamisen*. The Japanese term for these early pieces is *kumiuta*, 'songs consisting of assembled parts,' these being little poems and verses taken from many different sources. *Kumiuta* today are usually either despised for what is seen as their primitive textual structure or venerated like some mystical disclosure, performed as a rule only by one of the few still living Meiji-born artists.

Shamisen kumiuta are not primitive and later superseded experiments, but carefully structured works of art in their own right that form the very basis of *shamisen* music, the soil on which all later traditions grew and without which probably none of these traditions can be understood. I would go so far as to maintain that the *shamisen kumiuta* is the basis for practically all classical Japanese music composed since the beginning of the Edo period. Let me give the reasons for this contention. First, we must bear in mind that the *shamisen*, a small and easily transportable instrument introduced into Japan just before the Edo period, captured the fancy of the merchant class to such an extent that the laws of its melodies and rhythms permeated all aspects of the musical idiom of this most creative and artistically influential part of society. At the latest in the Genroku era (1688-1703), therefore, *shamisen* music can be called the incarnation of the Japanese musical spirit. Even when the *shamisen* in the nineteenth century began to lose its attraction and interest in other instruments increased, the musical idiom of Japan was so pervaded with

Within this thriving musical world, the *kumiuta* not only formed the starting-point and basis of *shamisen* art music, but also formed the core of the musical instruction of each new generation of professional blind musicians. In other words, *shamisen kumiuta* are model pieces and, it is only natural, therefore, to find the basic concepts of the *shamisen kumiuta* form incorporated in all other later *shamisen* music. Before going on to a concrete example of a *shamisen kumiuta*, let me add a few words concerning the link between the *shamisen kumiuta* and the professional blind musician who received his basic training through this art form. When the proto-*shamisen* was introduced into Japan from the Ryūkyū islands around 1562, it was a blind master in the city of Sakai near Osaka who transformed this Ryūkyū instrument by replacing its snakeskin body by one made of cat (or dog) skin. Furthermore, unlike its Ryūkyū predecessor which was plucked with a kind of nail, the *shamisen* strings were struck by a large plectrum, in other words, the *shamisen* came to be played in the same way as the lute *biwa*, the traditional instrument of the blind masters of old.

Ever since the fourteenth century, these blind *biwa* masters had formed organised groups and received systematic instruction in their art.[1] With the beginning of the Edo period, the organisation of blind musicians received official status, and at the same time the already strict conventions concerning the transmission of their musical art were further systematised. Particular importance was hereby attached to the certificates which permitted the novice to proceed from one degree of difficulty to the next. As, during the seventeenth century, attention shifted from the *biwa* to the *shamisen*, this system of instruction through an organised repertoire was adopted, and certificates were now also issued in the field of *shamisen* playing. In this way, the blind masters had a traditional and most effective tool to guarantee strict training in the 'secret of the strings,' a training that consisted of the study of basically 21 *shamisen kumiuta;*[2] and that was given both to prospective masters, and theatre musicians, as well as wandering minstrels and pleasure girls. Judging by the solemn faces we encounter nowadays during the performance of a *shamisen kumiuta*, one might think this type of art to be very ceremonial indeed. ... So let us consider a concrete example:

(One of the original 7 shamisen kumiuta, whose text appears for the first time in the song text collection '*Ōnusa*', 1685)[3].

Ukiyo-gumi

1.	tare mo ukiyo wa	for all of us this fleeting world
	kari no yado	is but a temporary abode —
	sanomi hitome o	why so avoid
	tsutsumumaji	being seen by others
	yoya kimi sharari	hey, don't linger!

2.	fumi mo yarumai	I'll no longer write you letters
	bingi mo semai	no longer send you word
	henji sae senu	not an answer do you give me
	usa tsurasa	[leaving me to] suffer pain —
	kimi o ba hito ni	I wish you once
	omowasete	fell in love:
	kahodo ni tsuraki mono zo to	[then] you'd know the pain one suffers,

186

onmoi omoi shirasede	[why] shouldn't I make you aware, aware —
to wa omoedomo	so I thought
mi no ue ni nareba	but as it's I [who love you]
sara ni omoi-kirarenu	to give you up would be unthinkable

3.
totemo tatsu na ni	rumours will spread anyway
nete gozare	so spend the night with me —
nezu tomo asu wa	no matter if you do or don't
neta to sandan sho	tomorrow 't will be said you did!
hana no odori o nō	hey! the dance of blossoms
hana no odori o	let's dance
hito-odori	the dance of blossoms

4.
ware wa kotsuzumi	the ko-tsuzumi[4] that's me
tono wa shirabe yo	my lord, he is the rope[5]!
kawa o hedatete nō	you cross the river, ho!
kawa o hedatete	you cross the river
ne ni gozaru	come to sleep with me —
hana no odori o nō	hey! the dance of blossoms
hana no odori o	let's dance
hito-odori	the dance of blossoms

5.
itoshi wakashu to	both charming young lads and
kotsuzumi wa	ko-tsuzumi drums,
shimetsu yurumetsu	by tightening and by loosening
shirabetsutsu	they are tuned —
ne-iranu saki ni	before they turn unusable
naru ka naranu ka	[I wonder] if they'll play or not
naru ka naranu ka	[I wonder] if they'll play or not

6.
mi-yama yarumai	you're not going [where you're out of reach], not to the mountains!
mi-yama-taki no mizu wa	the mountains' rushing waters
uchō tei tsuku	uchō tei tsuku[6]
chōdo uteba	firmly [the drums] are hit
uchō tei tsuku	uchō tei tsuku
tsukutsuku shin tan taratsuku	tsukutsuku shin tan taratsuku
chōdo utsu	firmly [the drums] are hit
wakashu-odori o nō	hey! the young lads' dance
wakashu-odori o	let's dance
hito-odori	the young lads' dance

The *ukiyo-gumi* is certainly not the sedate, solemn piece it appears to be nowadays on stage. But what about the reproach, levelled at *kumiuta*, that they are but a haphazard concoction of diverse and disparate poems and verses? Clearly, the *ukiyo-gumi* does not have a coherent text following an even and foreseeable course from beginning to end. It cannot be denied that there are abrupt jumps and leaps, and above all there is no topic holding the piece together as a whole. But if we look more closely, the jumps and leaps do not seem to be arbitrary. Thus the image of the dance in section 3 leads naturally to section 4 with its image of the most typical instrument for dance accompaniment, the small *tsuzumi* drum, while section 5 then appears as a conscious echo of the topic of section 4.

As to the overall structure, the *ukiyo-gumi*, like all other *kumiuta*, follows quite a clear pattern. Section 1 could be called an introduction; it is more or less impersonal in style and contains a reference to the *ukiyo*, undoubtedly, of course, the contemporary catch-word with double meaning, namely 'this miserable life' and 'the floating, transient world which we must enjoy.' (Incidentally, the title of the piece does not signify '*kumiuta* about *ukiyo*,' but '*kumiuta* that sets out with the image of *ukiyo*,' a *kumiuta* in principle taking its name from the first topic or image mentioned.) After the introduction, section 2 of the *ukiyo-gumi* can be understood as a kind of intensely emotional but on the surface subdued and somewhat dark beginning, in a way a picture of the *ukiyo* in the sense of 'wretched life.'

Sections 3 and 4 with their imperatives and their images of blossoms and music create an atmosphere of aimless play and increasing motion combined with increasing vivacity. Section 5 then, with its double meaning of *ne-iranu* and *naru* is a climax of emotion and playfulness (*ne-iranu* literally meaning both 'before the young lads lie down' and 'before the drums sound;' *naru* refers both to the drums and to making love, literally meaning both 'to sound' and 'to come to something, to succeed).' Section 6, finally, could perhaps be called a 'take-off' resulting from the continuous intensification of motion and emotion, a 'take-off' into a world beyond words, as it were. Beyond words lie the 'language' of musical instruments and the language of the body, in the first place dance.

All *shamiusen kumiuta* follow a structural pattern more or less similar to that of the *ukiyo-gumi*. However, each *kumiuta* draws on surprisingly different images. Space does not allow a discussion of this point, but suffice it to say that a study of all of the 21 basic *kumiuta* (most of them, like the *ukiyo-gumi*, consisting of 6 sections) would acquaint us with a large portion of the imagery that was to be used throughout the Edo period to depict frustration, resignation, determination, expectation, love, jealousy or joy, and to bring about the wish in a listener to move from the 'wretched' *ukiyo* to the 'transient *ukiyo*, which should be enjoyed.'

What can be said about the origin and background of *kumiuta* texts? Clearly, the *shamisen kumiuta* adhere to the norms of early and mid-seventeenth-century *odori-uta* (dance songs). In fact, many of *kumiuta* texts are (in part) identical with the texts of such dance songs; this may, for instance be seen if we compare them with the contents of song collections of the *onna kabuki* — the women's *kabuki* — of the 1630s. In women's *kabuki*, dance songs not only formed part of the entertainment programme of the various troupes of theatre artistes, but were quite clearly also meant to arouse the audience's interest in whatever the lady dancer might plan to do after the performance.

As mentioned, *shamisen kumiuta* texts are not coherent and are formed by combining small, pre-existing elements. Thus, our example *ukiyo-gumi* starts out in section 2 by picking up a little bit of text also found in the *onna kabuki odori-uta* (Dance songs for women's *kabuki*), published probably in the 1630s:[7]

fumi mo yarumai	I'll no longer write you letters
bingi mo shomai...	no longer send you word...

Incidentally, the text a few lines further on in this same *kabuki* dance song:-

naru to narazu to	will it come to something, come to nothing —
fumi o ba tsukuse	[no matter which, but] send a message!
kokoro-zuyo ya tsurena ya	you insensitive
	half-hearted [fellow]!
tonikaku ni	oh well,
ware wa kazu naranu	for nothing
mi ja hodo ni	do I count —
kimi ko ka	you plan to come? to come?
ko ka yuko ka	you plan to go?
kozuba mondoro yo	if you don't come then I return

finds its way into another *shamisen kumiuta* (the *koshi-gumi*), where it becomes section 4, the section marked by imperatives and often crude vivacity.

Section 3 of the *ukiyo-gumi* appears as a little poem in the song collection *Sōan kouta-shū*, published at the beginning of the seventeenth century:[8]

totemo tatsu na ni	rumours will spread anyway
nete oryare	so spend the night with me —
nezu tomo asu wa iyo	no matter if you do or don't, hey!
neta to sandan sho	tomorrow 't will be said you did!

Section 4 of the *ukiyo-gumi* is even more widespread and turns up in various documents — among others also in collections of country dance — since 1527:

mi wa kotsuzumi	the kotsuzumi drum that's me
kimi wa shirabe yo	[and you,] you are the rope!
kawa o hedatete	you cross the river,
ne ni oryare	come to sleep with me!

Section 5 of the *ukiyo-gumi*, finally, corresponds to a late Muromachi period dance song for *kyōgen* plays:[9]

itoshi wakashu to no	both charming young lads, yes,
kotsuzumi wa	and *ko-tsuzumi* drums,
shimetsu yurumetsu	by tightening and by loosening
shimetsu yurumetsu	by tightening and by loosening [they are tuned]
ne-iranu saki ni	before they turn unusable
naru ka naranu ka	[I wonder] if they'll play or not
chichi tappopoo popo	chichi tappopoo popo!
iya naru ka naranu ka	hey! [I wonder] if they'll play or not

The important point to be made is that, however heterogenous its elements may be, the *shamisen kumiuta* as a whole is not just one of many possible combinations of short verses and songs. In contrast to the texts for women's *kabuki*, for *kyōgen* or for country dance, the *shamisen kumiuta* is a carefully structured entity, made up of elements that have been selected and joined together for the purpose of being performed to the tune of the *shamisen* and in always exactly the same order. In other words, though we may find practically all the textual components of *shamisen kumiuta* in sixteenth and early seventeenth century song collections, once these components have been integrated into the *kumiuta*, they form an integral part of a fixed process of images corresponding to a fixed process of emotions. This process of emotions in turn corresponds to a carefully-structured musical line produced on the *shamisen*, an instrument which allows for far more sonorous and melodious differentiation than the flutes and drums used previously for the accompaniment of dance songs.

To conclude, let me give one further example to show originally loose elements being fixed within the strict overall structure of the *shamisen kumiuta*. In the comic *kyōgen* stage play *Utsubo-zaru* (known since about 1635) we witness a monkey dance performed to the singing of short songs. The sequence of short songs in the *kyōgen* play is (to a certain extent) variable, while also new elements can be introduced into the text, or existing ones eliminated. One of the possible forms that song and music of *Utsubo-zaru* can take while the monkey performs its pantomime and dance is as follows:[10]

asu wa jōzu mono	tomorrow it sets sail
fune ga jōzu mono	the boat sets sail —
omotage mo naku	you show no sign of loving me,
o-yoru tonogo yo	my sleeping lord!
o-yoru tonogo yo	my sleeping lord!

(then spoken text)

fune no naka ni wa	on the boat
nani to o-yoru zo	how do you spend your nights?
fune no naka ni wa	on the boat
nani to o-yoru zo	how do you spend your nights?

(spoken text, to the monkey)

tsūtto dete neyo neyo	come on, lie down! lie down!

(the monkey comes to the front of the stage and lies down)
(further spoken text)

toma o shikine no	a rush mat as a bed
kaji-makura	the oar as pillow .....
Hinda no Yokota no wakanae o	the seedlings in the rice-field at Hinda-Yokota

(spoken text)

shombori shombori ueta mono	I planted them alone, dispirited and forlorn

(spoken text)

ima kuru yome ga	the wife who now will come to me
karōzu yo no	yes, she'll reap the harvest
haradachi ya	maybe to your displeasure —
shikaku-bashira ya	four-cornered pillar!

190

kado-bashira	corner pillar —
kado no nai koso	someone who's not edgy, [who is yielding]
soi yokere	it is nice uniting with
soi yokere	it is nice uniting with
Hinda no odori wa	and so
kore made zo	the dance from Hinda goes
kore made zo	and so [the dance from Hinda goes]

A look at the *shamisen kumiuta* reveals the following: the element with the four-cornered pillar (C) is firmly integrated into one of the *kumiuta* (Hayafune) in what can be called position 3, the position of 'early stirrings of emotion and vivacity.' As for the verses *'asu wa jōzu mono...'* in the *kyōgen* play (marked A and B), they also find their way into a *kumiuta*, this time as the final climax of the *kumiuta Hinda-gumi:*

asu wa jozu mono	tomorrow it sets sail
fune ga jozu mono	the boat sets sail —
omotage mo na to	you show no sign of loving me,
aa o-yoru tonogo ya	my sleeping lord!
Hinda no odori o	let's dance
hito-odori	the dance from Hinda
hito-odori	let's dance [the dance from Hinda]

fune no naka ni wa	on the boat
nani to o-yoru zo	how do you spend your nights?
toma o shikine ni	a rush mat as a bed
kaji o makura ni	the oar as pillow —
Hinda no odori o	let's dance
hito-odori	the dance from Hinda
hito-odori	let's dance [the dance from Hinda]

Water — and by extension a boat and a car — are particularly sensual images. In this connection we may be reminded that it was to a very large extent the girls of the harbours — on rivers, lakes or at the sea shore — who forged that rich tradition of disarmingly plain and yet powerfully luring songs and dances that entertained the lonely traveller throughout Japan — and throughout a long period of Japanese history. The *shamisen kumiuta*, created towards the end of the seventeenth century, are at the same time the highest development as well as the end of this tradition of little songs and dances. The great pleasure-districts of the Edo period demanded more coherent and elaborate performances of the professional musician and dancer — yet they all evolved from the roots that were the original 21 *shamisen kumiuta* of the Genroku era.

31

Paradise at Kasuga

SUSAN C. TYLER

Kasuga Shrine was founded in the eighth century as the clan shrine of the Fujiwara. It is set against the hills to the east of the city of Nara. The most important feature of the landscape is Mikasa-yama, a small symmetrical hill immediately beyond the shrine. The Fujiwara clan temple was Kōfuku-ji, a short walk away. The shrine and temple are often shown together in paintings. As Buddhism spread in Japan, the Shinto deities were converted to the new religion along with the people and the two religions developed a symbiotic relationship. Shinto deities were seen as the particular Japanese manifestations of the eternal Buddhist deities. They protected Buddhism and received Buddhist offerings such as the reading of sutras. The deity of Kasuga received a bodhisattva title and, like many other Shinto deities, was called Daimyōjin.

I will discuss several paintings of Kasuga Shrine and its landscape and show in what way the shrine was a Pure Land. I will then discuss a painting of the deities of several Buddhist paradises and another painting which identifies Kasuga with Fudaraku, Kannon's mountain paradise. I will explain what Fudaraku meant to Gedatsu Shōnin (1155-1212), a Kōfuku-ji monk who was one of the most famous devotees of Kasuga.

As part of the very strong interest in the Buddhist paradises that developed in late Heian a number of Shinto shrines were rebuilt to suggest Pure Land temples, which in turn were modelled on Chinese palace architecture and on the palaces in paintings of Pure Lands.[1] Before these changes Kasuga may have looked like a *miya mandara* in the Nezu Museum. By the late twelfth century, Kasuga looked much as it does today. It had acquired delicate red-and-white and green-painted corridors and gates which surrounded or replaced the older Shinto fences and *torii*. These corridors and gates make the shrine look a little like the Byōdō-in, one of the few surviving Heian period Pure Land temples, or like a palace such as those shown in simpler Pure Land mandala. In literature and in art it is clear that Kasuga Shrine was in a general way paradise, and specifically the paradise of the Buddhist counterparts of the Shinto deities enshrined there.

In the conclusion of the *emaki Kasuga Gongen genki* (hereafter *Genki*) there is a passage which speaks of this quite clearly. It says:

'Since purity in accordance with the mind is itself the Pure Land, our own Kami are the Buddhas. How could the shrine not be the Pure Land? Thus Jōruri and Vulture Peak are there within the shrine fence. Why seek Fudaraku and Shōryōzan beyond the clouds? Surely that is why the venerable Myōe revered the Mountain as Vulture Peak, and why our Daimyōjin taught Lord Toshimori that it is the pathway to enlightenment.'[2]

If I had to define the goal of Shinto and of Buddhism in one word, I would have to say that the goal of Shinto is purity while the goal of Buddhism is enlightenment. The passage in the *Genki* makes it clear that these goals are one. Paintings of the landscape of the shrine show features which protect its purity and produce purity in the visitor. The journey to Kasuga shown in this painting begins at the first *torii*, which is the entrance to the area sacred to the shrine. Subsequent *torii* mark greater degrees of purity, if there is some accident, it is more serious the closer it is to the shrine. The many bridges crossing the path, covering the tiniest trickles of water or no water at all, are cleansing. The irregularities in the path keep evil influences out. These irregularities are most obvious close to the shrine. You must cross a bridge, go through a gate, around a fence, and over another bridge, not approaching the shrine directly. Even then you end up in between the shrines, not looking directly at any of them.

The passage from the conclusion to the *Genki* goes on to say that the mountain, Mikasa-yama, is the pathway to enlightenment. This has to do with one Toshimori whose story is told in Scroll 5 of the *Genki*. He had prospered because of his devotion to Kasuga. Once, when he came on a pilgrimage 'he reflected on the vanity of visiting the shrine in quest of wordly gain.' At this he heard a voice speaking from the shrine saying, 'The path of enlightenment is the path of my mountain.' Upon his death he achieved rebirth in paradise.

Enlightenment and purity, paradise and the shrine, Kasuga Daimyōjin and the Buddha are, in stories like this, brought into close touch with each other. Also, the rôle of Mikasa-yama is emphasised. In paintings the deities sometimes appear very close to the shrines, but often they appear hovering around the mountain.

There are several frankly Buddhist elements in Kasuga's landscape. There was at Kasuga a place called 'the six realms' at a bridge near the present 'Man'yō Garden,' and a 'hell' which may have been close to the main precinct in a ravine on the other side of the path. In the mountains behind Kasuga shrine there is a place that is still today called 'Hell Valley,' a name that is a reminder that the dead were once buried deep in the mountains here as they were behind other sacred mountains. There is disagreement whether it is the moon or sun which rises above Mikasa-yama but, if you take it as the moon, then the moon is the light of enlightenment. At the top of some paintings there is an invocation which tells of the creative mercy of Roshana in tempering his light and appearing to men as Kasuga-no-Daimyōjin.

The perceived geography of Kasuga, shown in part in paintings, is also interesting. A fourteenth-century painting in the Nōman-in of Hase-dera shows this geography most clearly, with a paradise above, the landscape of Kasuga below, and the hell that was below the plain suggested by Jizō's guiding a monk up from his shrine. This hell, rather like other hells, is illustrated in the *Genki*, Scroll 6. It was a private hell for devotees of Kasuga where they might count on special help if they had been serious in their devotion and where, even if they had been wicked, they might rely on the compassion of the Daimyōjin in finally attaining liberation. For monks there was a special low-grade paradise in the mountains just behind the shrine. Here they continued to study and debate as they had on earth, listening to the Daimyōjin preach until they achieved release.

The paradise in the upper part of the painting is curious. The passage in the *Genki* speaks of Vulture Peak, Shaka's paradise; Jōruri, Yakushi's paradise; and Fudaraku, Kannon's Paradise. Shōryōzan was another name for Wutai shan; and Wutai shan was the paradise of Monju. In the paradise shown in this painting the deities are arranged as they would be in a mandala of the five buddhas, but two of them are bodhisattvas. The centre figure, accompanied by Monju and Fugen, is Shaka; Jūichimen is in the upper left of the painting; and Miroku, shown as a bodhisattva, is on the upper right. Closer to us there are two buddhas, Yakushi and perhaps Amida. Jizō is shown raising a soul fo the paradise from the shrine below.[4]

Shaka is, along with Fukūkenjaku, the *honji butsu* of the first shrine; Miroku and Yakushi are both the second shrine; Jizō is the third shrine, Jūichimen is the fourth; and Monju is the most common *honji butsu* of the Wakamiya. Although Amida appears in only one other place as a *honji butsu* of the first shrine of Kasuga, he presides over the most famous of Pure Lands.[5]

Since Shaka is in the centre, the paradise should be Vulture Peak, the site of the preaching of the Lotus Sutra. The identification of the first shrine with the Shaka, rather than Fukūkenjaku Kannon, is attributed to Gedatsu Shōnin (also Jōkei). He and the Kegon monk, Myōe Shōnin (also Kōben), who lived from 1173 to 1232, are the two best-known devotees of Kasuga. Both men were visionaries and were eclectic in their beliefs, but both did see Kasuga as Shaka's paradise. Myōe particularly was known for his visions of Mikasa-yama as Vulture Peak. However, in this painting the presence of the other deities makes this identification difficult. It does not look like any other painting of Vulture Peak either. Instead, the painting looks almost like an illustration on the conclusion of the *Genki*. It declares that all the paradises of the *honji butsu* are available at Kasuga. The presence of Amida, which is unusual in art and literature concerned with Kasuga, is the strongest reason for understanding the painting to argue that all paradises are accessible through devotion to Kasuga. There is also a statement of rank made by putting Shaka in the centre and Miroku and Amida in subordinate positions, even though their paradises were more popular. This is in keeping with the single-minded concentration of Shaka in the *Genki*. By including the competition and placing even Amida in Kasuga's heaven, the impression is strengthened that Kasuga is a world all its own, looking only inward, complete with its hell, its earth, and a paradise so full that one need search no further.

While this painting shows a generalised paradise that might be simply called the Kasuga Pure Land, the *Kasuga Fudaraku-sen mandara,* a fourteenth-century painting owned by the Nezu Museum, shows Fudaraku floating above the actual landscape of Kasuga. This arrangement poses the problem of the identification of a particular landscape with a particular paradise.

Since early times Buddhist paradises have been established on actual mountains. Fudaraku has a geographical location and is supposed to be a place you can actually visit. Shaka's paradise is a mountain which can be found on a map, Vulture Peak in Rajgir. Monju's paradise was the Chinese mountain Wutai shan. These earthly paradises were established anew in the countries to which Buddhism travelled. Even more simply, in temples, the central world mountain was established in the platform on which the deities were placed, while Pure Lands and earthly paradises were also made, at times very elaborately.

Yet, the man was rare who climbed a sacred mountain such as Vulture Peak, understanding it fully as earth and paradise at once. The statement made by the mountain/paradise is one more phrasing of the statement that *samsara* and *nirvana* are equal: not a problem that has proved easy to solve. Placing the paradox in the landscape gives a physical urgency to its solution. If mountain and paradise are the same, why then am I not walking in paradise? Yet, even if they have climbed the mountain and seen nothing but mountain and the view from the top, people will continue to believe that Vulture Peak is Shaka's paradise.

Although Mikasa-yama was identified with Vulture Peak, Fudaraku was more important at Kasuga. The clearest expression of the significance of Fudaraku at Kasuga is found in the writings of Gedatsu Shōnin. Gedatsu is known for his identification of Shaka as the *honji butsu* of the first shrine, but this did not keep him from being an ardent believer in the presence of Kannon at the shrine. Although he was a scholar, he did not rely entirely on his scholarship, but was deeply devoted to Kasuga and to various Buddhist deities. Gedatsu wrote a refutation of the single practice of the *nembutsu* on behalf of the Nara Buddhist monks, but his own ideas partook of the same discouragement as Hōnen's over the capacity of men to work out their own salvation.[6] This perception led him to devotion to a different and more varied range of practices and deities than Hōnen espoused. In particular, it led him to devotion to Shaka (and Ryōjusen and relics), to Kannon (and Fudaraku) and to Kasuga Daimyōjin. His various devotions were not separate from his devotion to Kasuga. This is so much a foundation of his thinking that he seldom mentions it, yet it underlies many other statements. He was, after all, a Fujiwara and a Kōfuku-ji monk. When he does actually state his opinion of the relationship of his various devotions it is clear that he finds them essentially, and unnervingly, one devotion with several gates and several names.

In Gedatsu's early writings he spoke of his faith in many buddhas and bodhisattvas. If there was any concentration in this, it was an emphasis upon Shaka and Ryōjusen, and upon Miroku and the Tosotsu heaven. He seemed to desire most rebirth in the Tosotsu heaven. But Gedatsu was ill and growing older. His faith in his own ability grew less and Kannon came to occupy the central place in his devotion. In 1209 Gedatsu wrote, 'Fudaraku is in south India near the sea on the eastern edge of the Malaya mountains. It is roughly south-west from our country. It is in the same world as our own and there is no doubt that one of inferior capacity can be born into it.' He expressed a similar attitude towards Ryojusen as an earthly paradise.[7]

In a note written in 1201 Gedatsu told the story of one Gatō Shonin who longed for Fudaraku and often saw it in his dreams. In 1001 Gatō set sail with a disciple for Fudaraku. At this inspiring example, Gedatsu laments his own lack of faith. In fact he seems to have doubted that anyone really made it to paradise, even though birth in paradise was supposed to be the easiest path. People do not achieve rebirth, 'though this is not because the powers of the buddhas are weak, but because of their own insufficient faith.' He judges that the easiest practice is the oral *nembutsu*, and that the fastest way is the Amida *raigō*, but even this path, though it is supposed to be easy, is in fact difficult. He writes about going to Tosotsu and seeing Miroku, but says, 'I'm unripe and this birth is impossible for me. Let me be among men and serve near the Gongen [of Kasuga].'[8]

Though Hōnen and the other Pure Land devotees believed that Amida extended his grace to the most lowly, Gedatsu was not so sure. He felt that Amida would not save you if you were really bad, but that Kannon would, because Kannon in his mercy is kindest to people who've done a poor job in life. Although devotion in Kannon could lead you to any paradise you wished, if you failed to reach the one you wanted, you could still go to Fudaraku. The reason for Fudaraku's accessibility is that Fudaraku is on this earth and thus requires only the body, ability and aspirations of this earth. Because of Gedatsu's identification of Kannon with Kasuga Daimyōjin, which grew stronger late in his life, birth in the Daimyōjin's paradise was for him a humble form of birth in Fudaraku.[9] From Kaijūsen-ji, where he spent the last ten years of his life and where he died, Gedatsu could see Kasuga-yama. He, like many Fujiwara and as a devotee of Kasuga, paid devotion to Kasuga morning and night. In the year of his death he discoursed upon Fudaraku from his bed.[10]

In the Nezu *Kasuga Fudaraku-sen mandara*, Kasuga's landscape is painted in the lower part and above the landscape of Fudaraku floats. At the foot of the mountain there are buildings and people, and at the shore and a bit offshore there are boats. The sea figures in many Pure Land mandala as the separation between paradise and earth. In these paintings, too, though Amida's paradise is separated from earth by a great distance, the soul sometimes rides in a boat on its journey. The sea in Buddhist texts is a metaphor for the inconceivable crossing between practitioner and Buddha. As such, the stone boats and bottomless boats of the Zen monasteries make a half-humorous remark on both the difficulty of this crossing and the nature of this sea. The paradox expressed in the Nezu painting is not unlike that expressed by the stone boats of the Zen monasteries. There is no difference to be bridged between Buddha and monk or between Fudaraku and Kasuga. Yet in experience there is an inconceivable distance between them. Because both Fudaraku and Kasuga are of this earth the phrasing of the problem leaves the realm of ideas and takes on tangible strain.

The most important place associated with Fudaraku in Japan was Kumano and the Nachi waterfall. The waterfall and its shrine and temple complex are in the mountains a short distance from the sea. Nearer the sea shore there is a temple which marks the place from which small, round unsteerable boats are said to have set out for Fudaraku. It is easier in some ways to believe in a paradise that is impossible to visit except in visions, like Amida's Gokuraku. Nachi itself and Kasuga are both called Fudaraku. Why, then, does the devotee have to set off for Fudaraku in a boat or, in the case of Kasuga, wait for his death? Simply because everyone knows that in their normal, waking experience Kasuga Shrine and Nachi are not paradise. Fudaraku is a paradise that can be reached in the live, waking body, by a crossing over the sea, and Kasuga was a place Gedatsu could walk to, but he had stopped hoping to be enlightened and to really see Kasuga as Fudaraku before he died. The Nezu *Kasuga Fudaraku-sen mandara* is an exceptionally lovely image of the paradox that this world itself is paradise.

I have one last thing to mention about this painting. Both Fudaraku and Mikasa-yama are shown full of blossoming trees. Not only does this draw a link between them, it also reminds you that in paintings it is always spring at Kasuga. As a Pure Land, the shrine offers a glimpse of the original world when all was fresh, perfect and pure, when the gods stepped on the earth. If the shrine is the Pure Land and the path of enlightenment is the path of Mikasa-yama, paintings of the shrine, its deities and its landscape come to take on the meaning of Pure Land paintings, and even to explore enigmatic Buddhist truths.

32

On the Origin of *Wagaku* (Japanese Music) in the Heian Period

VLADISLAV SISSAOURI

The problem of the origin of *wagaku* (or *hōgaku,* 'Japanese music') created in the Heian period is one of the most difficult to solve. Mainly it is the problem of the origin of the Japaneswe scale-system. This paper limits itself to this particular question only.

There is no unanimous view on the problem of the Japanese scales' origin. Most scholars think that the system is indigenous and that it was fully formed before the seventh or eighth centuries, when continental music, *Gagaku,* was brought in. But Professor Tanabe Hisao suggested that the national musical mode is derivative and has roots in the Chinese one. He explained the formation of the Japanese mode in the following way. Two pentatonic modes were borrowed from China: the *ryo* (d-e-fis-a-b) and the *ritsu* (a-b-d-e-fis). In Japan the *ritsu* became very popular and was modified: in the descending direction the second and fourth grades became a semitone lower and in the ascending direction a semitone higher, which resulted in the formation of the Japanese national mode.[1]

Our analysis of the musical structures of the *Gagaku* and the *wagaku*[2] confirms that the national scale-system was foreign in character, but that the process of its formation differed from the one suggested by Professor Tanabe. The term *wagaku* indicates the indigenous origin of the music as opposed to the foreign *Gagaku*. The genres of the *wagaku* were vocal: *saibara, kagura, rōei, azuma-asobi* and some others. Their texts, as a rule, were based on ancient folk-lore.

In ancient Japan there were many rites and the definite poetical structure was formed. The rites were called *asobi*. The modern meaning of the word *asobi* is 'pastime, play, pleasure,' but in ancient times it meant 'ritual, ceremony.' The *Nihonshoki* (Chronicles of Japan) version of the myth of Ame no Wakahiko's death says: 'During eight days and eight nights they wept, cried, mourned and sang.'[3] In the *Kojiki* (Records of Ancient Matters) it is said: 'During eight days and eight nights they performed *asobi*,'[4] i.e. (funeral) ritual. The ancient word *uta*, usually translated as 'song,' meant a sort of poetical form consisting of five and seven syllable lines. It should be noted that modern scholars interpret the corresponding Chinese character in the *Nihonshoki's* version of Ame no Wakahiko's death not as 'sing,' but as *shinobu* (recall, remember). The ancient *uta* were inseparable from rituals and did not differ from prayers.

Some historical sources indicate that these ancient rites and songs had no musical characteristics (if we establish that music is based on a system of definite scales) and that the music of the *wagaku* in this sense, i.e. based on definite scales, was created only in the late Heian period. For example, the *Taigenshō* — compiled in 1511 by Toyohara Muneaki — cites the words of Fujiwara no Akinaka, minister for Shrine Affairs, who died in 1127: 'The ancient *kagura* had no musical modes. Recently a mode for the *kagura* music has been created in the capital. It was based on the *ichikotsuchō* and has been modified now.'[5]

This quotation is extremely important for our subject. It not only points to the late appearance of *kagura* music, but also to its foreign origin, since the *ichikotsuchō* was a mode of *Gagaku* music. This applies also to all other genres of *wagaku* music, since they are based on the same principles of musical organisation.

Besides, many historical sources (*Ryōjin hishō kuden, Sango yōroku, Jinchi yōroku, Kyōkunshō. Taigenshō* and others) state that the *saibara* pieces were sung on the melodies of the *tōgaku* and *komagaku* music, that is, on the melodies of the Chinese and Korean sections of the *Gagaku* repertoire. In his summary table Professor Hayashi Kenzō shows that 25 *saibara* pieces were versions of *Gagaku* music[6] (the total number of *saibara* pieces is 65). Therefore, the *saibara* may have been originally just simple poetical texts with the music created later. The sources mentioned above indicate that the first pieces of *wagaku* had to be simple arrangements of the borrowed music. The texts of *wagaku* were more ancient than its music. In the tenth and eleventh centuries the Japanese composed music for their native songs (texts) according to *Gagaku* principles and, by doing so, created the musical genres of the *wagaku* in the strict sense of the word.

The analysis of the musical structure of *wagaku* music and a comparison of it with instrumental *Gagaku* music throw some light on the process of the musical evolution in the Heian period. Let us begin with the main features of *Gagaku* music. Its musical structure is characterised by the combination of different scales and melodic patterns which have different origins (we do not deal here with rhythmical and architectonical principles). The parts of the zither *sō*, the lute *biwa* and the mouth-organ *shō* are based on the pentatonic scales without semitones. These scales stem from the main one: d-e-fis-a-b. The structure of the pentatonic scales is supplemented by two notes: cis and gis, and they are only auxiliary which can be demonstrated by the analysis of the parts of these instruments in the *watashigaku* (versions of the same piece in different mode).

This scale-system in Chinese in origin. The base-scale of *Gagaku* consists of the first five notes of the twelve sonore tubes (*lülü*). At the time of its infiltration into Japan, the Chinese scale system was highly developed, but it kept its pentatonic character. This can be seen, if we have a close look at *Gagaku* music.

When analysing the parts of the cylindrical reed-pipe *hichiriki* and of the flute *ryūteki*, we see that they are based on different scales. The most important elements of the *hichiriki* part are the patterns with sounds c,f,g, which generally are not used in the parts of the strings and the mouth-organ. These patterns are of two kinds: (1) descending trichords in two positions: e-c-b and a-f-e: (2) gruppetto with augmentative second above and minor second below in three positions with c,f,g, as basistone.

The structure of the trichords is the same as in ancient Greek trichords from which enharmonic tetrachords were derived. It may be suggested that the *hichiriki* sprang from the Greek aulos. We know the tuning of the aulos was e-c-b-a-f-e, which is the combination of the trichords of the Japanese *hichiriki*.

The gruppetto was probably Persian in origin. One comes across the same patterns in the music of the Near and Middle East, where it has the same rhythmical structure as the *Gagaku's* gruppetto.

It is more difficult to determine the origin of various formulae of the *ryūteki's* part. We can suppose that they are not Chinese in origin, because a diatonic scale with chromatic notes is used in its part while the Chinese elements were based on pentatonic scales.

It is extremely important to pay attention to the fact that the origin of the musical instruments and the origin of the elements of *Gagaku* are closely connected and the elements of any musical culture are present, as a rule, in the part of an instrument which was formed in the same culture. Thus, the Chinese scale system is present in the parts of the zither *sō* and the mouth-organ *shō*, the ancient Chinese instruments, created, according to Confucian tradition, by the legendary rulers. (There is only one exception here, the *biwa*, which is Persian in origin. But the tuning of the Persian lute, as well as of the Arabian one, was based on the cycle of fifths and fourths, that is, on the same principles as the Chinese scale-system. We think, that this was the reason why the Chinese could use the lute in the same way as their native instruments). The *hichiriki* was imported into China from western countries (probably, Kucha). From the historical point of view, the penetration of a Greek instrument into China through Iran and Eastern Turkestan is quite plausible.

We can state that the level of abstract thought reflected in musical practice in China and Japan was rather low. The musicians had no abstract conception of scale or melodic patterns: these musical structures were closely connected with the musical instruments. It was impossible, for example, to play the trichords of the *hichiriki* on the *sō*. The part of every instrument was limited by its original structures, although there were examples of some diffusion between the parts of different instruments. There are some pieces of *Gagaku* where the *hichiriki* and *ryūteki* parts are based on the Chinese elements, but there are no specimens left where the original patterns of wind instruments would be used in the string parts.

The analysis shows that the music of the *wagaku* created in the late Heian period derived from instrumental *Gagaku* music. The utilisation of the instruments of the *Gagaku* orchestra provoked the appearance of their original patterns in *wagaku* music. The *hichiriki* became the main instrument of *wagaku* genres (in this paper we do not touch upon the reason of this process), and subsequently its pattern became the most important for the structure of the new music. The line of this instrument was predominant in the vocal genres. For the *wagaku* the most important elements were the trichords. Even the gruppetti were not used in the *wagaku* music. The combination of the two trichords has resulted in the formation of the original scale of *wagaku* music. The particular character of this scale can be explained by its evolution from the *hichiriki's* trichords. In *Gagaku* music these formulae were strictly descending (as they were descending in Greek music), they were never used in ascending order and in this case were replaced by the anhemitonic pentatonic structure. The mode of *wagaku* music kept this peculiarity: it had the ascending variant which was pentatonic without semitones.

But, as the Japanese used the other instruments of the *Gagaku* orchestra in the vocal genres, it entailed the appearance of the other elements of instrumental music. Two opposite tendencies are evident in the development of *wagaku* music: one consisted of the gradual elimination of all other elements in favour of the *hichiriki's* trichords; another in preservation of their original patterns in the parts of different instruments. For example, because of the conservatism of musical thought, in the *saibara* orchestra the Japanese used all *Gagaku's* instruments (except for the percussion). The parts of the flute and the mouth-organ were transformed: in the modern *saibara's* structure they reproduced the line of the *hichiriki*. The strings are based, however, on the same patterns as in *Gagaku* music which contradicts the main line and gives the impression that the scale organisation is rather complicated. The Japanese understood this contradiction but, instead of modifying the parts of the strings in accordance with the wind instruments, they got rid of them. In all other genres of *wagaku* music the strings were not used. The instrumental ensemble of the *rōei* consists only of the *hichiriki*, flute and mouth-organ. In the *kagura* and the *azuma-asobi* the mouth-organ was rendered unnecessary too, and the monodic line was executed by the voices, the *hichiriki* and the flute. (We do not touch here upon the problem of the *yamato-goto*, which is very complicated and demands separate analysis).

Subsequently, the scale of *wagaku* music formed from the two *hichiriki's* trichords was considered to be the native Japanese scale, contrary to the anhemitonic pentatonic scales of Chinese music. In the *Tsurezure-gusa* it is said: 'There is in China the mode *ryo,* there is no mode *ritsu.* We have the mode *ritsu* and don't have *ryo.*[7] The *ryo* mode designates here the anhemitonic pentatonic structure and the *ritsu* — the mode, which was formed in *wagaku* music.

Coming back to Professor Tanabe's opinion on the formation of the national scale system, we can say that the process of formation of the *wagaku* scale did not take place in the theoretical sphere, but was determined by the concrete melodical patterns of the *hichiriki* which came from China. They were not of Chinese origin and it has determined the original character of the *wagaku's* mode. Contrasting with the Chinese anhemitonic structures, this mode was interpreted as a mode of national origin.

Japanese national music is the branch of continental music. The creation of the *wagaku's* musical style marked the end of a long period of borrowing and adapting continental music. One can distinguish the different stages in the process of this adaptation: the *saibara's* music was sufficiently connected with the instrumental music, whereas in the *kagura* the Japanese created the 'pure' national style. In spite of the strong general influence of Chinese culture, the national musical style differs substantially from the Chinese style, since the *wagaku* music was developed on the basis of the non-Chinese elements of the *Gagaku* music.

33

The Kachōga of Katsushika Hokusai

MATTHI FORRER

In the vast oeuvre of Katsushika Hokusai, *kachōga* take a small and yet important place. Apart from his treatment of this genre in book illustrations, he devoted two series of single sheets to the exclusive depiction of flowers and birds/insects. These two series are easily distinguished by their formats, a series in the *chūban tate* format popularly called the set of 'small flowers,' a series of the *ōban yoko* format generally known as the set of 'large flowers.'

Here, I would like to discuss the latter series of 'large flowers' in more detail, especially taking into consideration the compositional elements and its background. Designed in the early 1830s, the same period as Hokusai's large series of landscape prints, this group of prints takes a very special position in this artist's oeuvre. In comparison both with the works of his predecessors and his contemporaries — including himself in the set of 'small flowers' — the prints feature a sense of detail or rather close-up which is almost unparallelled in Japanese prints. At least, carried through to such an extent in all the prints of the set. And, in my opinion, it is exactly this effect of close-up which gives the designs the great dramatic power they have.

If we wish to study some of the designs more particularly, this is perhaps most obvious in subjects such as the peonies, the irises, the hibiscus and the poppies. In the design of peonies and a butterfly, there is an apparent breeze coming from the right, affecting not only the leaves but also every petal of the flowers as well as the butterfly. Although still clearly recognisable as peonies, the flowers appear in a sort of disorder. It is obvious that they were painted from life, in nature, and not faithfully drawn in the artistss studio. The effect of the wind is only enhanced by the presence of a struggling butterfly, its wings bent into semi-circles. Similarly, there is a strong wind in the case of the poppies. Here, the close-up renders two of its flowers almost invisible at the bottom of the sheet. As for this aspect, an inspection of all the designs in the set shows that the flowers reach most of the edges or are even cut abruptly at the sides. Especially in the designs where natural phenomena play an active part, a comparison with photography using a telephoto lens is very tempting. However, we all know that this could not be the case. The only instrument to have served the purpose at the time would have been a telescope. As regards the telescope, it is interesting to note that it had not only been introduced in Japan but was also quite widely known. A triptych by Torii Kiyonaga from the 1780s, for example, shows townspeople on a picnic party in the hills of Asukayama looking at the distant city through a telescope.[1] Hokusai also has a similar design of the picnic party by Takada, with Fuji in the distance, where three ladies have a telescope on a stand, figuring much more conspicuously in the foreground. It is one of his plates for the album *Ehon kyōka — Yama mata yama* of 1804. Earlier in his career, Hokusai had already depicted two ladies in a large-head portrait against a mica ground, one of whom is looking through a telescope. This is one of the two prints known from the series *Fūryū nakute nana kuse*.

In addition to such references demonstrating familiarity with a telescope, there is also evidence for the artists being acquainted with the working of the device. In the third volume of the *Hokusai gafu* (c. 1849), for example, there is a series of consecutive designs illustrating a whale hunt. The first plate shows a man seated in a hut with thatched roof, looking through a telescope, another man in the foreground swinging a large pole as if to give signals. Turning over the page, there is a double-page illustration showing a group of fishermen winding a large rope on a winch. Only in the third plate do we get to know what the man is watching and what the heavy load on the rope really is: a flotilla of small boats surrounds a captured whale.

Much more intriguing even is Yashima Gakutei's exploration of the possibilities offered by a telescope. In his album *Sansui kikan kyōkashū* of around 1820, Gakutei presents a number of landscapes with several details in close-up. Thus, we are first shown a Chinese landscape with mountains in the distance, a river running zig-zag from the top left of the page to the bottom right, houses and a bridge closer to the spectator. On the following double-page illustration, there is a close-up of a Chinese and a boy crossing the plank bridge with, on the far shore, the view of a man talking by a window, a man on horseback and another Chinese who just crossed a small stone bridge. When again we turn the page, there are three close-ups, one of a man talking to another man in a window, a traveller with hat and stick who is located near a house in the middle right in the original view, and one of the two men playing gō in the house in the foreground.

As well as other examples that could be cited, these show quite clearly that telescopes must have been known in wider — though certainly select — circles during the Edo period. That artists such as Hokusai and Gakutei with their keen interest in science and technology — as is witnessed in their generally great attention for detail and accurateness in the representation of all kinds of tools — were familiar with its working, may thus not surprise us. If we now accept that Hokusai was familiar with the working of a telescope — even though it seems unlikely that he possessed one himself — we might also imagine that the effects of seeing distant objects in enlargement may have been in his mind when making some of his designs. At least to me it seems very likely that this instrument has played a particular rôle in the series discussed here and may account for the rather unprecedented cut-outs and general atmosphere in the designs of some of the 'large flowers.'

34

Osaka Prints in Prague Collections

LIBUŠE BOHÁČKOVÁ

While the works of Edo *ukiyoe* artists have attracted the attention of both western and Japanese scholars and collectors since the second half of the nineteenth century the interesting Osaka school has been long neglected.

The situation has improved during the last 15 years, especially thanks to Professor Susumu Matsudaira who is systematically publishing monographic studies of Osaka artists as well as catalogues of exhibitions selected mainly from the Ikeda library collection. The institution also keeps an invaluable collection of *banzuke* or theatrical programmes, the *daichō* or scenarios and of the *yakusha hyōbanki* or critiques of actors.

Two hitherto published volumes of *banzuke* are of special importance as well as the exhibition catalogues — the *Kamigata ukiyoe nihyakunenten* of 1975, Hokushū to Toyokuni of 1983 and *Kamigata shibai eden zuroku* published for an exhibition of Osaka actor prints shown in the Tokyo National Theatre in January 1985.

It was actually a massive *kudari* of Osaka actors who presented themselves in a collective *kaomise* to the Tokyo audience — many of them for the first time as there were not only great stars who used to play in both areas — such as Nakamura Utaemon III or Ichikawa Ebizō V — but also actors who never played in Edo, such as the popular Arashi Rikan II.

Even if it was not the first exhibition of Osaka prints in Tokyo — the first one being the Nihyakunenten shown in the Riccar Gallery in 1975 — for most of the Tokyo theatre visitors it certainly meant the first encounter with the Osaka school and provided perhaps the first knowledge about its existence.

And yet the works of Osaka *ukiyoe* artists, even if close in style to the Katsukawa and Utagawa schools, have a special charm not to be found in Edo *ukiyoe*. There has always been a meticulous endeavour to characterise the actors by their personal traits — Roger Keyes speaking about the early masters of the school called it 'the harsh accurate likeness' — and it was the high level of Kansai engravers and printers which made such perfect characterisation possible.

The Osaka prints further excel in magnificent colour schemes often combined with fine embossing and the use of sparkling metallic pigments. The most gorgeous ones of these surimono-style prints were certainly not sold but distributed among friends and fans of the respective actors.

According to Roger Keyes — whose 1973 *Theatrical World of Osaka Prints* (actually a catalogue of the Philadelphia Museum of Art collection) is the standard and invaluable work on the subject — the lack of interest in Osaka prints was due to various reasons: their late character, the fact that the first full-coloured single prints appeared as late as the 1790s, their absolute scarcity and the fact that their themes were restricted to actor portraits.

The relative scarcity of Osaka prints in western collections is also on account of the fact that the western collectors bought their prints mostly in Tokyo. The most important Czech collector of Japanese art, on the other hand, the writer Joe Hloucha, stayed in Osaka in 1906 and also brought to Prague Osaka prints among other works of Japanese art and craft. These became the basis of what is now one of the four major public collections of Kamigata *ukiyoe* in the world, the others being, as already mentioned, Ikeda bunko, the Philadelphia Museum of Art and the Victoria & Albert Museum.

No wonder, then, that the first book in a western language dedicated to Osaka prints was written by a Czech. Lubor Hájek's *The Osaka Woodcuts* or *Hirosada* in the German version is still considered a pioneer work in *ukiyoe* research.

The larger part of the Prague collection of Kamigata *ukiyoe*, a total of some 500 prints, is kept at the Náprstek Museum, a smaller one, some 300 prints, at the Oriental Department of the National Gallery. This short report does not cover the whole of the Prague collection, the final evaluation of which will be given in a catalogue which is due to be published shortly. The following data are based only on the part kept at the Náprstek Museum.

With the exception of several prints, mostly representing actors of the chūshibai Kansai theatres, it was possible to identify the actors and the respective play, theatre and date of performance. There are 44 artists of the Osaka school represented in the Náprstek Museum collection, of which 25 were active during the Bunka through Tempo eras, while the remaining ones come from the late Kōka through middle Meiji eras. The second half of the collection, however, is much larger than the first one as it comprises a great number — 137 and 106 respectively — of works of two of the most prolific artists of the later period, namely of Gosotei Hirosada and Ichiryūsai Yoshitaki. These figures must be taken into account when the collection as a whole is evaluated. The predominantly late character of the collection and the absence of the single sheets of the early masters was reflected already in the selection for Lubor Hájek's book criticised by R. Keyes for giving 'an unbalanced picture of the school.'

It must be added that, while Hirosada's prints are gratifying, thanks to a vivid though conventionalised characterisation of the people depicted and to superb technical quality combined with gorgeous colour scales, Yoshitaki's work is represented for the most part by later prints executed in ugly analine colours and bearing clear marks of the 'tremendous pressure' under which this most busy Osaka artist worked.

Even if not so important as other collections as far as the development of the school is concerned, the Nāprstek Museum collection contains, nevertheless, several single prints and series of prints interesting from the point-of-view of the hitherto published material. To illustrate this fact several examples can be given:

The period of activity of Hokuroku, an artist known apparently only by name, could be guessed and his place in the master-pupil succession-line fixed. The museum specimen of a print published as anonymous by Keyes bears a signature of Enjaku, one of the late and rather rare artists. He is surprisingly well represented in the Prague collection. Several single sheets, for example, one of Sadanobu's *Miyako meisho,* will increase the number of lists of the known sets of prints.

From the rare 'twelve months' *surimono* series by Ashikuni there is a set of five sheets in Prague two of which have not yet been published but are probably kept also at the Waseda University. A pendant to the gallery of Chūshingura *ronin* portraits by Hirosada published in the Philadelphia catalogue is found also in the Nāprstek Museum. Besides two very close parallels it brings new faces and rôles to the set.

Not only series of prints but also several large compositions achieved by combination of standard single sheets could be completed by prints kept at the Nāprstek Museum, such as an interesting tetraptych with a group of actors walking in a temple garden by Shigeharu, a tetraptych representing a scene from the Nobunaga cycle by the same artist and a vertically arranged diptych by Kunihiro and Sadamasu depicting the popular scene with Ishikawa Goemon on the Nanzenji gate.

From what has been said it is perhaps evident that even if the publication of the Prague collection will bring no very exciting new aspects to the problematics of the Kamigatae research, it will certainly supply several new items of knowledge to the present state of this field of study.

35

Japan and Christian Mystery Plays: Christian Kōwakamai Reconsidered

THOMAS LEIMS

In 1940, Josef Franz Schütte published a Latin codex, the manuscript Reg. Lat. 459, which had been discovered in the Vatican Archives shortly before. Schütte identified Manoel Barreto, a Jesuit missionary, who went to Japan in 1570, as author of that manuscript. According to Schütte, it must have been written in 1591. A major part of the document provides valuable evidence of western contacts with, and influence on, Japanese *geinō* at the beginning of the *Edo* period.[1]

A complete description of the codex can be found in Schütte's publication. Therefore, we need only concentrate on those parts of the manuscript which deal with a description of the gospel and the passion of Christ. This paper, in fact, is intended to provide further information for the solution of a problem which *kirishitan* researchers, for example, Ebisawa Arimichi and even Shinmura Izura, have been discussing for a long time, that is, the use of dramatic forms by the Jesuits for the purpose of spreading the gospel in Japan during the Azuchi-Momoyama period.[2]

CODEX REG. LAT. 459 AND THE TRADITION OF CHRISTIAN MYSTERY PLAYS

Even Father Schütte, who is a historian and not a theatre expert, considers the 'Dialogues on the Instruments of Passion of the Lord,' a passage of the above-mentioned codex which provides the basis for this discussion, as a 'preliminary level' of the Christian mystery plays which had been flourishing in Japan since about 1560.[3] Schütte's interpretations can be agreed upon for several reasons: the author of the codex does not give a mere description but provides the conversation of the Virgin Mary and Mary Magdalen in dialogue form, which is, undoubtedly, the basic form for the dramatic arts. However. Schütte could and should have gone further in his interpretation, because these dialogues are not a 'preliminary step' in the development of mystery plays but a written record of a custom which had been in existence since 1561. The *Cartas* describe the celebration of Holy Week and Easter in Bungo with mystery plays.[4] The *Dic nobis Maria*, the same dialogue our manuscript is dealing with, is explicitly mentioned as one of the topics which was performed.

Normally, Jesuit records give no information as to the manner of the performance, the number of persons involved, the texts used, the shape of the stage etc. Therefore, the recorded version of the *Dic nobis Maria* as can be found in the Codex Reg. Lat. 459 is important for the analysis of dramatic form and contents of these mystery play performances. The question, how the codex is related to these problems, will be dealt with below.

'MAY NO FON'

Our knowledge of mystery plays would be much deeper if a work of the Jesuit Mission Press, the so-called *'May no fon'* (the Book of *mai*-Dances), could be rediscovered. This book, however, is no longer available, although there is ample proof of its former existence: Jōao Rodriguez, a contemporary Jesuit, quotes several times from it in his *Arte breve da Lingoa Iapoa* (1620), and the book is mentioned several times in contemporary Jesuit letters.[5] The *'May no fon'* is described in the major bibliography of Jesuit activities in Japan, the *Kirishitan Bunkō* as a work 'certainly printed but not preserved.'[6] Another prominent researcher, Doi Tadao, quotes Rodriguez's *Arte breve:* '...In order to enable the Europeans to study the Japanese language, we made our Japanese brethren translate many Japanese classics into the colloquial language, e.g. *Heike monogatari* and the *mai*, all of which are printed in our [i.e. *rōmaji*] types.'[7] From the evidence, Doi considers the *mai* as a means of studying the Japanese language.

The best idea of what the *'May no fon'* contained can be obtained however, from Manoel Barreto's codex: In the course of a description of the gospel, the *May no fon* is mentioned eight times with quotations corresponding to the appropriate gospel. Barreto even gives the corresponding folio number of the *May no fon*. Schütte makes the following comparison:

Quotations concerning *'May no fon'* in Barreto's MS	Contents of the respective passages
fol.6. vide May fol. 34	Natal no fi Luc. 2 (The Gospel of Christmas)
fol. 6v: pera pintar a pobreza da ?? nos may fol.9 (To show the poverty of ?? our *mai*)	The same gospel
fol.11 vide May fol.91,92	Gospel of the 12-year-old Jesus in the temple. The audience is astonished because of his learned answers.
fol. 22: vide May fol.17 como busca a Madanella (!) (as the investigation of Mary Magdalen)	The gospel of Easter ... 'Who will roll away the tombstone from the grave ...' They enter the grave.
fol. 49: vide May fol. 17.18	Gospel of the Thursday after Easter: Jesus appears to Magdalen.
fol.77: vide May fol.17.18	The end of the passion. The corpse of Jesus is handed over to Joseph by Pilat ...
fol.78: vide May fol.19.17. 18.30.58.59.66.91.92.	Start of the 'Dialogues on the tools of tormentation.' Mary talks to her son at the cross.
fol.91: vide May fol. 122 Taixoqua no May	Ascension of Mary into heaven. Mary and Martha
fol. 98v: Pera se pintar a pobreza da casa onde naceo, vide nos may fol.9 (to show the poverty of the house where /Christ/ was born, refer to our May ...)	A consideration of Christmas

The best description of mystery plays available at the time of Schütte's discovery was given in Luis Frois' *History of Japan*, which had been partly edited and translated into German as early as 1626. From this material, Schütte concludes that the *mai*-translations mentioned by Barretto must have been two different works 'because *"mai"* are dances and plays.' Here, Schütte agrees with Doi. Because the *kanji* were missing, Schütte, however, was not able to identify the *Taishoqua no may*.

Because of this deficiency, Schütte is criticised by Pierre Humbertclaude, who correctly identifies 'Taishoqua' as a piece from the *kōwakamai*-repertoire, 'Taishok (k) an.'[9] This *kōwakamai* deals with a jewel that Fujiwara Kamatari (*taishokukan*) had dedicated for the construction of a temple. His daughter, married to a Chinese emperor, sends this jewel by ship from China. During the crusade, the ship is attacked by the dragon gods of the sea. In order to recover the jewel stolen by these gods, Taishokkan lives in disguise among fishermen and divers for several years. Finally, Taishokkan's lover, a diver girl, finds the jewel at the bottom of the sea. But she is attacked by a sea snake. In order to hide the jewel in her bosom, the girl cuts open her breast. When she reappears at the surface, she is dead, but the precious jewel has been recovered. Taishokkan uses it for the decoration of Kōfuka-ji temple in Nara.

Humbertclaude explains the combination of *Taishokkan no mai* with the assumption of the Virgin in *'May no fon'* '...because there are undoubtedly transposable allusions', for example, the sumptuous funeral at the end of the play, the open heart of the lover as a symbol of the Sacred Heart of the Virgin or even the victory of the Virgin over the heathen dragon.

For the other occasions in the gospel, Humbertclaude looks for 'appropriate *kōwakamai* plays' which could symbolise for example the poverty of Jesus, or the opening of the grave of Jesus. However, he is not able to give one single title of a *kōwakamai*, dealing with such matters. He is even not aware of the fact that *mai no hon* is not only the title of a work from the Jesuit Mission Press but the generic term of a literary genre which flourished at the beginning of the Edo period. According to Schneider these *mai no hon* put difficult passages of classical texts (*shōhon*) into the colloquial, thus modernising the language of the Muromachi period to a considerable extent.[10]

At first sight, the analogy of these types of *mai no hon* with the *kirishitan 'May no fon'* mentioned by Barreto seems striking and plausible. However, for several reasons, we cannot agree with Humbertclaude:

The Christian *'May no fon'* must have been printed before the writing-down of Manoel Barreto's manuscript, for example before 1591. According to Schneider the genre of *mai no hon* as a general part of Japanese literature came only into existence at the beginning of the *Keichō* period, for example 1596. It must be strongly doubted that the Jesuits should have been able to pioneer a new literary genre by just printing one folio volume in *rōmaji* characters.[11]

Secondly, Humbertclaude is not able to give one single allusion between events described in the gospel and pieces of the *kōwakamai*

208

repertoire besides '*Taishokkan.*' In addition, his definition of *kōwakamai* as pure literature is only partly correct. The *Vocabulario de Lingoa de Iapam*, the famous Japanese-Portuguese dictionary of 1603, defines *mai* as 'stories of old times, for example romances, which are sung and danced.'

Finally, the Passion of Christ as mentioned in Barreto's manuscript, is the focus of Roman Catholic faith. To water it down by an 'appropriate' *kōwakamai* would, at least in the eyes of the Jesuits, be counter-productive for the Christian mission. Further evidence for the refutation of this theory can be found in considerable numbers in the *Cartas:* Holy Week is, with one exception which the Jesuits could not be held responsible for, always celebrated by plays in western style representing the event as it is described in the gospel.

Should we, therefore, agree with Schütte's theory that there must have been two different '*May no fon,*' one containing Christian mystery plays and another designed as a reader for language education and containing Japanese *kōwakamai* plays?

A close examination shows that Schütte's and Humbertclaude's theories need not be considered antagonistic. This statement needs further explanation. On the occasion of Christian holy days, Christmas, Easter, New Year's Day, Corpus Christi, etc. the *Cartas* report that mystery plays as well as purely Japanese dances were performed (For the exception of Easter celebration, see above). Therefore, there should be no obstacle in both mystery plays and *mai* being printed together in one volume. There is further evidence for that theory. In his grammar of 1604-8 Jõao Rodriguez makes ample quotations in Japanese from the gospel, Genesis as well as the Jesuit versions of 14 *kōwakamai* plays. There is no distinction between these two genres. Secondly, a certain Paolo Yofo is, according to Doi, the author of many *kirishitan monogatari*, for example *kurobune monogatari*, (Story of the Black Ship), *enpen monogatari* Story of a Wedding) etc.[12] These *monogatari* are quoted in Rodriguez's *Arte* as well. The same Paolo Yofo is the author or editor of the *Kirishitan* versions of *Heike monogatari*, *Taiheiki*, and *Roei zahitsu*, all of which appeared in the Jesuit Mission Press. He is, however, and this fact has until now been overlooked, mentioned as the author of a Christian mystery play which was performed in Shimabara as early as 1566.[13] Consequently, we can draw the conclusion that this Paolo Yofo is the author of Christian mystery plays as well as the editor of Japanese *kōwakamai* plays, both of which were printed together in one work. This would match with the quotations in the Codex Reg. Lat. 459 of the Vatican Archives which make no difference between purely Christian plays and the *Taishokkan.*

For the year 1593 there is an example of such a combination. At the time, the Jesuit Mission Press published a book containing the *Heike Monogatari*, *Aesop's Fables* and a collection of Japanese proverbs. The pagination of the volume keeps the sequence; at the end of the folio there is an index in alphabetical order, dealing with the three different chapters as a whole. Therefore, this volume must have been planned and designed as one single work, and it had not been bound together just by chance, as one might think. Combining western and Japanese topics for the use of the Jesuit mission in Japan, therefore, must be considered a common fact. There is enough evidence that the *'May no fon'* was no exception.

A further step in the right direction is James T. Araki's thorough investigation of the transfer of the *Odyssey* into the *kōwakamai* play *Yuriwaka daijin*.[14] In this article, Araki shows the second level of contacts, for example the amalgamation of western and Japanese dramatic arts. More evidence for Araki's theory will be given in a separate publication.

36

Japanese Traditional Culture and Today's Japan: The Internationalisation of the Kabuki Theatre and its Function in Modern Society

KAWATAKE TOSHIO

I shall limit my remarks to the theatre, or, more precisely, to Kabuki, my special field of research. I am convinced, however, that many of the problems I consider in relation to Kabuki are common to all traditional arts, that is, traditional Japanese culture in general.

The conflict between 'tradition' and 'modern' or 'contemporary' in the Japanese arts has been of much more importance than in western cultures. Nō and Bugaku, for example, can undoubtedly be considered classical arts, and this is exactly the way they have been perceived by the audience. Kabuki, in contrast, has always kept a subtle association with the times in which it has been performed; because of the immanent elements of modernisation during its development as well as the continuing changes within its audience, it has been alert to change. During the Meiji period, the theatre buildings were greatly enlarged and electric stage lighting equipment was introduced. As a consequence, the make-up of the actors and their way of acting changed to a certain extent. The time and length of the performances, too, had to be adapted to the changing social customs. While considering all these frictions and contradictions, I should like to deal with the question whether and how Kabuki can survive in present-day society by considering some important topics which took place recently in the Kabuki world. Generally speaking, they can be divided into domestic Japanese and overseas phenomena.

Domestically, Kabuki experienced three important events during 1985, the *shūmei* (name-awarding ceremony) of Danjūrō, the trial introduction of three performances per day (instead of two) at the Kabuki-za theatre, Tokyo, and the revival of real Edo Kabuki at a theatre on Shikoku island.

Danjūrō's *shūmei* ceremony took place at the Kabuki-za theatre and lasted for three months from April to June 1985. The profit from these performances is estimated to have been an unprecedented sum of 3,000 m ¥. In October 1985, the *shūmei* production was shown in Nagoya and in December in Kyoto; in April 1986 it finally went to Osaka, which meant that it had lasted for half a year in total. In addition, in July and August, *shūmei* memorial performances took place in the United States where the traditional *hirō kōjō* ceremony (formal greeting of the audience by an actor elevated to a new rank) took place in the same way as in Japan: Danjūrō, holding the *sanbō* (a small wooden stand) in one hand, had the traditional sharp look at the audience using the unique *nirami* technique. Evidently, the *shūmei* ceremony as a whole has to be considered as the biggest event the Kabuki world ever experienced. One reason for this tremendous success certainly is the name of Danjūrō which had the highest rank in the Edo Kabuki world. Thus, the whole event once again proved the existence of Kabuki to the world and served as a symbol of its unbroken popularity and prosperity.

By a system of succession and inheritance the importance of a 'traditional art,' its preservation and handing down to future generations can easily be understood. At the same time, such events can be considered a good way of enhancing the 'value' of Kabuki in a 'market' which is getting tougher all the time as well as being diversified by television and other media.

The feasibility of introducing three performances a day in order to increase the numbers because of audience needs is also part of the marketing challenge today. Traditionally, there were only two shows per day, the first starting at 11 am and the second at 4.30 pm. However, this pattern was no longer acceptable in a modern society: the length of the performances as well as their starting-time had to be adjusted. During the trial period, beginning September 1985, the curtain rose at 11 am, 2.30 pm and 6.30 pm. The structure of the show, too, was changed. A drama always alternated with a dance piece. As modern life has become busier and more hectic, the number of elements shown during any one performance had to be reduced in order to prevent Kabuki's traditional formal aesthetic values from disappearing into oblivion. Without taking the needs of the audience into account, no form of theatre can survive! Unlike, say, sculpture or architecture, the importance of the formal aesthetic content is deeply felt in the traditional theatre.

As had become customary in recent years, Kabuki performances took place in Shikoku on three days at the end of June 1985 at the Kanamaru-za which is better known under its popular name Konpira Shibai, a theatre which has a tradition going back more than 150 years. Nakamura Kichiemon was the principal performer. It is self-evident that this participation was aimed at promoting the revival of the Edo stage at its best, the preserving of the theatre and the original values of Kabuki. The small yet beautiful building, because of its poor condition had not been used for a long time as a theatre but as a cinema. Finally, after the reassessment of its value by the Nihon Engeki Gakkai (Japanese Academic Society for Performing Arts), an initiative for its preservation was started in 1969. In the following year the Kanamaru-za was designated an 'important cultural property' by the Bunkachō (Cultural Affairs Agency). In 1976, the building was relocated to a more suitable place and underwent complete reconstruction. Seating — made up of boxes on the floor — was kept in accordance with tradition; revolving stage, *suppon* and *seriage (lift mechanisms in the hanamichi* and in the main stage respectively) are still moved by hand as in former days. With the exception of the lighting equipment which had to be electrified everything was kept as close to the original as possible, and in order to maintain the atmosphere created by traditional lighting methods, performances have been limited to matinées using daylight only. As a result, Kabuki's traditional aesthetic values are being preserved, communication with the spectators is being strengthened and the new arrangement of three performances daily is very much appreciated.

In the Kanamaru-za the height of the proscenium arch as well as the measurements of the revolving stage match those of the standard Edo period theatres in the city of Edo. This theatre is, therefore, of great importance for research into the original forms of Kabuki.

Let us now move to events which have taken place in other countries. In 1985 America and Europe both experienced Kabuki performances. The fact that these shows were not perceived as mere spectacles but appreciated because of their acting techniques and their dramatic value, for example, as 'normal theatre,' is of major importance. During the European tour of the Ichikawa Ennosuke Ensemble, West Berlin saw the first ever *chūnori* (a traditional lift technique by which the actor is raised to the ceiling by draped wires and thus 'flies' over the *hanamichi*) outside Japan. In addition, the fact that only 'Yoshitsune Senbon Zakura,' a lengthy epic piece, was shown — and highly esteemed — as *tōshi kyōgen* (a production consisting of only one drama which is shown as a whole in contrast to showing highlights of several pieces) must not be overlooked.

The principal event of the US tour was, as already mentioned, Danjūrō's *shūmei* ceremony. The biggest response, however, was obtained by 'Sakura-hime Azuma Bunshō,' a *kizewamono* (a bourgeois play which deals with low-class people in contrast to historical plays which only depict people of the noble or warrior classes). Although the drama was cut considerably, the *tōshi kyōgen* performance still lasted about two hours. The appeal of Kataoka Takao, a young handsome actor of 'male' rôles, and the charm of Bandō Tamasaburō, a famous young female impersonator, played a major part, too, in the big success. The most breathtaking surprise, however, was the fact that the scenery was changed in such an energetic manner. Suicide because of love for the same sex, unfulfilled love, rape, murder, the principle of cause and effect — all the elements found in modern drama, meant a real shock for the audience and caused great excitement. This was mainly because of the fact that, within the frame of a beautiful yet formalised stage-set with all its effects, human instincts, satisfaction of one's desires and passion, (features common to mankind) were depicted and expressed in such an impressive manner. For many, up until then, Kabuki was merely a 'beautiful' spectacle with music and dance in abundance. However, through this performance, Kabuki could be experienced in a completely different way as a drama about the human condition.

Surprising as this reaction may sound, I have experienced similar audience reaction since 1960 when I accompanied Kabuki's first American tour. Since then, I have ascertained on several occasions that the pieces which were most appreciated during the 25 years of performances overseas were undoubtedly *'Shunkan'* and *'Chūshingura.'* *Buyō* (dance pieces) were expected to be even more successful, but this was not the case. The most important reason for the failure of dances is the absence of dramatic situations which have universal appeal. My personal impressions were further confirmed by an inquiry which I conducted in most of the countries Kabuki ever visited from America to Australia. So far, more than 6000 people have returned the questionnaire and their replies are at present being analysed by an institute for computerised statistical research. I am convinced that, by using this method, several interrelations and correlations will become clear. At the same time, I hope to be able to contribute to the better understanding of the Japanese people and Japanese theatre, its special characteristics as well as its universal features.

Some interesting facts are emerging; for example, the heightened liveliness of overseas performances is matched by a 'normal' interest in Kabuki at home. There is also the question of how Kabuki is influencing the world of drama generally, both in construction and representation. At the same time the remarkable progress that has been made in academic research has to be properly catalogued and coordinated.

In my opinion there are at least two reasons for these phenomena. One is certainly the tremendous economic growth of Japan after World War II. Since then, there has been a great interest in 'Edo' in general because the Edo-period bourgeois society's high-class culture was considered the spring-board for Japan's rapid modernisation. Secondly, because of its 'post-modern' formal creativeness, Kabuki can be considered as a convincing model for overcoming European and American modern realism. This second aspect has been especially confirmed by many western theatre pioneers, such as Max Reinhard introducing the revolving stage and Meyerholdt experimenting with the *hanamichi*. More recent examples of Kabuki's influence on foreign theatrical forms, are the French 'Théâtre du Soleil' which gained much attention for its Asian-style 'danced' versions of Shakespeare plays and 'The Importance of Being Earnest' — the latter being a production of the Theatre Department of Toronto University (Canada) where many Kabuki-like elements as well as aesthetic aspects of *Ukiyō-e* (wood-block prints) were used. Neither production can be considered as really mature. However, both aimed at the destruction of western as well as Japanese theatre traditions in a kind of 'Aufhebung' process, thus introducing the birth of a 'third' genre, the 'theatre of the future.' Surprising as it may sound, these productions can be considered one step in the realisation of the 'Theater der Zukunft' which was projected a hundred years ago by Richard Wagner in his *Gesamtkunstwerk*. Using modern terms we can consider these experiments as Kabuki's contribution to a 'total theatre:' to serve as a grand reservoir of 'natural resources' for post-modern theatre. This is Kabuki's international commitment.

As to scholarly research, Kabuki was for a long time behind Nō. The reason for this delay may perhaps be found in the fact that Japan's governing élite at the time limited westerners who came to Japan during the Meiji Period to seeing Nō drama as the only true clasical Japanese theatre. Kabuki wasn't 'liberated' in terms of cultural exchange until much later.

John Masefield's translation into English of 'Kanadehon Chūshingura' first appeared almost at the same time as Reinhard and Meyerholdt experimented with Kabuki elements. Masefield's version was, of course, more an adaptation than a real translation. But in a general sense, it can be considered as the beginning of comparative research, an achievement, however, which certainly did not result from a scholarly approach.

Original Kabuki research only really started after the end of World War II. Faubion Bowers, Earl Ernest from America, Charles Dunn and A.C. Scott from Great Britain, later Donald Keene, James Brandon and William Malm had the opportunity of including personal experience and contacts with Kabuki in their research, thus opening the way for an in-depth evaluation and analysis. Over the years, aspects ranging from 'Kabuki and *Ukiyō-e*' to *hyōbanki* (classifications of actors by attributing to them marks of popularity and ability, a system which was in vogue throughout the Edo period) have been published, and Kabuki research is gaining increased momentum especially from younger scholars. Among them some of the most remarkable study is being undertaken by Thomas Leims. This young German took up a new hypothesis by the Italian Benito Ortolani, namely that early Kabuki cannot be explained from existing indigenous genres only, but must have undergone some influence from western theatre. By using unknown materials and sources which are only available in Europe, he was able to prove the existence of such elements and influences. It is expected that a page of Japanese theatrical history will have to be rewritten as a result of his research.

The foundation of the 'European Kabuki Conference' can be considered as part of this new growing interest in the genre tendency. The first and second conferences took place at the Institute for Theatre Research, Vienna University, in 1981 and 1983 and a third conference is planned.

It must not be overlooked, however, that Kabuki research conducted by foreigners differs somewhat from Japanese approaches. The 'excavation' of documents, sources and materials which are out of reach for many Japanese scholars has to be considered as a rather unique path. I personally had a quite different yet amusing experience when more than ten years ago I made a speech in Cologne. In the question-and-answer session which followed my paper, I was asked by a young man, 'I have heard that the number of Kabuki actors totals about 1000. I have already listed up 600 of them. Is there any way of obtaining the remaining 400 names?' Well, I told him of the collection *Kabuki hyōbanki shusei*, the editing of which was under way at that time. As I was astonished at this unconventional question, I unfortunately forgot to ask this man why he conducted such research. However, I am convinced that such an approach which is a

214

testimony to the high esteem Kabuki has gained worldwide, would never even be considered by a Japanese scholar! If we accept the fact that western scientific research came into existence and developed out of a mere desire for the extension of basic knowledge and not for any real aims, we have to take seriously this kind of detailed, minute research which is based on one's personal tastes and preferences. It is all the more regrettable that Japanese scholars seem to have either no interest whatsoever in the results obtained by foreigners nor are they willing even to consider or criticise them. However, the combination of Kabuki seen from within Japan and at the same time perceived with the different eyes of a foreigner could bring about a confirmation of Kabuki's true aesthetic values for mankind. The continuing development of Kabuki research conducted by foreigners is therefore highly desirable.

Undoubtedly at the present time Japan is experiencing a rejuvenation and reappraisal of her traditions. The wearing of traditional Japanese clothing, for example, has become fashionable again. The classical beauty of Takagi Nō performances (Nō performed in torch-light at night in the open air) has become very popular. Normally, only a small number of those wishing to attend these performances can be admitted. Takagi Nō has recently been performed even among the modern buildings of Tokyo's Hibiya district. During 1985, this kind of performance took place several times and it has become even more popular since them. The Kabuki performances being held in Shikoku belong to the same phenomenon of reevaluating Japanese tradition.

However, this rejuvenation of Japan's traditions must not be interpreted merely as a tendency to go back to former times. In our modern society, where life is getting more and more standardised, there is a demand for aesthetic values which oppose modern times, i.e. a longing for 'anti-modern' beauty. This kind of desire is based on a willingness to reconsider the roots of one's own human nature. Within this context, Kabuki is certainly a traditional piece of culture unique to Japan. However, at the same time, given its appeal in the rest of the world, it has, in my view, a certain universality of content and construct which is common to both East and West. Thus, if this is the case, it is clearly highly desirable that an effective continuing exchange of research between Japanese and western scholars is ensured and is of an even higher standard in the future. This will result in a rediscovery of Kabuki in our modern world, and will also mean, of course, a great contribution to the future of Kabuki.

Translated and annotated by Thomas Leims

SECTION 4:
Literature

37

On the Problem of the Interrelation between Russian and Japanese Cultures (Leo Tolstoy and Tokutomi Rōka)

L. L. GROMKOVSKAYA

A well-known Japanese specialist in Russian philology, Yokemura Yoshitarō, in his article on the influence of Russian literature on Japanese literature[1] published almost a quarter of a century ago (1961), was quite right to say that the very fact of such influence is beyond doubt. The point is whether it was as deep as it ought to be, or partial and incomplete. According to the author, this question should have been cleared up.

In previous years, this problem has been explored to a great extent by scholars, both Japanese and Russian, but its full elucidation is yet to come. In literary science until now discoveries have occurred which fill in the lacunae or correct the known facts. The aim of the present paper is possibly to verify certain fixed judgements and versions considering the creative relationship between Tokutomi and Tolstoy.

The theme 'Tokutomi Rōka and Leo Tolstoy' has been attracting Soviet scholars for a long time. Not a few articles by prominent specialists both in Russian and Japanese philology have been published. A contribution, made by Academician N. I. Konrad, is of particular importance. Let us deal in brief with the history of relations between Tolstoy (1828-1910) and Tokutomi (1868-1927).

As is widely known, as early as the end of the last century (in 1897) Tokutomi Rōka wrote a book about Tolstoy which opened 'the epoch of Tolstoy' in Japan. His deep acquaintance with Tolstoy's works made Tokutomi first a sincere admirer and later an ideological follower of the great Russian writer. His great desire to converse with his idol led Rōka to Yasnaya Polyana. The five days spent with Tolstoy became a turning-point in Tokutomi's life. After his meeting with Tolstoy, he raised a public protest against the government by expressing indignation at the unjust death sentence passed on twelve socialists accused in the affair of Kōtoku Shūsui. Following the example of his teacher, Tokutomi moved to the village where he spent the rest of his days trying to realise the ideal bequeathed by Tolstoy: to live the peasant's life of labour.

Such is the actual canvas. We are far from ascribing all these actions exclusively to Tolstoy's influence. Rather we should mention that, in looking at the means by which Rōka's inner spiritual evolution expressed itself in his life, it is necessary to take into account the spontaneous, direct and strong influence of Leo Tolstoy; though the fact that Rōka 'repeated' Tolstoy in many respects was not simply a result of that influence. Nonacceptance of evil and the vigorous search for truth are the innate traits of Rōka's nature. And only thanks to this were Tolstoy's lessons mastered so thoroughly. As Confucius said, 'The same sounds respond to each other.'

Now let us consider the main topic which is to offer a new interpretation to the fixed statements which acquired the power of axioms in our field of science. We shall touch upon two of them.

It is accepted that there exists a correlation between Namiko, the heroine of Tokutomi's first novel 'The Cuckoo' (*Hoto gisu*) and *Anna Karenina*. We consider it more appropriate to observe such a correlation between Sadako in the novel 'Black Current' (*Kokuchō*) and the heroine of the immortal creation by Tolstoy. We should recall the story of Sadako. In *Kokuchō* Tokutomi exposed the 'feminine theme,' artistically completed, forcefully written. The story of Countess Kitagawa Sadako is a genuine 'novel within a novel' and could become the basis of an original work.

Sadako came from a noble but impoverished family. Sadako's mother, having lost her husband early on, was bringing up her daughter more strictly than usual. The girl was educated at home, acquiring all her knowledge and skill in history and literature from her mother, playing *koto* and studying calligraphy. But most important was her sense of duty. To Count Kitagawa young Sadako brought as a dowry her exquisite beauty, her education based on ideas of feminine modesty, and an ancient box where among few family relics was a dagger in a black varnished scabbard. All this — rare beauty, gentleness, being the best of feminine virtues, and the dagger — paved the way for her to a tragic finale: exhausted by the despotism at home and her husband's mockery, Sadako killed herself. Even such a brief outline of the story enables us to identify similar features in the characterisation of Anna and Sadako: both are married to high officials; both come from impoverished families; both meet the tragic end — suicide. It could be also mentioned that Sadako has a dissolute brother. But the main thing, it seems, is not the coincidence of subject lines or even traits of character — though all this is important enough — but comparative textological analysis. This does give an opportunity to estimate that 'melting' of the one poetological system into another which occurs in the process of one writer exerting influence upon another.

In *Kokuchō* there are a number of scenes reminiscent of Tolstoy. For example, the description of intense expectation on account of the delayed arrival of Count Kitagawa during Sadako's funeral, arouses associations with the scene in the church during the wedding of Levin and Kitty when the public with a growing bewilderment perceives the inexplicable absence of the fiancé. But we shall analyse only one scene — the death of both heroines. In Tolstoy's novel we read: 'She wanted to fall half-way between the wheels of the front truck which was drawing level with her. But the red bag, which she began to pull from her arm, delayed her, and it was too late; the truck had passed. She must wait for the next. A sensation, similar to the feeling she always had when she went bathing, before she took the first plunge, seized her and she crossed herself. The familiar gesture brought back a whole series of memories of her childhood; and suddenly the darkness that had enveloped everything for her, lifted and for an instant life glowed before her with all its past joys. But she did not take her eyes off the wheels of the approaching second truck. And, exactly at the moment when the space between the wheels drew level with her, she pulled aside the red bag and, drawing her head down between her shoulders, dropped on her hands under the truck, and with a light movement she would rise again at once, sank on to her knees.'[2] The description of Sadako's suicide reveals a distinct reversal from Tolstoy's text. While Tolstoy writes that 'life glowed before her with all its past joys,' Tokutomi tells how before Sadako's inner sight all her joyless life flies past in a moment; if Anna tries 'to pull off the red bag, delaying her,' Sadako turned around her hand; if Anna 'sank on to her knees with a light movement she would rise again at once,' Sadako fell on the dagger with all her weight.

Of course, such 'melding' of poetics usually takes place unconsciously, when one writer penetrates deeply into the artistic manner of the other, absorbing the very essence of the creative approach to his work. Not once did Rōka demonstrate his adherence and devotion towards Leo Tolstoy's works. It is of special interest to observe how he regarded the life in Yasnaya Polyana. Rōka felt as if he had got into a well-known place. In the surrounding environment and the people he constantly perceived the sources of literary situations and images, which speak of Rōka's enormous knowledge and his perfect ability to attune himself to Tolstoy's works. He remembers that the small river Voronka is mentioned in the novel *Anna Karenina*; the old nurse reminded him of Natalija Savitchna from the trilogy 'Childhood,' 'Adolescence' and 'Youth.'

The second point we should like to mention is an interpretation of the well-known words of Tokutomi about his departure from Tolstoy's place inserted in the work 'New Spring' (*Shinshun*). The words about leaving Tolstoy are usually regarded in the direct sense as a renunciation of Tolstoy's ideas and artistic principles. Certainly, after his visit to Yasnaya Polyana the personal contacts between Rōka and Tolstoy began to fade instead of increasing, as one would suppose. But we know that, after his meeting and conversations with Tolstoy, Rōka started a new life, and the words 'left his own self' means renunciation of his own past. Perhaps Rōka felt a desire to choose some other way and not exactly the one exposed to him by Tolstoy.

Nevertheless, an objective analysis of Rōka's works and their social rôle during the period following his visit to Yasnaya Polyana and till his last days, shows that in the 'new life' Rōka appeared closer to Tolstoy than before.

Following the chronological principle let us consider the first major works of this period — for example, 'The Idle Chatter of an Earthworm' (*Mimizu no tawakoto*). Really, the ironical tone in which Rōka presents aspects of non-resistance, such as the imbecile Hisa, or there is the main character of the short story 'Two hundred yen' (*Ni hyaku yen*), hints at a revision of certain of Tolstoy's precepts. But, even if this observation is true, its value cannot be compared to the conviction with which Rōka demonstrates his fidelity to Tolstoy in the famous essay devoted to agriculture. Its almost every line is aphoristic. The adherence to Tolstoy is manifested in the very theme — the theme of the soil. We also find here the direct citing and the paraphrase of Tolstoy's words concerning the Russian peasantry.

The book 'In Death's Shadow' (*Shi-no kage-ni*) reflected the inner crisis of the author. It also arouses involuntary associations with Tolstoy's spiritual searchings. Most brightly it can be seen in the Biblical legend about Jonah, given in the conclusion.[1] It is known that the story of the prophet Jonah was highly appreciated by Tolstoy who inserted it in the book *What Is My Belief*.

Tolstoy, dreaming of founding a new religion, was very close to Rōka in his programme work 'New spring,' the mystic colouring of which is evident. Rōka describes the ecstatic mood capturing his soul at some moments when he dreams of heavenly visions, when he sees himself and his wife Aiko as Adam and Eve. He is sure in his messianic rôle, believes that to enter the new life as Adam and Eve was prescribed to them from heaven — just as it was prescribed to him to travel round the world, since 'In my Father's house are many mansions.' These words are cited in the beginning of the book 'From Japan to Japan' (*Nihon-kara Nihon-e*). Similarly, Rōka followed Tolstoy's precept: 'the most important and useful thing for the people is some creation where the author depicts his own experience and thoughts' and began the line of confessional prose with his novel 'Black Eyes and Brown Eyes' (*Kuroi me to chairo-no me*) and ended up with the novel *Fuji* unfinished because of his death in 1926.

Tokutomi Rōka, the writer and citizen, has done great services for Japan. One of the most important, to our mind, is his 'presentation' in Japan of Leo Tolstoy, whose influence had serious implications for the development of Japanese literature.

38

Inoue Hisashi as a Literary Critic

JEANETTE TAUDIN CHABOT

In his article '*Kawabata Yasunari to sanji bungaku*' (Kawabata Yasunari and the literature of eulogy), Ueda Makoto points out that Japanese literature lacks a genre which can be termed *sanji bungaku*, literature of eulogy. He lucidly illustrates how Kawabata Yasunari is an exception to this rule by discussing why Kawabata produced many writings that are eulogistic in nature, what his rhetoric of eulogy is, and how his entire literary oeuvre can be seen as literature of eulogy. According to Ueda, Kawabata excelled in introducing new writers to the literary world and eulogising deceased ones. Although they are literary criticisms of a sort, because Kawabata avoids generalisations and abstractions, preferring instead to insert a personal anecdote or two, they give an essay-like impression. Kawabata's appraisals of authors are indirect, the only obvious expressions of praise being quotations from others. Yet, the reader is naturally drawn to take a positive view of the author whom Kawabata discusses.

Today, I consider Inoue Hisashi to be a champion of *sanji bungaku* as far as his literary criticisms are concerned. He seems to follow the path of Kawabata in that he produces literary criticisms without criticising, or finding fault with his subjects. This may sound contradictory, since nowadays we tend to think that any criticism should contain a sharp edge to uncover shortcomings. However, the first Oxford dictionary definition of criticism is 'judging merit of works of art and literature or of persons and things in general, expression or exposition of such judgement.' In other words, a critic does not necessarily have to assign faults to the work or person he reviews. In the case of Inoue Hisashi, it is more than not mentioning faults. His literary criticisms are so abundant in overt praise that they may even sound like fan-letters.

Inoue Hisashi (born in 1934) is well known more as a novelist, dramatist, and poet than as a critic. Even among Japanese writers who are known to be the hardest working in the world, Inoue stands out as one of the most prolific of them all, having released more than 65 titles in the last 15 years. He is both a social and literary critic. In this paper, however, I shall only deal with him as a literary critic, for as a social critic Inoue arms himself with quite a different set of weapons than as a literary critic.

Unlike Kawabata who preferred to deal with unknown or deceased writers, Inoue mostly plunges into relatively established, contemporary writers and their works. This immediacy of subject is one of the reasons for the fan-letter-like quality of his literary criticisms. Another reason for it may be the emphasis of personal experience as the reference point, for instance, 'After having read Mr Endō's *The Sea and Poison,* I couldn't eat meals for three days.....'[1] Another aspect to consider for this quality is that the bulk of his literary criticisms are in the form of interviews with the authors in question and *kaisetsu,* criticisms included in the book containing the work under review. The nature of these forums obviously limits the mentioning of negative factors. On the other hand, Inoue is just as outlandish in pouring out praise even in the literary review section of the newspaper which is often used by other critics to express negative as well as positive evaluations. Two excerpts from the literary review section of the *Asahi Shimbun:*

> 'There are many more, but if I allow myself to soak in the pleasure of listing them, I will be exceeding my space limitation right away. So I draw a line around here and say that I completely agree with the patterns that Shinoda extracts out of these twenty-six contemporary novels. No, the word 'agree' is such a conceited way of putting it. I re-state in an old-fashioned expression: scales came off my eyes.'[2]
>
> 'Immediately in front of us is always a milky future without visibility. Are there any walking sticks that can support us as we are daily forced to step into this future in which any incredible thing can take place? For instance, Ishikawa Jun's *Kyofuki* which he started writing nine years ago and recently finally completed is one such stick.'[3]

221

We have now seen that several elements account for the quality of a fan-letter in his literary criticisms. There is yet another aspect that makes his literary criticisms unique, namely characteristics of *gesaku*, entertainment stories of the Edo period.[4] Since his *Tegusari shinjū* (Handcuffed Suicide , 1972) based on an Edo *gesaku* won the Naoki Prize, Inoue has been named a *gesakusha* of the Shōwa period. Being an ardent admirer of *gesaku* and *gesakusha*, Inoue says that he does not deserve being considered as a *gesakusha*, since in today's Japan one has so much freedom to shape one's own life that there is no true frustration which is a seed of a *gesaku*.[5] He openly admits on many occasions, however, that he is not keen on the so-called modern Japanese literature as epitomised by *junbungaku* (pure literature), especially *shi-shōsetsu* (I-novels). He directly and indirectly employs several techniques of *gesaku* in his novels and dramas, and I feel he does the same in his literary criticisms as well. By *gesaku* techniques I mean in this case *shukō* (originality of setting or plot), exaggeration, verbosity (nothing is left unsaid), humour, sense of parody, catering to the popular taste, and the self-humiliating image of the author as a provider of mere entertainment.

Let us first examine how *shukō* is evident in Inoue's literary criticisms. He often reviews several books by different authors in a single article. The juxtaposition of chosen works is a big surprise to the reader. Yet more surprising is how Inoue weaves these totally unlike threads into a fabric with a genuine unity. For instance, in one case he deals with a scholarly book of literary analysis *Nihon no gendai shōsetsu* (Contemporary Japanese novels), a comic book *Jarinko Chie* (Kid Chie), and a book of interviews by an anthropologist called *Nijuseki no chiteki bōken* (The twentieth-century's intellectual adventures). This seemingly incongruous combination of works receives oneness through the theme Inoue superimposes, which is the title of the article: *'Fuhen no chūshutsu'* (Extraction of patterns). The discussion of one work leads naturally to the other and, in the last paragraphs, all of them are recaptured as integral elements in the exploration of the theme. Time and time again, Inoue uses this approach, but his *shukō* is not only limited to the combination of books. In illustrating a point, he may place a quotation from serious poetry next to the lyric of a pop song.[6] He tells about his experiences in Australia to illuminate the rhetoric of Miyazawa Kenji;[7] his analysis of Kita Morio's *Takami no kenbutsu* (View from higher up) is through the eyes of a cockroach.[8] These are all such original methods of reviewing serious works that the reader cannot help being fascinated.

Exaggeration, a common technique of *gesaku*, is inseparable from Inoue's literary criticisms. Here are two random examples:

Because his writing style is full of strength and suppleness and attentiveness, the reader can effortlessly jump over the wall of common sense which is supposed to be more difficult to cross over than the Mach barrier.[9]

'After that, I started considering Matsumoto Seichō to be an interesting author. That was about the time his *The Eye's Wall* came out; I read that, too. Ever since, I put Sōseki on the right side of my desk and Seichō on the left and repeatedly read his works.'[10]

These exaggerations seem to serve two related functions, at once providing a comic touch and making the critic himself appear a bit ridiculous in the eyes of the reader.

Another obvious aspect of Inoue's literary criticisms is his verbosity. In contrast to Kawabata who relies on the suggestive power of margins — what has not been said — to evoke the reader's sympathy, Inoue seems to turn over every stone and use every tool available to defend the work under review. He does not count on the reader's imagination to complete his work. Rather, he is a servant who does all the work for his master, the reader. The reader can just sit back and enjoy what is served by the critic. In playing such a rôle as writer, Inoue is being consistent with the image of *gesakusha* that he is an entertainer and craftsman, rather than an artist with more superior vision than the reader. Inoue himself says that he is a craftsman:

> 'Free lancer, writer, author, etc. — the name sounds attractive, but the essence of our sort of work can best be expressed with the term "indoor working craftsman." At least I consider myself as a craftman.'
> 'As long as there are orders or things that I want to produce, I hurriedly retire into my workplace after breakfast. I evaluate the materials, think of a way to bring the best out of these materials. The rest is finishing up the work patiently with papers and writing utensils.'[11]

By this time it may have become clear that Inoue's literary criticisms are geared towards the average reader, not to scholars or other critics. (The same can be said of his works of fiction which are mostly classified as entertainment stories and not as the so-called pure literature.) He is rarely abstract in his approach. Even when he introduces a rather metaphysical idea *kinshitsu no kūkan* (averaged-out-quality space), he explains in terms of the familiar image of a popular candy: 'no matter how or where you cut it, only the same face appears like a well-made Kintarō candy.'[12] So again, Inoue tries to reach the same kind of public as the *gesakusha* of the Edo period.

In the true spirit of *gesakusha*, Inoue places himself beneath his subject and the reader. His view is thus that of someone looking up. He praises, wonders, reveals jealousy.

> 'I have no intention of comparing Mr Seichō's inspirations and literature with my own. I am merely a reader. If I compare Mr Seichō and myself as writers, I might as well quit writing novels. Especially his short stories, the short stories produced between 1953 when he received the Akutagawa Prize and 1957/8, if I keep on reading them, I can only despair. Style, structure, immediacy of subject — on every point I cannot even reach his foot. There is no way of comparing. So I remain a mere reader of his works.'[13]
> 'Then I thought: Mr Kita's sense of humour is not only on the tip of his tongue. Mr Kita's existence itself is humour. So, just as there are not too many courageous people who can stop eating peanuts after having tasted only one, there are not too many courageous people who can put down Mr Kita's humorous stories after having read one page. Especially *Sailor Kupukupu's Adventures* is such a case.'[14]

Even what should be interpreted as weaknesses in an author or his work under review are magically transformed into something to be admired:

223

'...Not all eight stories can be called masterpieces, but at least five of them are the best one can expect today in the field of entertainment stories. 8-5, that's a phenomenal batting average.'[15]
'...To put it positively, its content is saturated. One can say negatively that it is chaotic or like a messy toy box. But it is also true that a reader who finishes reading it will be filled with a pure sense of happiness that makes him say, "I have indeed touched something important."'

Inoue not only places his colleagues on a pedestal, but deliberately pulls down his own position. He often uses phrases such as 'I have no technique nor courage to summarise efficiently a world supported by 1450 pages of manuscript, but let me only explain its set-up.'[17] According to Inoue, the *gesakusha* of the Edo period were consciously or unconsciously aware that no matter how clever or scathing their works may be, they could never be above what they were parodying.[18] In a similar way, perhaps Inoue Hisashi as a literary critic acknowledges that no matter how brilliant a criticism may be, it can (or should) never tower above the work it criticises.

Inoue delves into books on architecture, linguistics, and philosophy with the same intensity as with pure literature, comic books, or dictionaries. In this respect, he resembles Kawabata Yasunari who was criticised for supporting authors expressing opposing views or becoming a member of societies representing contradictory doctrines.[19]

The sub-total of such elements of *gesaku* combined with constant mingling of personal values in Inoue's literary criticisms creates a sense of suspense. He relentlessly piles on praises and doggedly plays the underdog. Because of accumulated effect, the reader begins to wonder when the explosion point is going to be reached. Is the work really worth this much praise? Is not the critic building this tower of praise only to kick it down with his foot once it is completed? Is Inoue contemplating his criticism to commit double-suicide with the work it is meant to review? Inoue is aware of this kind of mechanism in *gesaku*.[20] Despite this suspense, however, as far as I can perceive Inoue sustains the tension till the end and does not let his subject down.

We have seen that Kawabata Yasunari and Inoue Hisashi as creators of the literature of praise have some qualities in common, such as the bringing forth of personal experience, a non-abstract approach, and the acceptance of a wide range of subjects. Kawabata concentrated on new and deceased authors; Inoue likes to deal with his contemporaries. Their major difference, however, is in their rhetoric. While Kawabata remains indirect and suggestive from an artist's distance, Inoue is the embodiment of *gesakusha*. Thus both of them give distinct impressions, though firmly agreeing on one point as literary critics — 'criticism should consist of one statement, "a good work." To go into details is of no benefit and can only be harmful.'[21]

If what Kawabata produced can be termed as *sanji bungaku*, the literature of eulogy, maybe Inoue's literary criticisms can be named *betahome bungaku*, the literature of extolling. Why does Inoue choose to be a *betahome* literary critic while he is a sharp-tongued social critic? The answer to this question may be related to the essence of many of his fictional and non-fictional works — sympathy for common people who struggle on and distrust for those who abuse power. It seems then that, in Inoue's mind, the writers belong to the category of people who deserve acceptance.

39

Not Only Minamata: An Approach to Ishimure Michiko's Work

LIVIA MONNET

Ishimure Michiko, the author of *Kugai jōdo: Waga Minamata-byō* (Paradise in the Sea of Sorrow: My Minamata Disease) can hardly be called a popular writer. In the West she is virtually unknown. Nevertheless, I believe that she deserves to receive more attention, both inside and outside Japan. In order to establish her position in the contemporary Japanese literary scene two things are needed: a body of rigorous, sober criticism, which should include assessments not only of individual works, but of her whole oeuvre; and the truth behind the myth surrounding the writer's person. The criticism of Ishimure's work which one encounters more often than not in obscure literary journals seems, with a few exceptions,[1] to suffer not only from a very uncritical, boundless admiration for whatever the poet has turned out in the course of her literary career, but also from a chronic lack of interest in the substance of her work, viz., what it is that makes the latter valid as literature. This attitude is inextricably bound with what I would call 'the Ishimure myth.'

This myth, which came into existence after the publication of *Kugai jōdo* has, in various forms and appellations, such as 'the kataribe[2] of the Shiranui Sea' (*Shiranuikai no kataribe*), Ishimure the 'sorceress' (*miko*), or 'spiritualistic medium' (*reibai*) consistently impeded a real understanding of her art. It is essential that Ishimure's writings be approached with a minimum of extra-artistic data, which should be taken into account only in so far as they are indispensable for the evaluation and interpretation of the work in question. 'One cannot use the life to interpret the work,' writes Susan Sontag in her essay about Walter Benjamin.[3] Of course most of Ishimure's works, especially those dealing with Minamata, cannot be considered independently of her life, as they not only nourish upon it but are, in a more or less straightforward way, autobiographical. (Any work of art is 'autobiographical' in so far as the artist projects himself into it). But her childhood experiences, or association with the victims of Minamata disease, should not be made into a yardstick for evaluating her work. The unique qualities of the latter will emerge only when the mythical fog has cleared away and critics, journalists[4] and the public begin to see Ishimure, not as a sorceress, or a reincarnation of dead souls, but just as what she is: a poet with a profound sensibility and a remarkable talent.

In order to present Ishimure to non-Japanese readers, the additional work of translation must be done but not, as in the case of the Japanese criticism of her work, before demarcating the territory of myth from that of reality.

It will not do to assert that *Kugai jōdo* 'has already become a Japanese classic,' that it 'ought to become a world classic,' and in the same breath to say that it will never become a world classic like Harriet Becher Stowe's *Uncle Tom's Cabin* because it is a book 'which is difficult even for Japanese people to understand. All the more so for foreigners!' Similarly, it will not do to say that *Kugai jōdo* is written in 'an indigenous dialect which seems nearly impossible to translate,' and which again 'is difficult even for most Japanese to understand.'[5] While it is probably true that *Kugai jōdo* will never become a world classic, even if we were to be offered an excellent translation of it, it is not true that it is impossible to translate[6] and downright arrogant to assert that foreigners will not be able to understand it. Here is another stubbornly persisting myth: 'things Japanese' cannot be understood by non-Japanese. Sasayama Yutaka, who made the assertions quoted above goes on to give us another saintly portrait of Ishimure: 'Her tiny 150-centimetre frame endured many physical dangers in order to clear a path, confronting the polluting industries, standing up to local and central government.... Sometimes, just as it seems that she has a shy, sweet expression on her face like a little girl, she will suddenly give a sharp look that seems to peer into all the cracks and crevices of the human soul.'[7] While it is true that Ishimure has an enthralling personality, and that she has played an exemplary rôle in the struggle of the Minamata disease patients, this portrait is certainly exaggerated. Moreover, it does very little to further our understanding of her art.

I am not trying to say that the function of criticism is to destroy myths. Criticism is both a destroyer and a creator of myths, it constantly replaces old myths with new ones: think of Romantic criticism, think of Ruskin and Matthew Arnold, of Ortega y Gasset and André Breton, of Valéry, the Nouvelle Revue Française and the American New Criticism, of Sartre, Barthes and Susan Sontag. What I am trying to say is that the evaluation and interpretation of Ishimure's work should rest, not upon myths, but upon facts: the richness and originality of her style; her scathing criticism of contemporary Japan, and of the myth of modernisation and industrialisation; the episodic, fragmentary character of her prose; the narrow range of themes; symbolism and hyperbole and so on. However painful it may seem to divest Ishimure of her Romantic aura, it is imperative to do so, in order to have an unobstructed view of her literary achievement.[8]

Ishimure Michiko was born in Amakusa in 1927. When she was three months old, her family moved to Minamata. She spent her childhood and youth in great poverty. The misery of her family was compounded by her father's chronic drinking, the presence of her blind and insane grandmother, and the fact that one of her younger brothers suffered from neurosis. Ishimure has recorded the unhappy circumstances of her childhood, as well as the consolation she found in her unique relationship with her grandmother and other poor and victimised persons, and in the beauty of nature in autobiographical works like *Hahatachi e no bunjoshō* (An Introduction for Mothers, original title *Aijōron*, 1959-60), *Waga Shiranui* (My Shiranui Sea, 1968), *Tsubaki no Umi no Ki* (Journal of the Sea of Camellias, 1976) and *Ayatori no Ki* (Cat's Cradle Journal, 1983).

From 1943 to 1947 Ishimure worked as assistant teacher at two primary schools in Minamata. In 1954 she met Tanigawa Gan and began to take part in the literary discussions he organised at his house. She became a member of the literary circle Kyūshū Sākuru Kenkyūkai (Kyushu Study Circle), in which Tanigawa was a central figure and to which other aspiring writers and critics like Morisaki Kazue, Ueno Hidenobu and Kawano Nobuko also belonged. Her first essay about Minamata disease was published in *Sākuru Mura* (Village Circle), the magazine issued by this circle. Ishimure's literary talent reached maturity under the influence of the Kyushu Study Circle, especially that of Tanigawa Gan, whom she later mentioned along with historian Takamure Itsue as her spiritual mentor. All through the 1960s Ishimure continued to write about Minamata disease, to comfort the isolated and impoverished victims and to try to secure means to help them. Her first book about Minamata disease, *Kugai jōdo: Waga Minamata-byō*, was published in 1969. It had an enormous impact on the general public, and helped create an important grass-roots support movement for victims of the disease.

Kugai jōdo was made into a documentary film, which was shown on television on RKB Mainichi channel on 14 November 1970, and into several dramas, the most successful of which are those of *Sunada Akira*.[9] It was awarded the Kumanichi Literary Prize in the year of its publication and the first Ōya Soichi Prize in 1970. Ishimure refused both prizes, saying that she could not accept honours for herself while the agony of the Minamata disease victims continued, and that her work on their behalf was still not finished. In 1973 she was awarded the Ramon Magsaysay Prize in the Philippines.

Ishimure has written two sequels to *Kugai jōdo: Kugai jōdo: Dai ni bu* (Paradise in the Sea of Sorrow: Part II, 1970-71), which was left unfinished and *Ten no Uo* (Fish from Heaven, 1974). She has been a key figure in the struggle of the Minamata disease victims for adequate compensation and certification, acting both as their spokesman and as unsparing accuser of the inhumanity of capitalist industry and state.

Ishimure's works can be divided into three groups: First, autobiographical writings, the most important of which are mentioned above: Second, works on Minamata disease: apart from the *Kugai jōdo* trilogy, Ishimure has published a collection of essays entitled *Ryūmin no Miyako* (The City Roaming People Dreamed Of, 1973). She has also compiled two books about the struggle of the Minamata disease victims: *Waga Shimin* (My Dead, 1972) and *Ten no Yamu* (Even Heaven Suffers, 1974). The third group consists of works in which she focuses neither on her life, nor on Minamata disease, but on different themes such as the life of peasants during the Satsuma Rebellion of 1877, the mysterious life of Nature, the rôle of women etc. Examples from this group of works are: *Ishimure Michiko saijiki* (The Ishimure Michiko Almanac, 1978); *Seinan eki densetsu* (Tales of the Satsuma Rebellion, 1980); *Tokoyo no ki* (Eternal Trees, 1982); *Oen yugyō* (Oen's Travels, 1984) etc.

The *Kugai jōdo* trilogy is Ishimure's masterpiece, on which her reputation as one of the most original and, at the same time, least accessible women writers of post-war Japan chiefly rests. In the chapters '*Yukijo kikigaki*' (What Yuki Said), '*Ten no uo*' (Fish from Heaven) and '*Tsuchi no uo*' (Fish on Land) from the first, and most famous, part of the trilogy, in the chapters '*Ashibune noshō*' (*Reed Boat*) and '*Kamigami no mura*' (Gods' Village) in *Kugai jōdo*, Part II, and finally in the chapters '*Funa kanjin*' (Mad Boat People) and '*Hana Kanjin*' (Madness of the Time of the Cherry Blossoms) in *Ten no uo*, the poet's art shows a kind of consummate, self-contained perfection, which she did not reach again in subsequent works, except perhaps in *Tsubaki no umi no ki*, and in certain passages in *Seinan eki densetsu* and *Oen yugyō*. But it is not my intention to follow in the wake of those Japanese critics who have lavished praise on the trilogy without paying attention either to its imperfections or to its originality. Let me emphasise a few points, which seem to me essential for the evaluation and interpretation of Ishimure's work.

One of the most striking features of the three works which form the *Kugai jōdo* trilogy is their bewildering structural complexity. This looks on the surface like mere disorder, or inability on the writer's part to organise her thoughts: medical reports; minutes of city assembly sessions; quotations from newspaper articles and various books alternating with passages written in beautiful poetic prose; dialogues interspersed with dramatic monologues and flashbacks; abrupt changes of locale; a sombre epic mode which, together with an absurd, nonsensical mode disrupts the pervading lyrical mode of the works; chaotic chronological sequence; narrative or descriptive passages dropped abruptly and resumed without warning later in the course of the narration and so on. However, this is neither casual disorder, nor organisational inability on Ishimure's part: it is as carefully planned and deliberate a structure as any intelligent writer could conceive of.

Though she maintains that she writes in a kind of trance, completely dominated by an unknown power, Ishimure has also asserted that there is a great deal of deliberation and premeditation in her writing.[10] This reflects a contradiction which lies at the core, not only of the *Kugai jōdo* trilogy, but of the whole of Ishimure's work: human consciousness can control the chaotic flow of time and history through art, wars and other such radical acts of will, but this, needless to say, is an illusion. The most the artist, who is conscious of his impotence can do is become an 'arrested collective consciousness,' which mirrors both the flow of time and the mass of tiny human wills swimming in it, while skilfully manipulating the latter's illusions of power. The *Kugai jōdo* trilogy is an instance of such 'arrested collective consciousness,' the expression of Ishimure's ultimate distrust of human consciousness, of history and of all establishments ostensibly devised to maintain order, which she views as instruments of coercion.

The same, essentially modern distrust can be discerned in the style and language of the *Kugai jōdo* trilogy. Language is as illusory a structure as order and power, and as chaotic and unreliable as human consciousness (I am speaking of a general concept of consciousness, which subsumes the subconscious and the libido). Language has no underlying logic, and no unity. It cannot accommodate what you want to express. It is a tantalisingly inadequate vehicle.[11] Hence the fragmentary character of the trilogy, which consists of a series of unrelated episodes, narrated with a total disregard for the chronological sequence. Hence the disjunctiveness and extravagance of the style, which marries obscure symbolism with hyperbole, and allows the long dramatic monologues of the Minamata disease patients (Sakagami Yuki, Mokutarō's grandfather, Egoshita Kazuko's mother, the mother of the congenital patient Tanaka Toshimasa) to disrupt the 'modernity' of the narration like an invasion of elements from forgotten times. In view of the current misconception about Ishimure's peculiar oral idiom I feel compelled to add that these superb monologues are not faithful transcripts of what the patients told her during supposed long conversations with her. She is no more a compiler of *kikigaki* than she is a spiritualist medium.

The poet's distrust of language can also be discerned in her refusal to conform to accepted notions about what literature should look like, or be about. Not only does she write about Minamata disease, a theme which lends itself more readily to sociological, medical or political writing, but she embodies it either in very unconventional prose, neither documentary nor fictional, but a mixture of the two, intensely lyrical, and illuminated by an oral poetic idiom uniquely her own; or in pure poetry which, again, is rather difficult to distinguish from poetic prose.[12] Precisely because existing literary forms and genres cannot accommodate what Ishimure is trying to express, she attempts to create new ones. Her endeavour to create a new language and a new literary form has been recognised by some,[13] but by no means all, critics, most of whom assign the *Kugai jōdo* trilogy to the realm of documentary literature.

The *Kugai jōdo* trilogy, then, is not only about Minamata disease. It is also about the modern artist's distrust of human consciousness, history and language. And also about disruption. Watanabe Kyōji, one of the first critics to direct his attention to the multiple layers of meaning in *Kugai jōdo: Waga Minamata-byō* says that the book is also about the downfall of the world represented by the Minamata disease patients, the world of pre-modern Japan, with its traditional village communities, ancestor worship, naïve animism and synchretic Buddhism.[14] But *Kugai jōdo* is a book about multiple disintegration. What Ishimure so painstakingly portrays is not only the slow physical decay of the Minamata disease victims, the collapse of the pre-modern society and of the natural environment in which they lived, but also the breakdown of the contemporary industrial civilisation and, implicitly, the approaching end of the human race. She assumes for herself not only, as she says in a memorable passage in the first chapter of *Kugai jōdo*, Part I, the rôle of a 'sorceress cursing modern times,' but that of a visionary, a phrophetess. In *Kugai jōdo*, Part II, and *Ten no uo* there are apocalyptic visions of a great conflagration consuming the world, and of the extinction of humankind through abuse of technical progress. The solemn, apocalyptic tone of a good part of the trilogy is so insistent that it reminds one of passages in the Bible. Ishimure herself says that her writings about Minamata disease form a kind of new Revelation of St John the Divine, not about the advent of Jesus Christ, but about 'the loneliness and misery of being eternally unable to die.'[15]

Ishimure Michiko undoubtedly has a pre-modern sensibility. This is apparent first of all in her depictions of Tokyo as a gruesome theatre of monsters, or a modern version of Hieronymus Bosch's grotesque hell. Her fierce condemnation of Chisso (short for Chisso Kabushiki Kaisha, the company which caused Minamata disease through its discharge of mercury effluent into Minamata Bay) and the huge bureaucratic machine of the local and central governments also indicate the poet's intense dislike of contemporary society. In her eyes, the Chisso Company is symbolic both of the illusions and the suicidal drive in Japan's rush towards modernisation. As yet another form of defiance of the modern spirit, Ishimure attempts to emulate pre-modern literary forms — the *jōruri* of the Edo period, the *setsuwa* of *Konjaku monogatari* in her works.

She has also declared that she feels she has much more affinity with Shinran, Chikamatsu, Miyazawa Kenji and Yanagida Kunio than with any writer of the Shōwa period. She gives lavish, vivid descriptions of the pre-modern village communities in the Minamata area, emphasising the virtues of their inhabitants, and deploring their disappearance in the post-war rush for economic growth. Ishimure's beautiful portraits of the victims of Minamata disease, as well as the homage she pays to the fishermen living on the shore of the Shiranui Sea, calling them 'the last richness of humankind' constitute, of course, the most convincing evidence of her pre-modern sensibility. However, this sensibility forms, so to speak, only the upper stratum of the poet's undeniably modern consciousness.

Apart from the complex structure, and the disjunctiveness and fragmentariness of the style of nearly all her works, one can find any number of instances of Ishimure's 'modernity.' There is, for instance, the theme of loneliness of the individual in the modern world. One can also find recurrent images like hole (*hora ana*), crack or fissure (*sakeme, kiretsu*), crevasse (*kurebasu*), which reflect the decaying state of contemporary civilisation. Ishimure's attempt to install Woman as the 'fountainhead of life' (*seimei no minamoto*), and her frequent use of feminine imagery, both of which indicate a brand of feminism rather different from that of other women writers such as Morisaki Kazue may be cited as additional evidence of her modern spirit. However, in recent works like *Ayatori no ki* and *Oen yugyō*, she turns her back completely on the modern age in order to immerse herself in a utopian pre-modern Land of Bliss (the Shiranui Sea of her childhood, the imaginary Island of Ryūō, where the mad medium, Oen, lives). Because they lack the tension between modernity and pre-modernity, and the polarity of the *Kugai jōdo* trilogy, these works are not entirely convincing, despite the poet's effective use of 'poetic dialect.'[16] The *Kugai jōdo* trilogy may be said to be not only the most 'modern,' but also the most successful of her works.

For the reasons I have tried to sketch above — complexity of structure and style, pre-modern sensibility, peculiar poetic dialect, narrow thematic range — Ishimure's works will probably never become, as Sasayama Yutaka rightly suspects, 'world classics.' Not even the first part of the *Kugai jōdo* trilogy, which is an astounding piece of work. However, I feel that the latter at least, as well as *Tsubaki no umi no ki* should be accorded the rank of 'minor classics.' Ishimure is, to my mind, one of those 'great minor poets'[17] whose work, even if it may not leave a deep mark on their own time will endure beyond it.

40

The Emancipation of Women as Shown in the Novels of Sata Ineko

*I will write. I will write about the suffering
and sorrow of women ...* (II,64)[1]

This declaration of the heroine of Sata Ineko's most famous autobiographical novel *Kurenai* (Scarlet) can be regarded as the motto of her whole literary work. As this quotation shows, the most important theme of Sata's comprehensive work is the suffering of women because of their situation in society and family.

Sata Ineko was born in Nagasaki in 1904. From her early childhood onwards, she was forced to work. At the age of 24 she came into contact with members of the Proletarian Literary Movement, and started her literary career by describing both her experiences at different jobs and the lives of women of the working-class in general.

During the period of the Proletarian Literary Movement up to 1934, the female figures of Sata's novels differ quite a lot. On the one hand we have Osono, the heroine of *Tabako jokō* (Female Worker in a Tobacco Factory). She sympathises with the Proletarian Movement in which her husband plays an active rôle and reads all the pamphlets he brings home, but she herself does not become active in the movement. When she gives birth to a child while her husband is imprisoned because of his political activities, she interprets the birth of the baby as her own contribution to the movement, since the number of supporters would grow in this way. Osono's attitude is truly a very traditional way for women in patriarchal societies to support a political movement. On the other hand, Sata's later proletarian novels introduce professional female leaders and labour-unions. These women behave quite contrary to the traditional rôle of women, even

CEWJ—P

in the way in which they speak. For example, they address each other as *omae*, which is normally used only by men. Although Sata portrays women who try to liberate themselves from traditional women's rôles, there is no confrontation between the sexes in her proletarian novels, because at this time the solidarity of the members of the working-class is of first priority for her.

After the decline of the Proletarian Movement, Sata Ineko begins to write her best known autobiographical novels, which are based on her own experiences during particular periods of her life. One of them, *Suashi no musume* (Barefooted Girl), published in 1940, became a best-seller at once. The heroine, Momoyo, a girl of 14, has been working very hard in Tokyo with her grandmother, as well as with other relatives. As she cannot stand this life any longer, she leaves them to live with her father, who has a job in a small town. But even at her father's place, she does not get the freedom she desperately longs for. What 'freedom' means to her is expressed in the following quotation:

> 'How nice it would be to be free and act as one wants to. That doesn't mean that I want only to act according to my will. But if it weren't for the rumours of people, if there were no rules as to how a girl should behave, if one didn't have to submit to anyone, if everybody, men and women, could live as they liked to, if there was such freedom, how happy would I be!' (III, 58-59)

While the heroines of Sata's proletarian novels saw the reason for their suffering as stemming merely from class-difference, Momoyo is clearly aware of the fact that the limitations of her freedom are also rooted in the position of women. Living alone with her father, she is supposed to fulfil the rôle of a housewife and to serve him. She feels that, as the eyes of the neighbourhood are watching her, she must submit to the standards of behaviour set by society as to how young girls are to behave. Although she would like to go out and walk around, she has to stay indoors during the time when the young workers of the nearby factory return home, in order not to be seen by them. But like a horse that gallops off although it is being reined in, she knows that her desire cannot be controlled.

During the beginning of her stay at her father's place, Momoyo wishes to marry as soon as possible, as a way to escape living with her father, which was becoming more and more restrictive to her. But by and by she succeeds in freeing herself from the limitations imposed on her by society and family, by building up her own value system. People begin to call her *suashi no musume* (barefooted girl) since she is always seen without socks, even in winter. Finally, Momoyo is no longer content with waiting for a marriage-proposal. She returns to her grandmother and goes to work again. The novel ends when the heroine is happy that she has discovered her own identity. The title *Suashi no musume* expresses her eventual transformation into a girl, who is no longer willing to conform, and who has freed herself (at least to some extent) and has become a strong personality.

The novel *Chibusa no kanashimi* (Pain of a Mother's Breast), published in 1937, deals with the theme of motherhood. Sata wrote the novel in the form of a letter addressed to the daughter of her first marriage, in order to explain to her the reasons for her divorce. At the time of the marriage the writer has been a traditional wife, obedient to her husband, who treats her very badly. When she gives birth to a baby, she realises that she would not be able to raise the child under these unbearable circumstances. Her responsibility to the child affords her the luxury of even considering separating from her husband. She returns to her father's place with her daughter. Such behaviour was very unusual before the Second World War in Japan, as children were legally regarded as being their father's property. But for the writer, it was impossible to leave the child with a man whom she could not trust.

The fact, that she takes her daughter back to her family, however, does not mean that she wants to dedicate her whole life to her. When she falls in love with a man, she has to decide between him and her daughter, because to raise the child together would be impossible for them. So she asks herself:

'Should a mother dedicate her whole life to her child? ... Would you want me to give up all the joy of my life and bind my whole life to you? Does happiness mean to you to be raised by me?' (II, 318)

While her father insists that she should not get married for a second time, but live instead with her daughter, the writer realises that to sacrifice her own life would not be good for the child. She thinks it over:

'When you are grown up, surely you will, out of love, take pity on me. But one day you will have to live your own life. Then you must go your own way, without worrying about me.' (II, 319)

This attitude seems to be a very important point. The author not only stresses the emancipation of women but also emphasises the necessity of the independence of children. She does not leave her daughter with her husband whom she cannot trust but, when she starts a new life, she entrusts her daughter to her father and her step-mother, who would like to adopt their grand-daughter as their own child.

The novels *Haguruma* (Cog Wheel) and *Kurenai* (Scarlet) depict the process of development which the author went through until she became conscious of the problems of women's emancipation. *Haguruma* deals with the most trying period of the Proletarian Movement, when many members had gone underground or been imprisoned because of governmental pressure. The heroine of *Haguruma* appears to be a strong and (at least to some extent) emancipated woman, who supports her family as a writer of the Proletarian Movement. While her husband is imprisoned, she gives birth to a child. Sata Ineko has described such an experience in the novel *Tabako jokō* (referred to earlier) about three years before she finds herself in just the situation about which she wrote. She has anticipated her own fate in a fictional work. But the heroine, Akiko, of her autobiographical novel *Haguruma* reacts completely differently from Osono in that early proletarian novel. Akiko resents that she has to interrupt her activities within the movement because of the baby's birth. While recuperating from the birth of the child, she immediately returns once again to work. Unlike Osono, she is not content merely with giving birth to new supporters of the Proletarian Movement, as she knows that her active participation is required.

The most famous novel, *Kurenai*, is based on the time immediately after that depicted in *Haguruma*. During the absence of her husband, the protagonist, whose name is also Akiko, has become famous as a novelist. When he returns home from prison, life starts to become very difficult for her. She begins to suffer from the conflicting feelings of loving her husband and at the same time longing for the freedom of living alone.

Now that her husband, who is also a writer, has returned home, Akiko realises that she is beginning to act like a traditional wife again. During his absence, visitors, who entered the house, had been her guests, but now she finds herself serving tea to his friends and sitting silently beside them. As she knows by her own experience how much housework disturbs creativeness, she never urges him to take even a small portion of responsibility for the children and the household.

In theory, Akiko and her husband would like a relationship on an equal basis; and he even wants her to pursue her writing. But in practice both of them fall back time and time again into the traditional rôles of husband and wife. Therefore her existence as a writer becomes extremely endangered. Akiko now realises how difficult it is for women who have been brought up and conditioned from birth as traditional females, to put their own standards of emancipation into practice. Reacting against the traditional thinking which remains deeply ingrained within her, Akiko decided to cut her hair. Cutting the hair or changing the hair-style in Japan is often regarded as a symbol for an important turning-point in the life of a woman. When Akiko in *Haguruma* realises that her traditional hair-style does not suit a woman who has become as emancipated as she is, she has her hair cut. Thus, she had adapted her outward appearance to her inward attitude. But in the case of Akiko in *Kurenai*, it is just the other way around. She is not yet emancipated, and her altering her hair-style to a modern one, attempts to overcome her traditional thinking. However, she does not succeed.

When her husband says that he wants to leave her in order to live with another woman, she interprets this as his way of escaping into an easier life. She tells him: 'I've been proud of our way of life. But now you just want a normal wife.' (II, 66) She feels very disappointed that her husband has forsaken their common ideal of a relationship based on equality. As the author does not offer any solution for Akiko's dilemma in the novel, she is afraid that those women who are just at the point of trying to emancipate themselves, might be discouraged by reading it. Therefore she stresses in an essay that if one is prepared for, and aware of, the problems with which a working woman is confronted, one will be able to solve them.[2]

The fact that Sata regards the professional activities of women as being very important for their independence, is seen in the family novels, which she published in the fifties and sixties. These novels revolve around the young women in Sata's daughter's generation. Some of them are no longer forced to choose between having a job and having a family because their husbands help them with the household tasks. Even though the percentage of couples who share the housework is very small, it must be regarded as very important that this new social phenomenon is depicted in Sata's novels.

Reading the family novels of Sata, it becomes evident that the fact that women attained legal equality through the new constitution after the Second World War does not mean that they became suddenly thoroughly liberated. The author shows in her novels that traditional thinking continues to exist in people's minds, especially in those of the older generation, which of course inhibits the freedom of the younger. The two main types of women in the family novels are represented by the two sisters in *Jibun no mune* (Her Own Heart). Chizuko, the younger one, is the type of modern young woman who marries a colleague and shares the housework with him. The older sister, Fumiko, appears to be more traditional and very shy. The day when an *omiai*, a meeting with a prospective bridegroom, is arranged for Fumiko, Chizuko comes to help her with her make-up. When she puts lip-stick on the lips of her sister, Fumiko suddenly utters: 'Somehow it is terrible, I feel like a piece of merchandise!' (X, 228) The author stresses that even a girl, who at first sight seems to be very traditional, can have the consciousness of a modern woman. Sata does not condemn the system of *omiai* on principle, but criticises the way they are arranged. In her novels she presents many women who feel degraded into mere objects. The heroines of these novels accept the system of *omiai* only as a way to meet someone, and — once they get acquainted with each other — intend to make the final decision for themselves. When everything is arranged by their parents they feel treated like a puppet on a string. At this point they reject being obedient to their parents, because they have begun to regard their own identity as very important.

Even if some women in Sata's novels sacrifice themselves for the sake of their families for a certain period of time (for example, refraining from marriage because of having to care for younger sisters and brothers after their mother's death), in the end each of them finds a way to free herself and live the life she longs for. When the heroine of *Itoshii koibitotachi* (Dear Lovers), Tsugie, considers breaking off her relationship with a man in order to live together with her aged mother, he thinks: 'I have to make Tsugie aware that resignation is no way to happiness.' (VII, 166) This statement summarises Sata's message and ideals — that self-sacrifice is a destructive and self-limiting goal, which in the end brings only unhappiness and dissatisfaction. The female characters which Sata Ineko has created can truly be an inspiration to women, because they demonstrate that the power to better one's own circumstances lies within oneself. The literary works of this author can be regarded as an appeal to women to free themselves and search for their own way to self-realisation.

41

Tsubouchi Shoyo: His Literary Theory in Practice

KEIKO KOCKUM

Among the few subjects which were overlooked by the advocates of western civilisation, after the Meiji Restoration in 1868, was literature and, in particular, the writing of the novel.

The development of a new type of novel had to wait until the publication of *Shosetsu Shinzui* (The Essence of the Novel) by Tsubouchi Shoyo in 1886. In this work, Shoyo presented in detail his theory as to how the novel, the *Shosetsu*, should be written. Shoyo at the same time was also writing a novel so as to provide a practical example of his theory on novel-writing. This novel, *Tosei Shosei-katagi*, is generally considered to be a failure. Yet it is also generally agreed that *Shosetsu Shinzui* was the impetus for the emergence of the modern Japanese novel. Indeed, it was in 1887 that Futabatei Shimei, after literary discussions with Shoyo, wrote and published *Ukigumo*, which is regarded as 'the first modern Japanese novel.'

Throughout the Tokugawa period, there had been two categories of literature. Poems and prose written in classical Japanese or Chinese comprised one category; *haikai*, *kabuki*, *joruri* and fiction the other. The two categories are known by a variety of paired names, such as *ga-bungaku* and *zoku-bungaku* (elegant and vulgar literature), *bushi-no-bungaku* and *chonin-no bungaku* (the literatures of the ruling and the ruled classes), and even *bungaku* and *hi-bungaku* (literature and non-literature). A further classification might be into primary and secondary literature: primary literature had a didactic purpose and was strongly related to 'moral learning' based on the Neo-Confucian philosophy, which taught the ruling class how to rule and the ruled class to obey. Fictional prose was included among the secondary literature, because it was not Confucian in nature, nor did it teach people how to rule, and be ruled: it was referred to as *gesaku*, non-serious work, and was not considered as having any 'literary' value. A present-day judgement of Tokugawa literature might well be that the primary literature was lacking in novelty, while the secondary literature was lacking in literary quality.

There were several factors which contributed to the development of a new type of literature, where parts of each of the two previous literary categories combined together; the result was a new type of fiction, and the eventual result was the modern novel — *shosetsu*. Tsubouchi Shoyo called for literary reform, and his thesis *Shosetsu Shinzui*, suggesting the way towards achieving this, was published in nine volumes of booklets between September 1885 and January 1886 by the Shogetsu-do publishing company.

In the preface of *Shosetsu Shinzui,* Shoyo states his opinion that recently the writing of *shosetsu* he has seen have been of extremely poor quality. They are either reworkings of or imitations of the Tokugawa *gesaku.* His purpose in writing this work is to demonstrate to readers what a novel should be and, at the same time, to provide authors with a plan, so that from now onwards there will be an improvement in Japanese novels to the extent that they may eventually be able to surpass European novels in quality, and be of such a standard that they can take a glorious place alongside painting, music and poetry on the altar of the arts.

Shosetsu Shinzui is divided into two parts. Part one is mainly about the theory of the novel, and part two about methodology. Some parts of Shoyo's theory are contradictory, and other parts rather vague. But his main points are that the novel should deal with reality and not with convention, should be independent as an art form, and should not be used as a tool for moral education; a novel must have universal appeal, and should not be intended to cater to the tastes of one small segment of the reading public for a short span of time. The essential point in writing a novel is to portray *ninjo,* i.e. human feeling, and thereafter to portray *setai,* i.e. general social conditions. Shoyo makes a point that the way of portraying should be by the use of *mosha,* i.e. 'copying,' which will result in realism. We can also see that he was aiming at shaking contemporary society's prejudiced view of the novel as a literary form.

Based on this theory, Shoyo wrote a novel entitled *Ichidokku Santan, Tosei Shosei-katagi.* ('On the Character of Present-day Students, Read Once and Sigh Thrice).' It was published in seventeen paperback booklets between June 1885 and January 1886. Shoyo, who had graduated from Tokyo University two years previously, was already a known literary scholar. A strong public reaction, mostly antipathetic, followed publication of the novel. It was the most discussed novel of the year.

At the beginning of chapter 11, Shoyo replied to the criticisms he had received. To the criticism that it was unthinkable that a literary scholar should write such a low-class and vulgar work, Shoyo wrote:

'Those who criticise my *Shosei-katagi* as being vulgar do not know what a novel is. The novelists in the West have written about the lower classes, about prostitutes and about the 'inner world' of pick-pockets, to quote a few examples. The difference in novel writing between the West and Japan is that the western novelist has depicted the lower-classes because it is the novelist's duty to depict reality, while the Japanese novelist has written vulgar stories to meet the demand of uncultivated readers. This novel is written in the same manner as a western novel.'

To the criticism that a scholar should concentrate on more serious matters and, if he wishes to have anything to do with novels at all, the translation of a political novel, at least, would be more meaningful, Shoyo replied:

'This criticism is typical of those who regard the novel as a "useful art," and the Arts as a tool for politics. These are the words of those who do not know what a novel is, of those who are not moved by Victor Hugo's and Charles Dickens' novels. I do not wish to waste pages here on such people, though I am willing to discuss this topic at some other time and place.'

When he was criticised that the students in his novel are those of three or four years ago, while the students of today are neither as prodigal nor as lazy as those described in this novel, he answered,

'The story here is set in the 14th or 15th year of Meiji. The first part of the novel is about the past, and the story will gradually approach the present day. Thus, it can be seen that this criticism is also that of the reader who knows only about traditional Japanese fiction. I intend to describe how the students' characters progressively change, as well.'

When it was suggested that the novel must be based on the author's own experiences, and he was asked, 'Has a scholar's life really been like this?,' Shoyo wrote:

'Mr Dickens has written a novel about a group of pick-pockets. Do you think Dickens earned his living as a pick-pocket?'

Shoyo's primary intention seems to have been to portray student life, as is stated in the preface of the novel, but on the final page of the last chapter, chapter 20, he says that he could not fulfil his intention of writing about student life because of the limitations of the size of the book. He also says:

'The aim of this novel centres on the brother and sister finding each other. Maybe it sounds as if my aim has been running counter to what I have led the reader to expect when he takes the novel's title into consideration, but I have planned my plot to suit the reunion of a brother and sister, and not to suit the description of the characters of the students in detail.'

So, the novel is about the student, Moriyama, finding his sister from whom he was separated 14 years previously in the brief civil war which took place in 1868. However, the novel does not centre upon them. Moriyama's best friend, Komachida, falls in love with a *geisha* who later in the novel proves to be Moriyama's long-lost sister. Shoyo directs the focus of his interest towards the long-lost girl and her brother's best friend, and he contrives a grand finale where the problems besetting them are removed, and a happy future together is ensured.

This, however, contradicts Shoyo's own foreword to *Tosei Shosei-katagi* which clearly expresses his intention of writing a novel to describe different types of students, who have a variety of attitudes towards life, a novel by which he could instruct his readers how 'to judge, to discriminate between good and evil.' However, this didacticism was exactly what Shoyo, the literary scholar, was trying to liberate the modern novel from, so that it could become an independent art form.

We can also see the ambivalence of Shoyo's understanding of *ninjo*. The 'human feeling' that Shoyo was conscious of was, as is made apparent throughout *Shinzui* and the novel, similar to that seen in *Genji Monogatari*,

Tamenaga Shunsui's *Umegoyomi* and some English novels. It is obvious that by 'human feeling' what Shoyo meant was the love between a man and a woman.

One aspect of this love is 'passion,' which is carnal desire, and the other 'love' based on the admiration of someone's personality. In describing the students, therefore, Shoyo had to divide them into two groups: the students, whom Shoyo calls the 'immoral party,' whose *ninjo* was based upon 'passion,' and the students who controlled and suppressed their passion. Shoyo had no difficulty at all in writing about the students of the 'immoral party;' his language runs smoothly, and the dialogues are quite authentic, something which had not been previously seen in Japanese fiction. They are the characters who come alive in the novel and provide us with a vivid picture.

Shoyo's problem was how to present the other group of students. And, since Shoyo's ideal *ninjo* was to be felt by them, and since *ninjo* had to be described in a novel, and since a novel must have a hero (as stated in section ten of *Shinzui*), Shoyo chose his novel's hero from this group.

One of the standard criticisms of this novel is that it is a 'hero-less' novel. I cannot agree with this. Shoyo failed to present his hero and heroine sufficiently clearly so that the reader could understand them as such. The hero is Komachida whom Shoyo allows to fall in 'love' with the heroine and who is, therefore, the only male character in the novel who fulfils Shoyo's demands as a hero.

Shoyo, the scholar, demands that characters be described from within, but Shoyo, the novelist, failed to reach inside his characters' minds. Since 'a woman is a soothing agent,' a view expressed by a non-'immoral party' student, Shoyo did not have to develop her psychologically. On the other hand, Shoyo had to make his hero 'struggle' and 'agonise' to show his, the novelist's, insight into his character. The hero's 'agony' is, for example, shown in chapter 2, when the hero, Komachida, cries out in anguish, in a blend of Japanese and English. However, isn't it a little too grandiloquent, even for an intelligent student, to have him speak English in such a scene? The picture of the 'struggling and agonising' hero is rather comical, and scarcely arouses a reader's compassion.

Is it because Shoyo had never found any 'psychological insight' in the earlier Tokugawa novels, which he could use as a model when he came to apply it to his own novel? Is it because the only 'psychological insight' he has read, was in English? Or could it possibly be that students of his epoch really talked like that?

In composing the characters of his novel, he must have collected characteristics from the novels he had read, in the way he recommends as a good method in *Shinzui*, section 3. Could Shoyo have collected too much material? The reason for the failure of this novel is that its contents should have been spread over two different novels and the hero in one novel cannot also appear as the hero in the other.

Shoyo, the literary scholar, held that the novel as an art form 'should touch our hearts,' but the descriptions of students' life could hardly move his readers' hearts, so the maudlin theme of the reunion of a brother and sister was chosen as the main plot. It is evident from the fact that the *geisha*, Tanoji, is introduced at the very beginning of the novel, that Shoyo was intending to tell the story of a long-lost girl who had become a *geisha* and then is 're-found.' But such a theme had already become too common and well-worn both in Japan and, in a similar form, in the West, and was not suitable for a 'modern' novel. What Shoyo did was to adapt the then modern social class, the university students, as a sort of 'parallel plot,' to imbue his work with a 'modern flavour.' However, since he was not writing a report about student life, this had to be 'woven into' the plot 'skilfully' as Shoyo states in *Shosetsu Shinzui*. The 'thread' Shoyo used to 'weave' the 'student's life' into the plot was too thin, with the result that the work has fallen into two parts. They are barely connected to one another by the students' conversations about the hero, and their advice to the hero.

As we have seen, the failure of this novel is partly because of Shoyo's misinterpretation of certain fundamental literary concepts, and partly because of contradictions occurring when he came to put his own theory into practice. But the fundamental failure is that Shoyo no matter how hard he tried, could not shake off the idea that all literature should, in some way, 'guide' the reader towards moral improvement. The first stage of his literary development was based upon *gesaku*-works, as one can clearly see through his frequent mentioning of them both in *Shosetsu Shinzui* and *Shosei Katagi*. When the literary scholar's theory was put into practice by a novelist, who made *gesaku* the foundation for his story-telling, the last Tokugawa *gesaku*, spiced with the flavour of modern Japan, *Tosei Shosei Katagi*, was the result.

It is, in a way, a very unfortunate novel. The stylistic advance of the 'modern' atmosphere in the dialogue passages did not receive as much attention as it should have, because of the publication of *Ukigumo* the following year. As a result of *Ukigumo's* high reputation, *Shosei Katagi*, in comparison with this later work, has received an unfairly harsh critique.

Shoyo, by actually writing this novel, imbued courage into contemporary young literati who had for the most part been translating foreign novels, and spurred them on to attempt the writing of original novels themselves. They were guided by Shoyo through *Shosetsu Shinzui* theoretically but were unfortunately provided by Shoyo in *Tosei Shosei Katagi* with a good example of how not to put his theory into practice.

42

The Palimpsest of Memory in *Yoshino-Kuzu* of Tanizaki Junichirō

PASCALE MONTUPET

The hills of Yoshino, often celebrated in the Manyōshū are, as one knows, difficult to negotiate (located as they are at the entrance of the Kii peninsula) considered to be a place leading to the beyond. Indeed, the reader, plunged in a temporal labyrinth, glides towards the beyond, in search of the golden palm; a palm that the tale of *Yoshino-kuzu*, published during the sixth year of Shōwa (1931), seems to promise him. Actually, if the spatial field where Tsumura and the narrator-author are strolling along is situated in a precise country, that of Yoshino, then their journey goes astray in a time eroded by a shower of instants, to the extent that it becomes an illegible palimpsest in which we can hear the mingled voices of Tsumura, the narrator and Tanizaki speaking to one another, actor and spectator at the same time. And yet it is from this temporal diachrony that the unity of creation originates as an ideogram originates from a sequence of lines.

The first period of time travelled over is that of history, the troubled period of Nanboku-chō. Evoked by the figure of Jitennō, dominant in the first chapter, it reappears in the last as a necessary intermediary, but somewhat disguised; but, as Mikame remarks, Tanizaki introduces a few variations to historical reality. How can one explain this disguise? According to Hirayama, when Tanizaki asserts at the end of *Yoshino-kuzu* that he has not written a historical narrative, it is the confession of his failure, an opinion contradicted by the strong censure concerning anything written relative to the Emperor's person during the wars over Manchuria. On the other hand, for Mikame, this disguise is the proof that *Yoshino-kuzu*, far from being a historical narrative, is a work of fiction. Possibly Tanizaki did not wish to limit his book to a historical narrative but, being aware of its romantic usefulness, has used it as a sort of 'monumenta' to which the reader could refer. After that, it is easier to bring the said reader to accept a deceptive scenography, passing imperceptibly from the truth to probability, then to illusion, richer in possibilities. Moreover, we may notice the frequent repetition of the world *gensō* (illusion).

Thus, the actual repeated historical references to Nanboku-chō as written in *Gikei-ki* quickly become but a haze to the reader, representing some lost time. From the second chapter onwards, the first temporal web thickens with new fibres that we shall call collective memory. At least that is our own interpretation of chapters 2, 3, 4, 5. It resembles *The Garden of the Forking Paths* by Borgès: 'this web of times is quite dishevelled;

these times which draw nearer fork, criss-cross, embracing all possibililties.'

The reader of Yoshino-kuzu will thus recover the multiple paths of his memory, at once intellectual, sensorial, sentimental, and even Buddhist. Intellectual at first, the structure of *Yoshino-kuzu* is akin to a pastiche of anecdotal journeys during the Heian period. Tsumura and his companion arrive at the Yoshino site; they describe it; then the author discloses the state of mind of both travellers. There are many references to *meisho*, whether they be that of Yoshino as a place or, for instance, that of a temple standing at the top of the Kuragari pass. There are also numerous allusions to koji or the poems of the Elders, such as those blooming in *Manyōshū* and *Kokin-shū*, often quoted and commented on by Tanizaki in what Gérard Genette would call a hypertext. In short, a reader, fed on the literary tradition of Heian, will feel the presence of the Elders, supported by the indirect presence of the 'ego,' since, according to Roland Barthes, 'I don't think it wrong for the "ego" not to appear anymore, for one to penetrate and to lose oneself entirely in the masterpieces left by the Elders.' (*Critique*, November 1973).

These references to the Elders remind us of the stylistic brilliance of the *Kilin*. But the depth of the master's polish, and the transparent multiplicity of the different layers, and the reminiscences of the theatre emphasise this depth very soon by the gloss of the brocades. The arrival on the stage of Yoshitsune and his beloved Shizuka is equal to a powerful *'captatio benevolentiae.'* Earlier, I referred to the reader being charmed, the theatrical illusion not being the slightest artifice. This time Tanizaki appeals to the sensorial memory of the reader, the memories of *Yoshitsune-sembon-zakura* and of *Konkai* are mainly valuable because of the visual and auditory impressions relived, comparable to Marcel Proust's recovered sensations; sensations for which 'intelligence is quite powerless!'

Tanizaki often limits himself to indirect allusions, either by his mother's mouth or by Tsumura's, and the reader quickly perceives that, if the actual site of Imose enables the author to return to the theatre, it is the opposite of the play *Yoshitsune-sembon-zakura* which brings him back to real time, the time of a rediscovered childhood. In parallel, it is *Konkai* who brings Tsumura back to his childhood, the link binding them being the evocation of Shizuka, at the same time wife, mother and vixen. Thus, we go from the character on the stage to the real person, go back to a legendary figure, exactly as in *The Search* we go from a Venice of dreams to the real Venice.

But this time, rediscovered thanks to the theatre, it is soon limitless since it presents itself again by the magic of reincarnation. Thus, we understand the dream-like reminder of the Nō of *The Two Shizuka*, the dual aspect of the stage character seems to coincide with a permanent duplication of the text; *Yoshino-kuzu* becomes an actual hypertext of the Nō such as we have described; a hypertext of which Tsumura would be the *shite*, in search of his roots and 'I' the *tsure*. This poses the problem of the 'I'-Tanizaki relationship, a problem that we shall shortly be tackling.

For Tanizaki goes further now than the sensorial stage to reach his reader's heart, a memory which is no longer collective but individual, taking up a third of the book: chapter five entitled 'Kuzu.' It is at this moment that the reader hears for the second time the songs about the forest of Shinoda and remembers the games that they gave rise to. Which reader would remain insensitive to the admirable letter of Tsumura's grandmother, so tenderly poetic? We feel we are listening to Tanizaki's own heart. Finally, what power Tsumura's mother's face embodies, as a live portrait of the vixen-mother of *Konkai*, reincarnated with the features of Owasa!

We would like here to emphasise the romantic importance of the reincarnational phenomenon. In his work Proust also wakes some of his characters in order that they may live again; even Albertine, but this is done almost inadvertently. Tsumura's mother's resurrection with Owasa's features, on the other hand, is perfectly integrated into the temporal web of the narrative. This kind of procedure is not Tanizaki's own preserve. To convince oneself of this, one only has to turn over the pages of *The Temple of the Dawn* by Mishima, since its hero is reincarnated with the features of a little princess of Siam. This use of reincarnation is essential, in our opinion, to the realisation of what we understand as the timelessness of the narrative. Indeed, the notion of time as uniform, absolute, is annulled by the reincarnational phenomenon replaced by a temporal discontinuity, a spring of eternity, perhaps natural to a civilisation impregnated with Buddhism, but still difficult to understand for a civilisation stamped with Christianity, which conceives the resurrection of human beings quite differently. *Yoshino-kuzu* could well be a first step in the beyond.

These memories of Tsumura, this emotion of 'I,' brings us back to the problem mentioned previously: that of the relationship between 'I' and Tanizaki, and of the part played by Tsumura vis-à-vis 'I.' 'I,' as we said before, is exterior to Yoshino but is constantly involved in Tsumura's memories, to the extent that the latter's search ends up by being merged with the former's curiosity, as well as reflecting on the reader.

The last chapter bears testimony to the authenticity of Tanizaki's journey to Yoshino, since Hirayama says that he followed the same path linking Sannoko to Hachimandaira, and that he found it identical to Tanizaki's description. Thus 'I' would become merged with the author. Just a few details do not seem to coincide. For instance, the narrator walks through the pass of Obamine, and he is alone, whereas Tanizaki — at least this is what he writes to Okumura — goes through the pass with a carriage and a guide. Anyhow the narrator is never exactly the author and, *Yoshino-kuzu* not being a *shishōsetsu* but indeed a fiction, the coincidence between author and narrator is not essential.

On the other hand, the protective distance of fiction produces an effect of catharsis on the childhood fantasies of both Tanizaki himself and his readers. Such is the strength of this entanglement of time, of memories, where everyone may draw little fragments of himself, of his 'cultural identity.' Would not Ōe Kenzaburō writing *The Game of the Century* follow the same path?

The time of History is now both lost and regained, eternally present. After reading *Yoshino-kuzu*, it is impossible to read it again backwards in the manner of Proust. Proust's impressionism is erased because of a sharp sense of staging.

We should like to end this study by dealing with this very clever staging. Tanizaki has brought the Elders on the stage; he wrote himself in *Setsuyo-an-yawa:* '...The *meisho* play the part of those creating fantasies, the actual place known as Yoshino is not important; what is important is to see it with the eyes of remembrance.' He has staged his recollections of the theatre, read and perceived by the constant return of Yōshitsune and Shizuka's figures, duplicated even down to objects, including the *koto* for instance. He has also staged Tsumura and the narrator, sitting on a rock in Chapter IV, and they are still there in Chapter VI, as landmarks on the path of memories. He has even staged Nature, choosing the season of autumn, propitious to the melancholy of the journey in Heian times.

This theatrical aspect of the novel would not be complete, had Tanizaki not put himself on the stage. Indeed, the culture perceived one page after another, the fluttering heart of a child, the search of the woman-mother are really Tanizaki's — dare we say? — 'this modulated murmur,' as Bergson wrote, 'by which existence reveals its inexhaustibly-changing nature to the mind.'

43

The Rôle of Kokinshū Poetry as a Source of Allusion (*hikiuta*) in *Genji Monogatari*

GUNILLA LINDBERG-WADA

This paper concerns the rôle of *Kokinshū* poetry as a source of poetic allusion (i.e. *hikiuta*, poem alluded to) in the narrative, dialogue and letters of *Genji Monogatari*. The word *hikiuta* first appears in the commentary on *Genji Monogatari* called *Sairyūshō* by Sanjōnishi Kin'eda (about 1525). However, research on *hikiuta* goes back as far as the history of research into *Genji Monogatari*. The earliest commentaries *Genji Monogatari shaku* (also called *Koreyukishaku* or *Genjishaku*) by Fujiwara Koreyuki, and *Okuiri* by Fujiwara Teika, both completed in about the 1230s, deal almost exclusively with the relations between Genji Monogatari and the Japanese, Chinese and other literary sources that can be considered to be important for a proper understanding of the *Genji Monogatari* text.

The first scholar to give an exact definition of the term *hikiuta* was Motoori Norinaga (in *Genji Monogatari tama no ogushi*, 1796). According to him, *hikiuta* means an 'old poem' which is quoted in the text of a tale (*monogatari*). He says that the meaning of the whole poem, or part of it which is not cited in the text, is included in the meaning of the text. He defines *hikiuta* as referring only to the case where the meaning of the text cannot be understood without knowledge of the poem which is alluded to (*hikiuta*). Tamakami Takuya, on the other hand, in *Tokorobiki shiika butten* in Ikeda Kikan (ed.), *Genji Monogatari jiten'ge* (1960), takes into consideration not only the case in which the reader cannot fully grasp the meaning of a passage of the text (including the underlying meaning) without recalling a certain poem, but also each case in which it can be assumed that the author of the text recalled a certain poem to his or her mind while composing the text.

My criteria for selecting the *Kokinshū* poems already referred to have been: a) a prose passage of the *Genji Monogatari* text and a *Kokinshū* poem share a phrase or part of a phrase and b) as a result of the combination of a *Kokinshū* poem (the poem alluded to, *hikiuta*) and the *Genji Monogatari* passage, the scope of the *Genji Monogatari* passage is changed in one or both of the following ways: 1) a latent or hidden meaning of the *Genji Monogatari* passage becomes obvious; 2) the *Genji* Monogatani passage of text is brought into relation with a larger context, i.e. that of *Genji Monogatari* as a whole or of other works of literature or of human experience in general.

In *Genji Monogatari*, the prose text in itself can often be characterised rather as poetic or lyrical prose. Poetry as such, not only in the form of poetic allusion, also plays an important part in the text, as about 800 poems form part of it. Furthermore, there are not only allusions to *Kokinshū* in the text, but also to Chinese legends, Buddhist sutras, poetry from *Ise Monogatari*, *Wakan Rōeishū Kokin Rokujō Gosenshū* and *Shūishū*.

In accordance with the above-mentioned criteria, I have found 188 instances of allusion to poems of *Kokin (Waka)shū* in the *Genji Monogatari* text (128 *Kokinshū* poems alluded to on 188 occasions). Depending on characteristic traits, those 188 instances of *hikiuta* divide into two groups of about the same size as follows:

1) a. Dialogue, interior monologue or letters quoted or related. In a few cases narrative text.

    b. One phrase of the poem alluded to appears in the *Genji Monogatari* text, in order to invoke another part of the whole of the poem alluded to.

    c. *Aesthetic or implicit mode of expression*

2) a. Narrative text (but also in some cases dialogue, interior monologue or letters).

    b. Knowledge of poem alluded to not necessary for comprehension of the

text, but the scope of the *Genji Monogatari* text is broadened by poetic allusion.

    c. *Expanding mode of expression or means of recognition.*

The above two groups have been divided into four types of poetic allusion, mentioned in 1 c and 2 c above. Those are not meant to be absolute types, but are instead closely related to each other. 'The aesthetic mode of expression' and *hikiuta* as a 'means of recognition' constitute the two extreme ends of the unbroken continuum formed by the four types of poetic allusion (*hikiuta* as an aesthetic mode of expression, as an implicit mode of expression, as an expanding mode of expression and as a means of recognition). *Hikiuta* as an aesthetic mode of expression stands for poetic allusion only as a figure of speech, taking no account of extra-linguistic realities. *Hikiuta* as a means of recognition, on the other hand, is created in the borderland between linguistic and extra-linguistic reality, where the two mutually arouse expectations and confirm each other. Between those two extremes there is the bulk of the material — *hikiuta* as an implicit and as an expanding mode of expression. Although those types of poetic allusion are different from each other both in type of sentence and in the relationship between *Genji Monogatari* text and part of poem invoked, their function in the *Genji Monogatari* text is strikingly similar. The majority of *hikiuta* as implicit or expanding modes of expression are connected to the expression of feelings, often in the relationship between man and woman.

I have made this classification in order to make clear that poetic allusion, *hikiuta*, is not a type of stylistic device that always plays the same rôle in the *Genji Monogatari* text, but on the contrary plays quite a varied rôle. *Hikiuta* is a source of 'imagery' on the one hand and of 'signals' on the other hand. The *waka* images used frequently become symbols in the composition of *Genji Monogatari* — of *shukke*, of 'Uji' as a concept, of 'scent' as religious emotion and karma. *Hikiuta* also constitute signals to invoke more or less complex concepts in the *Genji Monogatari* text. The *Genji Monogatari* text can be read on different 'levels.' There is an explicit level and an implicit level, where the rôle of *hikiuta* can be seen in the interaction between the explicitly told and the meaning implied in the *Genji Monogatari* text. The rôle of *hikiuta* can also be seen in each confined context and in the larger context of *Genji Monogatari* as a whole — in the composition of the plot.

HIKIUTA AS AN AESTHETIC MODE OF EXPRESSION

(23 instances) The device of *hikiuta* may be used for an aesthetic purpose, to create refined language. Through allusion to poetry, the narrative becomes implicit and suggestive rather than explicit in its expression. Only a person of education (i.e. an urbanite) is able to use or understand this kind of language properly. *Hikiuta* as an aesthetic mode of expression is used in a social context, almost exclusively in speech or letter writing. A person who can allude to a poem properly is a person of good taste and education, while a person who is not good at this use of language is ridiculed. An example of the refined language used by the urbane aristocrat is the following scene in the chapter *Matsukaze:*
A party is held at Katsurain, with drinking and exchanging of poems, including an exchange of poems between Reizei-in and Genji, both alluding to the name of the place, the moon etc: 'As Genji was reciting to himself *"thriving on..."* he recalled Awajishima and cited Tadamine's poem...' (*'NAKA NI OITARU to uchizun-jitamau tsuide ni awajishima wo oboshiidete mitsune ga...'*) The words in caps in the above quotation allude to the following poem in *Kokinshū* (no. 968):
Because it is a village thriving on the moon I can confidently rely on the light (*hisakata no naka ni oitaru sato nareba hikari wo nomi zo tanomuberanaru*)

In this scene, the imagery of *Kokinshū* no. 968 among others forms the background to the poems which are recited. 'The one who knows' — the urbane aristocrat — knows how to allude to this specific poem, which shares the name of the palace with that of the *Genji Monogatari* context — *katsura*, and which, according to the head note in *Kokinshū*, was also recited in a situation similar to that in *Genji Monogatari*.

HIKIUTA AS AN IMPLICIT MODE OF EXPRESSION

(61 instances) The difference between implicit and aesthetic expression is a matter of degree. Allusions not only invoke the connotations of the poem alluded to, but also involve a shift in focus from what is explicitly stated to what is implicitly told. Sometimes the message conveyed by the *Genji Monogatari* expression does not have much in common with the poem alluded to except for the *waka* imagery. Because it is an implicit mode of expression, it is possible to express extremely complex states of feelings in a concise manner. Furthermore, it makes it possible to mention matters which would be rude, too bold or (for reasons of taboo) almost impossible to express in explicit language.

In the following scene in the chapter *Suetsumuhana*, *hikiuta* serves as a means of expressing complex feelings in a concise form:
Genji and Suetsumuhana are together in the morning after he has stayed the night:
'(Genji): "At least this year I think you could let me hear your voice even if just a little. Of course waiting for the voice of the *uguisu* is one thing; anyway I am eager to see your unkind attitude to me renewed," he said and at last she managed with great difficulty to say in a trembling voice: *"Spring with its chirping."'* ('*kotoshi da ni koe sukoshi kikaseta maekashi mataruru mono wa sashiokarete ōnkeshiki no aratamaran nan yukashiki to notamaeba SAEZURU HARU WA to karoojite wananakashi idetari.*') The words in caps in the above quotation allude to *Kokinshū* poem no. 28:
Spring with its hundreds of birds chirping
Each year it is renewed
While I am growing old
(*momochidori saezuru haru wa monogoto ni
aratamaredomo ware zo furiyuku*)
The meaning expressed in the *Genji Monogatari* text is not that of the phrase of the *Kokinshū* poem actually quoted ('Spring with its chirping,' '*saezuru haru wa*'); instead, it is the rest of the poem, especially the last part of it, that is invoked, 'Each year (spring) is renewed, *While I am growing old*' ('*haru wa monogoto ni aratamaredomo* WARE ZO FURIYUKU').

However, whereas the part of the poem invoked by Suetsumuhana expresses a general feeling of *mujōkan,* or the impermanence of life, in connection with the passage of time and the change of season, she gives it the far more private and restricted meaning 'You are getting tired of me.' This meaning, together with the wretchedness she is feeling, is accentuated by the contrasting phrase she actually quotes, 'Spring with its chirping' ('*saezuru haru wa*') with its vivid, fresh image of spring.

(75 instances) In this function, the expression of the *Genji Monogatari* text by way of *hikiuta* invokes the whole of a certain poem, which in turn widens and deepens this expression (phrase). The effect of this varies according to context. A *hikiuta* expression often climaxes a descriptive or narrative passage (which has been gradually built up) and by poetic allusion a whole situation or atmosphere, state of affairs, is summed up, comprised and clarified in concise language to set off a new turn in the narrative. Often the events of *Genji Monogatari* are made parallel to the literary background by *hikiuta*. (For instance, Genji's sojourn at Suma is overtly made parallel to Yukihira's sojourn at Suma and the poetry he is supposed to have composed there.)

It is quite common that a description of a scene or milieu is simultaneously a description of the inner state of feelings experienced by the tale's characters and expressed by way of poetic allusion. In the description of places and scenery outside Heiankyō, poetic allusion seems to have the effect of bringing into relief and rendering familiar and comprehensible a milieu or scene that would otherwise be difficult for the presumptive reader of the story to comprehend and grasp. The whole description is often built up exclusively around *waka* imagery.

The following passage of the chapter *Kagaribi* begins a new turn in the narrative, stating the season of the year and the situation:
It is during the period Genji visits Tamakazura to teach her to play the *koto*. The passage opens with:
'It became *autumn*. As *the first* cool *breeze* started *blowing the husband's hem* he felt a bit sad and was no longer able to stay away (from Tamakazura) but visited her often.' ('*AKI ni narinu HATSUKAZE suzushiku FUKI-idete SEKOGA koromo mo URA sabishiki kokochi shitamau ni shinobikanetsutsu ito shibashiba wataritamaite.*')

Up it blows, my husband's hem,
and shows the lining anew;
so fresh and novel,
the first breeze of autumn
(*wa ga seko ga koromo no suso wo fukikaeshi
uramezurashiki aki no hatsukaze*)

The wind is one of the main characteristics of autumn. This *Kokinshū* poem about the first breeze of autumn ('*aki no hatsukaze*') evolves around the concept of '*ura.*' *Ura* is the lining of the hem that blows up in the first breeze of autumn. Simultaneously it is part of the word '*uramezurashiki,*' meaning 'fresh and novel.' In this latter case *ura* stands for *kokoro* — the heart or mind that feels the novelty but which is hidden inside a person.

The passage of *Genji Monogatari* quoted above, starts out as a description of the season in general, but through the 'husband's hem' Genji becomes the subject and through the word '*ura,*' the description of the season turns into a statement about his feelings. The concept '*ura*' is here further used in one more sense of the word, namely 'hidden feelings.'

Genji is no longer able to stay away: he cannot suppress his feelings for Tamakazura ('*shinobikanetsutsu*'), with the result that he goes to visit her often.

HIKIUTA AS A MEANS OF RECOGNITION

(29 instances) *Hikiuta* as a means of recognition implies that poetic allusion is used not only to create concise expression or to compare personal experience to universal experience. The 'reality' of the world of fiction is the *Genji Monogatari* text is also recognised and interpreted — even shaped — in the terms of *waka*.

An example of this rôle of poetic allusion is the following scene from the chapter *Wakana*, part I. The day after the visit at Onna-san-no-miya's residence, Genji spends a day at Lady Murasaki's. After sending a poem to Onna-san-no-miya, attached to a spray of white *ume* blossom, Genji goes near the porch, dressed in white clothes and with some white *ume* blossom still in his hands, and watches the scenery outside:

'An *uguisu* that started out its early spring song quite nearby in the red *ume*-tree startled him, and the sight of him as he hid the flower, maybe thinking "*my sleeve smells indeed of the ume flower*," pushed up the screen and looked out was so young and charming that it was hard to imagine that this man was the father of a grown son as well as a man of such a high position in the state.' ('*uguisu no wakayaka ni chikaki kōbai no sue ni uchi-nakitaru wo SODE KOSO NIOE to hana wo hikikakushite misu wo oshiagete nagametamaeru sama yume ni mo kakaru hito no oya nite omoki kurai to mietamawazu wakō namameka shiki ōnsama nari.*')

In the above passage *Kokinshū* poem no. 32 is alluded to:

Because I just broke off a twig
my sleeve smells indeed of
the *ume* flower;
Maybe believing it to be here
the *uguisu* sings
(*oritsureba sode koso nioe ume no hana
ari to ya koko ni uguisu no naku.*)

By the use of the verb form '*oritsureba*' this poem gives the impression of just now being experienced: through the emphatic words *koso* and *koko ni* it implies that the action of breaking off a twig has just been completed. The whole little scene in *Genji Monogatari* is built up around this *Kokinshū* poem and includes every element of it.

The *Kokinshū* poem is the situational description of a moment that is complete in itself and that is the result of an action ('Because I just broke a twig,' '*oritsureba*') that calls for no continuation. In the *Genji Monogatari* context, however, this poem is transformed into a linear story that evolves into a new action: Genji hides the flower he actually holds in his hand. What was merely implied as a possibility in the poem has become explicit fact in the story of the *Genji Monogatari* context.

An interesting point here is that the '*waka* as a means of recognition' function of poetic allusion, is not restricted to the description of a scene as such, but that it also includes the fictive person of the story itself, as Genji's action of hiding the *ume* from the *uguisu* is described as directly induced by this poem.

CONCLUSION

The dominant tendency of *hikiuta* as a mode of aesthetic and implicit expression as occuring in dialogue and letters, suggests that this use of poetic allusion reflects the language spoken by the educated urbanites of the Heian era. The tendency of *hikiuta* as an expanding mode of expression and as a means of recognition is not as clear as the above; nonetheless, there is a preference for this use of poetic allusion in the narrative — suggesting that this reflects a stylistic trait of the narrative of *Genji Monogatari*, where *hikiuta* forms an integrated part of the narrative in prose.

An important precondition for the stylistic device of *hikiuta* was that there existed a kind of standardised *waka* language as a frame of reference common to both the author and the readers of *Genji Monogatari*. *Kokin (Waka)shū* played an important rôle in the creation of certain norms and a standardised *waka* language that was to have an influence on *waka* composing for centuries to come.

As I already mentioned, *hikiuta* play an important part in the description and expression of complex feelings in *Genji Monogatari*. It is especially common in connection with the relationships between men and women. It should be noticed, however, that allusion to poems of *Kokinshū* does not play this part equally in every relationship between man and woman in *Genji Monogatari*. Allusions to *Kokinshū* poems have a higher degree of frequency in 'unusual situations' and tend to contrast to 'everyday life,' where *hikiuta* are scarcer. For example, allusion to *Kokinshū* poems is scarcer in the relationship between Genji and Lady Murasaki or Genji and Lady Akashi than in his relationships with Yūgao, Asagao, Oborozukiyo and Suetsumuhana. The important rôle of allusion to *Kokinshū* poems in the story of Yūgiri and Ochiba-no-miya is also an example of its use in. circumstances opposed to everyday life. This connection between *Kokinshū* poems and 'unusual situations' can also be seen in the types of situation where *Kokinshū* poems are alluded to: partings, journey, unfamiliar surroundings. Examples of this can be seen in the Uji story, in Yūgiri's visits to Ono, and the description of Tamino-no-shima.

To sum up the rôle of *waka* poetry in the form of poetic allusion in *Genji Monogatari* (possibly also *waka* poetry as such in *Genji Monogatari*), *waka* represents a certain attitude towards life, a way of analysing life and the phenomena one encounters. *Waka* presents a form to shape material of a complex nature. This is the reason why *waka* is used to such a high degree in order to express or describe feelings. *Kokinshu* poetry offers a source of knowledge, acts as a guide in different situations. It offers a standard form to grasp and express overwhelming things like death and grief. It gives shape to and puts a confused state of emotions into order in a situation of parting or at the start of a new phase or change of milieu in the narrative or the life of the characters of *Genji Monogatari*. *Waka* poetry also is a way to mention the unmentionable like *shukke* or the possibility of death (unpure, taboo things, maybe).

44

The Genji-Intext[1] in Towazu-gatari

TSVETANA KRISTEVA

Since it was discovered in 1940 by Professor Yamagishi Tokuhei and published in 1950, Lady Nijō's *Towazu-gatari* has commanded increasing attention and provoked an important, if latent, controversy. On the one hand, there is the widespread opinion, shared by many Japanese scholars, that Lady Nijō's lyrical diary[2] is but an imitation or repetition of *Genji Monogatari*. Lady Nijō's enthusiastic admirers, on the other hand, while conceding that the link is undeniable, have somewhat timidly avoided direct confrontation and regard it as evidence of the later work's enhanced fictionality (*monogatarisei*.)

This paper is concerned with the textual interrelationship of the two narratives. By examining the various types of links and the valorisation of the *Genji*-intext in *Towazu-gatari*, I hope, firstly, to vindicate Lady Nijō's claim to originality and artistic merit and, secondly, to demonstrate in the light of recent developments in literary theory the *modus operandi* of the classical Japanese tradition.[3]

Duly noted by many scholars, the problem of *Genji Monogatari's* intextual presence in *Towazu-gatari* has been discussed most thoroughly by Professor Shimizu Yoshiko in her essay 'Why was *Towazu-gatari* written?'[4] In her excellent study, Professor Shimizu has set out to catalogue the *Genji* references in *Towazu-gatari* in order to demonstrate the immense influence of Murasaki Shikibu's narrative upon Japanese court life in the late thirteenth century, precisely the time when *Towazu-gatari* was written. However, since Professor Shimizu's starting-point was *Genji Monogatari* and her aim, reflected in the title of the series in which her essay was published, was to corroborate but one more exemplary function of *Genji* in classical Japanese literature, she did not discuss the actualisation of the *Genji*-intext in *Towazu-gatari* and thereby, perhaps, unintentionally detracted greatly from Lady Nijo's merits as a writer.

Thus, for example, in her discussion of the opening episode in which GoFukakusa leads away Nijō to his palace, Professor Shimizu points out the obvious reference to Genji and Murasaki and concludes that 'it attests to her Nijō's) tendency to imitate *Genji Monogatari* at all costs and by all means and continually to attune and adapt her own narrative to it.'[5] Later on, she gives the following explanation: 'Obviously, the writer of *Towazu-gatari* has memorised the context and the letter of *Genji Monogatari*. That is why every now and then we come across words and phrases from *Genji* as Nijō tries to imitate its characters and episodes. Of course, her education was not confined to *Genji Monogatari;* she also quotes poems from *Ise Monogatari, Sagoromo Monogatari, Shinkokinshū*, etc., but her dependence

251

upon *Genji* was particularly heavy, since here we have a case of profound structural influence rather than accidental citations.'[6] Professor Shimizu is quite right in that Nijō went far beyond citing (*in'yō*) in the classical Japanese sense of the term. Lady Nijō's citational practices, however, amount to a complex inter-textual relationship which, far from belittling her work, redounds to her credit.

Modern literary scholarship, inspired by Bakhtin's theory of the dialogue nature of the word or discourse,[7] has widely accepted the notion that every text is a mosaic of quotations which are actualised on various semantic levels. Every text absorbs and transforms other texts. Every text is constituted through references to other texts, styles, traditions, antecedent types of discourse, and literary methods depending on the historical and socio-cultural and axiological affiliations of the writer. Within the triad 'object — addressee — context (code),' 'each word (text) is an intersection of words (texts) where at least one other word (text) can be read.'[8] The dialogue nature or double-voicedness of any discourse and its ambivalence or polyvalence are essential textual features that have developed in a steady, if haphazard, fashion from antiquity to the present day. In this development, however, there have been periods when certain literary *exempla* acquired such a highly authoritative status or conventionality that resorting to the 'other's word' within the framework of the historico-cultural continuum was an artistic imperative rather than a matter of possibility or choice. As Bakhtin put it:

'It has not been possible in every epoch to wield direct authorial discourse, it has not been possible for every epoch to wield a style, for style presupposes the existence of authoritatively-sanctioned value judgements... Nor has it been possible in every historical situation for the creative artist in the last instance to express himself in direct or unrefracted or unconditional authorial speech. When there is no 'last' word of one's own, every artistic intent, every thought, feeling, and experience has to be refracted through the medium of the other's word, the other's style, or the other's manner, and it is impossible to identify oneself with them without reservations, distancing, and refraction... In such epochs, especially in epochs dominated by conventional discourse, the direct, unqualified, and unrefracted word seems barbarian, raw, and wild. The word/discourse of culture is always refracted through the authoritatively-sanctioned medium.'[9]

It is a critical common-place that *Genji Monogatari* absorbed the 'word of culture' and the poetic methods of its artistic antecedents and became a stylistic *exemplum* for Japanese court literature. That narrative was the highest convention and began to function as the obligatory immanent code within the framework of all the aristocratic literary texts that were to follow. *Towazu-gatari* was no exception since its socio-cultural roots lay precisely in that sphere of influence where *Genji* was the *exemplum* and, on the other hand, it belonged to an epoch (the late Kamakura period) in which court literature was declining or, in other words, 'direct authorial discourse' was impossible. One should also note the encoded textual presence of *Genji*, even in *Heike Monogatari*, the exemplary narrative of the new epoch, which attests to the continuity of the literary tradition. However, if that was a case of realised possibility, *Towazu-gatari* exemplifies the mandatory imperative of convention. Consequently, its artistic merits should not be defined in inverse proportion to the intextual presence of *Genji* but, rather, precisely with regard to the modes of textualising the other's word, style and manner, with all of which Lady Nijō did not identify her own discourse 'without reservation, distancing and refraction.'

Therefore, my purpose has not been to catalogue the instances of *Genji Monogatari's* presence in *Towazu-gatari*, since I can add very little to Professor Shimizu's list, but to demonstrate *how* the *Genji*-intexts are valorised in the new text, acquiring different functional meanings from the prototext and, at the same time, activating the textual body upon which they have been grafted.[10]

There are many valuable contributions to the poetics of the 'other's word.' Apart from Bakhtin and Julia Kristeva, the typology of the relations between the metatext and the intext has been discussed by Wierzbicka, Todorov, Lotman, Torop.[11] (Let me mention in passing that it is very difficult to draw a clear-cut distinction between the two terms.) The number of specific textual studies is even greater.[12]

The most detailed typology of the 'other's word' suggested by Torop, employs a pair of interrelated criteria, *mode* of linking and *level* of linking, and also takes into account whether it is just an element of the text or the entire text that is linked. The mode of linking can be affirmative or polemic, each of these further subdivided into explicit and implicit forms.[13] That wide variety of linking practices alone indicates that there can be no simple negative solution to the problem, i.e. the presence of intext(s) alone does not mean that the work in question has no independent artistic merit; moreover, plagiarism is only one of the possible cases of implicit affirmative linking and sometimes it is not even that as the arch-plagiarist James Joyce well knew.[14]

Let me mention another curious example. In his *Empire of Signs*, Roland Barthes has half-seriously demonstrated by means of his own photo how the 'other's discourse' is naturalised in the new context. Because of the hieroglyphic environment and the specific rituals of Japanese typography, Barthes's picture in the *Kobe Shimbun* looks more Japanese than that of the actor Tamba Tetsurō in the context of a European paper.[15]

And now we can go back to the Lady Nijō. It is not accidental that the very first episode of Book One of *Towazu-gatari*, that is, the beginning of GoFukakusa's love affair with Nijō, quite intentionally refers us to *Genji Monogatari* (especially to the 'Waka Murasaki' chapter). Far from being a sign of helplessness, the inter-textuality in that episode suggests a deliberate stylistic strategy, to wit, one of intextual containment and metatextual framing.

A warning is signalled with the preparations for the arrival of GoFukakusa since everyone knows of his coming *except Nijō*. Her perplexity is unresolved on the surface level of the narrative, but the context creates expectations and adumbrates the events to follow through a metatextual authorial reference to *Genji*: 'What a naïve child you are,' her father replied amid the general laughter. *'How was I to understand?'*[16] Compare with *Genji*: 'Please, sir. You forget yourself completely. She is

253

simply not old enough to understand what you have in mind.'[17] Later on, the narrator drops the veil of vagueness, and the associative reference becomes quite unambiguous. Compare the following passages:

	Towazu-gatari	*Genji Monogatari*
a)	Don't fall asleep before His Majesty arrives. Serve him well. **A lady in waiting should never be stubborn, but should do exactly as she is told** (p.4)	You are not to sulk, now, and make me unhappy...**Young ladies should do as they are told.** (p.109)
b)	...I suddenly awakened to find right beside me a man who **had made himself comfortable** (*nare gao-ni*)[18] and fallen fast asleep. (p.5)	I will be your watchman. You need one on a night like this. Come close to me, all of you. **Quite as if he belonged there** (*nare gao-ni*)[19], he slipped into the girl's bedroom. (p.104)
c)	When at dawn we heard someone say, 'His Majesty will be returning today, won't he?,' GoFukakusa muttered, 'Now to go back **pretending something happened** (*koto ari gao naru...*) and prepared to leave.(p.6)	It was still dark when the wind began to subside and he made his departure, and all the appearances were **as of an amorous expedition** (*koto ari gao nari ya*).(p.105)
d)	Your unexpected coldness has made me feel that the pledge I made long ago...was all in vain. You must at least behave in a way that other people won't find too strange. **What will people think** (*hito ikaga omowan*) if you seclude yourself.(p.6)	What a way to behave, what a very unpleasant way to behave. Try to imagine, please **what these women are thinking.** (*hito mo ika-ni ayashi to omouramu*).(p.181)

The sinuous movement of the intext in these four passages, situation – quotation – situation, culminates in *b* and *c* in the quoted *naregao* and *kotoarigao*. The direct reference to *Genji Monogatari*, reinforced by weaving the 'other's word' into the speeches of Nijō(b), her father Koga Masatada (a), and GoFukakusa (c,d), unmistakably recalls the famous 'Waka Murasaki' chapter. Furthermore, there is the metatextual intrusion of the narrator as if it was necessary to dispel any shadow of doubt: 'It seemed like an episode from an old tale.' (*mukashi monogatari meki*)(p.18). This episode (the beginning of the love affair between GoFukakusa and Nijō) looks like a case of positive linking and that is how it has been understood by scholars who have discussed it solely in terms of *Genji Monogatari's* influence or Lady Nijō's imitative tendencies. In order to understand the functional rôle of the intext, however, we have to assess it with regard to its contextual framing and then within the framework of the entire text.

The incipient affair between GoFukakusa and Nijō is paralleled in this episode by the clandestine affair between Nijō and Akebono (Sanekane), who at first remains unidentified. Sanekane's identity, however, is not withheld for the sake of secrecy, as some scholars have asserted, but *for artistic reasons*. The narration of the liaison between Nijō and Sanekane has in this first chapter a supplementary function; it provides the background against which the GoFukakusa-Nijō affair, constituted as an allusion to 'Waka Murasaki,' is actualised in the new text. Such an interpretation if supported by the heavy metatextualisation on the Sanekane-line. Filled with remorse, Nijō answers Akebono's (Sanekane's) love-letter: 'After I sent this I began to wonder what I had done.' (p.8) She accepts the gowns presented to her by him and resorts to a lie lest she should betray herself: 'My heart throbbed, but somehow I replied calmly, "They are from Her Highness, Lady Kitayama".' (p.3).

The first direct confrontation between the two lines occurs during GoFukakusa's second visit to Nijō:

'He lay down beside me and began to talk of what was uppermost in his heart, but I was so dazed that I could only worry about what would happen next. I was tempted to acquiesce quoting the line "If this were a world without lies," except for my fear that the person who had claimed he might die of grief (Sanekane) would consider my behaviour vulgar.'(p.8)

The confrontation is brought to a climax when Nijō is led away to GoFukakusa's palace (as Murasaki is led away from Genji):

'It hardly seemed the same place where I had lived for so many years as a child. Frightened and ill at ease now, I regretted having come and wondered what I might expect.'(p.10)

These remarks have crucial significance for the interpretation of the *Genji*-intext in the first chapter where it is very prominent. The references seem clear and straightforward; nevertheless, the *Genji*-intext as it is actualised in *Towazu-gatari* carries on an implicit ('hidden interior') polemic with the prototext of *Genji Monogatari* and adumbrates the tragic turn of events in Nijō's life. Nijō's affair with GoFukakusa is constituted as an allusion to Murasaki and Genji, but the *polemic character of the linking* is a reminder that hers will not be the happy fate recounted by the 'old tale.' Murasaki remains Genji's beloved throughout his life and he barely survives her, whereas Nijō does become the ex-emperor's favourite concubine for a time but is finally banished from the court by him.

Again, the *Genji*-intext (in this case the reference is to the 'Suma' chapter) is subject to a similar polemic linking at the beginning of Book Three of *Towazu-gatari*:

Towazu-gatari	*Genji Monogatari*
I was at this time so worried about **my affairs, which were proving to be an unending source of trouble** (*'yo-no naka ito wazurawashiki...'*), that I longed in my weariness to go and live beyond the mountains. Yet **the difficulties of giving up this life barred the way** (*'nao, sutegataki ni koso...'*).(p.121)	For Genji life has become **an unbroken succession of reverses and afflictions** (*'yo-no naka ito wazarawashiku...'*)... Unsettling thoughts of the past and the future chased one another through his mind. **The thought of leaving the city aroused a train of regrets** (*'ito sutegataki koto ōkaru naka-ni mo...'*)... (p.219)

255

Genji is banished from the palace as a result of plotting by Lady Kokiden, who is his father's (the emperor's) first wife and hates the very shadow of the dead Kiritsubo, Genji's mother. Nijō's banishment at the end of Book Three is effected with the collaboration of Higashi Nijōin, who is GoFukakusa's first wife and hates Nijō as much as the memory of her mother, although Nijō's own sins precipitate her destruction. Here again the intext is polemicised, and its function is to create expectations and to adumbrate the course of events.

One may conclude from these examples that as a rule intext on the level of content is not linked affirmatively, but is polemicised, its most frequent function being the adumbration of future events. This fact applies to *Towazu-gatari's* generic features, for the so-called 'hidden interior polemic' is usually pointed out as a characteristic of autobiographical writing.[20] As a result of this polemical intext, the narrative is bifurcated both spatially and temporally, the texture gains in depth and suggestiveness, and the 'unwritten' can be read by the readers, for whom *Genji Monogatari* is functioning as a model.

Intexts containing the 'other's word' themselves present a special emphatic case. Here is an interesting example. After her father's death, Nijō receives the following letter from Akebono (Sanekane): 'I have wanted to write to you every day, but I was afraid that my messengers would meet His Majesty's and cause him to wonder **if your heart had strayed...** (pp.32-3) *hi-wo hatezu mo mōshitaki-ni gosho-no mitsukai nado miaitsutsu koro to mo shirade ya oboshimesaren to...* — p.49). It may not be immediately clear why the Japanese *'koro to mo shirade ya'* should be rendered **'if your heart had strayed.'** The expression *'koro to mo shirade ya'* contains a reference to one of Kaoru's poems to Ukifune, who had a clandestine liaison with Niou:

nami koyuru	It still stands firm,
koro to mo shirazu	The pine-clad mount of Sue,
sue-no matsuyama	Thought I. And even then
matsuramu to nomi	the waves engulfed it.
omoikeru kana	(p.1003)
(vol.6, p.168)	

The point is that Kaoru's poem contains a hint at Ukifune's unfaithfulness since the polemicised *Kokinshū*-intext, the original poem (prototext) being a pledge of faithfulness. Here is that poem from *Kokinshū*:

kimi-wo okite	On the day
adashi kokoro-wo	That I am unfaithful to my vows,
waga motaba	May the waves break over
sue-no matsuyama	The Mountain of Waiting of Sue.
nami mo koenamu	

We are confronted, then, with a case of double linking and containment. By dint of this already two-voiced intext, the text of *Towazu-gatari* has become three-voiced or three-dimensional: on the one hand, there is the affirmative analogy which links the GoFukakusa-Nijō-Akebono triangle to the Kaoru-Ukifune-Niou triangle while, on the other hand, through the *Genji*-intext a further polemic link is extended to *Kokinshū* poem.

It is really strange, not to say inexcusable, that the presence of the 'other's word' in Japanese classical prose has hardly ever been studied, especially the intext on the level of content, which has been generally considered a negative feature. At the same time, all scholars acknowledge that the basic poetic techniques in Japanese classical poetry *waka*, such as *kake-kotoba, engo, honkadori,* are meant to create a kind of two-dimensionality, not just on the level of expression but, above all, on the level of content. So it turns out that, while we admire the two-voicedness of poetry, we deny, or at least ignore, it in prose, which after all is based on the same type of aesthetic perception. We can even discuss the problem of intext in Japanese classical prose, borrowing the basic poetic techniques of *waka*. Thus, for instance, Akebono's letter can be said to contain an *engo*-intext; the first episode of *Towazu-gatari* can be discussed in terms of a *honkadori*-intext, and so on. We can even find the *makura-kotoba* principle exemplified by many cases on the level of expression, where we have obvious cases of affirmative linking typical of medieval literature.

In both prose and poetry, ambivalence/polyvalence is effected through references to well-known expressions, images, characters, motifs, and situations. For *Towazu-gatari* and for the entire court literature following *Genji*, *Genji Monogatari* functioned as the 'authoritatively sanctioned' model text. It is worthwhile to observe that its exemplary rôle was not confined to letters alone but affected the behavioral code and the everyday life of the aristocracy as well. Professor Shimizu tells us that in the third year of the Kōan period (1280) a lively discussion known as the *Kōan Genji rongi* took place in the Fushimi Palace. The emphasis was not so much on analysing the text of *Genji* but, rather, on asserting one's own life in terms of it.[21] *Towazu-gatari* gives further evidence thereof: for example, the kickball game organised by GoFukakusa in honour of Kameyama (pp.92-93); the concert modelled after one in *Genji* (pp.96-98).

The fact that *Genji Monogatari* functioned as a model of court life in Nijō's time (the latter half of the thirteenth century) indicates that the intextualisation of *Genji* was a twofold process: in the first place, there is the simple linking *text - text*, in the second, the trinomial linking *text - psychological and behavioral patterns - text*, which calls for a special essay in cultural semiotics.

Notes

Chapter 2 J. L. BREEN *Heretics in Nagasaki: 1790-1796*
The author wishes to express his gratitude to Sr Kataoka of Junshin Women's University, Nagasaki, and the librarians of Nagasaki Prefectural Library for their invaluable help in obtaining documents used in the preparation of this paper.
I have used the following abbreviations:
NPL Nagasaki Prefectural Library NSSS *Nihon Seikatsu Shomin Shiryō Shūsei*, (Sanichi Shobō: *1972*)

1. Takatani Eizaemon's statement, *25.9.1790, NSSS*, p. 768.
2. Sakujirō's statement, 25.9.1790, *ibid.*, p. 771.
3. See, for example, *ibid.*, pp. 768 and 774.
4. 'Chūeimon hoka jūhachinin,' 12.8.1790, *ibid.*; also Urakawa Wasaburō, *Urakami Kirishitanshi* (Zenkoku Shobō: 1943), p. 22.
5. For Hikozaemon, see *NSSS*, p. 832. For Enkichi, see Paulo Enkichi in Kataoka Yakichi, *Kakure Kirishitan* (NHK Books: 1967), p. 42, and Takatani Eizaemon's statement 26.9.1790, *NSSS*, pp. 774-5.
6. ' Sakujirō describes his journeys to Amakusa and Ōmura in statements dated 23, 25, 29.9.1790, *ibid.*, pp. 765, 770-2, and 774.
7. See 'Hizen no kuni Sonogigun Nagasaki Urakamimura Kumejirō Kakekomi Uttae' (hereafter 'Kakekomi Uttae'), *ibid.*, p. 813.
8. Kataoka appears to err when he writes that the nineteen villagers remained in prison for two years ('Kumejirō no Shusso,' *Katorikku Kenkyū* (Tokyo, 1941), vol. 2, 21.1, p. 2). 'Kakekomi Uttae' (*NSSS*, p. 813) suggests that they were released before the end of 1790.
9. For the *Shōya's* punishment, see *Takatani Eizaemon hoka nime ishūto naiso ni tsuite akushitsu ari. Yaku torihanashi oshikomi mōshiwatashisho*, Document 11.173, NPL. For Sakujirō, Morinaga Taneo (ed.), *Hankachō — Nagasaki Bugyō no Kiroku* (Tokyo, Iwanami Shinsho, 1962), p. 104.
10. Such evidence did in fact emerge in the 1856 incident. See collected documents in *NSSS*, pp. 833-856.
11. 'Kakekomi Uttae,' *ibid.*, p. 813.
12. A *Kakekomi uttae* has been defined as 'a means of by-passing established court procedure . . . and appealing directly to . . . the central government. It was absolutely forbidden in any other than the most extreme circumstances.' *Nihonshi Jiten* (Kadokawa: 1982), p. 187.
13. Toya Toshiyuki, *Kirishitan Nōmin no Keizai Seikatsu* (Itō Shotenkan: 1947), p. 12, maintains that it did, but this is mistaken. Yasuzaemon was released, as Toya states, in the eleventh month of 1792, but as Kumejirō did not leave for Edo till the end of the next month, this cannot have been a result of the *Kakekomi uttae*. Kumejirō's journey to Edo was actually inspired by the fact that Yasuzaemon was re-arrested.
14. Clearly, the authorities suspected that Yasuzaemon's *kō* was a front for clandestine religious meetings.
15. Shōgorō's statements, 5.2.1792, *NSSS*, p. 795.
16. Risuke's statements, 14.2.1792, *ibid.*, pp. 781 and 790.
17. 'Oshiokiukagai,' *ibid.*, p. 828.
18. See n. 16.
19. 'Oshiokiukagai,' *ibid.*, p. 832, and *Ishū shinkō itashisōrō mono kaishin shōmon*, 2-12, NPL.
20. 'Oshiokiukagai,' *NSSS*, p. 827.

21. An interesting account of *nandogami* can be found in Kataoka, *Kakure Kirishitan*, pp. 220-256.
22. See *NSSS*, pp. 775-779
23. Heisuke's statement, 19.8.1790, *ibid.*, p. 777.
24. *Osoreirinagara Kōjōgaki*, Document, 11-173, NPL.
25. The diagram is taken from *Kirishitan Shiryō*, Document 315-172, NPL.
26. See Kataoka Yakichi, 'Nagasakikenka Kirishitan Bohi Sōran,' *Kirishitan Kenkyū*, 1934, p. 214, and 'Kakitsuke,' *NSSS*, pp. 816-820.
27. Only the lenient penalty given to Junyo, the priest of the Shōtokuji temple, for negligence, is recorded in the *Hankachō* (Kataoka Yakichi, *Nihon Kirishitan Junkyōshi*, Tokyo: Jiji Tsūshinsha, 1979, p. 527).
28. Kataoka, 'Bohi Sōran,' p. 211.
29. 'Osoreirinagara kōjōgaki' in Toya, *op. cit.* p. 19, and statements made by Shōzō and Senzaemon, *NSSS*, pp. 806 and 809.
30. Ebizawa Arimichi, *Christianity in Japan* (ICU and Tuttle: 1960), p. 73, and H. Cieslik et al. (ed.), *Kirishitansho Haiyasho*, Tokyo: Iwanami Shoten, 1970, pp. 613 and 623.
31. I have used the copy of the *Yasokyō Sōsho* in the Junshin University Library, Nagasaki.
32. Shōjiuemon's statements *NSSS*, pp. 801 and 803, and those of Takatani Eizaemon, *ibid.*, p. 807.
33. Genzaemon's statement 25.3.1794, *ibid.*, p. 802, and Kisuke's statement, 24.2.1794, *ibid.*, p. 799.
34. Senzaemon's statement, 8.9.1793, *ibid.*, p. 806; and Toya, *op. cit.*. p. 15.
35. 'Oshiokiukagai,' *NSSS*, p. 832.
36. *ibid.*
37. Kataoka, *Nihon Kirishitan Junkyōshi*, p. 549.
38. For the dates of the Nagasaki *fumi-e*, see *Nagasaki Saijiki*, 1796, in *Nagasakiken Shi* (Tokyo: 1963), vol. 4, p. 877, and Kataoka, *Fumie* (NHK Books: 1974). Kanzawa Taikan (1710-1795) describes the *fumi-e* he witnessed in 1795 in *Okinagusa, Nippon Zuihitsu Zenshū*, vol. 15, p. 638.
39. H. Cieslik, 'Nanbanji Romane der Tokugawa Zeit,' *Monumenta Nipponica*, 1943, pp. 36-7.
40. *Tsūkō Ichiran*, (Tokyo: 1923), vol. 195, p. 190.

Chapter 3 CATHARINA BLOMBERG *Thunberg: A Swedish Scholar in Tokugawa Japan*
1. *Resa uti Europa, Africa, Asia, förrättad åren 1770-1779*, 4 vols., Upsala 1788-91.

Chapter 4 A. A. TOLSTOGUZOV *Some Features of Japanese Feudalism*
1. *Istoriya stran Azii i Afriki v sredniye veka*, I., 1968, p. 51.
2. Boldyrev G. I., *Sinansy Yaponii*, Moscow, 1946, p. 27.
3. *Istoriya stran Azii i Afriki v sredniye veka*, p. 373.
4. *Ibid.*
5. Takayanagi Mitsutoshi, Takeuchi Rijo (eds.), *Nihonshi Jiten*, Tokyo, 1974, p. 1291.
6. *Sovetskaya istoricheskaya entsiklopediya*, t. 16, Moscow, 1976, stolbets 907.
7. *Istoriya stran zarubeshnoy Azii v sredniye veka*, Moscow, 1970, p. 178.
8. *ibid.*
9. *Ocherki novoi istorii Yaponii*, Moscow, 1958, p. 26.
10. Alayev L. B. 'Tipologiya feodalizma na Vostoke' in *Narody Azii i Afriki*, 1977, No. 4, p. 74.
11. Konrad N. I., *Izbrannye trudy: Istoriya*, Moscow, 1974, pp. 154-155.

Chapter 5 DEREK MASSARELLA *'The Loudest Cries': Knowledge of Japan in Seventeenth-century England*
1. Derek Massarella, 'James I and Japan,' *Monumenta Nipponica*, xxxviii, 1983, pp. 377-386.
2. *Idem*, 'The Early Career of Richard Cocks (1566-1624), Head of the English East India Company's Factory at Hirado (1613-1623).' *Transactions of the Asiatic Society of Japan*, third series, 20, 1985, pp. 1-46.

3.   G. R. Crone and R. A. Skelton, 'English Collections of Voyages and Travel Writings, 1625-1846,' in R. Lynam (ed.), *Richard Hakluyt and his Successors*, London, 1946, p. 91 and *passim*.

4.   Chicago, 1965 *et seq*.

5.   'When the Twain First Met: European Conceptions and Misconceptions of Japan, Sixteenth-Eighteenth Centuries,' *Modern Asian Studies*, 18, 1984, p. 536.

6.   Lach, *Asia in the Making of Europe*, ii, book two, p. 69.

7.   *The Trading World of the English East India Company 1660-1760*, Cambridge, 1978, p. 79. The view is restated in his *Trade and Civilisation in the Indian Ocean*, Cambridge, 1985, esp. pp. 82-83.

8.   F. C. Danvers and William Foster (eds.), *Letters Received by the East India Company*, 6 vols. London, 1896-1902, ii, pp. xv-xvi.

9.   E. B. Sainsbury (ed.), *[A] C[alendar of the] C[ourt] M[inutes of the East India Company 1635-1679]*, 11 vols., Oxford, 1907-1938, *1668-1670*, pp. 72, 180; William Foster, *A Guide to The India Office Records, 1600-1858*, London, 1919, p. 1ff; *idem*, *The East India House*, London, 1924, p. 51 &n.

10.   The depressing details of the weeding out can be followed through in I[ndia] O[ffice] R[ecords], Home Miscellaneous Series, 722, which makes it clear that the process had been underway since the early eighteenth century. On Rundall, see *ibid.*, pp. 24-27.

11.   'The Trade of the English East India Company in the Far East, 1623-84,' *Journal of the Royal Asiatic Society*, April, October, 1960, pp. 32-47, 145-156.

12.   I.O.R. E/3/11 ff. 207-210v, esp. ff. 207v-208v; Peter Pratt, *History of Japan compiled from the Records of the English East India Company*, ed. M. Paske-Smith, 2 vols., repr. London and New York, 1972, ii, pp. 119-126.

13.   C[alendar of] S[tate] P[apers Colonial Series], *East Indies, 1617-1621*, pp. 249-251.

14.   Pratt, *History of Japan*, ii, p. 137. The journal is now located among the I.O.R (L/MAR/A/XXIII).

15.   *C.S.P. East Indies 1625-1629*, pp. 261, 266, 267, 276, 359, 571, 599, 620, 656, 666; *ibid., 1630-1634*, p. 32.

16.   Pratt, *History of Japan*, ii, pp. 127-129; *C.C.M. 1635-1639*, p. 119; Bassett, 'Trade ... in the Far East,' p. 40; K. N. Chaudhuri, *The English East India Company*, London, 1965, pp. 58-59; Robert Ashton, *The City and the Court 1603-1643*, Cambridge, 1979, pp. 127-129.

17.   Pratt, *History of Japan*, ii, pp. 129-131. Cf. Bassett, 'Trade ... in the Far East,' p. 40.

18.   Pratt, *History of Japan*, ii, p. 131.

19.   This is treated more fully in Derek Massarella, '"A World Elsewhere:" Aspects of the Overseas Expansionist Mood of the 1650s,' in Colin Jones, Malyn Newitt and Stephen K. Roberts (eds.), *New Perspectives on British Politics 1640-1660: the Local, National and International Dimensions*, Oxford, 1986.

20.   *C.C.M. 1655-1659*, pp. 281-283, 286, 290, 297, 300 and.

21.   I.O.R., G/21/4 p. 5 pr. in D. K. Bassett, 'The Trade of the English East India Company in Cambodia,' *Journal of the Royal Asiatic Society*, April 1962, pp. 55-61, esp. p. 57; *C.C.M. 1655-1659*, pp. 282-285; *ibid., 1668-1670*, p. 105.

22.   *Ibid., 1655-1659*, p. 289; Bassett, 'Trade ... in the Far East,' pp. 145-146.

23.   Pratt, *History of Japan*, ii, pp. 133-134.

24.   I.O.R., E/3/11 f. 209v; *C.S.P. East Indies 1625-1629*, p. 372.

25.   Pratt, *History of Japan*, ii, pp. 135-137.

26.   *Ibid.*, pp. 141, 153-157. A series of edicts expelling the Japanese wives and children of Europeans, including those of the English, was passed from 1636. Even if these were not completely enforced it is inconceivable that any children who remained in Japan were aware of their Scots or Irish identity!

27.   *C.C.M. 1668-1670*, pp. 63, 105; I.O.R. G/30 p. 319

28.   *C.C.M. 1668-1670*, p. 111; Pratt, *History of Japan*, i. p. 479, 482-484, ii, p. 143n; N. Murakami (ed.), *Diary of Richard Cocks, Cape Merchant in the English Factory in Japan, 1615-1622*, 2 vols., Tokyo, 1899, ii, pp. 368-369.

29.   Pratt, *History of Japan*, ii, p. 164; Cyril Wild (ed.), *Purchas his Pilgrimes in Japan*, Kobe, 1939, pp. 156-157, 219-220.

30.   Pratt, *History of Japan*, ii, pp. 141-142, 161, 164.

31.   I.O.R. E/3/87, pp. 472-485.

32.   I.O.R. G/21/4, p. 110.

33.   William Foster, 'Samuel Purchas,' in Lynam (ed.), *Richard Hakluyt ...*, p. 56.
34.   Lach, *Asia in the Making of Europe*, i, book one, p. 214; C. R. Steele, 'From Hakluyt to Purchas,' in D. B. Quinn (ed.), *The Hakluyt Handbook*, 2 vols., London, 1974, i, pp. 80-81; Crone and Skelton, 'English Collections of Voyages and Travels,' p. 67.
35.   I.O.R. Home Miscellaneous Series 722, p. 25.

Chapter 6 S. I. VERBITSKY *Russian Notions About Japan*
1.   See H. A. Erofeyeva, *Tumanny Albion: Angliya i anglichane glazami russkikh, 1825-1853*. Moscow, 1982; A. B. Davidson, V. A. Markushin, *Oblik dalyokoy strany*. Moscow, 1975; R. Yu. Danilevsky, *Rossiya i Shveitsariya: Literaturnye svyazi*. Moscow, 1984.
2.   Ivan Reikhel, *Istoriya o yaponskom gosudarstve, is dostovernykh izvestiy sobrannaya*, Moscow 1773, p. 2.
3.   The first article about Japan — 'The Russian Embassy in Japan' — which dealt with the expedition headed by Lieutenant Adam Laksman was published in *Vestnik Yevropy* in 1803. Four issues of *Otechestvennye Zapiski* in the course of 1822 published 'The First Journey of Russians Round the World Described by N. Ryazanov, Ambassador Extraordinary to the Japanese Court.'
4.   *Otechestvennye Zapiski*, No. 1, 1873, 'Yaponiya i yeyo reformy,' p. 8.
5.   See N. Ya. Danilevsky, *Rossiya i Yevropa*, St Petersburg, 1889; K. Leontiyev, *Vostok, Rossiya i slavyanstvo*, St Petersburg, 1885.
6.   V. S. Solovyov displayed much interest in the history of Japan. His views are expounded in the article 'Yaponiya (Istoricheskaya kharakteristika),' *Collected Works*, 1886-1896, Vol. 6.
7.   L. I. Mechnikov, *Era prosvesheniya Yaponii. (Meiji), Delo*, St Petersburg, 1876, No. 10, pp. 135-170; 1877, No. 2, pp. 242-275.
8.   Nikolai, 'Syoguny i mikado,' in *Russki vestnik*, St Petersburg, 1868, No. 11, pp. 207-221; No. 12, pp. 415-560.
9.   Among the most significant works by M. Venyukov is *Ocherki Yaponii*, St Petersburg, 1871.
10.   Sipigus, *Beseda o porazhenii posle porazheniya*. Warsaw, 1909, p. 33.
11.   Most popular among them was a book by R. I. Frayerman, *Zhizn i neobyknovennye priklucheniya kapitan-letinanta Golovina, puteshestvennika i morekhodtsa*, published in 1946. *Tsunami, Shimoda*, and *Heda*, novels by N. P. Zadornov, were printed in the 1960s and the 1970s.

Chapter 7 H. J. MOESHART *The Shimonoseki Affair, 1863-1864*
1.   Mr Kleintjes.
2.   Letter in the National Archives, The Hague (damaged).
3.   Letter in the National Archives, The Hague.
4.   In the possession of Dr D. Wittop Koning, Amsterdam.
5.   Letter of Dutch Consul General to Ministry of Foreign Affairs, The Hague in National Archives, The Hague. (20 July 1863).
6.   Ibid, 8 August 1863.
7.   Ibid, 26 August 1863: No answers received from the Bakufu. Only the French Consul receives answers, but he has a fleet in the harbour!
8.   *Note Identique* in the National Archives, The Hague.
9.   Letter to Chōshū in the National Archives, the Hague.
10.   Report of the action by Captain Van Rees of the *Djambi* in letter to De Graeff in National Archives, The Hague.
11.   Sir Ernest Satow, *A diplomat in Japan*, Oxford University Press, 1968, p. 108.
12.   *Ibid*, p. 120.

Chapter 9 OLAVI K. FÄLT*Image of Japan in Foreign Newspapers Published in Japan Before the Meiji Restoration*
1.   Olavi K. Fält, *Eksotismista realismiin. Perinteinen Japanin-kuva Suomessa 1930-luvun murroksessa*. With an English Summary: From Exoticism to Realism. The Traditional Image of Japan in the Transition Years of the 1930s (*Studia Historica Septentrionalia* 5. Oulu, 1982), pp. 10-11, 320. See also Daniel J. Boorstin, *America and the Image of Europe. Reflections on American Thought* (New York, 1960), pp. 37-39; John P. Diggins, *Mussolini and Fascism*.

The View from America(Princeton, New Jersey, 1972), p. XVII; Harold R. Isaacs, *Scratches on our Minds. American Images of China and India* (New York, 1958), p. 381; Melvin Small, *Historians Look at Public Opinion* (Public Opinion and Historians. Inter-disciplinary Perspectives. Edited by Melvin Small. Detroit, 1970), p. 22; Roy Neil Schantz, The Image of China in the Age of Discovery (New York University Ph.D., 1962), p. VII; Cushing Strout, *The American Image of the Old World*, (New York, 1963), p. X.

2. Fält, *Eksotismista*, pp. 318, 337.

3. Olavi K. Fält, *'Japanism in Finland during the 1850s. The Emergence of a Concept of Japan in the Finnish Press.'* Proceedings of the First International Symposium on Asian Studies, 1979. Vol. II, Japan and Korea. Hong Kong, 1979, pp. 359-368.

4. Olavi K. Fält, 'Valkoinen' Yokohama vapaa-ajan pyörteissä vuonna 1874. (The social whirl of 'white' Yokohama in 1874.) *Faravid*, 8/1984, pp. 265-296.

5. On the state of research in the field, see Olavi K. Fält, Fascism, Militarism or Japanism? The interpretation of the crisis years of 1930-1941 in the Japanese English-language press, *Studia Historica Septentrionalia* 8. Jyväskylä, 1985, p. 12, especially notes 8-10; Olavi K. Fält, Western Views on the Japanese Expedition to Formosa in 1874, (*Asian Profile*, 1985). The following works deserve special mention: Albert A. Altman, Shinbushi: The Early Meiji Adaptation of the Western Style Newspaper (*Modern Japan. Aspects of History, Literature and Society*. Edited by W. G. Beasley, Tokyo, 1976); Hachiro Ebihara, *Nippon ōji shimbunzasshi shi*, (Tokyo, 1934); Grace Fox, *Britain and Japan, 1858-1883*, (Oxford, 1969); Jiro Hayasaka, *An Outline of the Japanese Press*, (Tokyo, 1938); Hisao Komatsubara, Japan (*The Asian Newspapers' Reluctant Revolution*. Edited by John A. Lent. Ames, Iowa, 1971); Yuga Suzuki, Meiji no eijishishikō (*Sophia kikan 1985 nen shunshi* 34/1); Yuga Suzuki, Meiji zenki eijishi to gaijin janarisutō, (*Shimbun Kenkyū*, 349, 1980/8); Yuga Suzuki, Meijiki eiji shimbun shirō, (*Shimbun Kenkyū*, 310, 1977/5); Harry Emerson Wildes, *Social Currents in Japan with Special Reference to the Press*, (Chicago, 1927).

6. *The Japan Herald*, 23 November 1861.

7. *The Travels of Marco Polo* (Translated and with an Introduction by Ronald Latham. Penguin Classics. Reprinted. Great Britain, 1967), pp. 243-249; G. B. Sansom, *The Western World and Japan. A Study in the Interaction of European and Asiatic Cultures*, (Reprinted. USA. 1965), pp. 115, 187-188; C. R. Boxer, *The Christian Century in Japan, 1549-1650, (Second Printing. Corrected. Berkeley and Los Angeles, 1967), pp. 33-40; They Came to Japan. An Anthology of European Reports on Japan, 1543-1640*, (Edited by Michael Cooper. Berkeley and Los Angeles, 1965), passim; Shunzo Sakamaki, Western Concepts of Japan and the Japanese, 1800-1854, (*Pacific Historical Review* 6, 1937), pp. 13-14; Fält, Eksotismista, pp. 38-39, 47; Olavi K. Fält, Japani länsimaisessa kirjallisessa tietoudessa ennen Japanin avautumista 1954, (Written records of Japan in the West prior to the opening of Japan in 1854), (*Faravid*, 6/1982), pp. 231-237.

8. Jean-Pierre Lehmann, *The Image of Japan: From Feudal Isolation to World Power, 1850-1905*, (London, 1978), pp. 45-50.

9. See Lehmann, p. 134.

10. On the visit of George Smith, see also Pat Barr, *The Deer Cry Pavilion. A Story of Westerners in Japan, 1868-1905*, (Bristol, 1968), p. 186; Pat Barr, *The coming of the Barbarians. A Story of Western Settlement in Japan, 1853-1870*, (Tokyo, 1972), pp. 88-89; Fält, Yokohama, p. 269.

11. *Nagasaki Shipping List and Advertiser*, 17 July 1861.

12. *Ibid.*

13. 'The Opening of the New Ports,' *Japan Herald*, 30 November 1861.

14. *Daily Japan Herald*, 10 March 1864.

15. *Japan Times*, 8 September 1865; *Japan Times' Daily Advertiser*, 13 September 1865.

16. *Japan Times' Daily Advertiser*, 2 October 1865.

17. *Japan Times*, 15 September 1865.

18. *Japan Times*, 20 October 1865.

19. *Japan Times*, 3 November 1865.

20. *Japan Times*, 17 November 1865.

21. Sansom, p. 305.

22. *Japan Times*, 1 December 1865.

23. *Japan Times*, 12 January 1866.

24. *Japan Times*, 26 January 1866.

25. *Japan Times*, 15 December 1865.
26. *Japan Times*, 5 January 1866.
27. *Ibid.*
28. *Japan Times*, 9 March 1866.
29. *Japan Times*, 28 April 1866.
30. *Japan Times*, 19 May 1866.
31. *Japan Times*, 30 May 1866. Second Edition.
32. *Japan Times*, 2 June 1866.
33. *Japan Times*, 16 June 1866.
34. *Ibid.*
35. *Ibid.*
36. *Ibid.*
37. *Japan Punch*, May 1862, p. 14.
38. *Japan Punch*, September 1865, p. 89.
39. *Japan Punch*, January 1866, p. 150.
40. *Japan Punch*, February 1866, p. 165.
41. *Japan Punch*, February 1866. p. 169.
42. *Japan Punch*, April 1866, p. 200.
43. *Japan Punch*, September 1866, p. 282.
44. *Japan Punch*, November 1866, p. 315.
45. *Japan Punch*, July 1867, p. 46.
46. *Japan Punch*, July 1867, p. 47.
47. *Japan Punch*, December 1867, p. 72.
48. *Japan Punch*, January 1866, p. 89.

Chapter 10 IAN NISH *Japan and European Brinkmanship, 1895*

1. I. H. Nish, *The Origins of the Russo-Japanese War*, London, 1985.
2. S. E. Zakharov, *Tikho-okeanskii flot*, Moscow, 1966, p. 30.
3. Shimanuki Shigeyoshi, *Fukushima Yasumasa to tanki Shiberiya ōdan*, 2 vols., Tokyo, 1979, vol. I, pp. 226-47.
4. Mutsu Munemitsu, *Kenkenroku*, edited by G. M. Berger, Tokyo, 1982, p. 244.
5. *Yamamoto Gombei to kaigun*, Tokyo, 1966, pp. 97-9.
6. *Kenkenroku*, p. 206.
7. *Kenkenroku*, p. 207.
8. *Yamamoto to kaigun*, p. 98.
9. Fujimura Michio, *Nisshin sensō*, Tokyo, 1973, p. 178; R. Hackett, *Yamagata Aritomo in the Rise of Modern Japan, 1838-1922*, Cambridge, Mass., 1971, p. 166.
10. Fujimura, *Nisshin sensō*, pp. 178-80.
11. *Yamamoto to kaigun*, p. 99. Also *Taiwan-tō kō-Nichi hishi* (Tokyo: Hara Shobō, 1979) and *Taiwan tōji gaiyo*, (Tokyo: Hara Shobō, 1979).
12. Senshi sosho, *Kaigunbu: Rengō kantai*, i, Tokyo, 1975, pp. 55-6. I have dealt with other aspects of this crisis in 'The three-power intervention of 1895' in A. R. Davis and A. D. Stefanowska (eds), *Austrina*, Sydney, 1982, 204-25 and in 'Britain and the three-power intervention, 1895' in John Chapman (ed.), *Proceedings of the British Association for Japanese Studies*, 1980, 12-26.

Chapter 12 VALDO FERRETTI *Sato Naotake's Mission to Rome in 1940*

1. Historical Archive of the Foreign Minister of Italy, (hereafter *ASMAE*), SP, b. Giappone 23, for connection between Paulucci's and Okura's missions.
2. Central Archive of the State (ACS), Rome, *Micup*, b. 80, f.4.
3. See G. Volpi di Misurata, L'Italia e l'Estremo Oriente, in *Bollettino dell'Ismeo*, n. 11, 1935, pp. 448-52.
4. *ASMAE*, SP, b. Giappone 12, 'Relazioni commerciali tra l'Italia e l'Estremo Oriente,' 22 January 1935, *Riservata*.
5. The material relating to Conti's mission is in *ASMAE*, SP, b. Manchukuo 2 and b. Giappone 17.
6. *Hō-Keizai Shisetsudan to Nichi-I Keizai Kankei Zōshin no Seijiteki Sōchi ni Kan suru*

Kōsatsu, 22 March 1940, *Ō 2*, *Gaikō Shiryō Kan* (GSK), K 2.1.0.*4-1-6*, *Honpōjin Kaigai Shisetsu Ryōkō Kankei Zakken*.
7.   On the *Asama Maru* incident, cf. Nomura Minoru, *Taiheiyō Sensō to Nihon Gunbu*, Tokyo, *1983*, *pp. 130-32*.
8.   *Nichi-I Kyōtei ni Kan suru Iken*, GSK, B.1.0.0.J/X2, 22 September 1937.
9.   *Nichi-I Kyōtei no Teiketsu ni tsuite*, GSK, *Honpōjin* ... cit., 1 April 1940.
10.   See Hosoya Chihiro, 'Satō Naotake no Koto,' *Nyōsuikai Kaihō*, 1980, n. 587, p.3. Actually Satō had started his diplomatic career on the eve of the settlement after the Russo-Japanese War, when Motono was ambassador in Moscow, and remembered with highest esteem and affection his old superior until late in his life. Cf. Satō Naotake, *Gaikō Hachijū Nen*, Tokyo, 1963, pp. 73-76, and Usui Katsumi, 'Satō Gaikō to Nitchū Kankei' in Iriye Akira and Aruga Tadashi (eds.), *Senkanki no Nihon Gaikō*, Tokyo, 1984, pp. 241-66.
11.   Kurihara Ken (ed.), *Satō Naotake no Menmoku*, Tokyo, 1981.
12.   For the text, in Japanese, of the communiqué, a memorandum of the Europe-America Office of *Gaimushō*, and a draft of *Italo-Japanese* treaty, GSK, *Honpōjin* ... cit.
13.   *Nichi-I kan Sogō Shiji Kyōtei Teiketsu ni kan suru Kōsatsu*, 4 June 1940, *Ō 2,GSK*, *Honpōjin* ... cit. Even if this document was written down a few days before the declaration of war, it seems to enlighten the attitude of Tokyo after 10 June.
14.   Cf. G. Krebs, *Japans Deutschlandpolitik 1935-41*, Hamburg, 1984, vol. 1, pp. 430-3.

Chapter 13 J. Y. KIM *The Kwanggaeto Stele Inscription*
1.   Szczesniak Boleslaw, 'The Kotaio Monument,' *Monumenta Nipponica*, vol. VII, no. 1-2, 1951, p. 253. Professor Szczesniak of Notre Dame completed a distinguished study on the inscription. Based on 'as much material as possible,' he undertook his study not only minutely analysing the different readings, but also comparing and collating them with the rubbings of the king's funeral stele. Szczesniak's reading of the inscription as primary material is introduced here in elucidating the context of the inscription of the King Kwanggaeto monument.
2.   Each part of the inscription consists of the following numbers of characters: First part (sentences 1 to 13): 174 characters including 6 illegible ones. Second part (sentences 14 to 18): 67 characters including 2 illegible ones. Third part (sentences 19 to 72): 881 characters including 183 illegible ones. Fourth part: 440 characters including 11 illegible ones. Fifth part: 200 characters, all legible. I (the author) prefer to divide the third part into twelve sections, as far as possible in accordance with the textual chronology in order to facilitate analysis, discussion, comparison with different view points, and to make criticisms in case of need. Section one gives the King's accomplishments in Manchuria and the northern part of the Korean peninsula, and section twelve records the King's achievements in Eastern Manchuria.
3.   Kiley Cornelius J., 'State and Dynasty in Archaic Yamato,' *Journal of Asian Studies*, vol. XXXIII. no 1, November 1973, p. 36.

Chapter 14 LOUIS ALLEN *Buryoku shori: The Japanese Take Over French Indo-China, 9 March 1945*
1.   Cf. J. Decoux, *A la barre de l'Indochine*, Paris, 1949, p. 484; Claude Boisanger, Decoux's diplomatic adviser, in *On pouvait éviter la guerre d'Indochine*, Paris, 1977, p. 141; and Georges Gautier, *directeur de cabinet* and later Decoux's Secretary-General, in the symposium *De Gaulle et l'Indochine, 1940-1946*, Paris, 1982, p. 225.
2.   General Charles de Gaulle, *Mémoires de Guerre*, III, *Le Salut*, 1959, pp. 163-164.
3.   Wada Tsuneaki, *Shōgen: Taiheiyō sensō*, Tokyo, 1975, pp. 134-135.
4.   *De Gaulle et l'Indochine*, p. 221.
5.   Mamoru Shigemitsu, *Japan and her Destiny*, tr. O. White, London, 1958, p. 330
6.   Cf. for the debate within the army and the developments of events, the relevant volume of the Japanese official history, *Sittang; Meigo Sakusen*, Tokyo, 1969.
7.   *Ibid.*
8.   'Cet homme épais, direct, sans nuances ...' *A la barre de l'Indochine*, p. 330, Boisanger calls him an 'esprit épais et obtus ... un jouet dans les mains du Commandant japonais.' Boisanger, op. cit., p. 95.
9.   Decoux, op. cit., p. 328.

10.   *Ibid*, p. 329.
11.   *Sittang: Mei-go Sakusen*, p. 624.
12.   Boisanger, *On pouvait éviter la guerre d'Indochine*, p. 101.
13.   Discussion of this paper with Colonel Hugh Toye, who has particular expertise in the field of Laotian affairs and supplied me with an invaluable reference to M. Caply's article 'Le Japon et l'indépendance du Laos (1945),' brought forward interesting doubts on the argument. 'Although there were contingency plans from early 1944, nothing was implemented until January 1945,' he writes, 'and if you go back to Case 3 in the Supreme War Council's hypotheses on 9 September 1944, you can infer that it was French rebelliousness that was one of the factors in the final decision ... No prudent military commander would have failed to have a contingency plan from 1942 at latest. In fact, the Japanese were still in doubt as to whether to act in January 1945. The fact of long preparation is irrelevant: the question is what triggered it off at that precise moment. The coup was really against Japanese military interests: troops drawn from Meiktila hurt them in Burma and although that was for Thailand, not FIC, the fact of having to produce overwhelming force in FIC undoubtedly stretched them. Of course, plans existed ... Surely they would not have taken over FIC anyway: they had to have a compelling reason.' (Letter to the author, 22 July 1985).
14.   Taylor, *Awakening from History*, London, 1971, p. 280.
15.   Peter M. Dunn, *The First Vietnam War*, London, 1985, chs. 2, 3 and 4.
16.   Ben trovato as this episode appears, doubt has been cast on it by Terence O'Brien, who was involved in organising air supply to clandestine groups in South-East Asia. 'About a dozen aircraft were out on SD (special duty) work that night,' he writes, 'the weather was appalling and only two were able to find their drop zone. To believe that US night-fighters shot down the missing three is to credit them with radar of longer range than existed in Europe, or of quite exceptional luck in finding their targets on such a black night, and to accept that the Liberators were also exceptionally lucky to escape without a single weather casualty on such a tempestuous night — particularly when you realise that out of the 30 aircraft we lost on Special Duty, there are 24 that were certainly caused by weather over target or passage. Dunn told me his documentary evidence was not available, it was in storage, so I can't assess its value. I could believe the story, but the evidence would need to be irrefutable not only to me, but to many others in the SD squadron.' (Letter to the author, 16 September 1985).
17.   L. Allen, *End of the War in Asia*, p. 110.
18.   Dunn, *The First Vietnam War*, p. 15.
19.   *Ibid*, p. 14.
20.   On Captain Kaneko, An Butai and the activities of Nakano School graduates in Indo-China, cf. Hatakeyama Seikō, *Hiroku Rikugun Nakano Gakkō (zoku)*, Tokyo, 1972, pp. 191-207, and Sano Yuji, 'Yue no senjō wo kakeru,' In *Rekishi to jinbutsu*, Tokyo, August 1983, pp. 264-71.

Chapter 15 I. A. LATYSHEV *Controversial Problems of Japan's Post-War History in the Works of Soviet Historians*
1.   We have in mind the following publications: Ye. M. Zhukov, *Yaponya, 1940-1950 godov*. Lectures read at the Higher Party School of the CC of the AUCP (B), Moscow, 1951; P. P. Topekha, *Antinarodnaya politika pravykh liderov yaponskoy sotsialisticheskoy partii*, Moscow, 1954; Kh. T. Eidus, *Ocherki novoi i neveishei istorii Yaponii*, Moscow, 1955.
2.   Works which, in our view, idealise the reforms of the period of occupation include, for example: E. M. Martin, *The Allied Occupation of Japan*, New York, 1948; Chitoshi Yanaga, *Japan since Perry*, New York, 1948; E. O. Reischauer, *The United States and Japan*, Cambridge, Mass., 1950.
3.   As an example, one may refer to the book by D. V. Petrov, *Vneshnyaya politika Yaponii posle vtoroi mirovoi voiny*, Moscow, 1965, pp. 28, 29, 30 and fol. Kh. T. Eidus, *Istoriya Yaponii s drevneishikh vremyon do nashikh dney*, Moscow, 1968, pp. 186-188.
4.   See *Istoriya Yaponii, 1945-1975*, Moscow, 1978, p. 10.
5.   Thus, for instance, a prominent American historian of Japan, Hugh Borton, wrote: 'One of the chief objectives of the victors was to bring about far-reaching political changes in Japanese life. The Occupation authorities attempted to create to the extent possible new democratic institutions and to foster an atmosphere in which democracy could grow and prosper.' (See *Japan Between East and West*, New York, 1957, pp. 1-3). Further, elaborating

the same idea, the author states that all reforms were undertaken under the pressure and on the initiative of the Occupation authorities and that any new initiatives of that kind sprang from MacArthur's Headquarters.

6.   This fact is acknowledged by a former member of the MacArthur Headquarters, Harry Wildes, according to whom the aim of Headquarters was to complete the working-out of the Constitution and have it, if possible, approved before the Commission for the Far East sent proper instructions. H. E. Wildes, *Typhoon in Tokyo*, London, pp. 41, 44).

7.   Japanese journalist, N. Inoue, as far back as 1952 published an article in *Kaizō* where he wrote that MacArthur was going to frustrate the plans of the Far Eastern Commission which would accept a republican constitution and liquidation of the monarchy with the help of a peace provision unheard-of in international practice. (*Kaizō*, 1952, no. 6, p. 29).

8.   See *History of Japan, 1945-1975*, p. 31.

9.   V. I. Lenin, *Collected Works*, 5th edition, vol. 26, pp. 218-219.

10.   See *Vosproizvodstvo obshchestvennogo produkta v Yaponii*, Moscow, 1970, p. 6.

11.   We may find an example of such an understanding of 'modernisation' in John Hall's paper 'Changing Conceptions of the Modernisation of Japan' in *Changing Japanese Attitudes Toward Modernisation*, edited by Marius B. Jansen, Princeton, 1969, pp. 7-41.

12.   On this point one might fully agree with the assessment of the theory of 'modernisation' by the Japanese scholar, Inoue Kiyoshi. Criticising J. Hall, W. Rostow and E. Reischauer, he writes that it is characteristic of their views on 'modernisation' that in 'their theories' they actually regard capitalist modernisation as the way of development for the entire human society, intentionally negating the socialist road of progress. According to Inoue, their 'modernisation' means, to put it briefly, development along the path of capitalism. (Inoue Kiyoshi, *Nihon kindaishi no mikata*, Tokyo, 1969, p. 280).

13.   L. D. Grishelyova and N. I. Chegodar, *Kultura poslevoyennoi Yaponii*, Moscow, 1981, p. 158.

14.   See I. I. Kovalenko, *Ocherki istorii Kommunisticheskoi partii Yaponii posle vtoroi mirovoi voiny, 1945-1961*, Moscow, 1981, p. 83.

15.   *Ibid,*, p. 128.

16.   *Ibid.*, p. 203.

17.   Kajima Morinosuke, author of the *Short Diplomatic History of Modern Japan*, adhered to an identical interpretation of the San Francisco and the Security Treaties (see, for instance, his *Modern Japan's Foreign Policy*, Tokyo, 1970, p. 137.

18.   Among Japanese historians sharply critical of the San Francisco Peace Treaty and the Security Treaty are, for example, Fujii Kōichi, Ishii Kinichirō and Ogawa Shinobu, authors of *Nihon gendaishi*, vol. 2, Tokyo, 1966, p. 342; Tatsuya Naramoto, author of *Gendaino Nihonshi*, Kyoto, 1966, pp. 157-158; the authors of the popular *History of Japan* edited by Akido Yoshio, Inoue Kiyoshi, Eguchi Bokurō, Wakamori Tarō. (*Nihon no rekishi*, vol. 13, Tokyo, 1968, pp. 135-8).

19.   See *History of Japan, 1945-1975*, pp. 96-97.

20.   Authors and editors of the eight-volume work on the State-Monopoly Capital of Japan are among students of Japan's post-war history who treat the 1950s and 1960s as the period of gradual restoration of the independence of Japanese imperialism (see *Nihon no kokkadokusen shihonshugi*, vol. 4, Tokyo, 1970, pp. 230-232).

21.   For instance, Soviet historian of Japan D. V. Petrov in his book on Japan's foreign policy writes: 'Normalisation of relations with the Soviet Union manifested a new stage in the diplomatic history of the country. Broad vistas of a radical revision of her foreign policy and of a course which would be in full conformity with the tasks of ensuring peace, independence and the interests of the bulk of the Japanese people, opened up to Japan' (D. V. Petrov, *Vneshnaya politika Yaponii posle vtoroi mirovoi voiny*).

22.   Soviet scholar A. M. Sharkov, author of a book on Japan and the US comes to the following conclusions: 'The post-war alliance of the reactionary forces of Japan and the United States underwent an evolution. In the first years it had been openly unequal. Subsequently, as the Japanese economy became consolidated, the build-up of strength by Japanese monopoly capital and its rôle in the world economy and politics grew, the situation changed more and more. The early 1960s were a prominent landmark in this process. By that time (1960) the Security Treaty and the military-political alliance had been revised to be in force for a long period. The revised Security Treaty became essentially a pact of a military-political alliance, with the US playing a dominant and leading rôle. At the same time it was clear that during the 1960s Japanese monopoly capital, using and expanding the

position gained at the time of the revision of the treaty, proved able gradually to shift the focus of its policies to the insurance of its own interests (A. M. Sharkov, *Yaponiya i SShA. Analiz sovremennykh ekonomicheskikh otnoshenii*, Moscow, 1971, p. 6).

23.   See *History of Japan, 1945-1975*, p. 218. See also S. I. Verbitsky, *Yapono-amerikansky voyenno-politichesky soyuz, 1951-1970*, Moscow, 1972.

24.   See I. I. Kovalenko, *op. cit.*, p. 205.

25.   See D. V. Petrov, *Yaponiya v mirovoi politike*, Moscow, 1973.

26.   The late historian, Tarō Wakamori, a frequent participant in our discussions, believed that in contemporary Japan there was no basis for the revival of militarism and negated the existence of the militarisation process. (*Nihon no gunkokushugi o kangaeru*, Tokyo, 1972, pp. 42-43).

27.   Prof. Jū Ui of the Tokyo University reasoned, for instance, in the following way: 'One may say that Japanese militarism is really reviving. As at present Japan's military might is not able to break that of any East Asian country, plans for using it in conjunction with the armed forces of several other countries are being evolved. In future these forces will be used as a powerful fist in South-East Asia' (*ibid.*, p. 24).

28.   This question was most accurately and broadly discussed in the collective work by Soviet students of Japan, *Yaponsky militarizm* (Japanese Militarism), published in Moscow in 1972, edited by Academician Ye. M. Zhukov.

29.   We have in mind Soviet scholars Ya. A. Pevzner, A. M. Sharkov, P. D. Dolgorukov, A. I. Dinkevich, S. K. Ignatushchenko, etc.

30.   See, for instance, P. P. Topekha, *Rabocheye dvizheniye v Yaponii, 1945-1971*, Moscow, 1973, p. 280.

31.   *The Emerging Japanese Superstate, Challenge and Response* by Herman Kahn, Professor of the Hudson Institute (1970) as well as Ezra Vogel's book, *Japan as Number One, Lessons for America*, (Cambridge, Mass., 1974) may be cited as examples of such publications by American social scientists.

32.   *SSSR — Yaponiya: K 50-letiyu ustanovleniya sovetsko-japonskikh diplomaticheskikh otnoshevii, 1925-1975*, Moscow, 1977, p. 6.

Chapter 18 RUTH LINHART *Modern Times for Ama Divers*

1.   K. E. Müller, *Die bessere und die schlechtere Hälfte: Ethnologie des Geschlechterkonflikts*, Frankfurt, 1984, pp. 261, 297f.

2.   Müller, pp. 15ff, 298.

3.   Interview with Otawa Tamako, 4 August 1983.

4.   Segawa Kyōko, *Ama*, Tokyo: Mirai-sha, 1975 (Reprint of 1955 edition), p. 31.

5.   All remarks about *ama* and *ama*-work in Katada are based on daily conversations with the people of Katada and especially an interview with the head of the fishing-corporation, with officials of the women's section of the fishing-corporation and with other *ama* during my stay in Katada in July and August 1983.

6.   Tanaka Noyo, *Amatachi no shiki*, published by Katō Masaki, Tokyo: Shinjuku Shobō, 1983, p. 12.

7.   Iwata Junichi, *Shima no ama*, Toba: Shima Bunka Kenkyūkai, 1971 (Reprint of 1939 edition), pp. 1f.

8.   Müller, pp. 331ff.

9.   Müller, pp. 304f.

10.   Segawa, p. 3.

11.   Alice Schwarzer, *Frauenarbeit-Frauenbefreiung: Praxis, Beispiele und Analysen*, Frankfurt, 1973, p. 11.

Chapter 23 JOHN B. CORNELL *Japanese Burakumin: Civil Rights Policies in the Post-war Era*

1.   Isomura Eiichi et al., *Dowa taisaku shingikai chōsabu hōkoku*, 1965.

2.   Isomura, pp. 17-21.

3.   Yoshino R. and S. Murakoshi, *The Visible Invisible Minority: Japan's Burakumin*, 1977, p. 63.

4.   Isomura, p. 33.

5.   Buraku Liberation Research Institute, ed., *Long-suffering Brothers and Sisters, Unite!*, 1981, pp. 49-61.

6. H. Wagatsuma, 'Postwar Political Militance' in G. Devos and H. Wagatsuma, eds., *Japan's Invisible Race: Caste in Culture and Personality*, Berkeley, 1967, p. 72, citing Naramoto in *Buraku*, 1961.

7. Yoshino and Murakoshi, pp. 90-1.

8. The law's contents are presented in detail in J-F. Sabouret, *L'Autre Japon: les Burakumin*, Paris, 1983, pp. 85-7; Yoshino and Murakoshi, pp. 83-9.

9. Harada Tomohiko, *Buraku Mondai Gaisetsu*, 1976, pp. 66-7.

10. For a more sceptical view of government funding practice, see C-D. Hah and C. C. Lapp, 'Japanese Politics of Equality in Transition: the Caste of Burakumin' in *Asian Survey*, 1978, pp. 487-504.

11. S. Murakoshi, 'A Note on the Special Measures for Dowa Projects' in *Long-suffering Brothers and Sisters, unite!*, p. 38.

Chapter 24 IAN NEARY *A Legal Solution to the Buraku Problem?*

1. See reports of the Buraku Liberation Research conference held in October 1981, *Buraku Kaihō*, No. 176, January 1982, pp. 104-114.

2. For example the article by Takano Masumi, 'Dowa Taisaku Rippo no Genten to Genten,' *Buraku Kaihō*, No. 207, January 1984, pp. 26-51.

3. See J. Suginohara, 'Chitaiho Kigenkire ni mukete' *Buraku*, No. 37, March 1985, p. 7.

4. For further discussion of the 'Control Law' see *Buraku Kaiho no Tenbō o mezashite* — the report of the special committee on the Basic Law for Buraku Liberation, Osaka, 1985, pp. 7-11, 81-119. Also T. Matsumoto, 'Sabetsu Teppaiho ni Muketa Koso,' *Buraku Kaihō Kenkyū*, October 1983, No. 36, pp. 33-55.

5. Buraku Kaiho no Tenbō, p. 106.

6. Takano Masumi, 'Buraku Kaihō Kihonhō: Rippoka no haikei to Tenbō *Hogakū Seminar*, March 1985, No. 363, p. 31.

7. 1985 Nendo Undo Hoshin, *Shakai Shimpō*, 26 December 1985, p. 9.

8. *Buraku*, No. 36, August 1984, pp. 103-4.

9. J. Suginohara, 'Chitaiho Kigenkire ni mukete,' p. 11-12.

10. *Nippon Keizai Shimbun*, 23 March 1985, p. 13.

11. Takano, 'Dowa Taisaku Rippō ....,' pp. 34-5.

12. *Hōgaku Seminar*, p. 33.

13. Inoue Kiyoshi, 'Kaizen to Kaihō,' *Koperu*, No. 93, August 1985, pp. 12-13.

14. For detailed analysis of two major kyūdan tōsō of recent years, see F. K. Upham, 'Instrumental Violence and Social Change,' *Law in Japan*, Vol. 17, 1984, pp. 185-204

15. Kohshin Otani is the chief priest of the Jodō Shinshū sect, Honganji temple.

Chapter 25 ROGER GOODMAN *Returnee Children in Japan*

1. For a fuller exposition of this idea, see Goodman, 'Is there an "I" in Anthropology? Thoughts on starting fieldwork in Japan' in *Journal of the Anthropological Society of Oxford*, vol. xv(2), 1984, pp. 157-68.

2. Mombushō Kyōiku Joseikyoku Zaimuka Kaigaishijo Kyōikushitsu, *Kaigaishijo Kyōiku no Genjō*, 1985, p. 56.

3. E. Ohnuki-Tierney, *Illness and Culture in Contemporary Japan: An Anthropological View*, Cambridge, 1984, p. 43.

4. Minority Rights Group, *Japan's Minorities (Burakumin, Koreans, Ainu, Okinawans)*, Report No. 3, 1983, p. 4.

5. E. Vogel, *Japan as Number One: Lessons for America*, Cambridge, Mass., 1979, p. 243.

6. E. O. Reischauer, *The Japanese*, Tokyo, 1983, p. 421.

7. The 6th *Ibunkakan Kyōiku Gakkai*.

8. J. I. Kitsuse, A. E. Murase and Y. Yamamura, 'Kikokushijo: The Emergence and Institutionalisation of an Education Problem in Japan' in J. W. Schneider and J. I. Kitsuse (eds.), *Studies in the Sociology of Social Problems*, Norwood, N.J., 1984, pp. 162-79. I must acknowledge a particular debt in this paper to Professor Kitsuse's 'constructionist' approach to the study of social problems.

9. I am unsure of the strength of this organisation's case. Almost all Japanese I have asked deny there is any connotation in the word *'shijo'*, though some think it a slightly odd choice. It is quite possible, therefore, that the word was originally selected on the grounds

of euphony rather than to create a tone of discrimination.

10.   Kyoto University, Zaigai kikokushi jo no tekiō ni kansuru chōsa, Kyōiku Gakubu, Kobayashi Tetsuya. Five reports between 1975 and 1978.

11.   Murase has made the same discovery. See A. E. Murase, 'Higher Education and Life Style Aspirations of Japanese Returnee and Nonreturnee Students,' Sophia University, Bulletin of Foreign Studies, No. 19, 1984, p. 3, note 5.

12.   Mombushō, pp. 58ff.

13.   This is a particularly interesting reaction when one considers the difficulty many Japanese (and particularly it might be assumed schoolchildren) have with understanding the concept of identity. When the notion is introduced into a written text, for example, it is common practice to write the English word in katakana with a kanji approximation (mimoto) following it in brackets. A somewhat analogous performance is often necessitated by the introduction of the concept into conversation.

14.   See H. Befu, 'Internationalisation of Japan and Nihon Bunkaron' in Befu and Mannari, The Challenge of Japan's Internationalisation, Tokyo, 1983, pp. 245-8.

15.   Mombushō, pp. 107-8.

Chapter 26 JOY HENDRY Politeness and Communication in Modern Japan Attendance at the EAJS Conference in Paris, where this paper was presented, was made possible by an Overseas Conference Grant from the British Academy, with some additional support from the Oxford Polytechnic Conference Fund.

1.   See, for example, W. J. Rodney 'Some Universals of Honorific Language with Special Reference to Japanese,' University of Arizona, PhD thesis, 1982.

2.   Kusakabe Enta, Keigo de haji o kakanai hon (A book about using keigo without disgrace), Tokyo, 1983, pp. 3-5.

3.   Bunkajo, Keigo Kotoba Shiriizu (Language Series), 1, 1974, pp. 9-10.

4.   Kusakabe op. cit.

5.   Ōishi Hatsutarō, Keigo, Tokyo, 1975.

6.   Ōishi Hatsutarō and Hayashi Tarō, Keigo no Tsukaikata. (The Way to Use Keigo), Tokyo, 1975, p. 2.

7.   Bunkajo, op. cit.

8.   Bunkajo, op. cit., pp. 10-11.

9.   Befu Harumi, 'Civilisation and Culture: Japan in Search of Identity' in Umesao Tadao et. al. (ed), Japanese Civilisation in the Modern World, Senri Ethnological Studies, No. 16, Osaka, 1984.

10.   Bunkajo, p.2.

11.   R. A. Miller, Japan's Modern Myth, New York and Tokyo, 1982, pp 155-64.

12   Miller, p. 70.

Chapter 27 JAN VAN BREMEN Religious Nature of Popular Confucianism in Japan

1.   D. Sperber, Le Savoir des Anthropologues. Trois Essais, Paris, Hermann, 1982, p. 32.

2.   C. W. Mills, The Sociological Imagination, 1959, p. 143.

3.   R. M. Keesing, Cultural Anthropology: a Contemporary Perspective, New York: Holt, Rinehart and Winston, 1981, p. 5.

4.   R. Needham, 'Essential Perplexities,' delivered before the University of Oxford, 12 May 1977, pp. 9, 11.

5.   S. B. Ortner, Sherpas through their Rituals, Cambridge: University Press, 1978, pp. 1-2.

6.   Ibid, p. 171, 2, 3.

7.   B. Malinowski, Magic, Science and Religion, New York: Doubleday, 1948, pp. 237-54.

8.   P. Rabin, Primitive Man as a Philosopher, 1957, pp. xxi-xli.

9.   The choice of the term 'genre ethnography' is most likely an outcome of a study of ukiyo-e which I made in 1964. I find it interesting to see contemporaries entertaining similar notions. P. Metcalf (1982:263), for example, uses the term 'vignette.'

10.   Sperber, op. cit., pp. 15-48. 11.   Sperber, op. cit., p. 72.

Chapter 28 B. V. POSPELOV Ideological Structure of Nationalism in Japan

1.   Nihon wa sekai no moderu ni naru ka, Osaka, 1983, pp. 34, 68, 72 etc.

2.   Ezra Vogel, Japan as Number One: Lessons for America, Cambridge, Mass., 1979.

Chapter 29 V. SAUNDERS *Research Problems Experienced by a Foreigner in Japan while using Macro-Sociological Research Data Collection Techniques*
1.   C. Nakane, *Japanese Society*, London, 1971.
2.   E. Laumann, *Prestige and Association in an Urban Community*, Indianapolis, 1966.
3.   Organised by the College Women's Association of Japan, and held in Tokyo. The title of Professor Abbeglen's lecture was *Prospects for Japan's Economy: Continued Dynamism or Affluent Maturity*.
4.   E. Vogel, *Japan as Number One: Lessons for America*, Cambridge, Mass., 1979.
5.   Y. Sugimoto and R. Mouer, 'Japanese Society: Stereotypes and Reality,' in *Papers of The Japanese Studies Centre*, Monash University, No. 1, Melbourne, 1981,.
6.   See for criticisms of I.Q. testing: L. Edson, 'jensenism, n. — the theory that I.Q. is largely determined by the genes' in R. W. Mack (ed.), *Prejudice and Race Relations*, Chicago; 1970, and also T. F. Pettigrew 'Race, Mental Illness and Intelligence: a Social Psychological View' in R. H. Osbourne (ed.), *The Biological and Social Meaning of Race*, San Francisco, 1971.
7.   See for example, K. Tominaga, *Nihon no Kaiso Kozo*, (Japan's Social Stratification System), Tokyo, 1984; and also M. Matsusaka, *Shi Min Seikatsu*, (City People's Lifestyle), 1985.
8.   M. Morishima, *The Production of Technologists and Robotisation in Japan*, booklet published by London School of Economics, 1985.
9.   T. Sodei, 'Sex Rôle Differentiation at Work and at Home,' public lecture as for Abbeglen (see above).
10.   For a good discussion on dependency among Japanese people, see T. Doi, *The Anatomy of Dependence*, Tokyo, 1976.
11.   K. Odaka, 'The Middle Classes in Japan' in R. Bendix and M. Lipset (eds.), *Class, Status and Power*, London, 1966, p. 551.
12.   R. Steven, *Classes in Contemporary Japan*, Cambridge, 1983.
13.   R. Ohashi, *Nihon no Kaikyū Kosei*, (Japan's Class Composition), Tokyo, 1971.

Chapter 30 PETER ACKERMANN *Let's Dance a Dance — Song Texts for Basic Instruction in Shamisen Music*
1.   Katō Yasuaki,' *Nihon mōjin shakai-shi kenkyū*' Tokyo (Mirai-sha), 1974.
2.   Apart from these there existed a number of 'secret' pieces, and from the early 18th century onwards also a body of *naga-uta* — pieces whose text exposes a single topic from beginning to end — was used for instruction of professional blind musicians.
3.   The version of *Ukiyo-gumi* given here is the one found in the song text collection 'Matsu no ha' (Kyoto 1703), reprinted in: Asano Kenji: *Matsu no ha*. In: '*Chūsei kinsei kayō-shū*', Tokyo (Iwanami Shoten), 1959, [*Nihon koten bungaku taikei* Nr. 44], pp. 365-366.
4.   Small, hourglass-shaped drum; here the drum body is meant.
5.   The rope that holds the two skins against the top and the bottom of the drum body.
6.   Imitation of the sound of the *taiko* drum.
7.   '*Nihon shomin bunka shiryō shūsei*', V., Tokyo (San'ichi Shobō), 1973, p. 467.
8.   This and the next example is taken from Asano Kenji (op. cit.), pp. 334 and 365.
9.   Takano Tatsuyuki (ed.): '*Nihon kayō shūsei*', V., Tokyo (Tōkyō-dō), 1942, p. 285.
10.   Kitagawa Tadahiko, Yasuda Akira: '*Kyōgen-shū*.' Tokyo (Shōgakkan), 1972, [*Nihon koten bungaku zenshū*, Nr. 35], pp. 124-127.

Chapter 31 SUSAN C. TYLER *Paradise at Kasuga*
1.   Sasaki Kōzō, Okumura Hideo, Satō Masahiko, and Haino Akio, *Shintō no bijutsu: Kasuga/Hie/Kumano*, Nihon bijutsu zenshū, Vol. 11, Tokyo, 1979, p. 175.
2.   Royall Tyler's unpublished translation, 'The Miracles of the Kasuga Deity.'
3.   Conversations with Ohigashi Nobukazu, a Shrine priest, in winter and spring of 1983.
4.   This painting is discussed by Kameda Tsutomu in the article 'Hase-dera Noman-in no Kasuga jodo mandara,' in *Nihon bukkyō bijutsushi josetsu* Tokyo, 1970, pp. 372-80. The identifications of the figures are his.
5.   There is a large sculpture of the Kasuga *mishōtai*, a deer with a *sakaki* on its back. In the mirror in the *sakaki* there are five figures, the centre one identified as Amida by the authors of the Nara National Museum Catalogue, *Suijaku bijutsu*, Tokyo: Kadokawa Shoten,

1964, p. 183. This is the only place I know of where the first shrine is identified as Amida.

6.   See Robert E. Morell, 'Jōkei and the Kōfukuji Petition', in *Japanese Journal of Religious Studies*, Vol. 10, No. 1 (March 1983), pp. 6-38.

7.   In what I have written on Gedatsu I have relied on an article by Tomimura Takafumi, 'Gedatsu Shōnin to Kannon shinkō,' *Risshō shigaku* (Risshō daigaku shigakukai.), No. 40, March 1976, pp. 21-32. My quotations are from excerpts of Gedatsu's writings in his article. The translations are mine. Here Tomimura is quoting *Chigu Kannon kōshiki*.

8.   *Ibid.*, p. 26. Tomimura seems to be quite sure that for Gedatsu, Kannon is the presence at Kasuga, so he conjectures that this is a desire to serve Kannon, as humbly as possible.

9.   *Ibid.*, pp. 26-28.

10.   *Ibid.*, p. 23.

Chapter 32 VLADISLAV SISSAOURI *On the Origin of Wagaku (Japanese Music) in the Heian Period*
1.   Tanabe Hoisao, *Nihon ongaku kōwa*, Tokyo, 1926, pp. 248-59.
2.   Our musical analysis is based on the scores published by Shiba Sukehiro. Shiba Sukehiro, *Gosenfu-ni yori gagaku sōfu*, 3 Vol., Tokyo, 1968-71.
3.   *Nihonshoki*, 2 Vol., Nihon koten bungaku taikei, 67-68, Tokyo, 1967, Vol. 1, p. 136.
4.   *Kojiki*, Nihon koten bungaku taikei (Kojiki, Norito), 1, Tokyo, 1968, p. 117.
5.   *Taigenshō*, 4 Vol., Nihon koten zenshū, Tokyo, 1933, p. 1117.
6.   Hayashi Kenzō, *Gagaku (kogakufu no kaidoku)*, Tōyō ongaku senshū, V. 10, Tokyo, 1969, pp. 480-1.
7.   *Tsurezure-gusa*, Nihon koten bungaku taikei (Hōjōki, Tsurezure-gusa), 30, Tokyo, 1970, p. 253.

Chapter 33 MATTHI FORRER *The Kachoga of Katsushika Hokusai*
*An even earlier illustration of a telescope is to be found in one of Saikaku's novels, the *Kōshoku ichidai otoko* of 1682. I am much indebted to Mr K. B. Gardner for drawing my attention to this point.

Chapter 37 L. L. GROMKOVSKAYA *On the Problem of the Interrelations between Russian and Japanese Cultures (Leo Tolstoy and Tokutomi Roka)*.
1.   Yokemura Yoshitarō, 'on the question of the influence of Russian literature on Japanese literature' in *The Newsletter of Academy of Sciences of the USSR. (Literature and Language Section), Vol. XX, 1961, pp. 97-110.*
2.   L. Tolstoy, *Anna Karenina* in collected works in 22 volumes, Vol. 9, Moscow, 1982, pp. 363-364.

Chapter 38 JEANETTE TAUDIN CHABOT *Inoue Hisashi as a Literary Critic*
1.   Inoue Hisashi, *Shōdan shōhatsu* Tokyo, 1978, 'Kami to yūmoa', p. 222.
2.   Inoue Hisashi, *Kotoba o yomu* Tokyo, 1982, 'Fuhen no chūshutsu,' pp. 48-9.
3.   Inoue Hisashi, *Ibid*, 'Kako no kanata ni aru mirai,' p. 28.
4.   The *gesaku* of the Edo period (entertainment literature mainly catering to the merchant class) came in such forms as *yomihon, kibyōshi, sharebon, kokkeibon* and *ninjōbon*. Often they were delivered in instalments by *kashihonya* (book-lending merchants). Some of the characteristics associated with *gesaku* and *shukō* (cleverly constructed plot), *oto no makujime* (closing with a sound), *mojiri* (parody), *dajare* (puns), *jiguchi* (puns on proverbs), *goro-awase* (consecutive puns), *joku* (accumulative clauses) and frequent use of onomatopoeia. Inoue uses such techniques fully in his fiction dealing with the Edo period, such as *Tegusari shinjū* and *Gesakusha meimeiden* (Individual biographies of gesakusha, 1979).
5.   Inoue Hisashi, *Shōdan shōhatsu*, 'Edo no shomin bunka o saguru,' p. 28.
6.   Inoue Hisashi, *Kotoba o yomu*, 'Kinshitsuna jikan to kūkan no nakade,' pp. 13-17.
7.   Inoue Hisashi, *Fūkei wa namida ni yusure*, Tokyo, 1982, Nihongozukai no tatsujin to shiteno Kenji,' pp. 145-8.
8.   Inoue Hisashi, *Ibid*, 'Kita Morio: Takami no kenbutsu,' pp. 208-14.
9.   Inoue Hisashi, *Ibid*, 'Kita Morio ni okeru jojō to yūmoa,' p. 161.
10.   Inoue Hisashi, *Ibid*, 'Seichō bungaku: miryoku no subete,' p. 172.
11.   Inoue Hisashi, *Hon no makura sōshi*, Tokyo, 1982, 'Shinshun ni omou,' p. 185.

12. Inoue Hisashi, *Kotoba o yomu,* 'Kinshitsu na jikan to kukan no nakade,' p. 8.
13. Inoue Hisashi, *Fūkei wa namida ni yusure,* 'Seichō bungaku: miryoku no subete,' p. 174.
14. Inoue Hisashi, *Ibid,* 'Kita Morio, Sailor Kupukupu no bōken,' p. 205.
15. Inoue Hisashi, *Kotoba o yomu,* 'Monogatari no tanjō,' p. 130.
16. Inoue Hisashi, *Ibid,* 'Ikiiki toshita sōwa,' p. 171.
17. Inoue Hisashi, *Ibid,* 'Kako no kanata ni aru mirai,' p. 28.
18. Inoue Hisashi, *Shōdan Shōhatsu,* 'Gesaku no kanōsei,' pp. 114, 130.
19. Ueda Makoto, 'Kawabata Yasunari to sanji bungaku' in *Bungaku* 1982, pp. 111-12.
20. Inoue Hisashi, *Shōdan Shōhatsu,* 'Gesaku no kanōsei,' pp. 116-17.

Chapter 39 LIVIA MONNET *Not Only Minamata: An Approach to Ishimure Michiko's Work*
1.   See, for instance, Fujikawa Jisui, 'Shiranuikai no karayuki, jo,' *Kumamoto kyōiku,* June 1975; Sakai Tadakazu, 'Ishimure Michiko to Minamata,' *Kyūshūjin,* November, December 1975; Habu Kōji, *Kindai e no jujutsushi: Ishimure Michiko,* Tokyo, 1982; Arai Toyomi, 'Kugai jōdo: Shiron 4, 6,' *Ankaruwa* 62, 65 1981-2. These critics examine Ishimure's work from an overall perspective. Arai attempts a comparative approach within the confines of Japanese literature. Habu is one of the few critics who offers an analysis, albeit rather superficial, of Ishimure's style. However none of these critics is completely emancipated from the spell of the Ishimure myth.
2.   *Kataribe* were professional reciters and transmitters of the oral literature of Japan before the introduction of Chinese characters. Their profession persisted until the fourteenth century.
3.   'Under the Sign of Saturn,' *A Susan Sontag Reader,* New York, 1983, p. 386.
4.   An example of journalism's flattering portrait of Ishimure Michiko can be found in Mishima Akio, *Nake, Shiranui no umi,* Tokyo, 1977. Ishimure is presented as nothing short of a saint, a sort of Jeanne d'Arc of the struggle against Minamata disease.
5.   Sasayama Yutaka, 'Ishimure Michiko,' *Japan Quarterly,* 25, 1978.
6.   There are English, Spanish, and French translations of excerpts from Ishimure's works. See 'Pure Land Poisoned Sea,' James Kirkup and Nakano Michio (trans.), *Japan Quarterly,* 18, 1971, pp. 299-306; Fujimoto Kazuko, 'Discrimination and the Perception of Difference,' *Concerned Theatre Japan,* 2, 1973, pp. 125-135; 'Quo Vadis Homo Nipponicus,' Tashiro Yasuko and Frank Baldwin (trans.), *Japan Interpreter,* III, 1973, pp. 392-395; 'Canción de la patria en ruina,' Michiko Tanaka (trans.), *FEM,* IV, 1980, pp. 19-20; 'Desde la ribera del mar de la vida eterna,' Michiko Tanaka (trans.), *Estudios de Asia y Africa,* XVII, 1982, pp. 119-139. Takahashi Osamu used excerpts from *Kugai jōdo* in his play *Kokuhatsu: Minamata-byō jiken* (Accusation: The Minamata Disease Incident), Tokyo, 1970, which appeared in the French translation by Catherine Cadou (1977). Finally, there is my own translation of *Tsubaki no umi no ki, Story of the Sea of Camellias,* Kyoto, 1983, which, unfortunately, contains a number of infelicities which should not have been there.
7.   Sasayama, op. cit.
8.   In fairness to reviewers of Ishimure's work, it should be said that she herself has contributed to a certain extent to the creation of the myth surrounding her person and work: apart from several passages in her work in which she asserts that she was haunted by the souls of the Minamata disease victims, she has often declared in newspaper, radio and TV interviews that she wrote *Kugai jōdo: Waga Minamata-byō* in a state of trance. This need not be taken literally by the critic trying to see through the complexities of her work.
9.   Shingeki playwright and actor Sunada Akira was so deeply affected by *Kugai jōdo* that he decided to leave Tokyo, settle down in Minamata and devote himself to working on behalf of the victims of the disease. He now lives in Fukuro, Minamata City, dividing his time between farming, writing and acting. Apart from his plays based on Ishimure's writings 'Kugai jōdo' (1971) and 'Umi yo haha yo kodomora yo,' also entitled 'Ten no io' (1980), he has published two books about his experiences as a farmer in Minamata, his association with the Minamata disease patients and the meaning of Ishimure's work: *Oya-sama no kuni: Minamata kara,* Tokyo, 1975, and *Umi yo haha yo kodomora yo,* Tokyo, 1983.
10.   See, for instance, the transcript of her talk with Kuroi Senji, 'Toshi no kabe o hau mono: "Ten no uo" o megutte,' *Ki no naka no oni* (The Demon Inside the Tree), Tokyo, 1983.
11.   The poet's dissatisfaction with the inadequancy, and present state of disruption, of the language compels her to search for the original human language, undefiled by progress

272

and civilisation. The search for a pristine language (*gengo*), which Ishimure imagines was spoken by the poet-priests of ancient times echoes through many of her writings. In 'Hahatachi e no bunjoshō' we find the following passage: 'I try hard to remember the language I heard before I was born. Vexation comes up my throat.' However, no matter how hard one searches for the pristine poetic language of humanity one will never find it. The awareness of the inadequacy of language is unbearable: 'Broken words. They convey nothing, link nothing ....' See 'Hahatachi e no bunjoshō,' *Ryūmin no miyako*, 2nd ed., Tokyo, 1978, pp. 99 and 110.

12.   See *Minamata: Umi no koe* (Minamata: The Voice of the Sea), Tokyo, 1982, a long poem illustrated by the well-known painters, Maruki Iri and Toshi.

13.   Watanabe Kyōji, Kikuchi Masanori.

14.   Watanabe Kyōji, 'Ishimure Michiko no sekai,' *Chiisaki mono no shi*, Fukuoka, 1975, pp. 218-219.

15.   *Ten no uo*, Tokyo, 1980, p. 40.

16.   The expression 'poetic dialect' was used by Anthony Liman in his discussion of a short story by Ibuse Masuji. See 'Pilgrim's Inn,' *Approaches to the Modern Japanese Short Story*, Tokyo, 1982, p. 97.

17.   This expression was used by some English and American critics in their efforts to re-assess T. S. Eliot's place in contemporary literature. Though I believe Eliot was not a 'great minor poet,' but simply a great one, the phrase strikes me as appropriate for Ishimure's case.

Chapter 40 HILARIA GÖSSMANN *The Emancipation of Women as Shown in the Novels of Sata Ineko*

1.   All quotations are taken from *Sato Ineko zenshū*, Tokyo, 1977-9. Roman numerals denote volume numbers; arabic numbers denote page numbers.

2.   Sata Ineko, *Onna no jikaku*, in *Josei dokuhon*, 1935-36. (XVI, 390).

Chapter 43 G. LINDBERG-WADA, *'The Rôle of Kokinshū Poetry as a Source of Allusion,'* (*hikiuta*) in *Genji Monogatari*. If not otherwise stated, translations into English are my own, the quotations in Japanese are taken from Nihon Koten bungaku taikei, *Genji Monogatari* 1-5, Tokyo, 1975. This paper is based on my thesis 'Poetic Allusion — Some Aspects of the rôle played by Kokin Wakashū in *Genji Monogatari*', Stockholm, 1983, from which further bibliographical information may be obtained.

Chapter 44 TSVETANA KRISTEVA*The Genji-intext in Towazu-gatari*

1.   This term has been proposed by Z. Shmidt and further developed by P. Torop in his essay 'Problema intexta,' *Text v texte*, Uchonie zapiski tartuskogo gosudarstvenogo universiteta 567, Tartu, 1981, where it is defined as a 'semantically saturated part of the text which is subjected at least to double reading and is thus a double-text', p. 39.

2.   I discuss the generic significance of this term in my 'Japanese Lyrical Diaries and the European Autobiographical Tradition,' *Europe Interprets Japan*, Gordon Daniels ed., Tenterden, Paul Norbury Publications, 1984, pp. 155-162.

3.   Cf. Umberto Eco's *A Theory of Semiotics*, Thetford, 1977, where he discusses the functioning of literary tradition as follows: 'Even in the idiosyncratic personal activity of memorising previous semiotic experience, there is a continuous activity of extra-coding. There are a lot of phrases and indeed entire discourses that one no longer has to interpret or decode because one has already experienced them in analogous circumstances or contexts,' p. 136.

4.   'Towazu-gatari shippitsu-no imi,' *Koten toshiteno Genji monogatari*, Musashi, 1979.

5.   *Ibid.*, p. 147.

6.   *Ibid.*, p. 153-4.

7.   Bakhtin's term *slovo* has been variously translated as 'word' and/or 'discourse.' For this and other Bakhtinian terms, see the Glossary appended to his *The Dialogic Imagination*, by Michael Holquist (ed.), Austin and London, 1981.

8.   Julia Kristeva, *Desire in Language*, New York, 1980, p. 66.

9.   Mikhail Bakhtin, *Problemi poetiki Dostoevskogo*, Moscow, 1979, pp. 223, 235.

10.   Cf. Lotman's 'text v texte', *Text v texte*, Tartu, 1981, p. 10.

11.   Cf. Todorov's *Poetics*, Lotman's *Text v texte*, Torop's *Problema intexta*, etc.

12.   I would like to mention but one study, 'Homo Citans,' *Godishnik na Sofiiskiya*

Universitet, tom 74, Sofia Univ. Press, 1984, by the Bulgarian scholar, Nikola Georgiev.

13.   A very interesting and useful classification has been suggested by P. Torop in his *Problema intexta*, p. 38.

14.   I am indebted to the *wake*fool Bulgarian translator of James Joyce and Bakhtiniologist, Nikolai B. Popov, for this and other stimulating remarks.

15.   Cf. Roland Barthes, *Empire of Signs*, Richard Howard (trans.), London, 1983.

16.   *The Confessions of Lady Nijo*, Karen Brazell (trans.), Stanford, 1973, p. 4.

17.   *The Tale of Genji*, Edward G. Seidensticker (trans.), Tokyo, 1979, p. 104.

18.   *Towazu-gatari*, Fukuda Hideichi kochu, Tokyo, 1978.

19.   Nihon koten bungaku zenshu, *Genji monogatari*, Shogakkan.

20.   Cf. Bakhtin's *Problemi poetiki Dostoevskogo*, pp. 228-231.

21.   Cf. Shimizu Yoshiko's *Towazu-gatari shippitsuno imi*, p. 163.

Urakami Shōtokuji temple　　Fukahori Yasuzaemon narabi ni kinpen bosho zumen
Urakamimura Yonogo　*(See page 14)*

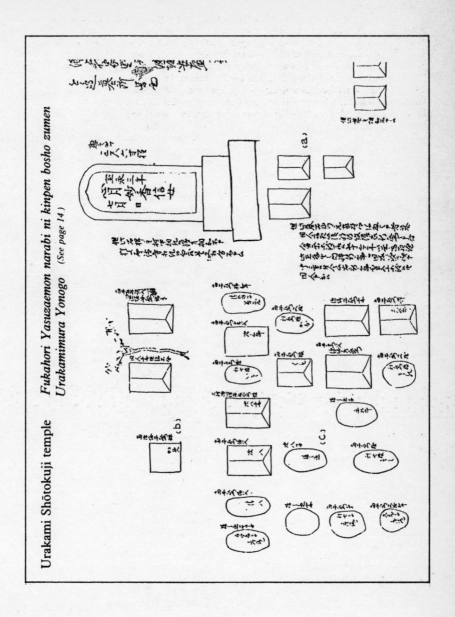

275

Index